M000187780

Strange Cocktail

Michigan Studies in Comparative Jewish Cultures emphasizes the dynamic interplay of Jews as historical subjects, Judaism as faith and practice, and Jewishness as a repertoire of cultural practices with other peoples and cultures. It addresses a wide range of cultural forms, including art and theater, music and film, in relation to literature and history.

Series Editors:
Jonathan Freedman, University of Michigan
Anita Norich, University of Michigan
Scott Spector, University of Michigan

Strange Cocktail

TRANSLATION AND THE
MAKING OF MODERN
HEBREW POETRY

Adriana X. Jacobs

University of Michigan Press
Ann Arbor

Published in the United States of America by the
University of Michigan Press
Manufactured in the United States of America
Printed on acid-free paper

First published August 2018

A CIP catalog record for this book is available from the British Library.

Library of Congress Cataloging-in-Publication data has been applied for.

ISBN 978-0-472-13090-0 (hardcover : alk. paper)
ISBN 978-0-472-12403-9 (e-book)

This publication was supported by a generous grant from
the Frankel Center for Judaic Studies at the University of Michigan.

For David and Lev

Contents

Acknowledgments

This project really began in the summer between my freshman and sophomore years of college, which I spent in the (very humid) town of Williamsburg, Virginia, translating into English the poetry of a group of Ecuadorian Modernists known as *Los decapitados*, a project funded by a National Endowment for the Humanities research grant. In addition to my translations—eleven in total—I had to prepare an extensive essay, providing historical context for these texts and also discussing my translation process. My advisor Kirsten Silva Gruesz recommended that I read George Steiner's *After Babel*, as well as John Felstiner's *Translating Neruda*, which combined the creativity of translation with incisive poetic analysis. Translation as a discipline still felt very new, but from that moment on, I had found my home in literary studies.

By the time I began my doctoral work at Princeton, I had made the switch to Hebrew, but my interest in translation continued, developing into a dissertation project on the relation between twentieth-century Hebrew poetry and translation and the figure of the poet-translator. I also continued to translate poetry, this time from Hebrew into English. Then, as now, the practice of translating poetry shaped my thinking about the choices translators make and how poems are made, and without a commitment to that practice, this would have become a very different book.

At Princeton, I was fortunate to work closely with Barbara Mann, whose seminar on space and place in modern Hebrew literature introduced me to the poetry of Esther Raab. It was Barbara who invited me to submit my seminar paper on Raab's multilingual poetics to *Prooftexts*, which became the cornerstone of this project. My advisor Sandra Bermann not only cheered this project to the finish line but also encouraged me to do the extra work required to make this project accessible and appealing to non-Hebrew readers. I also have Sandie to thank for including me in the early stages of the development of Princeton's Program in Translation and Intercultural Communication. This platform gave me the opportunity to work closely with David Bellos, who showed me first-hand how to combine translation theory and praxis in the classroom and in my work. I also extend appreciation to C. D. Blanton, Daniel Heller-Roazen, Alan Mintz, z"l, Jussara Menezes Quadros, and Richard Sieburth for their generous feedback and criticism at that early stage.

Before graduate school, I had the chance to work with Michael (Miki) Gluzman as his research assistant as he prepared *The Politics of Canonicity* for publication. Our weekly meetings in Tel Aviv gave me an indispensable foundation for my future work on modern Hebrew literature. Miki taught me to read Hebrew within a broad comparative framework and to be bold in drawing relations between authors and texts. Complimentary Lechem Erez sandwiches for lunch didn't hurt either.

As I was preparing this book, I was fortunate to have the following friends and colleagues in my corner: Riki Avidan-Traum, Alaina Browne, Shahar Bram, Jessica Cohen, Yali Dekel, Shai Ginsburg, Natasha Gordinsky, Shiri Goren, Karen Grumberg, Liora Halperin, Annie Kantar Ben-Hillel, Lily Kahn, Lisa Katz, Sarah Lariviere, Lital Levy, Dory Manor, Shachar Pinsker, Na'ama Rokem, Adam Rovner, Allison Schachter, Sasha Senderovich, Ronen Sonis, Shira Stav, Ilana Szobel, Giddon Ticotsky, and Naama Zahavi-Ely. *Spasibo bolshoi* to Asya Graf for her unflagging support and friendship over the years, which included reading large sections of this manuscript (and the book proposal) many times. Rachel Galvin pushed my theoretical thinking beyond my comfort zone, and for that gift I owe her *mil gracias*. And a *toda raba* to Rachel S. Harris for the hard truth that sometimes you need to start over to make the work better, and to Eran Tzelgov for asking the questions that make you think harder and translate better.

I am also grateful to my colleagues at the Faculty of Oriental Studies and the Oxford Centre for Hebrew and Jewish Studies for providing a supportive environment for teaching and research these past five years. At Oxford, the research program Oxford Comparative Criticism and Translation has been like a second home, and I want to thank Matthew Reynolds for welcoming me into this community where I have had the opportunity to share my work on Hebrew literature and translation in a vibrant comparative context. And a thank you to my friends on Facebook, both those I know in real life and those I may never meet. Social media *is* a distraction but also a source of meaningful intellectual inquiry, and I have been moved by the generosity and enthusiasm of friends and strangers who have answered my queries, offered suggestions, and inspired new ideas on behalf of this book.

I am grateful to the University of Michigan Press for taking on this book and want to thank Anita Norich, Jonathan Freedman, and Scott Spector in particular for welcoming *Strange Cocktail* into their Comparative Jewish Cultures series and for their enthusiasm for this project. Over the years, I have had the opportunity to publish parts of this project and wish to acknowledge here the editors and publishers who supported *Strange Cocktail* in its early stages and the anonymous readers whose critical feedback shaped the development of the book's central arguments. A section from the introduction draws from my chapter "The Go-Betweens: Leah Goldberg, Yehuda Amichai and the Figure of the Poet Translator," *The Blackwell Companion to Translation Studies*, edited by Sandra Bermann and Catherine Porter (Malden, MA: Blackwell, 2014), 479–491 (reprinted by permission of John Wiley & Sons). Earlier versions of chapters 2 and 4 began as conference papers and later developed into articles in the following publications: "Paris or Jerusalem: The Multilingualism of Esther Raab," *Prooftexts: A Journal of Jewish Literary History*, vol. 26, no. 1–2 (2006): 6–28 (reprinted by permission of Indiana University Press) and "Hebrew Remembers Yiddish: The Poetry of Avot Yeshurun," *Choosing Yiddish: Studies in Yiddish Literature, Culture and History*, edited by Lara Rabinovitch, Shiri Goren, and Hannah Pressman (Detroit, MI: Wayne State University Press, 2013), 296–313 (reprinted by permission of Wayne State University Press). I thank the publishers for their permission to reprint this material.

The writer Ehud Ben-Ezer, nephew and biographer of the poet Raab, has opened his home and personal archives to many Raab scholars over the years. To keep original documents in the best condition possible, he transcribed most of Raab's letters and journals and made them available as digital files, which proved invaluable in the preparation of this book. A few years ago, he generously allowed me to take a look at the original manuscripts of Raab's Baudelaire translations and photograph a few pages. I thank him for permission to include a reproduction of one of these pages here, and for permission to include other materials related to Raab. I am also grateful to Helit Yeshurun for her permission to republish material by her father

Avot Yeshurun, including a Yiddish letter written by his mother. Harold Schimmel graciously gave me permission to republish some of his early English-language poems as well as poems from the collections *Ar'a* (Siman kri'a) and *Lo'el* (Chadarim/Galeriya Gordon). His translations of poems by Raab appear here by permission of Peter Cole and Adina Hoffman, who published a collection of Raab's poems through their press Ibis Editions. My thanks also go to Michal Blum of Ha-kibbuts ha-me'uchad and Yair Landau, trustee of the Leah Goldberg estate, for permission to reprint Goldberg's poems and manuscript materials. I also extend my gratitude to Hila Tzur of the Archives of the Hebrew Writers Union ("Gnazim"), who has come through on many occasions with hard-to-locate materials and at a later stage kindly updated reference numbers for many of the materials reproduced here by permission of the Institute.

I have my parents Robert Tatum and Marcela Espinosa to thank for encouraging my bilingual upbringing and always fulfilling my extensive book wish lists. The English–Spanish relays across our dinner table always felt completely natural and sparked a love of languages and translation that remains to this day. I also thank my step-mother Chiraporn Tatum and in-laws Erica and Mark Jacobs for their encouragement and wisdom as my academic career developed over the years.

So many acknowledgments end with the names of those to whom the book is dedicated and mine will be no different. I am deeply grateful that I get to start and end every day with David and Lev. The work I do in the hours in between is sustained by their support and love, but especially by the model that David provides to our son of an interested and engaged partner who cares about what I do and ensures that I have the space, time, and opportunity to do it. Lev (age seven) very much wanted to contribute a blurb to this book, so here it is: "Hebrew poets like to translate … but what happens next?!" And on that note, let's turn the page.

Note on Translation

It will come as no surprise that a book that concerns translation involved a great deal of translating—of words, paragraphs, and, of course, poems, from Hebrew mostly, but also from Yiddish, French, German, Russian, and even Spanish. In the course of doing so, I also faced the question of whether or not to make use of someone else's translation or produce my own. When a text was not available in English translation, the decision to translate from scratch was very straightforward, but the inclusion of existing translations was more complicated and now requires some explanation.

The figure of the poet-translator is central to this book, and for that reason, I chose to include several existing translations (from Hebrew, Russian, German, and French) and to do so without alteration. I wanted to give other translators a voice in this project and to put my own translations and critical readings in dialogue with translation *and* translators. I have seen many scholarly works that include modified versions of translations, usually to bring them closer in line to the way that the author is reading the work. Although I used to employ this practice, I have since come to feel that doing so is deeply problematic and misguided. A scholar would not think to modify an original text, and yet it has become a common practice to do so with translations. This reflects, in part, a still pervasive perception in academia of translations as less creative, secondary, and unoriginal. And yet, it is my position that translation is the result of a number of intertwined decisions, and modifying a single word can have an unraveling effect. I hope that stating so in this commentary will encourage my fellow scholars to pursue a different practice. In my case, where I felt that I wanted to make such modifications, I used these instances as opportunities to engage the translation in my critical reading rather than change the translation itself. In the case of Avot

Yeshurun's "Memories are a House," I opted to translate my own version and received Helit Yeshurun's permission to do so (though in the endnotes, I direct readers to Leon Wieseltier's fine translation of the poem). With respect to Charles Baudelaire's "Bohémiens en voyage," I needed a translation that was a bit more literal than those that I was finding, and J. Kates very generously obliged my Facebook request for a "well-behaved, academic translation." Harold Schimmel's translations appear throughout this project for reasons that soon will become clear. I am grateful for his permission to include them here.

A word on my own translations: I have been translating poetry for over twenty years, and my preferred translation mode is creative, bold, and sometimes mischievous. Readers of Hebrew will not always find direct, linear equivalences between my translations and the Hebrew texts that accompany them. In fact, I hope they do not. This is not to say that I am presenting the non-Hebrew reader with a radically transformed text in translation, but rather to highlight that translation is a process with many turns and digressions. In my reading of the poems included in *Strange Cocktail*, I address my own translation choices. They not only reflect my understanding of a poem, but also my way of thinking about translation. In many instances, I offer a range of alternatives or cite the choices of other translators to give readers a sense of the distances a word can travel and the different forms it can take. Where possible, I have included original and translated poems in their entirety, so that readers can participate in the kind of reading across and in translation that was the original spark of this study.

PART I

Where You Take Words

Introduction

Poetics and Practices of Translation in Modern Hebrew Poetry

THE TRANSLATED NATION

On July 22, 1952, the Hebrew poet Leah Goldberg gave a talk on literary translation at a gathering of the Higher Council of Culture (*ha-moʻatsa ha-ʻeliona le-tarbut*). As she herself admitted, her presentation was "pretty superficial," but she was nonetheless rattled by the vituperative response of Avraham Kariv, a fellow poet and critic who was in the audience.[1] Goldberg recorded what transpired in her journal:

> האיום הוא התפרצותו של קריב המכוונת נגדי, כ"נציגה טיפוסית של הזרם הזה" הרוצה ב"אומה מתורגמת". נגד כל אלה שאין להם צורך ב"שורשים" בארץ, היודעים מה עשו לנו הגויים, וכורעים ברך לפני גוי. למה לנו הבאלזאקים והסטנדאלים האלה! ואין לנו שום צורך בשום באלזאקים, הם טובים רק לשם שיחה מנוונת בבתי קפה. כל התרבות האירופית הזאת איננה שווה פרוטה, ול.ג. והעיתון שלה יש לו 50 שבועות בשנה "יארצייטן" לאיזה גוי, ומפי אלה הם חיים … והאסון הזה שמתרגמים את כל ההבל הזה הקרוי קלאסיקה וכד' וכד'.

> The worst was the outburst Kariv directed against me in particular as "the epitome of a trend" that desires a "translated nation" [*uma meturgemet*]. Against those who have no need for "roots" in this country, who know what the *goyim* [non-Jews] did to us and still genuflect before them. What use do we have for these Balzacs and Stendhals! We have no need for these Balzacs; all they are good for is degenerate chatter in cafés. European culture isn't worth a cent and yet for 50 weeks a year Leah Goldberg and her paper [*Mishmar*]

light a *yahrzeit* [memorial] candle for some *goy* and live off of this …
What a catastrophe that they are translating these so-called "classics,"
etc, etc.[2]

Kariv had immigrated to Mandatory Palestine in 1934, a year before
Goldberg, and was himself a translator of Russian primarily, but also of
Yiddish.[3] His translations from Russian included *Piotr pervyi* (Piter ha-
rishon, Stybel, 1936–1937), Alexei Tolstoy's sweeping historical Russian
novel that appeared in installments in the journal *Novyi mir* between 1929
and 1934 and won the Stalin Prize in 1941.[4] At first glance, this credential
would suggest that a double standard is implicit in Kariv's objections to
Goldberg's translation choices. After all, the non-Jewish Tolstoy was a member of the Russian elite, and his novel was a celebration of a way of life that
ran counter to the egalitarian ethos of Jewish nation-building. But in the
decade following the publication of his translation, one of many works he
translated from Russian, the Holocaust had irrevocably altered Kariv's relationship with European literature. Now better known as a literary critic and
editor, his response highlighted a major tension with regard to the status of
translation in Israel's national literary culture. For Kariv, Goldberg's translations of Stendhal and Balzac betrayed her dedication to a European (and
specifically Western European) canonical authority that Hebrew literature,
now a national literature, no longer required. He further insinuated that her
translation activity profited from a culture (and here he invokes "Europe"
more broadly) that had inflicted catastrophic harm on the Jewish people.
Kariv's comments were not the thoughts of a "crazy person," Goldberg wrote,
but rather were representative of the "cultural fascism" that she observed in
the literary culture of her time, which for her brought back memories of
the xenophobic rhetoric that took hold in Germany in 1933.[5] It was that
increasingly repressive climate that had prompted Goldberg to immigrate
to Mandatory Palestine in 1935, shortly after the publication of her debut
collection *Taba'ot 'ashan* (Smoke Rings) in Tel Aviv. And once more, in
Kariv's words, echoes of this past had reached her.

Two days earlier, in stark contrast to Kariv's outburst, she had enjoyed a
conversation with Martin Buber on Hebrew translations of Greek classics,
and, in particular, of the works of Plato and Thucydides. This conversation,
which Goldberg described in the same journal entry, took place at the Buber
residence, where his daughter Eva and her husband Ludwig (Arie) Strauss
were also in attendance. Strauss (1892–1953), a German-Jewish writer,

also had immigrated to Palestine in 1935. Like Goldberg, his own writing addressed the zones between Europe and Palestine, between Hebrew and the diasporic languages of its immigrant writers.[6] Later that year, Goldberg would take up an academic position at the Hebrew University, and together with Strauss would begin setting in motion plans for the establishment of a department of comparative literature, the first of its kind in Israel. The novelist Aharon Appelfeld counted them among his teachers in those years, recalling that "Leah Goldberg and Ludwig Strauss ... had much to say about the dichotomy of having two languages and two homelands. They were poets and spoke like poets."[7] In any event, it is hardly incidental that Goldberg juxtaposes the Kariv and Buber encounters in her journal entry: together they encompass two divergent but coexisting views on the status of translation in the still-new State of Israel.

The phrase "translated nation"—*uma meturgemet*—stands out in this account, because when Kariv levels this accusation at Goldberg, his intent is to cast her interest in translation as anti-Zionist, as evidence of her resistance to a Jewish national culture and to Hebrew monolingualism. The irony here is that Goldberg's Hebrew translations were vital to the development of modern Hebrew literature in the early to mid-twentieth century, but at the same time, Goldberg often resisted external demands to focus her attention on specific texts and authors, as chapter 3 explores. She also knew "full well" the future that awaited a culture that rejected foreign and diasporic voices and placed restrictions on the production and circulation of translated texts. She understood intimately the dehumanizing effect of this repudiation, what became of a society that was no longer receptive to the outside voices that translation mediates and the transformative effects that can result from these encounters. A year later, the publication of Goldberg's translation of *War and Peace* (Milchama ve-shalom), the master work of the other, better-known Tolstoy, positioned literary translation as a still vital, necessary, and possible activity in Israel. While I am in no way claiming here that Goldberg's Tolstoy translation was a direct response to Kariv—her project was well underway when she delivered her remarks on translation—the timing highlights the blind spots in Kariv's critique and, more importantly, the inconsistencies that shaped the politics of Hebrew translation and its reception in this period. In fact, a glance at Kariv's publications shows that he continued to publish translations well into the late 1960s.[8]

Strange Cocktail: Translation and the Making of Modern Hebrew Poetry offers a translation-centered reading of modern Hebrew poetry that explores how the relation between translation and writing shaped the development of twentieth-century modern Hebrew and Israeli poetry. In the chapters that follow, I show how the implicit and explicit translation practices of modern Hebrew poets—that is, the poetics of translation that shapes their original work, as well as the praxis of translation—not only situate them in more expansive literary constellations but also, in the process, become synonymous with Hebrew writing itself. Through both a poetics and praxis of translation and by applying strategies of translation in their original Hebrew works, modern Hebrew poets created multilingual, heterogeneous, and even radical poetic languages that allowed for a wide range of literary networks and affiliations to circulate in the field of Hebrew literature. Some of these, like the Anglophone and French vectors, have not received the attention given to German, Yiddish, Russian, and Arabic in modern Hebrew literary scholarship, but are, as I show in chapters 2 and 5, vital to understanding that the development of modern Hebrew poetry was not only engaging or responding to tensions between multilingualism and monolingualism, diaspora and nation, or mobility and territoriality but also advancing an understanding of poetry that was fundamentally relational, bringing into its fold the work of poets across many languages and literary traditions, often in ways that productively, and often politically, disrupted and unsettled the language of the Hebrew poem.

A focus on translation also allows us to appreciate how views on literary translation developed and changed both in modern Hebrew literature of the late nineteenth through the twentieth centuries and in the oeuvres of poets themselves. In a period of Jewish nation-building in Palestine, literary translation, in Chana Kronfeld's words, "enriched, indeed enabled, the production of a modern literature in the newly revived Hebrew language," but this was also the case for Hebrew writing in the nineteenth century, as the following chapter will show.[9] Writing in a rapidly changing literary vernacular, modern Hebrew translation practices throughout the diaspora, and later in Palestine, were deeply embedded in the act of modern Hebrew writing itself, particularly in the production of poetry.[10] In this respect, a translation-centered reading reveals to what extent the translation practices of poets had a transformative effect on the circulation and reception of poetry, not to mention the ways in which the Hebrew poem itself was renewed by and in translation. As political Zionism advanced the Jewish nation-building project in Palestine, the translation practices of poets, more so than prose writers, reveal a more complicated relation between the desire for territory and settlement, on the one hand, and the translatability of the Hebrew poem, on the other.[11] Through their translation work, twentieth-century Hebrew poets not only acknowledged the multilingual strata of the Hebrew language or "the polyphony of Jewish culture," as Benjamin Harshav described it, but also carried the unsettled, diasporic, and multilingual status of translation into their own Hebrew writing, and it is in this respect that translation is also implicit in original Hebrew works.[12]

My chapters on Esther Raab (1894–1981), Goldberg (1911–1970), Avot Yeshurun (1904–1992), and Harold Schimmel (1935–) interweave two major strands in this work. The first is an exploration of how the relation between Hebrew translation and poetry developed in the twentieth century, looking closely at the translation practices of these poets. The second examines the distinct poetics of translation that their own work articulates, the various translation strategies, forms, approaches, and theories that shape their own writing in Hebrew, as well as the themes, figures, and languages of translation that pervade their texts. This selection of poets also represents the kind of constellation of writers that a translation-centered reading encourages. Schimmel, the subject of my final chapter, envisioned his English translations of Hebrew poetry as part of an expansively translational and transhistoric "poetic map," which included his own original Hebrew poetry.[13] The fact that Schimmel translated Raab, Goldberg, and Yeshurun into English organizes this very project to a large extent. By giving primacy to the figure of the poet-translator, I have been able to gather these poets around their shared understanding of translation as a creative practice, of the poem as translation, and thereby call attention to the relations and chain reactions that are activated when poets translate poets. My constellation offers an alternative to canonical order, acknowledging that many different configurations of a translation-centered reading are possible, while also drawing relations between the individual and multiple theories of translation that the works of these poets engage and develop.[14]

The expression "strange cocktail" comes from Raab's own characterization of her poetry and its literary influences as a *kokteil ketsat meshune*, a somewhat strange cocktail.[15] This expression first appears in her 1972 letter to the scholar Reuven Shoham, where she explicitly uses it in the context of her influences: a mix of French, German, and Swedish writers, as well as Hebrew poets of the period. But Raab was also referring to her iconoclastic tendencies, particularly her rejection of the quatrain, sonnet, and, in general, traditional Hebrew prosody. In her 1972 essay "Milim ke-tsiporim nedirot" ("Words Like Rare Birds"), Raab described her poetic language as a *gidul pere*, a wild growth, a parasitic and invasive trope that rejects claims to continuity and the linear affiliations that determine literary "genealogies" (usually patrilineal in the case of Hebrew).[16] Comparing herself to her modern Hebrew contemporaries, what made her poetry "strange," in Raab's view, was her native-born status (she was born in Ottoman Palestine) and her claim to being a native speaker of Hebrew, which both distinguished and excluded her in a predominantly immigrant literary culture. At the same time, Raab's work calls attention to ways in which the very idea of a "mother tongue," like a strange cocktail, is a concoction of real and imagined elements and a site of multilingual encounter.[17] The Israeli sociologist, poet, and translator Zali Gurevitch has called attention to this implicit multiplicity in the context of Israel's fraught language politics: "Mother tongue is but one generic name for the sundry and diverse voices that enter each individual voice, and which makes this individual voice a native-voice, 'our voice.'"[18] In this respect, Raab's "strange cocktail" also gestures to the uncanny, restless, and implicit intertextual and multilingual layers that shape the works of these poets, aptly describing what transpires and emerges when translation and original writing slip, mix, and combine.

Following the historical overview that chapter 1 offers, *Strange Cocktail* introduces, in chapter 2, the work of the poet who inspired its title. There, I focus my reading on the composition of *Kimshonim* (Thistles), Raab's debut collection published in 1930, which she undertook alongside her translations of German and French poetry, notably translations from Charles Baudelaire's 1857 collection *Les Fleurs du mal*. I show how the process of working intimately with Baudelaire's poetic language encouraged Raab to push her own writing in radically new directions, resulting in poems—and translations—that were ahead of their time in terms of form and idiom. These translations also allowed Raab to negotiate a middle ground between her "native" Hebrew identity and the other cultures, languages, and geographies that circulated in her Palestinian childhood. Today, Raab is still best known as a "Land of Israel" poet, whose work celebrates the pioneering spirit of the pre-Statehood period, but my reading of *Kimshonim* focuses attention on the cosmopolitan and multilingual currents that run through this collection. Though they remained unpublished in her lifetime, Raab's translations of Baudelaire, and my reading of these translations alongside her original poetry, challenge the nativist reading that Raab herself promoted and that prevailed in studies of her work until more recent years. While previous studies of Raab have acknowledged her affiliation with Baudelaire, my reading offers the first close study of the translations themselves and their specific, intertextual relation to the poems of *Kimshonim*.

In chapter 3, I address Goldberg's wide-ranging output, which demonstrates how early modern Hebrew poets engaged a poetics and a praxis of translation in order to reclaim, as well as fashion, personal narratives that did not accord with the demands of a national literary culture. Themes and figures of translation are prominent in Goldberg's poetic oeuvre and correspond as well with her expansive practice of translation, which included Hebrew translations of Dante, Petrarca, and Dostoevsky, among others. For Goldberg, the translation of poetry and its circulation ensured the vitality of Hebrew literary culture but also resisted the demands of territorial nationalism by insisting that Hebrew literary culture remain world-oriented. Although Goldberg was committed to developing a national literary culture, she also came into conflict with her own milieu by holding on to the idea of Hebrew as a European, diasporic language and literature and refusing to accede to a "negation of the diaspora" (*shlilat ha-galut*). Her translation activity, I show, not only worked on behalf of this position but also found a place in her own writing. My reading of Goldberg's 1952 poetic cycle "Ahavata shel Tereza di Mon" ("The Love of Teresa de Meun") and her iconic poem "Oren" ("Pine") departs from previous scholarship, which tends to emphasize Goldberg's reckoning with the home/exile binary. Rather, by placing translation at the center of my reading of these poems, I show how relations between nation and diaspora, home and exile, and Hebrew and Europe remain productively complicated and intertwined in Goldberg's oeuvre.[19]

Chapter 4 offers a new approach to reading Yeshurun's poetry that brings together recent work on disability, mobility, and the epistolary genre. Here, I propose prosthetic translation as a critical framework for reading Yeshurun's hybrid and multilingual poetry, and, in particular, his elegiac collection *Shloshim 'amud shel Avot Yeshurun* (1964, Thirty Pages of Avot Yeshurun), a work dedicated to the family he lost in the Holocaust. The relation between prosthesis and translation traces back to the work of Walter Benjamin, Theodor Adorno, and Jacques Derrida, but has been more explicitly and more precisely articulated by David Wills.[20] In his 1995 book *Prosthesis*, Wills, who has translated Derrida into English, describes the prosthetic aesthetic in terms that blur any distinction between translation and writing: "the writing of prosthesis ... is inevitably caught in a complex play of displacements; prosthesis being about nothing if not placement, displacement, replacement, standing, dislodging, substituting, setting, amputating, supplementing."[21] In Yeshurun's epistolary poems, many based on actual letters from his family, he traces the permutations that single lines in Yiddish undergo from poem to poem, from Yiddish to Hebrew, with translation serving as one of several strategies by which Yeshurun revives and attempts to reintegrate the fractured relationship between his Hebrew and Yiddish. In the process, this prosthetic translation creates and marks sites of relentless linguistic discomfort and phantom pain that persist in the Hebrew textual body. In this chapter, I also bring these poems into relation with the remnant of a lost, original Yiddish poem that Yeshurun claimed to have written and its rich textual afterlife in his Hebrew poems.

Chapter 5 brings us to Schimmel, an American-born Israeli poet who began his career writing in English but turned to Hebrew following his immigration to Israel in the 1960s. In the 1970s and the early 1980s, Schimmel's commitment to the English translation of Hebrew poetry laid the foundation for his own writing in Hebrew, but also unsettled his project of self-Hebraization. And while Israeli literature continued to privilege Hebrew, the demand to "become Hebrew" had become outmoded by this period. In this context, I consider Schimmel's Hebrew poetry alongside his English translation activity and its relation to the output of Anglophone poets living in Israel in the 1960s and the 1970s. This discussion also includes an overview of the intertwined poetry and translation of *Ha-mishpacha* (The Family), a group of Israel-based poets that included Schimmel, British-born Dennis Silk, Tel Aviv-native Arieh Sachs, and German-born Yehuda Amichai. Schimmel's poems often incorporate unmarked and embedded Hebrew translations of his Anglo-American mentors, notably Robert Lowell, to whom Schimmel dedicated his 1986 sonnet collection, *Lo'el* (Lowell). *Lo'el* is a revisionary poetic bildungsroman, over the course of which Schimmel corrects the mistake of writing, in his early Hebrew poems, "as though I had had no past before Hebrew and before this land."[22] In *Lo'el*, the line between translation and writing blurs entirely, as in Lowell's own work, and this convergence of translation and writing creates what Matthew Reynolds has called "a poetry of translation," a hybrid, multilingual poetic language for the real and imagined languages, histories, and geographies of the poet.[23]

In the work of Yeshurun, for example, the migration of translated language (usually Yiddish into Hebrew) into a poem often goes unmarked. In these instances, a line between original and translated language cannot be drawn, although in many other instances, its broken, fragmented, and disquieting language could be construed as a sign of translation activity. The interwoven histories of poetry and translation also report that poet-translators have a tendency to refer to translations, and particularly their own translations, as creative, original texts. I elaborate this point in my chapter on Goldberg, who was keen to formulate a typology of translation, but also acknowledged that the translations of poets often claimed the status of an original. Roman Jakobson likewise recognized that the translation of poetry was more creative than "translation proper" allowed.[24] In fact, although Jakobson was otherwise skeptical of claims to untranslatability, poetry, like dreams and magic spells, presented conditions that entangled creativity in the question of translation. Indeed, Jakobson himself asserted that with poetry only "creative transposition" is possible.[25] Because the translation of poetry requires a willingness to recast the poem in another language, it may come as no surprise that most of its practitioners have been poets. For the twentieth-century Brazilian modernists, for example, translation was more than a movement from one language to another, but rather a strategy toward a radical, counter-colonial revision of Brazilian literature's relation to its European precursors. In his landmark 1928 text "Manifesto antropófago" ("Cannibal Manifesto"), the Brazilian poet Oswald de Andrade invokes the Tupi people, who reportedly ate their enemies to absorb their power and strength, to propose aggressive strategies of translation that create—or *trans-criar* (transcreate)—texts that complicate, recontextualize, and multiply their relation to their predecessors.[26] This transcreative process is also energized by the translatability of the original poem, a possibility that for some poets entirely blurs the line between original and translation, as the twentieth-century Mexican poet Octavio Paz noted in his proclamation, "No text can be completely original because language itself, in its very essence, is already a translation."[27]

In the latter half of the twentieth century, increased attention to the visibility of translators and translations prompted new approaches to theorizing the relation between translations and originals, as the primary status of original texts and authors was called into question and even rejected. In Israel, translation studies advanced in the 1970s primarily through the pioneering research that came out of Tel Aviv's Porter Institute of Poetics and Semiotics, particularly through the work of Harshav, Itamar Even-Zohar, and Gideon Toury, and the development of the "polysystem" theory of literature. With its roots in the Russian formalist tradition, polysystem theory situated literature within a heterogeneous and interconnected social, cultural, and historical framework. Even-Zohar's work, in particular, focused considerable attention on the critical role of translation in shaping literary culture and economies, even going so far as to argue that translation activity was such a central and integral part of the literary polysystem that "no clear cut distinction is maintained between 'original' and 'translated' writings."[28] In the 1980s and the 1990s, Israeli translation studies continued to develop along sociological and historiographic lines in the work of scholars Nitsa Ben-Ari and Zohar Shavit (whose historiographical research I address in the next chapter), calling attention to the relation between translation and ideology, the role of translation in Israeli pedagogy, and the status and value of translation in the Hebrew literary economy in Mandatory Palestine/Israel. Alongside this work, scholars like Aminadav Dykman, whose essay on Goldberg's translations I reference in chapter 3, continue to use translation as a lens through which to read Hebrew literature in multilingual and comparative contexts. Dykman is also a literary translator in his own right (of classical Greek, Russian, and Latin, to name a few of his languages), thereby bringing theory and praxis together in contemporary translation studies.[29] Over the decades, the work of Shimon Sandbank has stood out in particular for its attention to textual relations between Hebrew and European literature, with an emphasis on poetry. In his landmark study, the 1976 essay collection *Shtei brekhot ba-ya'ar: kesharim u-makbilot bein ha-shira ha-'ivrit ve-ha-shira ha-eiropit* (Two Pools in the Wood: Hebrew Poetry and the European Tradition), translation emerges as a constitutive relation in Sandbank's comparative reading of Hebrew, German, Italian, and English poetry of the twentieth century. For Sandbank, a poetics of translation develops out of practices of translation, which are distinct for each poet, and in this respect, among others, *Strange Cocktail* has been in dialogue with his work since its earliest stages.[30]

Blurring the lines that demarcate translation and original and calling into question a text's claims to originality and authority are critical interventions that one observes in various strands of translation theory in the twentieth century, but in my work I have found Benjamin's assertion that "to comprehend [translation] as form, one must go back to the original, for the laws governing the translation lie within the original, contained in the issue of its translatability" to be a particularly productive point of departure for my own inquiries.[31] Benjamin's expression "laws governing translation" acknowledges translation as both a separate text and also one that remains in a very close, arguably synonymous, relation to its original, a relation that carries serious implications in national contexts. If translations are bound by the laws of the original, this would appear to complicate their status within the laws and borders of the languages and cultures into which they cross, thereby begging the question: In what ways does translation transgress the rule of law of a target culture? But Benjamin's language of law also assigns a complicated authority to translation because the translation, no longer contained within its source language and culture, is now free to bend and impose its own rules in as many contexts into which it is translated.

In this respect, translation is a practice that can work on behalf of hegemonic social and literary structures or resist them entirely, introducing and producing alternative narratives of canon formation and tradition and tracing new, sometimes radical and transgressive, relations between texts and authors. This potential for transformative transgression has motivated postcolonial approaches to both the study and practice of translation. "I remain interested in writers who are against the current, against the mainstream," Gayatri Spivak wrote in her 1993 landmark essay "The Politics of Translation." "I remain convinced that the interesting literary text might be precisely the text where you do not learn what the majority view of majority cultural representation or self-representation of a nation state might be."[32] Here, Spivak called attention to the need to translate works that are not canonical, whose marginal or excluded status means that they are precisely the kind of works that challenge (literary) institutional authority. And yet, for minor languages like Hebrew, the translation of canonical literature can be politically charged as well, as the disagreement between Goldberg and Kariv reveals.

In the past few years, fractures and tensions have become visible in the contemporary Hebrew poetry scene in Israel between Ashkenazi (European) and Mizrachi (Arab/Middle Eastern) poets, the latter group redressing decades of European, and primarily Western European, hegemony in Israel's literary culture through persistent challenges to "The State of Ashkenaz," as the poet Roy Hasan writes in one of his signature poems.[33] The poetry collective Ars Poetika has been particularly vocal and active in challenging the primacy Ashkenazi poets have claimed in various institutions of Israeli literary culture, from their disproportionate inclusion in university and high school curricula to their representation in the publishing industry and the economy of literary prizes. Their challenge to the Ashkenazi literary elite is implicit in their very name, where *ars* not only invokes the Latin *ars poetica* but also the pejorative *'ars*, a word that comes into Hebrew from the Arabic (where it means "shepherd" but also denotes "pimp" in its modern usage) and refers to young men, usually of Middle Eastern background. As I have prepared this book, I have been mindful of the fact that it brings together four poets of Ashkenazi background, and where possible, I address the rich traffic between Hebrew and Arabic, particularly in the chapters on Yeshurun and Schimmel, where the legacy of Arabic on the development of Hebrew poetry allows for different options and strategies toward a more inclusive poetry.[34] Arabic is not one of the languages in my linguistic toolbox, but I hope that the translation-centered model that I offer in *Strange Cocktail* encourages new configurations and constellations of writers that put Hebrew into relation with a wider array of languages.[35]

The Israeli poet and scholar Almog Behar has observed that current East/West orientations in contemporary Hebrew poetry share "an opposition to the hegemonic project of 'the negation of the diaspora' in contemporary Israeli culture."[36] To a large extent, this opposition is also present in Western-oriented Hebrew poetry throughout the twentieth century, as my book highlights throughout in its attention to how, through and in translation, the poets of *Strange Cocktail* have asserted a wide range of relations both within and outside of the European frame, as well as the Anglophone tradition, in the case of Schimmel. In these cases, a resistance to canonical authority and the politics of gatekeeping is evident not only in the choice of translations but also in how and in what contexts literary translation occurred. For instance, Baudelaire may be a central figure in the Western European canon, but in her translations of his poems, Raab insists on making her own aesthetic choices visible. Her versions remain among the most radical translations of Baudelaire in Hebrew, but because they were unpublished in her lifetime, a serious appraisal of these works, and Raab's translation practices in general, has been long overdue.

Hebrew poets who translate approach the enterprise of translation, as poets have for centuries, as a laboratory for their own poetry. In the case of the poets of this study, their own writing on the matter confirms that they were attuned to the problematics of translation: issues of fidelity, the calculus of loss and gains, and the persistent afterlife of diasporic languages in Hebrew translation, as well as the ways in which translation shaped original

Hebrew texts. But these poets also acknowledged the extent to which their own texts constituted "a priori translating," to use Derrida's term, or, in Reynolds's words, "poem translations."[37] "One of the limits of theories of translation," Derrida cautioned, "[is that] all too often they treat the passing from one language to another and do not sufficiently consider the possibility for languages to be implicated *more than two* in a text."[38] What Derrida is rejecting here is the very idea of a monolingual text; rather, its language is implicitly, and even explicitly, multilingual. This is not only a condition of language itself—for example, the way languages migrate and develop over time through their contacts with other languages—but also a condition of an individual's relation to language, which is constantly changing and multiplying. Therefore, a poetics and a praxis of translation are not mutually exclusive, nor can they be separated from the work of original composition. Edwin Gentzler's entry on the "poetics of translation" in the *Routledge Encyclopedia of Translation Studies* contends that "the poetics of translation is concerned with the relationship between the poetics of a source text in its own literary system and that of the target text in a different system."[39] But the problem with this formulation is that it insists that the original and the translation are separate texts, rather than consider the possibility that these distinctions can, and often do, blur and collapse, particular in the writing and translating of poetry.[40] In *Strange Cocktail*, I call for an understanding of a poetics of translation as it surfaces *from* and operates *within* "original" literary texts. That three of the four poets whose work I examine are also literary translators (in the "proper" sense of the term) is not incidental; the practice of translation, as I show, makes them acutely aware of the ways in which writing poetry, and specifically, writing poetry in Hebrew, is itself a translational, multilingual practice. For these poets, to write in Hebrew in the twentieth century is to engage, at times reluctantly, with what Robert Alter has termed the "Jewish echo chamber."[41] As these poets moved between different registers and layers of Hebrew and its multilingual fusions and inflections, writing in Hebrew became an act of translation.[42]

Yet, for all four poets, translation also serves as a crucial and antihegemonic mode of cultural, linguistic, and transhistoric exchange, thereby constituting a politics of translation that is inseparable from its poetics.[43] For these poets, translation blurred the line between translation and original writing in ways that transgressed the prevailing aesthetic and ideological demands of their time, which varied for each poet in significant ways, as I will show in part II. However, working in a minor literary vernacular, the translation strategies that modern Hebrew poets like Raab, Goldberg, Yeshurun, and Schimmel employed also allowed them to inscribe their Hebrew writing into more expansive constellations, thereby "forging," as Jahan Ramazani observed with regard to modernist notions of literary citizenship, "alliances of style and sensibility across vast distances of geography, history, and culture."[44] In the zone that opened between translation and original, modern Hebrew poets were able to activate new and sometimes radical relations that not only reflected and engaged the multilingual currents that remained active despite the Zionist demand for national monolingualism but also arguably ensured that this demand would remain unfulfilled.

TRANSLATION AND THE IN-BETWEEN

I begin this section where the previous one closes—in the zone of the in-between, a space that has become the paradigmatic location of translation and translators. In his landmark collection *The Location of Culture*, Homi Bhabha describes the in-between as an "interstitial moment," where "the intersubjective and collective experiences of *nationness*, community interest, or cultural value are negotiated."[45] This now ubiquitous formulation of the in-between resonates in contemporary reconsiderations of modern Hebrew and Israeli literary history, particularly with regard to language politics, literary identity, and canon formation.[46] In her introduction to the collection *Between Languages and Cultures: Translation and Cross Cultural Texts*, Anuradha Dingwaney formulates an understanding of in-betweenness as "that space of translation where the self or one culture encounters, and, more importantly, interacts with an 'other' or another culture. It is a fertile space, and disquieting, because, if explored fully, it proves to be a sphere (or zone) in which one both abandons and assumes associations."[47] Here, the word "disquieting" stands out for the ways that it accords with the tensions and currents that underlie my use of the expression "strange cocktail." Throughout this book, my use of the term "in-between" not only addresses translation as a movement *between* languages, cultures, histories, and so on, but also acknowledges positions and articulations of in-betweenness *within* linguistic, geographic, and cultural texts and contexts. In postcolonial studies of translation, in-betweenness often lies at the interstices of conveniently and clearly demarcated "source" and "target" languages and cultures and their respective geographies. This is a problem, Maria Tymoczko argues, because it displaces "the actual physical and cultural space that the translator occupies."[48] And yet, while it is the case that translators stand firmly in specific cultural and social contexts that inform how, why, and what they translate, translation also has the (inconvenient) tendency to unsettle, displace, and transform its sources and targets.

Tymoczko's critique of the in-between includes a skepticism of turns in translation studies that attempt to characterize the translator as a creative agent:

> Rather than promoting a view of a translator as embedded in and committed to specified cultural and social frameworks and agenda, however broad, the discourse of translation as a space between embodies a rather romantic and even elitist notion of the translator as poet. If the place of enunciation of the translator is a space outside both the source and the receptor culture, the translator becomes a figure like the romantic poet, alienated from allegiances to any culture, isolated by genius.[49]

The phrase "translator as poet" stands out in Tymoczko's argument, not for the literal relation that it implies—in fact, in her reading, she does not concern herself with poetry at all—but rather because "as poet" functions here as a metaphor for the creative potential of translation, of which the history of poetry translation offers many examples. But this is a formulation that relies on long-standing, negative generalizations of poets—and translators—as figures who stand outside of culture, time, and even language, further reifying the more pernicious generalization of poetry's untranslatability. Even more problematically, Tymoczko insinuates that ascribing a creative role or agency to translation excludes it from cultural and social contexts, thereby ignoring how creative approaches to translation have been responsible for some of the more radical shifts and turns in literary history (e.g., the vernacularization project of the sixteenth-century Pléiade poets, the ongoing and multilingual legacy of Petrarchism, and the "cannibalistic" poetics of the Brazilian modernists). The "in-between" remains a productive location for twentieth-century and contemporary poets and translators, for whom it is hardly a static, "neutral" space, but rather a zone of transformative, transgressive, and transhistoric relation and movement.

In her research on Amichai, Kronfeld discovered an unpublished qua-train, wherein the poet imagines life's gatekeepers as translators, *turge-manim*, who accompany the speaker through life's journey until the end when these guardians go to sleep and the speaker's heart returns "to its first home," *el beito ha-rishon*.[50] These guardian translators move in the space between life and death, but they are not impassive bystanders. This space of translation contains the fullness of an active life. By extending the metaphor of translation to the cyclical journey of life and death, Amichai advances a metapoetic argument. The "first home" to which all lives return at death is also the *bayit*—Hebrew for stanza—of the poem, thereby underscoring the intimate, inclusive relation between originals and translations, source and target, writing and translating.

Why Amichai opts for the Aramaic-inflected *turgeman* and the his-torical and cultural associations that this particular term carries, rather than modern Hebrew's *metargem*, is elucidated further in the poem "Ve-lo nitlahev" ("And Let Us Not Get Excited"), where the translator—also a *turgeman*—no longer shadows the poet but now serves as a figure for the poet himself:

וְלֹא נִתְלַהֵב, כִּי לֹא יִתְלַהֵב
תֻּרְגְּמָן. בְּשֶׁקֶט נַעֲבִיר
מִלִּים מֵאָדָם לְאָדָם, מִשָּׂפָה לִשְׂפָתַיִם אֲחֵרוֹת,

וּבְלִי לָדַעַת, כְּמוֹ אָב שֶׁמַּעֲבִיר
קְלַסְתֵּר פְּנֵי אָבִיו הַמֵּת לִבְנוֹ,
וְהוּא אֵינוֹ דוֹמֶה לִשְׁנֵיהֶם,
הוּא רַק מְתַוֵּךְ.

And let us not get excited, for a translator
must not get excited. Quietly, let us pass on
words from one to another, one tongue (*safa*) to other lips (*sfatayim*),

unawares, the way a father passes down
the features of his dead father's face to his son,
yet he doesn't resemble either of them:
he's just a go-between (*metavekh*).

(Translated by Chana Bloch and Chana Kronfeld)[51]

During the Babylonian exile (sixth century BCE), the use of Aramaic as a Jewish vernacular increased considerably, and it continued to be a major vernacular of Jewish communities in Palestine and the diaspora in the post-texilic period. As a result, Jewish congregations could not rely solely on Hebrew for religious instruction and liturgy, necessitating the services of a *meturgeman* (also, *turgeman*). The *meturgeman* would provide oral translations of Hebrew biblical texts into Aramaic but was not restricted to literal translation (in fact, literal translation was often expressly prohibited); rather, the *meturgeman* would expand the translation with commentary and references to relevant, topical events.[52] Amichai is aware of this history, and his use of the word *turgeman* allows him to invoke an understanding of translation that encompasses not only verbal but also cultural and historical mediation and transformation. In modern Hebrew, *metavekh*, which Kronfeld and Chana Bloch translate as "go-between," also carries the meaning of "broker," in the financial sense, further underscoring Amichai's understanding of culture, language, and tradition as economies of exchange, gains, and losses. In this respect, Kronfeld argues, an understanding of contemporary translation comes down to "what it means for a human agent, be it a reader, a poet, a translator or a poetic persona, for that matter, to activate, interpret, critique and rewrite the constitutive texts of a culture."[53] But the poet-translator participates in these exchanges *be-sheket*, quietly, and without getting too "excited" (like the inconspicuous Talmudic *meturgemanim*). In other words, the poet-translator does not lay claim to an original voice or to the demand that he or she leave a visible historical and cultural imprint. Instead, both the poet and translator participate in cultural and linguistic *michzur*, recycling, a process that is derivative—in other words, unoriginal—but also transformative and creative.[54]

In "Ve-lo nitlahev," Amichai positions the poet-translator at the center of this chain of cultural and linguistic transmission, between the past (the grandfather) and the future (the son), a position that allows the poet-translator to participate actively in a cultural economy, while also creating new linguistic, cultural, and historical associations and relations. In fact, Amichai is likely challenging here the patrilineal model that dominated Hebrew literary historiography until the late twentieth century.[55] In modern Hebrew, the expression *klaster panim* is a fixed expression often translated as "countenance," but it has an etymology that opens Amichai's *klaster pnei aviv*, "the countenance of his father," to suggestions that the poet is playing with and arguably critiquing ideas of inheritance. Indeed, by rendering *klaster panim* as "features" in their translation, Bloch and Kronfeld tie the expression to the themes of mediation and circulation that shape the poem.

Despite its Germanic or Yiddish inflection, the word *klaster* is not Semitic in origin. It is likely a Hebraization of the Greek κρύσταλλος (*kristalos*) or the Latin *crystallum*, and its presence in this poem constitutes a translational moment. It makes its way into Hebrew through rabbinic literature, where it appears several times. In one notable instance, in the Talmudic tractate *Berakhot* (Benedictions), the expression *klaster panim* appears in a discussion on Moses and the *matan Torah*, the giving of the Torah at Mount Sinai.[56] In a glossary that accompanies *Berakhot*, the famed French medieval rabbi Shlomo Yitzhaki (Rashi) offers the biblical expression *karan 'or panav* as a kind of translation or definition for *klaster panim*.[57] In the biblical book of Exodus, where the *matan Torah* is related, it is stated that as Moses came down the mountain, *karan 'or panav*, an expression that lends itself to various English translations and interpretations, including "the skin of his face sent forth beams" (Jewish Publication Society) or "the skin of his face shone" (King James Version).[58] But like Amichai's *turgeman*/father figure, Moses *lo yada*, did not know, that his face was shining when he addressed the Israelites (Exodus 34:29).

Amichai's recontextualization of this biblical and rabbinic material invokes, but also critiques, a long-standing narrative of transmission and inheritance on which Judaism has staked its identity for millennia, bringing questions of belonging and tradition to bear on postwar and postindependence anxieties of influence and legacy that were, and still are, particularly charged in Jewish Israeli society. On the one hand, post-1948 Israeli literary culture was motivated to dissociate itself from its diasporic roots but, on the other hand, it remained very much indebted to a textual tradition of exile and diaspora. The presence of the word *klaster*, as well as the Aramaic expressions that appear in the rest of the poem, also underscore, Harshav's words, "the ironies of reterritorialized language" and the deeply multilingual layers that shape Hebrew vernacular writing, which Amichai likens here to a practice of linguistic and cultural translation.[59]

The words *klaster* and *turgeman* mark dynamic intertextual moments that not only substantiate an idea of translation as mediation but also understand translation to be creative—that is, literally giving birth to a new "face" or legacy. A possible context for this understanding of *klaster* is the Talmudic tractate *Nidda* (Separation), which concerns menstruation and the female observance of ritual purity. Here, the word *klaster* first appears in a discussion on miscarriage and the specific circumstances that determine whether or not a woman is required to observe ritual purity following a miscarriage.[60] This discussion includes poetic details on the shape of the embryo at different stages of gestation, with one commentary, attributed to Rabbi Simlai, likening an embryo in an advanced stage of gestation to "a folded writing tablet" (*pinkas she-mekupal*).[61] This preoccupation with embryonic features, and their relation to composition, segues into a passage that enumerates the characteristics that parents bestow on their children. It marks this tractate's only instance of the expression *klaster panim*:

תנו רבנן שלשה שותפין יש באדם הקדוש ברוך הוא ואביו ואמו אביו מזריע הלובן
שממנו עצמות וגידים וצפרנים ומוח שבראשו ולובן שבעין אמו מזרעת אודם שממנו
עור ובשר ושערות ושחור שבעין והקדוש ברוך הוא נותן בו רוח ונשמה וקלסתר
פנים וראיית העין ושמיעת האוזן ודבור פה והלוך רגלים ובינה והשכל וכיון שהגיע
זמנו להפטר מן העולם הקדוש ברוך הוא נוטל חלקו וחלק אביו ואמו מניח לפניהם

Our Rabbis taught: There are three partners in man, the Holy One, blessed be He, his father and his mother. His father supplies the semen of the white substance out of which are formed the child's bones, sinews, nails, the brain in his head and the white in his eye; his mother supplies the semen of the red substance out of which is formed his skin, flesh, hair, blood and the black of his eye; and the Holy One, blessed be He, gives him the spirit and the breath, *beauty of features* [*klaster panim*], eyesight, the power of hearing and the ability to speak and to walk, understanding and discernment. When his time to depart from the world approaches the Holy One, blessed be He, takes away his share and leaves the shares of his father and his mother with them.[62]

For this use of *klaster panim* ("beauty of features"), Rashi offers *ziv*, light, as a synonym, which Israel W. Slotki renders as "beauty" in his English translation. In this passage, these intangible features are a divine patrimony, but Amichai's poem also suggests that, in addition to the genetic material that determines eye color and hair texture, uncoded, nonmaterial traits also pass between generations, though their transmission—or translation—is not contingent on linear continuities. Amichai was certainly aware of the politics of continuity that shaped the modern Hebrew literary canon and language politics in the twentieth century. Asserting an uninterrupted line of Hebrew textual history and linguistic transmission proved critical to the territorial politics of Jewish nation-building in the early twentieth century. In this context, the inclusion of the polyphonic *klaster* in a poetic line about inheritance suggests that, from one generation to another, narratives of continuity are fashioned, refashioned, revised, and retranslated.[63] The poet-translator occupies the hinge (or hinges) where a narrative turns toward new possibilities, and also where it turns back in an act of revision. This is certainly evident in Amichai's work, but the role of translation in shaping new lines of influence and tradition is also central to the work of Goldberg and Schimmel, as I will show in chapters 3 and 5.

Writers who employ a poetics of translation in their own work—an outstanding feature of bilingual and multilingual writing, as well as "minor literatures"—are explicitly rejecting a "romantic sensibility" that privileges originality and monolingual authority.[64] Amichai's 1989 poem "Bindidat 'amim" ("In the Migration of Peoples") acknowledges the multiple voices and experiences that comprise a national space/text:

וְאַף עַל פִּי שֶׁגַּרְנוּ לְאֹרֶךְ אוֹתוֹ הַפְּרוֹזְדוֹר
בְּאוֹתוֹ הַבַּיִת, נִפְגַּשְׁנוּ רַק כְּמוֹ שְׁנַיִם
שֶׁנִּפְגָּשִׁים בִּנְדִידַת עַמִּים שֶׁל יְמֵי קֶדֶם
בְּמִקְרֶה.

. . . .

אַתְּ לוֹקַחַת אֶת הַמִּלִּים מֵאוֹתוֹ מָקוֹם כָּמוֹנִי,
אַךְ הַמִּלִּים שֶׁלָּךְ שׁוֹנוֹת מִשֶּׁלִּי.

And though we lived in the same corridor
In the same house, we met only as two strangers
Meeting in the migration of peoples in ancient times,
By chance.

. . . .

You take words from the same place as me,
But your words are different from mine.

> (Translated by Barbara and Benjamin Harshav)[65]

Although Amichai engaged in literary translation throughout his career, it is in his own "original" poetry that his most extensive and sustained work of translation takes place, and this is the case as well for the poets of *Strange Cocktail*.[66] This translation is not the work of a neutral, detached bystander, but rather of someone who occupies the space of translation bodily, moving language *mi-safa li-sfatayim*, from lip to lips, from one language to many. In Hebrew, *safa* is both language but also lip. In the plural, the grammatical dual suffix *ayim* in *sfatayim* denotes doubling—two lips. The plural of languages, on the other hand, is *safot*. Amichai cleverly plays with these associations, conveying the doubling and multiplying of languages that occurs in the act of translation, and that is always implicit in the poetic text.

◆ ◆ ◆

The role and status of translation in the development of modern Hebrew poetry remains a relatively unstudied area in Hebrew literary scholarship, in part because of the particular challenges that reconstructing this work presents. From the nineteenth to the early twentieth century, poetry translation mostly circulated in newspapers, pamphlets, and journals, while book publishers primarily encouraged and invested in translations of prose. In addition to this circulation, translation was also implicit in the work of a number of poets for whom Hebrew was not a native language. The translation work and practices of modern Hebrew poets not only signals the presence of outside influences that potentially shape their own writing but also reveals relations that carry the original Hebrew poem into new linguistic, cultural, and historical contexts, sometimes doing so against the demands of the Hebrew nation-building project, and certainly against the demands of their own contemporaries, as the Kariv and Goldberg episodes that open this chapter illustrate. This is still the case, as my afterword highlights, for the current translation turn in contemporary Hebrew poetry. A number of poets today are engaged in a programmatic recharting of contemporary Hebrew poetry through a generative translation practice, and in so doing, they are continuing work that perhaps in the end is simply inherent, as this book argues throughout, in very act of writing (Hebrew) poetry.[67]

By bringing together four poets whose work covers the better part of the twentieth century, *Strange Cocktail* advances a transhistoric, comparative, and multilingual framing of modern Hebrew literature that considers how canons change and are undone when translation occupies a central position—how lines of influence and affiliation are redrawn and literary historiographies are revised when the work of translation occupies the same status as an original text, when translating and writing go hand in hand. By focusing on poetry, *Strange Cocktail* highlights the range of these contexts and further expands the ways in which modern Hebrew literature, and poetry in particular, continues to be framed and studied. In the zone that opens between translation and original, modern Hebrew poets were able to activate new and sometimes radical relations that *Strange Cocktail* now reactivates through a translation-centered reading of their work.

CHAPTER I

Voices Near and Far

Historical Perspectives on Hebrew Poetry and (Its) Translation

Nothing is lacking where there is creative work, even a work of translation.

—YAAKOV SHTEINBERG[1]

To further contextualize the poetics of translation that *Strange Cocktail* elaborates, I will offer here a distilled history of modern Hebrew literary translation and its practices, and specifically the translation of poetry, from the nineteenth-century Haskala, or Jewish Enlightenment period, to the early decades of the twentieth century, from the European and Russian diaspora to Mandatory Palestine.[2] I will highlight the critical role that translation assumed in creating a vibrant and flexible literary vernacular in modern Hebrew and the particular status that the translation of poetry asserted in these developments.[3] What I offer here are a few snapshots from the history of modern Hebrew poetry that illuminate the broader concerns of this book and also address specifically, and through a reading of key episodes, how thinking about translation, and particularly the translation of poetry, not only developed in modern Hebrew literature but also was a constitutive component of its development.[4]

MASKILIC TRANSLATION AND THE POETRY OF *HAʿATAKA*

While translation was a prominent practice during the Jewish Haskala, and one that was explicitly related to the vernacularization of Hebrew, there is little extant translation criticism that would illuminate how *maskilim*, Hebrew Enlightenment writers in the late eighteenth and nineteenth centuries, thought about or approached this activity; namely, how they distinguished between the translation of religious and scientific texts and literary translation. But even a cursory reading of maskilic journals and almanacs provides evidence of certain translation patterns and approaches, which illuminate how these writers identified, framed, and named literary translation, particularly toward the end of the Haskala when literary translation became a more widespread practice.

One of the more intriguing contributions of the late Haskala to Hebrew's translation lexicon is the use of the term *ha'ataka* to characterize literary translation. In modern Hebrew, *le-ha'atik* typically refers to duplication, replication, imitation, and copying, but its biblical usage is richly polysemous, where we find it applied to the idea of proceeding, moving forward, and moving on, as well as removing (as in furniture). Wilhelm Gesenius's lexicon offers a definition for the root ע-ת-ק that could encompass linguistic translation, "to transfer, to transcribe from one book to another."[5] Gesenius also acknowledges "to take away," with a reference to Job 32:15, *he'etiku mihem milim*, "they left off speaking," meaning they were silent.[6] In Marcus Jastrow's entry for *'atak*, we encounter translation, editing, and interpretation, the latter a meaning that takes hold in medieval and rabbinic literature.[7] In these later works, a sharper distinction is drawn between the interpretation of sacred texts and acts of linguistic translation, although slippages between the two certainly occur.[8] Aside from the ubiquity of the term *ha'ataka*, there is no consistent typology for literary translation in the Haskala. Instead, until late in the nineteenth century, one finds a variety of expressions for translation: for example, *mi-shirei* (from the poems of), *'al pi* (after, following, according to), *ne'etak mi-shir shel* (copied/transferred from the poem by) or *ne'etak mi* (copied/transferred from), and *targum* (translation). These terms were all in use, and in some cases, remain so today.[9] Nevertheless, what distinguishes *ha'ataka* from the now standard modern Hebrew verb for translating, *letargem*, is that *ha'ataka* explicitly suggests that translations can replace or stand in for original, foreign texts.

Daniel Weissbort has written that in Western literature "the nineteenth century ... is not generally thought of as a great age of translation," despite energetic debates on the topic and the German contribution, via Johann Wolfgang von Goethe and Friedrich Schleiermacher, to translation criticism, discussions which continue to resonate in contemporary debates on translation.[10] Nineteenth-century German translation, with its emphasis on proximity to the original text, encouraged a reciprocal relationship between translations and originals. In the *West-Östlicher Diwan* (West-Eastern Diwan), his 1819 collection of lyric poems (*diwan*) inspired by the Persian poet Hafez, Goethe acknowledged a meaningful relationship between originals and translations, specifically translations that "identify" with the original. In his words: "Inside [this circle] the coming together of the foreign and the native, the unknown approximation and the known, keep moving towards each other."[11] But this approximation also provoked what Weissbort calls an "anxiety of creativity."[12] With original and translation "moving towards each other," the gap between the two becomes indistinct and potentially irrelevant. For Goethe, this was the point: for German translation to house or domesticate foreign literature, thereby becoming a true *Weltliteratur*, world literature. On the other hand, Schleiermacher, in his landmark 1813 lecture "Über die verschiedenen Methoden des Übersetzens" ("On the Different Methods of Translation"), cautioned against overstating this approximation and stressed the importance of retaining the visibility of the foreign, of translation: "[J]ust as the inclination to translate cannot arise until a certain foreign language ability has been established among the educated, so too will the art of translation grow and its aim be set higher and higher when connoisseurship and the taste for foreign works become more widespread."[13] According to Susan Bernofsky, who has translated this essay into English, "to translate in this mode is to promote xenophilia."[14] Bernofsky is addressing nineteenth-century German literary culture specifically, but her argument resonates in Leah Goldberg's concern, voiced almost a century and a half after Schleiermacher's essay first appeared, that a rejection of foreign and diasporic texts and languages motivated and reinforced a resistance to Hebrew literary translation in early twentieth-century Palestine.

These debates on translation nevertheless offer a context for thinking about Hebrew literary translation in the nineteenth century and how it developed alongside the secularization and vernacularization of the Hebrew language. Indeed, an inclination to engage and appropriate foreign literature in Hebrew translation is evident in the major literary journals of the Haskala, notably in *Ha-me'asef*, which was based in Berlin.[15] For the most part, this activity is sporadic—particularly in the realm of poetry, where one finds single poems—and usually short poems—translated into Hebrew but little evidence of full collections of translated poetry. In that respect, the kind of comprehensive "transplantation" that German, French, and (to some extent) English poets engaged in the nineteenth century was not as explicit in the Hebrew context. Nevertheless, when one begins the work of tracking the circulation of translations in the journals and almanacs of the period, a close link between translation and original Hebrew writing becomes apparent.

The work of the Galician *maskil* Max (Meir) Letteris (1800–1871) stands out in this period. Letteris was born in Zolkiew, then part of the Austro-Hungarian Empire, and studied German, French, and Latin literature on the recommendation of Nachman Krochmal, a fellow Galician who also encouraged his poetry. He settled in Vienna where he published original poetry in both German and Hebrew, as well as several works of translation.[16] His first Hebrew poetry collections, *Divrei shir* (*Lyrics*, 1822) and *Ayelet ha-shachar* (*Morning Star*, 1824), included his translations of Friedrich Schiller and Homer, among many others.[17] If we go by the number of poems that are followed by the German preposition *nach*, "following" or "after," and a particular author's name, Letteris's *ha'atakot* constitute about a third of his published output. The 1860 collection *Tofes kinor ve-ugav* (*The Harp and Organ Player*) gathered his two previous books as well as additional poems, and included notes that suggest that some of these poems are reworkings of previous texts, including one that is a Hebrew translation of a poem Letteris originally wrote in German.[18] In many instances, Letteris also helpfully notes the title of the German poem that he has recast into Hebrew, though in many other cases he provides only the name of the original author (e.g., *nach Schiller*). As Gideon Toury noted, "[t]he range of activities, strategies and texts associated with translation [during the early to mid-Haskala] was thus both broad and highly diffuse, especially as many compositions which did not draw on foreign texts in a one-to-one fashion were still collations of parts of existing texts in another language."[19] Indeed, one of the methodological challenges of working with journals, almanacs, and periodicals of the Haskala is that often translations are not indicated as such in a table of contents; rather, the title of the poem is followed by the name of the translator *as* author. This is not simply a matter of the translator replacing the author, but rather indicative of the liberties that were often taken in the translation of these texts, thereby supporting a claim to authorship. Matthew Reynolds has shown this to be the case for eighteenth-century English translations of Greek and Latin literature. By the nineteenth century, the term translation begins to amplify, as Reynolds observes, "[to] describe a kind of writing that involves the transformation of words into other words as part of a continuous, if misguided, process of composition."[20] In fact, in the Hebrew literature of the same period, and well into the late nineteenth century, translations of poetry could be misread as original Hebrew texts, with Hebrew translators assuming the status of an original author. There are many documented instances where the original author's name appears before or after the translated text and in very small print, while the translator's name is positioned in much larger type below the text. Quite frequently, though this was not always the case with Letteris, the title of the original poem would not appear. Because these Hebrew translations often veered far afield from the original text, tracing them back to an original source can be tedious work, though this was not necessarily the case for the maskilic reader of these texts. Nor is it clear that a reader of these texts would have found it necessary to engage in this kind of forensic reading. "In fact translations have always been taken as substitutes," argues Reynolds, "that is, as texts that in some circumstances can be read instead of their originals."[21] As Haskala scholar Moshe Pelli has noted, in the early decades of the Haskala, authors practiced translation into Hebrew to prove that the language was capable of modern, contemporary expression.[22] And yet, as a twenty-first-century scholar of poetry and translation, I am struck by the extent to which certain practices of maskilic translation accord with the more radical, creative practices of translation that poets today utilize.[23] Comparing Letteris's Hebrew translations to their German sources reveals an expansive, fluid, and creative understanding of translation. In his introduction to *Ayelet ha-shachar*, Letteris was clear that he had departed from "the way of the translators" (*derekh ha-ma'atikim*): "[T]hrough much toil I made them work in my own voice, and with a free spirit I will declare publicly: this is my sound."[24] What Letteris meant by "way of the translators" is not entirely clear, but his comments imply that he may have had an understanding of a faithful, literal translation in mind, perhaps one that approximated the role of the Talmudic *meturgeman*. Instead, Letteris was adamant that his readers understand that these translations reflected his own poetic voice.

I turn now to an episode that marks, in my view, a transitional moment from the diffuse and varied approaches of maskilic literary translation to the more programmatic translation practices that emerged in the late nineteenth and early twentieth centuries. This episode concerns the journal *Ha-asif*, which was published annually between 1884 and 1889 (and briefly reemerged in 1893) under the editorship of Nahum Sokolow, a formidable editor, author, and translator who became a major leader of the Zionist movement. Although not directly aligned with the Jewish nationalist movement, *Ha-asif*'s literary section, "Otsar ha-sifrut" ("Treasury of Literature"), supported the work of late maskilic writers as well as writers associated with the *Hibbat Zion* (Love of Zion) and *Techiya* (Revival) movements.[25] The 1885 second volume of *Ha-asif* included the poem "Tochelet nikhzava" ("Hope Deceived"), a translation of Schiller's "Resignation" (the original title) by Natan Shapira (1817–1887).[26] Shapira was the descendant of a venerated seventeenth-century rabbi and Kabbalist from Kraków after whom he was named. At the time of his death, Shapira was remembered in the pages of *Ha-tsefira*, also edited by Sokolow, as an accomplished translator, despite his minimal published output.[27]

Schiller's poem appeared in 1784 in *Thalia*, a short-lived journal that he had edited, but it is evident that Shapira's translation draws from a later modified version, dating to 1800, which omits two stanzas.[28] In Schiller's poem, the recently deceased speaker approaches a heavenly tribunal to make an account of his life. In the course of the poem, we learn that the speaker had renounced his true love and sacrificed earthly pleasures for the promise of a rich afterlife, only to learn that there is no compensation in the hereafter. The title of the poem refers, in this context, to psychological resignation—the acknowledgment that one has come short of certain goals and aspirations—a feeling that can produce either despair or calm, as well as resignation in the German Protestant sense of the term, the submission of one's will to God. The speaker also imagines a dialogue with the divine where he is asked to "resign" his youth and love (named "Laura," a nod to Petrarca), but a band of mockers rebukes him, reminding him that "six thousand years hath Death reigned tranquilly!, /Nor one corpse come to whisper those who die, /What *after* death requites us!"[29] I will return to Shapira's translation in a moment, but want to note here that though there are expected modifications to Schiller's language and imagery, Shapira keeps to Schiller's ABAAB rhyme, a scheme common to the quintet, which was in wide use in sixteenth- and seventeenth-century European poetry. From his translation, one can surmise that he is at home with both the German and the Hebrew—no glaring errors stand out. In fact, a Hebrew translation of Schiller's "Die Ideale" ("The Ideals"), also translated by Shapira, follows this text, and this translation also showcases Shapira's skills as a translator, and of German poetry in particular.

The fact that this translation exists is hardly remarkable, but what distinguishes this translation from others that I have encountered from this period is that in the following volume of *Ha-asif*, dated 1886, we encounter Schiller's "Resignation" once again, but this time in a translation by K. A. (Konstantin Abba) Shapiro.[30] Born in Grodno in 1839, Shapiro, a Christian convert, made his living as a professional photographer (Leo Tolstoy was among his clients). He also published Hebrew poetry of some high regard in the 1870s and the 1880s and was closely affiliated with *Hibbat Zion* (which promoted Jewish immigration to Palestine); indeed, his literary profile would outlast Shapira's (His poem "Be-shadmot beit lechem" ["In the Fields of Bethlehem"] became a popular twentieth-century song lyric.). Although the capacious *Ha-asif* could afford to devote space to a retranslation, publishing two translations of the same poem in consecutive volumes nevertheless warranted some explanation.

In an editorial note that accompanied this translation, Sokolow explains to the reader that this poem has been translated into *leshon ha-kodesh* (the holy tongue, i.e., Hebrew) many times before, and acknowledges its inclusion in the previous volume of *Ha-asif*, but stresses that the editors felt that Shapiro's translation exceeded all previous efforts.[31] In this instance, the translation and original German text (following Schiller's modified 1800 version) are published side by side, "so that a discerning reader can see and judge for himself the merits of this translator's work."[32] Among the countless Hebrew journals of the nineteenth century, this translation of Schiller's poem stands out for many reasons, chief among them that Sokolow's editorial commentary constitutes an early articulation of modern Hebrew translation criticism. Publishing two Hebrew translations of the same German poem back to back invites a comparison of the translations, which are of course very different, as is often the case with the translation of poetry. The differences are not simply a matter of style and interpretation, they also reflect fundamentally distinct approaches to translation— between fidelity and adaptation—which preoccupied nineteenth-century European translation culture. Shapira's translation follows the form of Schiller's poem—it even manages to follow the German word order in some instances—but while faithful to the main content of the poem, it also tends to neutralize Schiller's specific references.[33] For example, the name of the speaker's beloved, "Laura" in the German original, becomes in Shapira's translation *ra'ayatkha*, your beloved or bride. Compare that with Shapiro's rendering, "Sara," an explicitly Jewish name. The inclusion of the German

אמרתי יש־לי תקוה *)

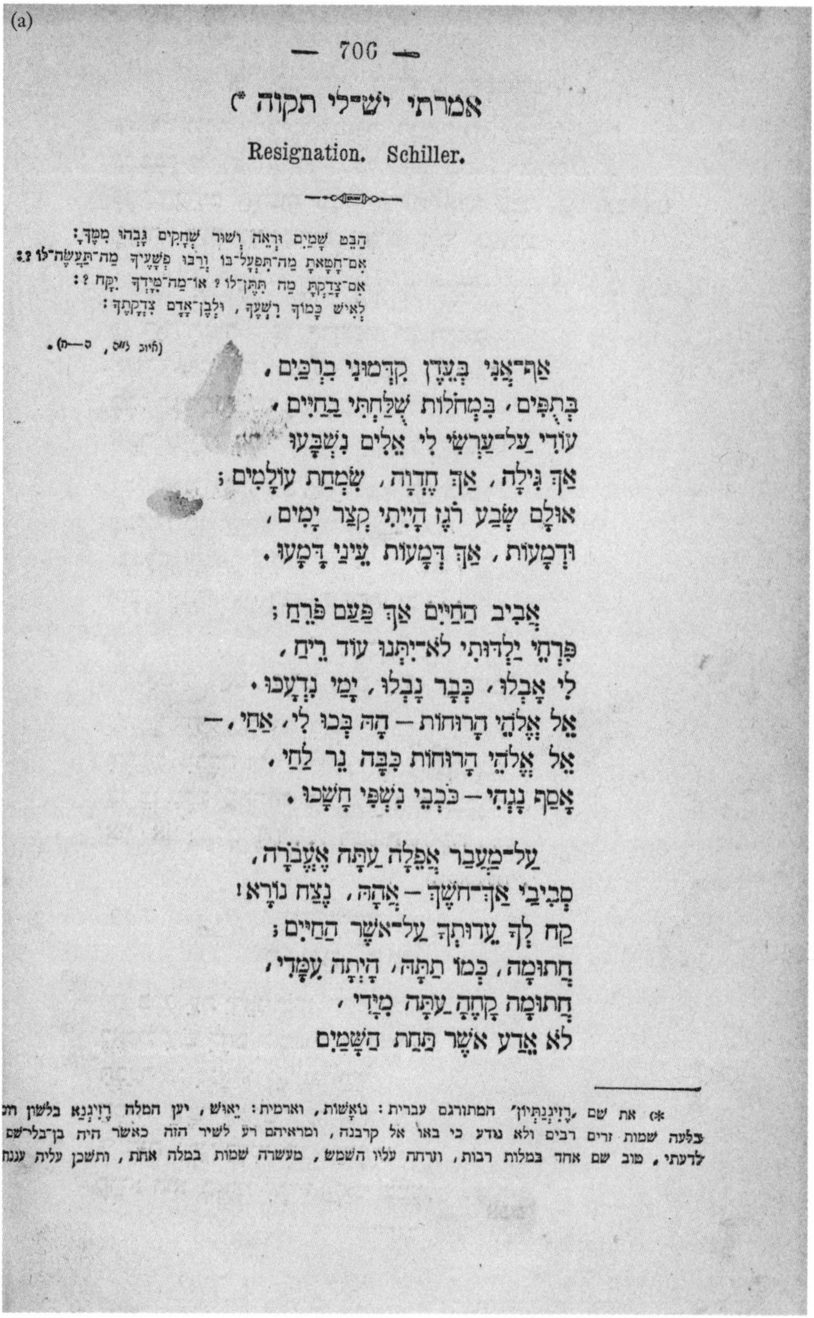

Resignation. Schiller.

הַבֵּט שָׁמַיִם וּרְאֵה וְשׁוּר שְׁחָקִים גָּבְהוּ מִמֶּךָ.
אִם־חָטָאתָ מַה־תִּפְעָל־בּוֹ וְרַבּוּ פְשָׁעֶיךָ מַה־תַּעֲשֶׂה־לֹּו ??
אִם־צָדַקְתָּ מַה־תִּתֶּן־לֹו ? אוֹ־מַה־מִיָּדְךָ יִקָּח ?
לְאִישׁ כָּמוֹךָ רִשְׁעֶךָ, וּלְבֶן־אָדָם צִדְקָתֶךָ :

(איוב ל"ה, ה׳—ז)

אֵד־אָנִי בְּעֵדֶן קַדְמוֹנִי בְרַכִּים,
בְּתָפִים, בִּמְחֹלוֹת שִׁלַּחְתִּי בַחַיִּים,
עוֹדִי עַל־עֶרֶשׂ לִי אֵלִים נִשְׁבָּעוּ
אַךְ גִּילָה, אַךְ חֶדְוָה, שִׂמְחַת עוֹלָמִים ;
אוּלָם שָׁבַע רֹגֶז הָיִיתִי קְצַר יָמִים,
וּדְמָעוֹת, אַךְ דְּמָעוֹת עֵינַי דָּמָעוּ.

אֲבִיב הַחַיִּים אַךְ פַּעַם פֹּרֵחַ ;
פִּרְחֵי יַלְדוּתִי לֹא־יִתְּנוּ עוֹד רֵיחַ,
לִי אָבָלוּ, כְּבָר נָבְלוּ, יָמַי נִדְעָכוּ.
אֵל אֱלֹהֵי הָרוּחוֹת — הָה בְּכוּ לִי, אֲחַי, —
אֵל אֱלֹהֵי הָרוּחוֹת כִּבָּה נֵר חַיַּי,
אָסַף נָגְהִי — כֹּכְבֵי נִשְׁפִּי חָשָׁכוּ.

עַל־מַעֲבַר אֹפֶל אֵפְלָה עַתָּה אֶעֱבֹרָה,
סְבִיבִי אַךְ־חֹשֶׁךְ — אֲהָהּ, נֵצַח נוֹרָא!
קַח לָךְ עֵדוּתְךָ עַל־אֲשֶׁר הַחַיִּים ;
חֲתוּמָה, כְּמוֹ תַתָּהּ, הָיְתָה עִמָּדִי,
חֲתוּמָה קָחֶהָ עַתָּה מִיָּדִי,
לֹא אֵדַע אֲשֶׁר תַּחַת הַשָּׁמַיִם

---

*) אֶת שֵׁם „רָזִיגְנַאצִיוֹן" הַמְתֻרְגָּם עִבְרִית: נוֹאָשׁוּת, וַאֲרָמִית: יָאוּשׁ, יַעַן חֹמֶל רָזִיגְנַא בִּלְשׁוֹן וכ׳
בְּלַעַז שְׁמוֹת זָרִים רַבִּים וְלֹא נָדַע כִּי בָאוּ אֶל קִרְבֵּנוּ, וּמַרְאֵיהֶם רַע לַשִּׁיר הַזֶּה כַּאֲשֶׁר הָיָה בֵין־בְּלִי־שֵׁם
לְדַעְתִּי, טוֹב שֵׁם אֶחָד בְּמִלּוֹת רַבּוֹת, וְתַחַת עָלָיו הַשֶּׁמֶשׁ, מְעֹרָבָה שְׁמוֹת בְּמִלָּה אֹתָהּ, וְתִשְׁכֹּן עֲלֵית עֲנָנָה

Figure 1.1. (*a* and *b*) Hebrew Translation of Friedrich Schiller's "Resignation" by
K. A. Shapiro, in *Ha-asif*, 3 (Warsaw: Isaac Goldman, 1886): 706–707

(הערת המו"ל)

השיר „רעזיגנאציאָן" נעתק כמה פעמים ללה"ק , וגם בהאסיף משנה
שעברה נמצאה העתקתו , אולם ההעתקה הנכחית עולה על כולנה . וע"כ
נתנו לה מקום בהאסיף הזה . והננו מציגים פה גם את נוף השיר האשכנזי ,
למען יראו הנבונים וישפטו על יקרת מעשה ידי המעתיק .

Resignation.

Auch ich war in Arkadien geboren,
    Auch mir hat die Natur
An meiner Wiege Freude zugeschworen;
Auch ich war in Arkadien geboren,
    Doch Thränen gab der kurze Lenz mir nur.

Des Lebens Mai blüht einmal und nicht wieder;
    Mir hat er abgeblüht.
Der stille Gott — o weinet, meine Brüder —
Der stille Gott taucht meine Fackel nieder,
    Und die Erscheinung flieht.

Da steh' ich schon auf deiner finstern Brücke,
    Furchtbare Ewigkeit!
Empfange meinen Vollmachtbrief zum Glücke!
Ich bring' ihn unerbrochen dir zurücke,
    Ich weiß nichts von Glückseligkeit.

Figure 1.1. Continued

original also highlights the extent to which Shapiro's translation departs from Schiller's form and meter. Instead of Schiller's quintets, Shapiro opts for sestets, which understandably alters the rhyme scheme (to AABCCB, a pattern common to the Spanish *sextilla*).

The translation "Sara" is consistent with the ways in which Shapiro recasts Schiller in a more explicitly Jewish context, a domesticating translation strategy that was consistent with the maskilic view of translation as part of the project of Jewish renewal and acculturation.[34] Take, for example, Shapiro's addition of the following epigraph, from the Book of Job:

הַבֵּט שָׁמַיִם וּרְאֵה וְשׁוּר שְׁחָקִים גָּבְהוּ מִמֶּךָּ:
אִם־חָטָאתָ מַה־תִּפְעָל־בּוֹ וְרַבּוּ פְשָׁעֶיךָ מַה־תַּעֲשֶׂה־לּוֹ:
אִם־צָדַקְתָּ מַה־תִּתֶּן־לוֹ אוֹ מַה־מִיָּדְךָ יִקָּח:
לְאִישׁ־כָּמוֹךָ רִשְׁעֶךָ וּלְבֶן־אָדָם צִדְקָתֶךָ:

Look unto the heavens, and see; and behold the clouds which are higher than thou.

If thou sinnest, what doest thou against him? or if thy transgressions be multiplied, what doest thou unto him?

If thou be righteous, what givest thou him? or what receiveth he of thine hand?

Thy wickedness may hurt a man as thou art; and thy righteousness may profit the son of man.

(Job 35:5–8, KJV)

Shapiro's epigraph constitutes a revision of the German *resignation* (the word is subordinated to the Hebrew title) and its explicit relations to German Protestantism. It also raises the question of how readers of Hebrew, by and large Jewish readers, would have received this poem. Shapiro addresses this fact in his footnote to the Hebrew title:

את שם "רֶזִיגְנַתְּיוֹן" המתורגם עברית: נוֹאָשׁוֹת, וארמית: יֵאוּשׁ, יען המלה רֶזִיגְנָא בלשון רומי בלעה שמות זרים רבים ולא נודע כי באו אל קרבנה, ומראיהם רע לשׁיר הזה כאשר היה בן־בלי שם לדעתי, טוב שם אחר במלות רבות, וזרחה עליו השמש, מעשׂרה שמות במלה אחת, ותשׁכן עליה עננה

The word "resignation" translates into Hebrew as *no'ashot*, and into Aramaic as *ye'ush*, because of the Latin word *rezigna* which swallowed many foreign languages, unaware that they had become her victims, but their likeness is unsuitable for this poem [which is] like an illegitimate son [*ben bli shem*, without a name]. In my view, better one word in many words, *and if the sun be risen upon him*, than ten words in one, *and let a cloud dwell upon it.*[35]

This footnote offers a fascinating critique of Hebrew's relation to European languages, while advancing an important critique about translation. Shapiro begins by acknowledging that a translation for the German *resignation* exists in Hebrew and Aramaic—in other words, in traditionally Jewish languages—but that these words are indebted to the invasive influence of Latin (*lashon romi*). The Latin migrates through these other languages, both Romance and Semitic, like an illegitimate child—in other words, disconnected from its origins. For Shapiro, this poses a major translation problem. The Hebrew *no'ashot* may be a "likeness" of the German *resignation*, but it is an imperfect copy. Instead, Shapiro espouses a view of translation that privileges creative multiplicity—"one word in many words"—which he illustrates in the longer, Hebrew title that precedes the German.[36] The alternative—"ten words in one"—is followed by a line from Job 3:5, a passage where Job laments the day that he was born. Put another way, a translation that simply duplicates the original would be "as infants which never saw the light" (Job 3:16), to invoke the Hebrew euphemism for publication, *latset le-or*, "to go into the light."

That the Shapira and Shapiro translations articulate distinct, and even competing, strategies of translation—adaptation and domestication, respectively—can be observed in their translations of Schiller's line "Hier öffne sich die Heimat dem Verbannten" (stanza 6, line 26), "here a home/homeland opens for the exiles," which becomes in Shapira's translation "le-ish meshulach ve-ne'ezav po yipatchu delatayim," "here doors will open for the abandoned and forsaken man." Shapira rhymes this two lines later with "shamayim," combining these end-rhymes to create an image of the "delatei shamayim," "the doors of heaven," from Psalm 78:23. Psalm 78, the second longest of the biblical psalms, carries the superscription *maskil le-asaf*, the wisdom of Asaph, and recounts the long-standing, dramatic tension in the biblical narrative between God and the children of Israel and their inconsistent observance of his commandments. In the passage that Shapira alludes to, which invokes the exodus out of Egypt, God arguably satisfies the hunger of the Israelites so that they will feel more acutely the sting of his punishment. This message resonates in the central argument of Schiller's poem: favor in this life is not a reflection of divine favor nor does it guarantee any rewards in the afterlife. Psalm 78 is also traditionally known as one of the *maskil* or wisdom psalms, which raises the possibility that Shapira is drawing a correlation between sacred and secular Hebrew maskilic traditions. On the whole, his use of allusion and intertextuality is considerably more opaque here than Shapiro's translation of the same line, "po sha'ar tsiyon le-khol-gole patu'ach," "here Zion's gate is open to every exile." While both translators observe the maskilic practice of introducing Jewish themes and language into their Hebrew translation, Shapiro's approach is to do so more directly and through more invasive reworkings of the original German. In this particular case, Shapiro's rendering translates Schiller's line as if it were a *Hibbat Zion* poem, hinting at the politics of translation that would begin to shape Hebrew translation activity in the twentieth century.

This seems to be Sokolow's design: to invite the reader to compare translation and original, and translation and translation, but framing these comparisons in terms that grant the Hebrew translator authority over and above any demands of the original, foreign text. At the same time, he positions Shapiro's Jewish *ha'ataka* of Schiller as superior to Shapira's translation (though refrains from making explicit his reasons why). Whether this is evidence of an ideological shift in the last years of the Haskala remains unclear. What is evident is that in the European space of translation and translation criticism, Hebrew poet-translators and their texts could move— and did move—in multiple, alternative directions that remain unexplored. Following these movements could open new possibilities for moving through and beyond the space that still seems to separate the nineteenth and twentieth centuries of modern Hebrew literature.

A GIFT FROM SINAI: TRANSLATION AND NATION-BUILDING

In the years that followed the Haskala, Hebrew translation activity became a more visible practice, as well as a crucial and valuable component of the modern Hebrew literary economy. Between 1910 and 1933, the Hebrew literary enclaves of Europe and Russia began to move and consolidate their operations in Palestine, and for much of this period, particularly between 1908 and 1920, translation was a major, indispensable component of modern Hebrew literary production. According to Zohar Shavit, such was the role and status of translation that it was, in her words, "designated to fulfill part of the functions of an original literature."[37] The translation of different kinds of texts—scientific, historical, linguistic, and literary—also encouraged the development of distinct linguistic and literary registers in Hebrew. Shavit, in an article cowritten with Yaakov Shavit, cites a wonderful passage from an article by Ze'ev Jabotinsky (published in *Haaretz*), in which he calls for sensitivity to style and tone in translation. "There are different levels in the development and understanding of a language," he writes. "One must accommodate the style of a translation to these levels. Dickens must be translated in a far richer language than 'Sherlock Holmes.'"[38] Editors and publishers established strict standards for the kinds of works they sought to publish, investing primarily in what they considered to be classics of world literature (with an emphasis on translations from German, Yiddish, and Russian) to generate a corpus of translated work that could serve as a model for original writing, and also to effect transformative changes in original Hebrew works through the influence of these translations.[39] In this respect, translation took on the status of creative, literary labor.

Although not well represented in the early twentieth-century Hebrew book market, poetry and poetry in translation circulated widely in literary journals and almanacs, as well as the Hebrew press.[40] As the previous section discussed, this had been the case throughout the better part of the nineteenth century and continued throughout the twentieth century (in fact, poetry—original and translated—appears regularly in the Hebrew press today). Such was the state of Hebrew poetry and poetry in translation that the Hebrew and Yiddish poet Yaakov Shteinberg (1887–1947), whose observation on translation opens this chapter, argued that Hebrew translators needed to prioritize prose translation over poetry. In his view, Hebrew poetry was much further along in its development than prose, which fell short of the standards observed in other literary traditions.[41] Shteinberg regarded translation as a fundamentally creative activity and was convinced that translation would have an immediate influence on the development and improvement of original modern Hebrew literature, and prose in particular. While translations of poetry continued to be published and circulated in these decades, a glance at the publication listing for Stybel, by far the most prolific publisher of Hebrew translations in this period, indicates that poetry in Hebrew translation represented a very small percentage of the translated books it published between 1917 and 1946.[42] Stybel was not the only Hebrew publishing house invested in translation, but given its distribution and relative financial stability, we can draw a fairly accurate picture of the state of poetry translation in the Hebrew book market in the early decades of the twentieth century. In this context, then, it is notable that in 1918, in a list of sixteen titles that Stybel considered a "high priority" for translation into Hebrew, one finds Aleksandr Pushkin's Russian novel-in-verse *Evgeny Onegin*, which was published in serial form between 1825 and 1832.[43]

The translator for this forthcoming volume is not stated in this list, but the letters that passed between Avraham Yosef Stybel and David Frischmann, *Ha-tekufa*'s editor between 1918 and 1922, reveal that they had reached out to the Hebrew (and also Yiddish) poet Chaim Nachman Bialik (1873–1934) to translate this work.[44] They were insistent that Bialik do this on the grounds that only a poet of his caliber could do justice to Pushkin (1799–1837), who, despite his death at a relatively young age, is still widely regarded as one of the greatest Russian poets and one of the founders of modern Russian literature. Bialik brought his own credentials to the project. Born in Radi, Volhynia, then located in the Russian Empire, Bialik moved to Zhitomir at the age of seven not long after his father's death. Although raised in an Orthodox home, Bialik was attracted to the Haskala and joined the *Hovevei Zion* movement, which shaped his early "longing for Zion" poems. The 1901 publication of his debut collection *Shirim* (Poems) met with wide acclaim among Hebrew readers, and for the next two decades Bialik embarked on a successful literary career as a poet (in Hebrew and Yiddish) as well as an editor and publisher. By the time Frischmann approached him with this translation project, Bialik was already regarded as "the poet of the national renaissance," a title minted by the critic Joseph Klausner.[45]

The idea that a poet would be best equipped to translate poetry is hardly a new claim (I explore it at length in chapter 3.). In his 1916 essay, "'Al ha-targumim" ("On Translations"), M. (Moshe) Ben-Eliezer argues: "Only a poet is capable of translating a classic work of poetry, one whose soul contains the sparks (*nitsotsot*) that exist in the soul of the poet he is translating."[46] The word "sparks" vividly captures here the relation between poet and poet-translator, suggesting that the resulting translation is the product of creative inspiration. Frischmann himself had tried to render *Onegin* into Hebrew and was dissatisfied with his efforts, and he was convinced that Bialik, who was already being compared to Pushkin, would succeed where he had failed. Hebrew translations from the Russian became more widespread as the Haskala extended eastward into Galicia and czarist Russia in the nineteenth century, so it is not surprising to find that by the twentieth century, Russian was one of the primary languages from which Hebrew writers, like Frischmann and Bialik, translated. But Pushkin's status in Russian literature—and later, European literature—also cannot be understated, and this fact certainly would not have escaped Stybel.[47] Although affiliated with Romanticism, Pushkin's work is often read as a bridge between the nineteenth and the twentieth centuries, a status that Bialik's Hebrew output had assumed in his own lifetime. A translation by Bialik, therefore, would have validated the value that Frischmann had placed on literary translation and his insistence on including first-rate Hebrew translations in *Ha-tekufa*, but it also would have made a statement about the status of Hebrew as a full-grown twentieth-century literature. However, the comparisons to Pushkin may have deterred Bialik, who was intent on forging his own identity in Hebrew literature, and while it appeared that for a time he would undertake this project, in the end, his translation did not materialize.[48]

Despite his resistance to this project, Bialik was a prolific translator of both poetry and prose into Hebrew. In fact, the maxim that reading a text in translation is "like kissing through a handkerchief" (*neshika mi-ba'ad le-mitpachat*) is often attributed to him. As is the case for most translation maxims, including Robert Frost's infamously misquoted suggestion that "poetry is what is lost in translation," Bialik's cautionary words have a far more complicated source (and, indeed, variations of this metaphor exist in other languages).[49] In fact, locating an origin for this phrase is difficult given that Bialik himself repeated variations on the "kissing through a handkerchief" metaphor in a variety of contexts, almost as often as he referred to translation as an act of (biblical) creation. As a Jewish metaphor for translation, this handkerchief can represent a space between distance and intimacy, like the bridal veil, or mark a dividing line, like the *mechitsa* (partition) that separates men and women in some synagogues.[50] But Bialik also understood that translations took on their own life, apart from their originals, and in this respect, the handkerchief also suggests the thin, sometimes transluscent, space of mediation between original and translation.

In 1917, Bialik delivered a speech at a gathering of *Hovevei sfat 'ever* (*Lovers of Hebrew*), which took place in Moscow that year, shortly after the February revolution. In his remarks, which were later published under the title "'Al 'uma ve-lashon'" ("On 'Nation and Language'"), Bialik offers what appears to be, at first glance, a scathing repudiation of translation, wherein he also invokes the metaphor of the handkerchief:

יש יהודים "מקוריים" הקשורים לקרקע נשמתה של האומה, ויש יהודים "מתורגמים",
החיים את חייהם לא בשפתם הם, אלא בשפות נכריות. מיגואל סירוונטס אמר: "התרגום
היותר טוב הוא רק הצד התחתון של הרקמה". מי שמשתמש בלשון נכריה, מי שמכיר
את היהדות בתרגומה – הרי הוא כאלו מנשק את אמו דרך המטפחת. כל מי שמציץ
דרך התרגום – אינו אלא רואה מתוך אספקלריה מטושטשת ואינו מרגיש את כל
הטעם בה ואת כל מאווי נשמתה, כי היא, הלשון, רק היא שפת הלב והנפש. מי שעמדו
רגליו על הרסיני זה, מי שכרת ברית-אהבה ראשונה עם לשונו הלאומית וקשר עמה
את חלומות נעוריו ומשאת-נפשו, – הוא לא יבגוד עוד בעמו לעולם.

There are "original" Jews who are bound to the foundation of the national spirit, and there are "translated" Jews who live their lives not in their language but in foreign tongues. Miguel Cervantes wrote: Even the best translation is only the reverse side of a tapestry [exact quote: *el traducir de una lengua en otra ... es como quien mira los tapices flamencos por el revés*-translating from one language to another ... is like being the person who looks at the reverse side of a Flemish tapestries]. He who uses a foreign language, who knows Judaism only in translation—that person is like someone who kisses his mother through a handkerchief. Anyone who glances through a translation is just looking into a blurred mirror and can't appreciate its full flavor and the full longings of the spirit, because this language (*lashon*) alone is the language (*safa*) of the heart and soul. He who has stood on this Mount Sinai, who forged a covenant of first love with his national language and to it bound the dreams of his youth and his ideals—this person will no longer forsake his people.[51]

Bialik's language of a "translated Judaism" resonates in Kariv's expression, "a translated nation," which we encountered in the opening of the Introduction. To be a translated Jew, according to Bialik, is to be cut off from the full experience of Jewish tradition, and to remedy this condition, Bialik was committed to *kinus*, Jewish cultural ingathering, that is, the reconstruction of a Jewish canon that would form the basis of modern Hebrew national culture.[52] To this end, in 1901, Bialik cofounded Moria, a Hebrew publishing house based in Odessa. Although World War I interrupted its operations, it was briefly revived between 1917 and 1918, the period when this address took place.[53] The Hebrew translation of key Jewish texts written in other languages, including Yiddish, was a major component of this project. In fact, the reference to Miguel de Cervantes's remark on translation is a nod to Bialik's own Hebrew translation/adaptation of *Don Quixote*, the first volume of which appeared in 1912, published by the aptly named Turgeman, an Odessa-based press that Bialik also cofounded. Nevertheless, despite the Zionist ideology underpinning his remarks, Bialik had yet to settle in Palestine. In fact, aside from a visit in 1909, Bialik spent most of these years in Odessa where he was committed to the diasporic Hebrew literary economy, a crucial stage, Bialik believed, of the emerging national culture in Palestine. When he emigrated in 1924 and settled in Tel Aviv, so did Dvir, his publishing house. What interests me about Bialik's remarks is that they do not repudiate translation as a whole; rather, Bialik objects to the translation of Jewish life, rituals, and experiences into other languages.[54] (Years later, the Hebrew writer and Nobel laureate S. Y. Agnon would tell the American Saul Bellow that translation into Hebrew would ensure the afterlife of his work. "The language of the Diaspora will not last," Agnon warned him.[55]) But translating into Hebrew also serves the aim of creating a new linguistic beginning for an emerging Hebrew national culture, one in which these Hebrew translations will assume the status of original texts.

When *Onegin* did appear in Hebrew translation in 1937, the centennial of Pushkin's death, it did so under remarkable circumstances—in *two* separate translations. The first was by Avraham Levinson, a Hebrew writer and translator, who had completed the translation much earlier but was not successful in publishing it.[56] His translation, however, was eclipsed by the other Hebrew *Onegin*, this one translated by Avraham Shlonsky. Shlonsky, a Russian-born Hebrew poet who had settled in Mandatory Palestine in 1921, had become a central figure of the *moderna*, the Hebrew modernists.[57] Shlonsky's participation in the Hebrew literary culture of this period marks an important shift in the culture of poetry translation, which began to take on greater urgency, prominence, and visibility in the 1920s and the 1930s. Although poetry in Hebrew translation did not make a major financial contribution to the Yishuv's literary economy, its cultural capital was unquestionable, and the *moderna*'s investment in its translation had much to do with this.[58]

Although the focus of the Hebrew publishing industry in the early twentieth century was on original and translated prose, the poem nevertheless held the status of national genre. Poets were the major representatives

of the emerging national canon, and it was in the arena of poetry where
the more polemical discussions on language and culture took place. In
fact, Shlonsky's debates with Bialik, who had been anointed the Hebrew
meshorer le'umi (national poet), mark a pivotal shift in the development of
modern Hebrew poetry in ways that also implicated translation. Shlonsky
famously derided Bialik's *nusach* (poetic style), which represented a move
away from the *melitsa* (allusive language) and *shibuts* (ornate biblical intertextuality), conventions that had characterized Hebrew poetry and translation of the Haskala.[59] In Shlonsky's view, Bialik never successfully replaced
the Haskala model with one that could form the basis of a truly modern
Hebrew poetic idiom. But the differences (as Shlonsky perceived them)
between the two poets also rested in their divergent views with regard to the
status of Hebrew in the Yishuv.

In 1927, Bialik, who had been appointed president of the Hebrew
Writers Union (Agudat ha-sofrim ha-'ivriyim), gave the keynote address in
Tel Aviv at a reception in honor of the Yiddish writers Sholem Asch and
Perets Hirshbein. Although Bialik strove to be diplomatic, he reproached
the language politics that preoccupied the younger generation (Shlonsky
included) when he remarked "language is just a part" of nation building—
not "everything."[60] He then went on to describe the relation between Yiddish
and Hebrew in terms of translation, noting that translations from Hebrew
to Yiddish and vice versa had, over the course of the nineteenth and the
twentieth centuries, enriched both languages. He also invoked the figure of
the Talmudic *meturgeman*:

התלמוד אומר, שמתורגמן קורא חייב לתרגם גם את רשימת השמות, שלכאורה
אינם זקוקים לתרגום, שנים מקרא ואחד תרגום. וב"חדר" היו מתרגמים כל מלה
עברית לאידית, ואפילו אם המלה נשארת בצורתה גם בתרגומה.

The Talmud tells that the *meturgeman* is obligated to translate even
a list of names, which ostensibly do not require translation, *shnayim
mikra ve-echad targum* [twice Torah and once Targum]. But in the
cheder [Jewish study house] they would translate every Hebrew word
into Yiddish, even if the word remained unchanged in translation.[61]

The expression "twice Torah and once Targum" comes from the halakhic
(Jewish law) obligation that the weekly Torah portion should be read at least
twice in that week, as well as in translation (specifically in the Targum, the
Aramaic translation/interpretation of the biblical text). Bialik transposes

the Talmudic *meturgeman* to the Eastern European *cheder*, the traditional study house for young Jewish boys, the very space that the *maskilim* repudiated in their pursuit of secular education and European cosmopolitanism. Bialik brings his audience back to this space, arguably to remind his audience of the family ties the languages share and to reestablish a continuity between the spaces of Jewish diasporic tradition and Hebrew national culture in Mandatory Palestine. In this respect, Bialik's attempt to accommodate both Hebrew and Yiddish in the project of *kinus* marked a shift from his 1917 push for Hebrew monolingualism, but Bialik also intended to illustrate tactfully to the Yiddish writers and their supporters in attendance that Yiddish writing could not escape the trace of Hebrew. Shlonsky naturally understood from these remarks that the reverse also held true: it could be argued that Hebrew contained the irrepressible presence of Yiddish.

Bialik's address sparked heated debate, particularly his now infamous assertion: "there is between the two languages a kind of match made in heaven (*zivug min ha-shamayim*) that can't be divided."[62] In his response, published in the journal *Ketuvim*, Shlonsky declared: "We never accepted this 'match' between the languages, so we're not going to dance at their wedding ... We view this catastrophe of bilingualism as we would tuberculosis, gnawing away at the lungs of the nation. We want our *Erets Yisraeli* (Land of Israel) breath to be purely Hebrew. With both lungs!"[63] I discuss the implications of this rhetoric of disability and disease in chapter 4, but it is important to note here that although Shlonsky repudiates multilingualism as a literary option for Hebrew writers, his own multilingual poetry, as well as his own practices, indeed poetics, of translation, contrasted sharply with his public statements on language politics in the pre-Statehood period.[64]

This brings me to another key historical episode in this brief history of modern Hebrew literary translation: the 1942 publication of the anthology *Shirat Rusiya* (Russian Poetry), edited by Goldberg and Shlonsky. This collection represented a collaboration of seventeen translators—including Shlonsky and Goldberg—and offered a sampling of thirty-four Russian poets, representing primarily the Silver Age (such as Anna Akhmatova and Osip Mandelstam), as well the Futurists (such as Vladimir Maykovsky and Velimir Khlebnikov) and state-sanctioned Soviet poets, a combination that would have been unprecedented in the Soviet Union at the time.[65] At the same time, the selection of poets and poems reflected, in part, the editors' own personal and biographical connection to the Russian literary tradition (e.g., Goldberg's affiliation with Russian acmeism). For Nina Segal, who has written on this collection, "the structure … undoubtedly represents an émigré 'outside' perspective on Russian poetry in its historical evolution … [and] also reflects the 'inside' view of the cultural situation in Jewish Palestine at the beginning of the 1940s."[66] This balance is also evident in the ways these texts were translated—both faithful to the varying styles and idioms of these poets and adapting these texts in several instances to realities in Mandatory Palestine.[67]

The appearance of the anthology during World War II is hardly incidental and, in fact, Shlonsky and Goldberg explicitly frame the anthology as a collective response to the war. They assert the power of poetry to "shed light," as they put it, in dark times, illustrating this point through their reading of specific poems and poets that engage and respond to Russian and Soviet political upheavals (beginning with the assassination of Tsar Alexander II in March 1881).[68] The underlying objective of their historical survey is to show, through the example of Russian poetry, the pivotal role that poets can and should play in national life. Shlonsky and Goldberg characterized their objective as follows: "the offering of a portrait of a generation, a biography of its tradition, which in every nation and language one discovers in the best poetry."[69] This portrait, however, served a dual purpose: it gave Hebrew readers a key collection of late nineteenth- and twentieth-century Russian poetry, and also served as a portrait of a generation of Hebrew poets inspired and shaped by these very works. In the pre-State period, anthologies of this kind also reflected a desire to create "an imagined national community" consistent with particular ideologies and politics.[70] The specific language that Goldberg and Shlonsky use in their introduction—*matan demut deyokano shel dor*—the offering of a portrait of a generation—is fairly innocuous at first glance, until we reach the end of the introduction where they conclude on this note: "Destruction surrounds us, our hearts are alarmed by the apocalyptic signs announcing, as it were, the end. But it is in such times that poetry has known how to decipher these signs with light, and not with darkness."[71] The revelatory power of poetry, and in this case, poetry in Hebrew translation, suggests a relation between this offering and the *matan Torah*, a relation that I also address in the previous chapter. By casting—indeed, translating—the "light" of revelation onto the political and cultural concerns of the Jewish community in Palestine, *Shirat Rusiya* positioned poetry and its translation prominently in the nation-building project, while also reasserting the prophetic role of the poet.

Like the poet-*turgeman* in Amichai's "Ve-lo nitlahev," their work brings this past into the present to chart a new future for modern Hebrew poetry.

The poet Haim Gouri, who was born in Mandatory Palestine in 1923 to Russian parents, recalls that although Russian was never spoken at home, the publication of *Shirat Rusiya* returned to him the Russian past of his parents but in "our Hebrew."[72] For a younger generation of poets, like Gouri, this collection offered the possibility of carrying Hebrew poetry in a new direction, paving the way for the Statehood Generation that would emerge shortly thereafter. That it did so in what Gouri refers to as "our Hebrew" is a critical contribution of this anthology, for, in their translations, Shlonsky, Goldberg, and the other translators strove to represent, as well as to create, varied registers and styles of poetic language in modern Hebrew as a way of bringing these possibilities to the attention of the next generation of Hebrew poets.

Two years later, Goldberg published an essay on Bialik that further contextualizes her understanding of the role of translation in the development of modern Hebrew poetry. In "Ha-meshorer ha-leʾumi" ("The National Poet"), Goldberg advances a poignant portrait of Bialik as a cultural translator and mediator, a *metavekh*:

הוא החזיר לעם ישראל את ילדותו. השירים הזכורים את הילדות, "זוהר" ו"ספיח" ואותה הרגשה ממשית של עולם ממשי של ילדות, בקרוא האדם לראשונה שמות לדברים,—כל אלה ניתנו לנו בשירתו בלשון העברית. הוא תירגם את ילדותנו לעברית, עד אשר היתה למקור,—ובאורח הזה לימדנו לדעת, כי-אכן אפשריים הם חיי אדם שלמים למראשיתם בלשון הזאת, בתרבות הזאת...

[Bialik] returned to the Jewish people their childhood. Poems that recall childhood, "Zohar," and "Safiach," and that same real feeling of the real world of childhood, by giving it a name for the first time—all these things were given to us through his poetry in the Hebrew language. He *translated* [tirgem] our childhood into Hebrew, until it became the origin—and in this way, he taught us that a full life from the very beginning is possible in this language, in this culture....[73]

The two texts that Goldberg refers to here, "Zohar" (1900) and "Safiach" (published between 1908 and 1923), a poem and an autobiographical novella, respectively, are narrated from a child's perspective and address the inner world of childhood and its boundless imaginative potential. Both texts are concerned with language, specifically the gap that breaks open between the language of this inner life of childhood and the language of adulthood, which Bialik engages as an act of translation that is both creative and distorting. Goldberg acknowledges how writing in Hebrew in the early twentieth century could be a translational and revisionary act—in this case, as a way of rewriting the Jewish diasporic past to create a new Hebrew beginning. This translation is interlingual, between the languages of this past and modern Hebrew, situating Bialik's diasporic Hebrew as the point of origin for what later becomes a territorialized, national Hebrew. And while this passage could be read through the lens of Zionist rebirth and renewal, by explicitly referring to Bialik's composition of these texts *as* translation, Goldberg calls attention to the ways in which translating and writing are mutually inclusive and transformative practices in modern Hebrew poetry. "Surely," she writes, "this is the first step toward a new life."[74]

PART II

The Go-Betweens

CHAPTER 2

Paris or Jerusalem?

Esther Raab, Baudelaire, and the Writing of *Kimshonim*

כָּל קְפוּל בְּשִׂמְלָתִי/לִי יִלְחַשׁ
Every pleat in my dress/whispers to me

—ESTHER RAAB[1]

The poet Esther Raab was born in 1894 in Petach Tikva to Hungarian immigrants who had arrived in Ottoman Palestine between 1860 and 1875 and were among the founding settlers of Petach Tikva, the first Jewish agricultural colony (*moshava*) in the Yishuv (today located east of Tel Aviv).[2] This status had earned Petach Tikva the sobriquet *em ha-moshavot* (the Mother of the Moshavot). The 1930 publication of Raab's debut collection *Kimshonim* (*Thistles*) was widely hailed as the first major literary work published by a native Hebrew speaker, and in these poems, Petach Tikva appears as a cultural and linguistic tabula rasa, a space free of diasporic influence, where an authentic and autochthonous Hebrew identity emerges; a closer reading of these texts, however, as well as Raab's prose accounts of her childhood, indicates that a steady influx of immigrants and visitors also ensured that Petach Tikva served as a meaningful site for cosmopolitan, multilingual encounters. In "Paris o Yerushalayim?"—a short prose account of her childhood published in 1952—Raab offers a detailed glimpse into the multilingual culture of the Yishuv and her own complicated place within it.[3] In what follows, "Paris o Yerushalayim?" serves as a point of departure for my reading of *Kimshonim* and the ways in which Raab's multilingualism, and how it related to her lifelong interest in translation, shaped its composition from its earliest stages.

In "Paris o Yerushalayim?," Raab describes her childhood home as a regular gathering place for visitors, including tourists, Zionist leaders, local intellectuals, and artists. Almost fifty years after the events she describes, Raab recalls: "[Mother] would wipe off the sand stuck to my bare feet and rush towards the living room, where a mishmash of words in Yiddish, German, and Russian tumbled out. This was a regular event at our place."[4] On such occasions Raab would be summoned to entertain the guests, as she does on the particular evening that opens her account with her rendition of "Esa 'einai el he-harim" (Psalm 121). Raab describes the song as "a selection from Psalms, to which my Russian teacher added the tune of the Ukrainian national anthem," a description that encapsulates the linguistic and cultural milieu in which Raab positions herself as a native Hebrew-speaking child.[5] The performance is a success, and Raab takes pride in her flawless and clear enunciation of "the words of this ancient text" and the ease with which she hits its highest notes, a feat that sets her apart from her classmates, who, in her estimation, often finish the song "on a slightly hoarse *pianissimo*."[6]

The combination of the song's Hebrew lyrics and its Ukrainian musical score exemplifies the complex linguistic and cultural interactions between Raab, the native-born child of the Yishuv, and her foreign-born audience, which includes her parents and even many of her peers. Though Raab presumably chooses to perform this piece because it showcases her flawless and effortless Hebrew, the song itself juxtaposes multiple historical, national, and linguistic affiliations. Psalm 121 belongs to a group of psalms (Psalms 120–134) known as *shirei ha-ma'alot*, the songs of ascents, after the phrase that opens each text. The speaker of Psalm 121, the most famous among them, declares a desire for protection and safekeeping that is initially addressed to the land. Its lyrics have found their place in the Jewish liturgical tradition, from the *ma'ariv* (evening) prayer to the *kri'at shem'a 'al ha-mita*, a bedtime prayer, as well as in the custom of reciting this psalm during the birth of a child and placing it, among other prayers, around the newborn's crib. Ancient Israelites may have recited these psalms during their annual pilgrimages to Jerusalem during Passover, Shavuot, and Sukkot, which together constitute the *shelosh regalim* or three pilgrimage festivals. These invocations of Psalm 121 accord with Zionism's emphasis on the relation between immigration and rebirth, but Psalm 121's arrangement with Ukrainian musical notation explicitly turns the performance into a complicated expression of nationalist desire, a surrogate anthem. In the essay, Raab locates herself between the land, described as "empty and silent," and this congregation of delegates from around the world, with the acute awareness that her nativeness is a mark of difference, setting her apart from her contemporaries.

After the performance, an unnamed visitor—whom Raab's nephew and biographer Ehud Ben-Ezer identifies as the Zionist leader Menachem Ussishkin—approaches Raab and, with "a strange, cold stare and a harsh voice," inquires: "Tell me, my child, where would you rather live, Paris or Jerusalem?"[7] The question puzzles her. Why has she never heard of this place? She wonders if perhaps Paris is "an Arab village near Gedera."[8] In Raab's personal cartography, as she recalls it, Paris does not register as a major European metropolis but rather as an unnamed locale in an isolated corner of the Yishuv (as was the case for Gedera at the time). The term "Arab village" also underscores here that "Paris" is excluded from a specifically Zionist cartography. Her personal map precludes foreign coordinates, both diasporic and local, or renders them marginal and irrelevant. Yet as Liora Halperin has observed, it was not uncommon for the Jewish home in Palestine to be "a space for multilingual relaxation," as is vividly described in this essay.[9] Additionally, Raab's spotless performance, if we take her word for it, sets her apart from her own generation of predominantly immigrant classmates, who presumably struggle with the same Hebrew text. Raab's nativism, however, is not invariable: the multilingual milieu of the salon, the Ukrainian tune of a now Hebrew song, and the immigrant background of Raab's parents and guests all bring diverse geographies and languages into view.

The question "Paris o Yerushalayim?" underscores the complicated, and at times ambivalent, interaction of native and foreign influences in Raab's oeuvre, but Raab's observations on her multicultural and multilingual childhood also illustrate how she constructed and negotiated the relation between the foreign and the native in ways that further entangled, rather than polarized, these terms. In the 1880s, Baron Edmond James de Rothschild (1845–1934), a member of the French branch of the Rothschild banking family, had administered Petach Tikva during the crucial early years of its founding. Through his patronage, a number of key figures in the colony's development traveled to France to further their study of agronomy and horticulture. But as Derek J. Penslar has shown, the influence of French culture on Ottoman Palestine can be traced back to the establishment of a network of Alliance Israélite Universelle schools throughout the Middle East, an initiative undertaken by the Paris-based organization with the express aim of furthering the cultural advancement of Middle Eastern Jewry. The first of these schools to open in Ottoman Palestine was Mikveh Yisrael, an agricultural school founded in 1870 and supported by the Rothschild family.[10] The Alliance was also active in Egypt, where French was the lingua franca of the haute bourgeoisie and business class, to which Raab's first husband belonged. According to Joel Beinin, the considerable cultural capital that French conferred made its acquisition a contributing factor to the "de-Arabization" of Egyptian Jews in the nineteenth and the twentieth centuries, thereby turning Jewish Cairo into a Western European enclave (which later explains, in part, how Raab comes to assign a diasporic status to Cairo).[11] It is therefore highly improbable that Raab was unaware of Paris and its cultural status. Furthermore, the cultural traffic between France, Egypt, and the Yishuv in this period tells us that French was not exclusively identified with diasporic Europe; on the contrary, it was a language meaningfully integrated in Middle Eastern Jewish life and commerce, including in Petach Tikva.

The question "Paris o Yerushalayim?" frames my reading of how Raab positioned French, which she had studied as a child, as a language vital to her cultural and literary development as a Hebrew writer. In this chapter, I will elaborate Raab's encounters with French: first, by relating the role of French, for Raab, in Ottoman and Mandatory Palestine, and later in Cairo, where she moved following her marriage, as well as in the various periods that Raab visited and lived in Paris, which are intertwined with her Cairo years. Raab's engagements with the French language, and the sites where these encounters occurred, elucidate the ways in which Raab understood and constructed—but also contested—the narrative of her native Hebrew identity in the polyglot, immigrant culture of the Yishuv. In a relatively early reappraisal of Raab's work, the scholar Dan Miron described Raab's poetic language as "dynamic, ambivalent, 'open' and fluid" and argued that the early nativist reading of Raab's work failed to take into account both her multilingual background and the influence "foreign poets" (*meshorerim lo'azim*) exerted on her blank verse and free rhythms.[12] While Miron focused more on her relation to other modern Hebrew poets (particularly Avraham Shlonsky and Chaim Nachman Bialik), his observations marked a major, unacknowledged lacuna in readings of Raab, which later work on Raab has engaged (e.g., Chana Kronfeld's positioning of Raab as modernist paragon and my reading of her multilingual poetics).[13] Kronfeld argues that "writing in a newly revived language (as Hebrew was in the 1920s), writing as the first native poet (male or female) in that reborn language, all the while remaining a self-conscious participant in French modernism make it impossible for Raab to take anything for granted—syntactically, semantically,

Figure 2.1. Esther Raab, Membership Card, The Association of Hebrew Writers, Palestine

Source: Gnazim-Hebrew Writers Archive, Israel, File 242/3549/5

pragmatically, and, not least of all, prosodically."[14] Through close readings of select poems from *Kimshonim*, Kronfeld demonstrates how Raab's daring syntactical contortions and "minimalist lexical, figurative and thematic strategies" are signs of more complex influences—both native and foreign—at work in *Kimshonim*.[15]

In her work on Yiddish in the Yishuv, Yael Chaver acknowledges the status of Yiddish as Raab's first language, a subject that Raab discussed at length in her 1971 interview with Ziva Shamir.[16] But Raab's engagement with French and German—through reading, writing, and translation—followed the arc of her literary career in ways that were more sustained and substantive than her relationship with Yiddish, though the role that French and German played in Raab's linguistic background and literary development require more extensive study.[17] In the mid-1920s, Raab translated, but did not publish, several poems by Charles Baudelaire and later claimed that Baudelaire's notorious 1857 collection *Les Fleurs du mal* (*The Flowers of Evil*) inspired the title and imagery of *Kimshonim*.[18] Raab's translations of Baudelaire, which she undertook during the composition of *Kimshonim*, are a crucial but neglected example of how a prolonged and active encounter with French and French literature shaped Raab's affiliation with Western European modernism and a cosmopolitan Middle East.

A close examination of the relation between these translations and the composition of *Kimshonim* not only addresses the non-Hebraic and non-Jewish influences that shaped Raab's early poems, but also demonstrates the extent to which in Raab's poetry, which was more closely affiliated with German and French literature, developed a poetic idiom distinct from the Russian-influenced output of the most prominent Hebrew poets in Palestine in the 1920s and the 1930s (e.g., Leah Goldberg and Shlonsky). For example, Raab's writing is full of rich, natural detail, but scholars of her work have long noted a decompositional mode, a penchant for weeds, thistles, desert flora, and spaces that Baudelaire may have inspired.[19] In my reading of Raab's translations, alongside the poems of *Kimshonim*, I argue that a poetics of decomposition—which is fundamentally creative and generative—was vital to Raab's crafting of her native persona and a self-fashioned, "native" Hebrew poetic idiom.[20]

BECOMING NATIVE

Although Raab actively promoted the canon's assessment of her work as nativist, her feelings of outsiderness—as both an "outsider within" the Yishuv and vis-à-vis the Jewish Diaspora—frame a native *eretsyisre'eli* (*Land of Israel*) self-identity and set the terms of her location within Hebrew literature early on, which coincided for Raab with the *moderna* (Hebrew modernism).[21] Despite the tireless efforts of the *moderna* to import a wide variety of international literary models into Hebrew, its major representatives—Goldberg, Shlonsky, and Natan Alterman—nonetheless remained, as Kronfeld has argued, "associated quite exclusively in the canonical literary picture with modernist developments in the countries with which they had the most biographical and cultural contacts."[22] Whereas modernism privileged exile, the *moderna*, at least in its public discourse, was a poetry of immigrant arrival and settlement. This emphasis would have set apart a writer like Raab, who could not claim the transformative immigration experience of her contemporaries. This is where Raab's multilingual, cosmopolitan experiences in Cairo and Paris proved vital in her literary development because they allowed her to problematize her native outsider status in the pre-Statehood canon and, ultimately, enabled her to claim her own diasporic ties.

Early in her career, Raab acknowledged that her native status placed her at the margins of the *moderna*, despite the fact that much of her early work was shaped by and aligned with international and Hebrew modernist models. For instance, in a letter to Reuven Shoham, in which she responds to a negative review of *Kimshonim*, she identifies key differences between her background and that of her immigrant contemporaries:

שלונסקי, אלטרמן, היו תקועים ברוסיות – וכן רוב הסופרים היה להם רקע מחוץ לארץ, לי בעצם לא היה כל מטען –יחפה, בחלל –במחלות, תחת אוקליפטוסים, בארץ ריקה מכל – ארץ מלאה רעיונות ושאיפות וקומץ אנשים נאחזים בציפורניים באידאלים שלהם, ומגשימים בגופם הקודח משימות גדולות, משימות שהפכו לאבני דרך – ואב שהיה – סמל בשבילי.

Shlonsky [and] Alterman were stuck [*teku'im*] in their "Russianness"—and indeed most of these writers had a foreign background [*rek'a mechuts la-arets*], I really did not have this burden—[I was] barefoot, in an open space—through illnesses, under the eucalyptus trees, *in a land empty of all things*—a land full of ideas and aspirations and a handful of individuals who clung to their ideals by their fingernails, with feverish bodies that realized great tasks, tasks that became milestones—my father was—such a symbol for me.[23]

The barefoot child running through an empty landscape embodies an unburdened native Hebrew belonging that characterizes many of the poems in *Kimshonim*, but the imagery in this passage specifically recalls the 1929 poem "La-av" ("To the father") that Raab wrote to commemorate the fiftieth anniversary of her father's arrival in Petach Tikva:

לְאָב

במלאת חמשים שנה לעלותו על אדמת פתח תקוה

בְּרוּכוֹת הַיָּדַיִם
אֲשֶׁר זָרְעוּ
בְּבָקְרֵי־חֹרֶף,
לְאוֹשֶׁת זַרְזִירִים עָטִים –
שַׂדְמוֹת־חַמְרָה אֲדֻמּוֹת;
אֲשֶׁר הִבְרִיכוּ הַגֶּפֶן בַּעֲנָוָה

וְשָׁתְלוּ אֶקָלִיפְּטִים כְּדִגְלֵי נִיחוֹחַ
עַל מֵי יַרְקוֹן;
אֲשֶׁר רִסְּנוּ הַסּוּס
וְהִצְמִידוּ רוֹבֶה לַלֶּחִי
לְגָרֵשׁ אוֹיֵב מֵעַל סֻכָּה דַּלָּה,
סֻכַּת־שְׁלוֹמִים מוֹלֶכֶת
עֲלֵי חוֹלוֹת וְיַמְבּוּט;
וּבְעַיִן יְרֻקָּה עַזָּה
יְפַקַּח עַל הָאֶפְרוֹחִים:
דּוּנָמִים רַכִּים זְרוּעֵי כַּרְשִׁינָה
וּשְׁוָרִים מִסְפָּר רוֹבְצִים בְּמֵי־בִצָּה...
חוֹרֵשׁ הַתֶּלֶם עַל אַף הַמִּדְבָּר
בּוֹקֵעַ רִאשׁוֹן בְּאַדְמַת־בְּתוּלָה:
בְּרוּכוֹת הַיָּדָיִם!²⁴

To the Father

Fifty years on the soil of Petach Tikva

Blessed are the hands
that sowed
on winter mornings,
to a rustle of starlings swooping—
fields of red loam;
that caused the vines to bend with fruit
and planted eucalyptus like flags of fragrance
along the waters of the river Yarkon;
that bridled the horse
and pressed rifle to cheek
to chase off an enemy from a meager hut,
tabernacle-of-peace that reigns
over dune and screw bean;
and a bold green eye
watches over the fledglings:
soft dunam seeded with vetch
as a few oxen squat in swamp-water...
plows the furrow despite the desert,
first cleaves virgin soil:
blessed are the hands!

(Translated by Harold Schimmel.)²⁵

Marking the anniversary of a colony's founding with a written act of commemoration was a common practice that shaped local historiographies and collective memories.[26] Yehuda Raab had the distinction of being the first Jewish resident to break the ground of the new settlement (boke'a rishon), an act that the poem documents. "La-av" begins with a blessing that takes its language from Genesis 1:11–12: "Berukhot ha-yadayim/asher zar'u" ("Blessed are the hands/that sowed").[27] These words pay homage to Raab's biological father as well as to all of the "founding fathers" of the Yishuv, both the pioneers and, in its possible allusion to Bialik's poem "Birkat 'am" ("The Blessing of the People"), the literary forefathers of modern Hebrew poetry.[28] Like the Australian eucalyptus tree, which was imported to Palestine, the elder Raab and his generation pave the way, through their tenacious dedication to the land, for the next generation of Labor Zionists. Their bare hands prepare—literally and sexually, "split open"—untouched eretsyisre'eli space to make way for a new, but fundamentally organic and native, expression: "Choresh ha-telem 'al af ha-midbar/boke'a rishon be-adamat-betula," "plows the furrow despite the desert,/first cleaves virgin soil" (l.18–19), in Harold Schimmel's translation. The father's first furrow—ha-telem ha-rishon (also the title of Yehuda Raab's memoir)—marks the beginning of a poetic language native to the land, to which his daughter, the representative of the first native generation, gives full expression.[29]

The relation between the work ('avoda) of settlement and poetic labor pervades much of the poetry of the Yishuv—the works of Rachel Bluwstein and Shlonsky come to mind, among others. In his poem "'Amal" ("Toil"), Shlonsky famously coined the expression paytan solel, poet paver, and thereby, as Michael Gluzman has argued, "the rebuilding of the land and the writing of modernist Hebrew poetry are perceived by Shlonsky as synonymous."[30] In "La-av," agricultural labor transforms the diasporic Jewish body. The father's plowing both consummates the immigrant's relation to the land but also suggests, in the way the hands dig into the earth, a burial of the diasporic body, which returns in a new and native state. Raab's poem memorializes this event, as well as the transformative translation of immigrant to native, from which her native Hebrew poetry emerges.

Underpinning this native attachment to a national and linguistic beginning, both in "La-av" and in the prose passage quoted earlier, are selective textual and contextual elisions and denials. For example, while the figure of the father epitomizes the late nineteenth-century Zionists who had settled in Ottoman Palestine and laid the foundations for a native and normative *eretsyisre'eli* existence, elsewhere, Raab recalls another side of her father: "He was like a goy. They called him 'Yehuda Goy'. He came wearing fancy clothing from Europe. He was pedantic in his way of dressing. And he had greenish-blue eyes, which I inherited."[31] Nevertheless, in this poem, Petach Tikva is both a point of arrival and a point of origin that replaces all others: just as the land is "empty of all things," so, too, are its immigrants emptied of their diasporic affiliations.[32] And yet, as Hannan Hever has argued in his work on Raab's "invented" nativism, "establishing that nativism is a beginning, the start of something new, means recognizing that there was something 'prior' to it, next to which this 'beginning' is itself an innovation."[33] At the end of the poem, the reiteration of "brukhot ha-yadayim" signals a return to a point of origin (the poem's first line) that the poet has rewritten but not erased—what is "prior" nonetheless remains. This return is indicated in the repetition of the line, as well as thematically, through the imagery of land labor, which brings this new landscape and text into fruition. The furrows that the father's hands plow are textual; they create lines for composition, a relation that becomes more explicit in the English translation of the poem. Indeed, the Latin *versus*, from *vertere* ("to turn") refers to the turn of the plow, and it is from this word that the English *verse* derives. But *vertere* also means to convert, transform, and translate.[34] Raab's claim to an unfettered beginning may have entrenched her in the margins of pre-Statehood literary culture, but "La-av" reveals that underlying this claim to a native Hebrew poetry is a revisionary and translational act of composition. In fact, in a later revisionary move, Raab claimed, in a letter to Shoham, that "La-av," a poem dated 1929, was her first published poem, though that status actually applied to three poems published in 1922 in the journal *Hedim*.[35]

Dana Olmert argues that the way that Raab asserts the pioneering labor of her own writing requires that "La-av" become her "pioneer" text. However, Olmert takes issue with Miron's reading of the poem, which argues that the father's dismembered body represents a shattering of a pre-Oedipal semiotic continuity that precedes the symbolic order.[36] As Miron describes it, semiotic continuity is created the moment an infant comes into bodily contact with her surroundings, and specifically her parents; this encounter sets roots that remain attached to a pre-Oedipal layer of development and that are realized, at this level, in pre-grammatical and pre-hierarchical language. According to Miron, "[in 'La-av'] Raab breaks apart the image of the revered father and turns him into a bundle (*tsror*) of synecdoches, that is into a pile of limbs separated from the whole image [of the father], those very limbs with which she first came into contact [with the world]."[37] Hamutal Tsamir agrees with this reading and observes that the final repetition of "bruchot ha-yadaim" confirms that by the end of the poem, the father "has disappeared [from the poem] entirely."[38] She further notes that the limbs specified in the poem (hands, eye, and cheek) are all female nouns in Hebrew, as well as limbs connected to "intimate contact," thereby suggesting that the land has replaced the daughter in the father's affections.[39] Breaking apart the body of the father challenges the relation between the land and patriarchal order, which is also enacted linguistically, and in the process, as Miron suggests, allows for a new female poetic order to assert itself. Olmert's objection is that this constitutes a misreading of this repetition and continues to give the father the final word, as it were. Instead, Olmert argues, "the blessed hands also mark the place of contact between [the father's] hands and the hands of the daughter, the poet, who describes them in *her* words."[40] Olmert is right that the father's dismemberment creates a space that the daughter-poet occupies prosthetically, so that it is her hands that arguably close off the poem. These hands embody an act of textual conversion and translation—evoked in and enacted by the turning of the plow—that generates a new beginning.

In the introduction to his English translation of *Kimshonim*, Schimmel elliptically but aptly observes that "[Raab] is more varied than her first book allows."[41] Despite the cosmopolitan contexts in which many of the poems were written (e.g., Paris and Cairo), the collection as a whole positions itself in a "native frame" that overshadows them.[42] On the whole, *Kimshonim* celebrates, through the eyes of a poetic speaker who is seemingly provincial in her sensibilities, an empty, mute land slowly coming into fruition through the labor of Jewish immigrants and their indigenous progeny. But in the following section, we will spend time with Raab in Paris and Cairo and examine closely how she constructed a diasporic, cosmopolitan identity from the experience of living in these cities and how these places shaped the writing of *Kimshonim*. We will begin in Cairo, where French, in part, catalyzes the breakdown of Raab's relation to the Hebrew language, a process that the poet described as radically transformative.

THE GRADUAL CONQUEST OF FRENCH

In a letter dated June 1921, Raab's paternal cousin and future husband Isaac Grun (יצחק גרין) complimented Raab on her fluency in French: "I so hope that you will be able to understand me, because from what I hear you are quite well-versed in French. To my great disappointment, I cannot make the same claim about my knowledge of Hebrew."[43] Although Grun had been born in Ottoman Palestine to a family of Galician origins, he had moved to Cairo at the age of 16 and had quickly adopted French as his primary language, using it almost exclusively, though his Yiddish and Arabic were also fluent. The Grun family ran a prosperous pharmaceutical company (his death certificate lists Grun's occupation as "merchant") with several branches in the Middle East. Ben-Ezer described Grun as a "Levantine," though it is not entirely clear how he is applying this term. The word *levant* originated with French and British colonialism, simultaneously encompassing a colonial geography (the *levant*, the East or the land of the "rising sun") and designating a cultural condition that applied to colonial subjects caught between the East and the West.[44] In a series of articles written between the 1950s and the 1970s, the Egyptian Jewish writer Jacqueline Kahanoff rehabilitated "Levantism" as a positive, multilingual, and multicultural state, marking an identity that was not bound by geography but rather constituted, in her words, "a prism whose various facets are joined by a sharp edge of differences."[45] It is possible that when Ben-Ezer applies this term to Grun that he is referring to the latter's assimilation of a cosmopolitan Egyptian identity—the fact that his French was better than his Hebrew being one indication of his distance from the cultural developments in the Yishuv.

But how and where did French enter Raab's linguistic milieu? Many of her early teachers were at the forefront of the Hebrew vernacularization project, and she herself had spoken basic Hebrew prior to beginning formal schooling, thereby observing first-hand Hebrew's development as a modern vernacular. The *riv ha-leshonot* (language debate) between Hebrew and Yiddish was hardly settled in this period, and at home the Raabs spoke primarily in Yiddish, the language in which Raab and her future in-laws would communicate as well. In addition to Yiddish, the other major diasporic language that dominated Raab's early linguistic experiences was French, as it was required by her school's curriculum, which was hardly surprising given the colony's ties to the Rothschild administration:

ואחד היה מוגרבי [חיוון], ואני סחטתי את הצרפתית שלו. הוא הוסיף גוון של חוץ וזה הגביר עוד את השורש בפנים. הוא היה זר לי. בכל היה זר. השפה שלו היתה זרה, המראה שלו היה זר, הידיים שלו היו זרות, כאלה מטופלות, בשעה שאני ראיתי רק ידיים עובדות חזקות.

One of the instructors was The Mugrabi [North African], and I squeezed out his French. He imported a tinge of the outside that only strengthened (my) internal roots. He was foreign to me. In all respects, he was foreign. The language that he spoke was foreign, his appearance was foreign, and his hands were foreign, as though they had been pampered, at a time when I only saw strong, working hands.[46]

"The Mugrabi" was the nickname of the educator David Chayun, who was brought to Petach Tikva to modernize the religious curriculum of the local Jewish Colonization Association school, which Raab attended. Chayun, in fact, was a Jewish native of Damascus, and was a teacher of French culture and language. French, unlike German, Polish, or Russian, was in use by both Ashkenazi Jews as well as Sephardic and Mizrachi populations, and functioned as a lingua franca between both groups in the Ottoman period. Nevertheless, for young Raab, Chayun represented the alienating and enervating effects of diasporic influence that contrasted sharply with her father's generation of land laborers and pioneers. Raab's description of Chayun's hands, when compared to the "blessed hands" of "La-av," further underscores his "strangeness." Yet, the very elements that constitute his difference—the French language, his "pampered" and bourgeois hands, and his Mizrachi background—are later appropriated by Raab, particularly in the period that she lived in Cairo. In other words, in the years predating the publication of *Kimshonim*, Raab would come to incorporate into her own identity several qualities of this cultural "other," notably an intimate attachment to French culture and language. But what this passage also suggests is that the "root" for this attachment was internalized in these early years.

In his biography of Raab, *Yamim shel la'ana u-devash* (*Days of Gall and Honey*), an indispensable source of these accounts, Ben-Ezer explains that letters written in French were found soon after her death in her private archives.[47] They form part of an epistolary exchange between Raab and her childhood friend Laurette Pascal (1895–1923), who committed suicide at the age of twenty-seven in Petach Tikva.[48] Pascal's father, Peretz, was a Romanian Jew who had studied horticulture in France under Baron de Rothschild's patronage, and through her mother, Miriam, she claimed ties to the Jerusalemite Rokeach family.[49] The Pascal family's French connections fascinated Raab, and she later admitted to Ben-Ezer that her friendship with Pascal had made her particularly receptive to French culture and had contributed to her early fascination with Western Europe:

לורת, שלומדת לימים בקולג' צרפתי ומבקרת בנעוריה בפריז, מביאה לאסתר מרוח העולם הגדול, עוזרת לה בלימוד הצרפתית, ומשפיעה עליה רבות; היא מספרת לה על צזאר פראנק, ועל הרקדנית איזאדורה דונקן, שאותה הכירה אישית. בחלומותיה של אסתר באותה תקופה, כפי שסיפרה לי לימים, מצטרפים יחד אהבה הריקוד, איזאדורה דונקן, והליכה הגלילה, לירדניה.

Laurette, who had studied in a French lyceum and visited Paris in her youth, gave Esther a sense of the wider world, helped her with her French studies, and had a great influence over her. She told her stories about César Frank and the dancer Isadora Duncan, whom she knew personally. Esther's dreams at this time, as she often related to me, featured her love of dance, Isadora Duncan, and excursions to the Galilee [halikha ha-galila], to Yardenia.[50]

In this passage, the juxtaposition of Isadora Duncan and the pilgrimage into the Galilee region illustrates, as in the earlier example of "Esa 'einai el he-harim," the non-binary interplay of foreign and native elements in Raab's early cultural experiences. Like Raab, Pascal had been born in Ottoman Palestine to an immigrant father but also claimed genealogical ties to Palestine through her mother, a native Jerusalemite. Following his studies, Peretz Pascal returned frequently with his family for professional reasons. Consequently, from a young age, Laurette Pascal spent her time divided between France and the Yishuv.

Pascal tutored Raab in French and maintained a daily written exchange with her in this language. In fact, Ben-Ezer surmises that a young Arab woman who worked for the Pascal family may have acted as a courier between the Pascal and Raab residences, and her role as an intermediary is one of many reminders that we find in such accounts of the diverse linguistic traffic that was typical of this period.[51] Pascal also tutored Raab in German, a language that Yehuda Raab encouraged his daughter to study: "[He] forced me to read Goethe, Schiller, and Heine," Raab recalled.[52] After Pascal's suicide in 1923, Raab observed: "Perhaps it was her influence, but I began to fill my journal with mystical sayings and German poems."[53] It is crucial to underscore that Pascal's affiliation with the French language and Western European culture was not native. In other words, Raab's increasing attachment to French, and later to a Western European cultural sensibility, was mediated through Pascal's own cultural and linguistic hybridity. In Raab's accounts, Pascal succeeds in elevating the status of French, and also German, from an irrelevant and strange diasporic language to one that later played an integral role in Raab's literary development and formed part of a more fluid cultural identity.

In July 1921, at the age of 27, Raab traveled to Egypt to visit the Grun family. She married Isaac later that year and settled in Hilwan, an industrial suburb of Cairo, where she lived for about five years and studied French intensively.[54] In 1990, *Haaretz* posthumously published a piece by Raab titled "Be-Kahir" ("In Cairo"), originally written around 1970.[55] In this essay, Raab recalls:

התקפלתי בהרמת ברכיים עד לסנטר, פתחתי את המאוורר, קריר היה, וקראתי צרפתית – ירחונים, עיתונים, ספרים, ושמעתי בסביבה שכנים מדברים צרפתית. התחלתי לדבר בפעם הראשונה שפה, שידעתיה רק מקריאה. פשוט פתחתי את פי, והמילים יצאו בלי קושי, באופן טבעי – ואני ברת [בת, כבר-הכי] צרפתית וגודש של מילים ברשותי, אני בוחרת אותן בהבנה וזה טבעי לגמרי – היה זה כיבוש שבא עלי כחתף והתמקם בי והעברית נעלמה מפי כמעט, רק יידיש דיברתי קצת עם ההורים. עם איזק דיברתי צרפתית, והוא בלע את דבריי והילל את הסיגנון המעולה – זה כמובן רומם את רוחי, והארץ איבדה לאט-לאט את זרותה בפניי.

I curled up, lifting my knees to my chin, turned on the fan, [the air] was cool, and read in French—monthlies, newspapers, books—and I could hear the neighbors around me speaking French. For the first time I began to speak a language that previously I had only read. I simply opened my mouth and the words came out effortlessly, naturally—I was [like] a French native and [had] a surplus of words at my command. I chose them deliberately in a way that felt completely natural—this [linguistic] conquest came over me suddenly and found a place inside of me. And *Hebrew almost vanished from my lips,* I only spoke some Yiddish with the parents. With Isaac I spoke French, and he absorbed my words, praising my excellent style—this, of course, lifted my spirits, *and the country very slowly lost its strangeness in my eyes.*[56]

Once reluctantly "squeezed out," French now comes "effortlessly" (*bli koshi*) and "naturally" (*be-ofen tiv'i*) for the adult Raab. Through the French language, Cairo—or at least a certain stratum of elite, European,

Figure 2.2. Raab and Isaac Grun in Giza, Egypt in 1925
Source: Gnazim-Hebrew Writers Archive, File 242/92702/8

cosmopolitan Cairo—becomes familiar, but does so at the expense of
Hebrew. This change occurs through a process that Raab does not resist but
rather understands as a natural outcome of living elsewhere: in order to be
at home in French, Hebrew must become a stranger. Becoming at home in
French and in "diasporic" Cairo allows Raab to assume a cultural position
more in line with that of her immigrant contemporaries. In that respect,
I argue that staking a claim in this diasporic position casts Raab's return
to Palestine in 1925 as a form of *'aliya* and motivates a process not of self-
Hebraization, as was the norm for many of her contemporaries, but rather
of re-Hebraization. The fetal image in "Be-Kahir" embodies the lingual
event Raab describes, in other words, the replacement of one's mother
tongue with another. In the essay "Cat in the Throat," the contemporary poet
Caroline Bergvall describes this as a "spitting out," which catalyzes "a whole
process of re-embodying one's language's spaces":

> As many of us are finding ourselves with increased frequency living
> in countries in which we were not born, or where we are first or

second generation citizens, or long-standing residents, or new arrivants, there is an interrupted sense of the past and of the living locale, whether we do or don't experience ourselves as diasporic. Whoever needs to create an allegiance or a correspondence, sometimes seemingly from scratch, or from access-points hidden from view, to a mixed cultural background, to a complex living jigsaw of multiple markers and untranslated biographical circumstances, will often question what linguistic belonging means, what fluency entails.[57]

Raab's "curled up" fetal posture imagines the process of linguistic "conquest" as both a submission and a rebirth. The use of synecdoche, invoking "lips" to represent a linguistic identity in flux, highlights the simultaneous processes of linguistic life and death—this is arguably true as well for the use of synecdoche in "La-av," where the father's hands (the fragmented body) are translated by *and* into the hands of the daughter (the compositional body). The process of embodying French as a natural language requires Raab to disembody Hebrew, but doing so later allows Raab to incorporate this diasporic experience. Doing so, however, does not replace the native Hebrew body with an immigrant one; rather, it creates out of these various identities—French Raab, Hebrew Raab, immigrant Raab, native Raab—a plurilingual body.

It is vital to underscore that Raab's description of linguistic rebirth did not imply her full acculturation into Cairene life. According to Raab, one of her conditions for marriage was the opportunity to study in Paris, a plan that Grun readily supported. During their ten-year marriage, Raab visited Paris for long stretches of time (attending classes at the Sorbonne, by her account) and continued to do so in the years following his death.[58] Though his death appears to have disrupted Raab's connection to Cairo, these years in Cairo provided her with the linguistic and cultural resources that carried into her later work, and were certainly present in *Kimshonim*, which she dedicated to Grun. Although Raab did not sever her ties to the Yishuv during those years, it becomes apparent from her own accounts that this period abroad allowed her to complicate the very elements that constituted her nativeness, and to acquire and incorporate the immigrant sensibility that she had lacked as a Hebrew native. In Hever's astute assessment, "Raab's nativism is rooted in the paradox that arises from the contradiction between, on the one hand, the claim of organic kinship to a place and, on the other hand, the support that this claim finds on the level of culture."[59] This paradox accounts, in Hever's view, for Raab's ambivalent accounts of her childhood, the way she oscillated, sometimes within a single interview, between claiming her parent's immigrant baggage as her legacy and simultaneously distancing herself from their past. If Raab ultimately found a compromise between her articulation of nativism and Hebrew modernism's privileging of exile and immigration, she did so in ways that anticipated postmodernism's commitment to flux and multiplicity.

In 1972, in a biographical sketch that Raab prepared for Shoham, she included details of her visits to Paris between 1936 and 1938. In her account of Parisian university culture of that time, Raab invokes the theme of the second homeland that also underlies the essay "Be-kahir," and, as is also the case for that essay, she describes here the processes of linguistic and cultural self-fashioning:

הזדהיתי לגמרי עם האטמוספרה של הנוער המובחר שהתאסף מכל קצווי-תבל סביב האוניברסיטה – לא הייתי צעירה אבל הייתי צעירה בידיעות – ומלבד החוויייה של העלייה השנייה היתה זאת החוויייה החשובה בחיי, כל האטמוספרה שנשמה תרבות והתרוממות, העם הפשוט היה מלא הומור וחן, התיאטרון האוונגרדי ביותר, היכרתי שחקנים שהיו גאונים כמו לואי ז'ובה (על הבמה) שמעתי דיעות צעירות ותוססות – של נזירים, ציירים שנלחמו על פת לחם ונעשו אחר כך מפורסמים יצרו אסכולות לעיניי הרגשתי את צרפת כמו מולדת שנייה (בתור עם) ואמרתי תמיד: יש זיקה לעם הצרפתי אל העם היהודי שניהם אוניברסאליים, רחבי-מבט שומרי-צדק ושפעם יהיו שני העמים ידידים – ניבאתי – וכך היה – זיקה אמיתית! אמרה לי פעם אחת הסטודנטיות: את צרפתיה וגם יהודיה וזה צירוף יפה מאוד ואנושי-רם.

I identified completely with the atmosphere of young elite students from all over the world who gathered at the university—I may not have been young but I was young in my knowledge of things—and aside from the Second 'Aliya, this was the most important experience in my life, the entire atmosphere exuded culture and excitement, simple people full of beauty and humor, the most avant-garde theater, I met great actors, geniuses like Louis Jouvet (on the stage), I heard the young and lively opinions of ascetics, painters who fought for a slice of bread and later became famous, creating schools of painting before my very eyes, I felt as though France were my second homeland (with respect to the people) and I always said: there is an affinity [zika] between the French and Jewish people, both are universal…. One of the [female] students once said to me: you are French and Jewish and that is a very beautiful and eminently humane combination.[60]

Figure 2.3. Raab's postcard of Paris, France, with a classic view of the Eiffel Tower, n.d.
Source: Gnazim-Hebrew Writers Archive, 242

This account brings together memories from several visits to Paris, but what stands out here is the young female student's characterization of Raab as both "French and Jewish." Raab's Jewish affiliation is clear, but in what ways was Raab "French"? Raab was not a French citizen, but the student could be referring here to the poet's linguistic fluency. Are we meant to understand that Raab's command of French was such that it could be misidentified as native? Or was there some other way in which Raab projected a French identity?

For Raab, Paris promised a necessary, even imperative, opportunity to expand her cultural horizons beyond the native frame (even though French and French culture also circulated within it). It gave her the opportunity to become a cosmopolitan subject, and it is to this lack that Raab may be referring when she writes, "I may not have been young, but I was young in my knowledge of things."[61] In a postcard dated 1937, she vividly described her experience of Paris to the Yiddish and Hebrew writer Moshe Stavsky (Stavi): "Right now I am sitting in the Jardin du Luxembourg—at the moment, in full bloom—a diverse array of wonderful languages against the background of painterly green. So many languages surround me: Chinese, Japanese, Yiddish, etc. How strange to observe this gathering."[62] When the anonymous student remarks, "You are both French and Jewish," her words validate Raab's place in this cosmopolitan, multilingual milieu.

A short story set in this period, "Ahava be-Zaltsburg" ("A Salzburg Romance"), complements, but also problematizes, Raab's anecdote of her Parisian education and experiences.[63] Raab's own 1935 excursion to Salzburg provided the material for this text, which relates a young woman's mysterious and romantically charged encounter with a stranger during a Mozart concert. "Ahava be-Zaltsburg" begins as the protagonist's train approaches the city, allowing her to observe in some detail the green landscape and slow curve of the River Salzach. In keeping with Raab's style, the speaker, who has traveled from Mandatory Palestine, pays considerable attention to the landscape and singles out its key elements. She describes her trip in terms of a pilgrimage"—ʿaliya le-regel—that unites "all those whose spirit is tied by a true bond to the world of theater and music."[64] This love for the arts, the protagonist argues, is a bridge between all nations, attenuating all differences in culture, national identity, and language.[65] In an autobiographical essay written in the same period, "ʿOlei ha-regel be-Zaltsburg" ("Pilgrims in Salzburg"), Raab attends a Mozart concert and marvels at the diverse audience that gathers to honor his music: "This is no standard audience, originating from the same place, [they are] delegates of all nations and all peoples, of all those who cherish art."[66] In this sentence, the shift from singular to plural—from *kahal* (audience) to *tsirei kol ha-artsot* (delegates of all nations)—further underscores this multicultural gathering.

Raab's protagonist soon discovers, however, that this common ground is an illusion. During the concert's intermission, a stranger strikes up a conversation with her in French and immediately discerns that she is a foreigner. The possibility that he may be a foreigner as well adds a touch of irony to their dialogue. "Mademoiselle, what you are wearing suggests that you have come from a distant land, haven't you?" he inquires. The protagonist replies: "Yes, Monsieur, I am from the Land of the Hebrews (מארץ העברים אני)." To this, the man responds, "You are very much a stranger—but also familiar—an artist, if I am not mistaken."[67] As they walk silently along the River Salzach, a feeling of weightlessness comes over the protagonist: "the stones of the street rolled imperceptibly under my feet, as though I were walking on water."[68] But the magic of the moment fades when the stranger declares his love and begs the protagonist to remain with him. "The man did not hear what he was saying," she observes, "... [a]nd all that divine music fled from my heart as though it had never been there."[69] Speaking hurriedly in terse and disjointed phrases (another breaking apart of this illusory flow), she gives him the primary reason for her refusal: "[F]or just a moment ago I was tangled in this dream ... now the dream has ended—and, you see, the entire point of this encounter is the magic ... so, good night, Monsieur!"[70] As the protagonist walks away, she looks back and sees him "stuck in his place (*taku'a bimkomo*), his eyes looking ahead without seeing me."[71] On her way back to her hotel, the weight of her evening shoes against the pavement crushes her toe, resulting in a "sharp pain," and there the story ends enigmatically with the words, "I rushed to my room so that I could extricate [my foot from the shoe]."[72]

Although this is not one of Raab's better stories, it contains language that stands out when read alongside her autobiographical prose. For instance, the phrase *taku'a bimkomo* may be considered in the context of Raab's description of her contemporaries and how they were, in her view, "stuck" in their diasporic cultural affiliations. Raab's protagonist is ultimately repelled by the stranger's offer, and the description of feet weighted down and damaged by "evening shoes" contrasts sharply with the "barefoot girl" of Raab's childhood memories, a figure that represents her freedom from diasporic attachment. At the same time, the encounter in Salzburg leaves its mark in the "sharp pain" that lingers after the man and woman go their separate ways. In the space that opens up between them, the protagonist of Raab's story has come into an awareness of her own attachments and, in the process, has acquired her own diasporic wound.

TRANSLATING BAUDELAIRE

In February 1972, Raab prepared for Shoham an autobiographical sketch that contextualizes the composition of *Kimshonim* in the 1920s. With regard to her literary influences in the postwar period, Raab explained (employing the present tense): "I swallow books in German and French, discover Russian literature in German translation—write poems under the influence of a poet named Walter Calé. I identify with him, and discover Baudelaire and Verlaine."[73] She also recalled how "foreign books" would find their way to Petach Tikva and pass from hand to hand, constituting an informal circulating library that shaped her early literary background.[74] A close reading of Raab's journals, which date from 1919 to 1935 and include the period in which she wrote the poems that comprise *Kimshonim*, corroborate the influence of these and other writers on her early poems. Alongside drafts of the *Kimshonim* poems, Raab also included drafts of her translations of Calé (1881–1904), Baudelaire, the Czech poet Otokar Březina, and Zvi Schatz, a Russian-born Jewish poet whom Raab knew personally.[75] These translations, and those of Baudelaire in particular, sit alongside her original Hebrew poems and were reworked and revised over a period of almost ten years though they do not appear in the final, published version of *Kimshonim*.

It is not clear that Raab ever intended to include the translations in the final version, but their presence in the *Kimshonim* notebooks offers evidence of the fact that Raab took translation seriously, testing out different word choices and line breaks, though perhaps less rigorously than she did her own original poetry. The presence of these translations suggests that Raab's readings of German and French poetry informed the poems of *Kimshonim*. More importantly, they also reveal the extent to which Raab applied her own aesthetic sensibilities to her translations, resulting in a translation practice that differed notably, particularly with regard to prosody, from that of her contemporaries.[76] Raab's translations raise a number of important questions. How attuned was the poet to the reception and translation of Baudelaire in Hebrew, German, and Russian, and to what extent did they inform her own readings and translations? Or do Raab's translations constitute an alternative reception to Baudelaire and a different approach to translation in general in Hebrew literary culture of the early twentieth century? Or, an even more urgent consideration: How does one reconcile the

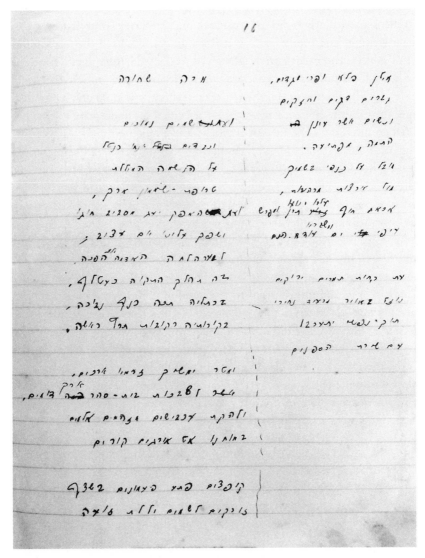

Figure 2.4. Part of Raab's Hebrew translation of Baudelaire's "Spleen," from the *Kimshonim* Notebooks (translation is on the left-hand column)

Source: Ehud Ben-Ezer, personal archive

reception of *Kimshonim* as a native Hebrew text, and Raab's own framing of her work as native, with the foreign texts and translations that were part of *Kimshonim*'s very composition?

In the 1973 essay "Milim ke-tsiporim nedirot" ("Words Like Rare Birds"), Raab cites Calé, the French author Germaine Beaumont (1890–1983), and Bialik as major influences on her early work, and made frequent reference to them, particularly Calé ("who came to me at the right time, it seems"), in later writings and interviews.[77] But Raab, in general, used the term "influence" ambivalently, particularly when it contradicted her frequent assertions of being free from influence and tradition, "a kind of wild growth" (*eize gidul pere*). Of the French poets, she remarks in this essay, "they only nourished me, they didn't influence me."[78] But Raab may be understating here her lifelong interest in the French language and French culture. Raab's readings and early translations of Baudelaire—which remained unpublished during her lifetime—certainly informed her own writing in Hebrew.[79] At the same time, her own emerging language and style shaped her Hebrew translations of Baudelaire (as well as those of the aforementioned poets), as is evident in the particular translation choices and strategies that she employed. According to Ben-Ezer, unlike Shlonsky and Goldberg, "[Raab] didn't feel any pedagogical obligation to be a translator."[80] Shlonsky, for example, regarded the production of literature in (good) Hebrew translation as a major contribution to the nation-building enterprise and was actively involved in developing a dynamic Hebrew translation culture in the Yishuv.[81] Although she did not promote her translations as she did her own work, an examination of her notebooks and correspondences suggests that translation was not an entirely minor practice for the poet. In her lifetime, she submitted her translations of Březina and Beaumont for publication and appears to have planned a larger translation project.[82] Her interview with Shamir contains the following exchange:

ש. לעניין התרגומים. הזכרת קודם לכן את תרגום ז'רמן ביאמונט. האם יש בידיך
מלבד תרגומי בודלר ותרגומי שירת ז'רמן ביאמונט, עוד תרגומים?

ת. לא. כתבתי פעם צרפתית, ופעם שלחתי והם כתבו לי שאשלח אבל לא רציתי
לערבב את התחומים, זה לא אמר לי הרבה לכתוב בצרפתית. לא היה לי בשביל
מי לכתוב בצרפתית.

ש. האם העצת לפרסם את תרגומי השירה של ז'רמן ביאמונט?

ת. תרגמתי כמה שירים ב"מאזניים". יש לי צרור של שירים שלה. אולי פעם
אציע את זה.

ש. והאם תרגמת פעם שירה עברית שלך או של אחרים לצרפתית, ידוע לנו שהיתה
זו משאלה כמוסה שלך?

ת. כן, אבל לא הצלחתי כל כך בזה...

Q. With respect to translation—you mentioned earlier your translations of Germaine Beaumont. Do you have other translations, in addition to those of Baudelaire and Beaumont?

A. No. Once I wrote [in] French, and once I sent [these writings] and was told to send more but I didn't want to mix these areas, I was not compelled to write in French. I didn't have anyone for whom to write in French.

Q. Have you attempted to publish your translations of Beaumont?

A. I translated a few poems for *Moznayim*.[83] I have a collection of her poems [in translation]. Maybe one day I'll try to.

Q. Have you ever translated poetry—your own or of others—into French? We know it was a secret wish of yours.

A. Yes, but I didn't get very far with this...[84]

If Raab's interest in translating Hebrew poetry was a "secret wish," how is it that it was known to Shamir and others? In what contexts did she share this interest? In a letter to the poet and editor Avraham Broides, dated June 17, 1952, she writes, "How are you? What is the news from our literary scene? [Raab was in Paris.] Is the promised collection coming out?—before I left I saw some announcements of its impending publication—After all this, my dream—to translate Hebrew poetry into French—can't be realized—there's no energy [for it]. I am preoccupied with medical treatments—it seems that I have gallstones."[85] In 1969, following the publication of one of her poems in the journal *Moznayim*, Raab offered to send the poet and translator K. A. (Kalman Aharon) Bertini her translations of Beaumont.[86] A week later, she dispatched another letter to Bertini, in which she remarked with regard to her translation output: "In fact, I have yet to publish any translation, either of Beaumont or others—I have started to translate only recently."[87] The translations in the *Kimshonim* notebooks dispute Raab's timeline. In fact, her letters clearly indicate that Raab had an ongoing, though largely (and possibly deliberately) private, interest in translation throughout her writing career. Furthermore, the letters to Broides reveal that Raab's interest in and command of French and French literature continued throughout her life, and that she even may have been invested in promoting Hebrew poetry, and her own poetry, in French translation. As the interview continues, Raab tells Shamir that she had translated Hebrew poems (whether her own or by others is not clear) about Mount Gilboa (located in lower Galilee) into French and published these translations in various places. She had planned an anthology of *shirat Gilbo'a* (Gilboa poems), but again, whether this was meant to be a French translation project is not specified in the interview. This work of French translation, including the revelation, in Shamir's interview, that Raab even wrote in French, is astounding, as it opens other possibilities for considering the relation between writing and (French) translation in Raab's work.[88]

The case of Raab's translations of Baudelaire offers a way of thinking about the role of translation in Raab's self-fashioning as a native Hebrew poet, and suggests a way of situating her Baudelaire translations, which have received cursory attention to date, in the uneasy translation and reception of Baudelaire in Hebrew literature. Although individual translations of Baudelaire into Hebrew were published in various journals in the late nineteenth and early twentieth centuries (by David Frischmann and Uri Nissan Gnessin, among others), a full translation of *Les Fleurs du mal* did not appear in Hebrew until 1962, in Eliahu Meitus's translation.[89] The language of illness, decay, and ennui found in and inspired by Baudelaire's work circulates in the work of late nineteenth- and early twentieth-century Hebrew writers such as Bialik, Gnessin, and Yosef Chaim Brenner, particularly in their critiques of the spiritual condition of diasporic Jews as well as life in the Yishuv. And yet, Hebrew literature's reception of Baudelaire in this period was selective, evading the anti-national, individualistic position of French and Russian decadence, of which Baudelaire was a major influence. In an essay written in 1922 for the periodical *Ha-tekufa*, the Hebrew poet and critic Jacob Fichman (1881–1958) remarked, "[Baudelaire] is too *French* for us ... It's no wonder that up to now there have been few attempts among our writers to translate the poetry of Baudelaire."[90]

Fichman's observation touches on a clearly palpable tension in the early Hebrew reception of Baudelaire between the desire to engage and emulate the poet as a paragon of European literature and a resistance to the implications of his poetics of decomposition and decadence on literary and political Zionism, which increasingly relied on the tropes and language of health, wholeness, and settlement.[91] But Baudelaire proved to be "too French" in a more literal respect. Gnessin translated several selections from Baudelaire's prose poems but was not proficient in French and relied on

Russian translations. In fact, most Hebrew poets and translators of the late nineteenth and early twentieth centuries engaged with Baudelaire's oeuvre primarily through its Russian translation. Russian was the "first language of European culture," to use Hamutal Bar-Yosef's formulation, for poets such as Bialik, Shlonsky, Alterman, and Goldberg.[92] Indeed, in her work on Hebrew literature and decadence, Bar-Yosef observes that the reception of Baudelaire among Hebrew poets was largely shaped and mediated by Russian literature and Russian translations of Baudelaire, *even* when writers (e.g., Alterman and Goldberg) were capable of reading Baudelaire in the original French. In this respect, Baudelaire was more "like a Russian poet" than a French poet in their estimation."[93] Bar-Yosef also has suggested the possibility that Baudelaire's language, imagery, and ideas so pervaded Russian literature of the fin de siècle that they eventually circulated indirectly into the work of Hebrew poets.[94]

Early Hebrew translators of Baudelaire focused primarily on his prose for reasons that remain unclear but may have had something to do with this Russian influence and Russian translations of Baudelaire. According to Adrian Wanner, the publication of Baudelaire's *Petits poèmes en prose* (also known as *Le Spleen de Paris*), more so than *Les Fleurs du mal*, influenced the development of Russian literature in the 1880s, in the years before Russian's own decadent movement emerged. "The genre of the prose poem with its fragmentation and oxymoronic subversion of the traditional prose-verse dichotomy proved to have a special appeal in this period of crisis," Wanner observes. "It seemed to offer a way out of the stagnation that had affected traditional verse poetry."[95] Beginning in the 1950s, with the emergence of new Israeli readers and translators working closely with the original French, as well as writers who encountered Baudelaire in other languages, translations of Baudelaire began to shift away from the Russian influence. The shift from prose to poetry translations was also notable.

The major exception to this preference for translating Baudelaire's prose, aside from Raab's translations, was Frischmann's essay on Baudelaire, which was published in the journal *Ha-dor* in three installments under the pseudonym Shaul Goldmann.[96] Frischmann (1859–1922), a highly regarded writer, critic, editor, and translator, had assumed editorship of *Ha-dor* under curious conditions. In exchange for editing the weekly, Frischmann, who was committed to European Jewish culture and promoting Hebrew as a European literature, agreed to adhere to the publisher's pro-Zionist platform and keep his name out of the masthead. Frischmann nevertheless remained invested in educating Hebrew readers on trends in contemporary European literature, a commitment that was evident in his selection of literary texts and criticism. His appraisal of Baudelaire emphasizes the aesthetic qualities of his work, which Frischmann openly admires, while carefully evading any identification with the poet's moral positions and lifestyle. His essay is a comprehensive reading of Baudelaire's oeuvre, striking in its frank discussion of taboo Baudelairean subjects—such as prostitution, lesbianism, Satanism—as well as remarkably generous in its selection of translated texts, which include excerpts from Théophile Gautier's biography of the poet and Baudelaire's journals and essays.

Frischmann's essay also includes several translations of Baudelaire's poetry, which he rendered in a prose translation. This option would have been a common practice in this period, but doing so also allows Frischmann to use his translation as a kind of gloss or interpretation of the poem. In some cases, he unpacks an image or phrase; in others, he leaves out parts of a poem that are not as relevant to his reading. But there is a sense, in reading Frischmann's essay and the attention that he pays to rehabilitating the term "decadence," that he is also conscious of the concerns that Baudelaire's work raised for a Hebrew reader, particularly in the decade following the publication of Max Nordau's *Degeneration*, which included a scathing critique of Friedrich Nietzsche, whose work Frischmann had translated into Hebrew.[97] In his translation of "Spleen," for example, Frischmann pointedly does not translate the word *ennui*, one of the keywords in Baudelaire's oeuvre. In another passage, he offers a humorous portrait of "the astute critics" who decry the cultural, moral, and spiritual "descent" or "decline"—in his Hebrew, *yerida*—of the fin de siècle, a decline that they date back to 1821—in other words, the year of Baudelaire's birth. Frischmann points out that every age claims that it is in a state of decline, and yet human beings remain creative— "because man just doesn't decline, he's not able to, for there is an imperative that supersedes all others and it is called 'development' (*hitpatchut*)." At the same time, Frischmann's use of the Hebrew term *yerida*—the opposite of *'aliya* or Jewish immigration to Palestine—suggests that Frischmann is also challenging Zionism's critique of diasporic Jewish culture.[98] Although his reading of Baudelaire is measured, Frischmann's translations of the poems advance an understanding of Baudelaire's poetry of decomposition as fundamentally creative, a breakdown from which "eize davar chadash"—some new thing—emerges.

Frischmann's article, however, is not an original work. As the scholar Ronen Sonis unveiled in his unpublished dissertation, it is a translation of an essay by the German critic Paul Goldmann, which was published on February 24, 1901, in the Viennese periodical *Neue Freie Presse*.[99] To what extent Frischmann was trying to pass this translation off as his own original is debatable; Sonis refers to this slippage as a "mistake."[100] Certainly, Frischmann had no trouble crediting himself when it came to translation, and the byline "Shaul Goldmann" suggests an intentionally mischievous Hebraization of the German writer's forename (the New Testament apostle Paul also went by the Hebrew name Shaul).[101] On the other hand, Frischmann never responded in print to discerning readers who were troubled by his failure to credit Goldmann as the original author. Instead, over time, the name Shaul Goldmann was understood to be one of a few pseudonyms that Frischmann employed in his long career. Since Frischmann appears to have translated from Goldmann's German, Raab can claim the status of being among the earliest modern Hebrew translations of Baudelaire's *Les Fleurs du mal* that engage directly with the French originals. Additionally, Raab translates Baudelaire in ways that explicitly reject the Russian model that was an influence for her contemporaries.

The *Kimshonim* notebooks include Raab's translations of the following poems by Baudelaire: "Causerie" (Sicha), "Parfum exotique" (Re'ach ha-merchakim), "Spleen" (Mara shechora), "Hymne" (Himnon), and "Le Jet d'eau" (Kilu'ach ha-mayim).[102] The translations appear in the third notebook, between translations of Calé and Raab's own original writing.[103] Aside from the poem "Le Jet d'eau," which appears later in the third notebook, the translations are grouped together. Edited versions of "Spleen," "Parfum exotique," and "Hymne" are also included in the third notebook as separate attachments.[104] The fact that Raab included diacritical marks in these last versions does not necessarily mean that she intended them for publication, but it does strongly suggest that she considered them to be advanced drafts, and perhaps even final versions (In fact, these are the versions that Ben-Ezer included in *Kol ha-proza*.). On the other hand, the fact that these poems were written out on separate sheets of paper at the end of the notebook may suggest that at some point she no longer considered them to be part of the *Kimshonim* corpus.

Raab's translations of Baudelaire emulate the compact and restrained *vers libre* that characterized her own poetry. Raab's rejection of Baudelaire's formal prosody was consistent with her disregard for prosody in general, particularly the quatrain, and signaled a major break from the poetic conventions of modern Hebrew poetry in this period. In a letter to Shoham, Raab shares her thoughts on and resistance to rhyme, which may illuminate her decision to translate these works—and write her own—in this manner:

ובכן אני גם לא ידעתי מה אני עושה – לא עשיתי כלום, הלכתי אחרי רגשותיי
והריטמוס הפנימי שלי – ואפילו הצטערתי לפעמים שאיני כותבת "בחרוזים יפים"
כמו כולם, חשבתי זאת לחולשה אבל משהו דחף אותי לכתוב דווקא כך. כאילו
"להכעיס" במקצת, לפעמים הייתי כותבת בחרוזים וזה צלע ולא מצא חן בעיניי –
כאילו ניטל כל רוח החיים מן השיר ואז השתחררתי ונתתי חופש לעצמי ואז באו
השורות הקצרות הקווים והמילים הבודדות בתור שורה, משהו דומה לתווי-נגינה
היה בזה....
החריזה היא מלאכה, כל אחד חורז. זה מכאיב את האוזן.
התוכן נמס, המנגינה נמסה בשיגרת החרז. החרוז הופך את התוכן לנדוש.
בשיר חשוב הריתמוס, המיסטיקה ולא התוכן המושגי. הזמר הפנימי –
הוא החשוב.

Well, I also didn't know what I was doing—I didn't do anything, I followed my feelings and my inner rhythm (*ritmos*)—and I was even sorry sometimes that I didn't write "in beautiful rhymes" like everyone else, I thought that it was [my] weakness but something pushed me to write in spite of that. As if "to infuriate" a bit, I would write sometimes in rhyme and it was somehow flawed and didn't please me—as if the life spirit had been taken from the poem and so I released myself and gave myself the freedom and then came the short verses, the lines and the solitary words within the line, somewhat like musical notes....

Rhyme is craft, everyone rhymes. It pains the ear.

The content dissolves, the tune dissolves with the habit of rhyme. Rhyme makes content trite.

In a poem what is important is rhythm, the mystical quality and not the conceptual content. The interior song—that is what matters.[105]

In addition to eschewing rhyme, Raab frequently breaks Baudelaire's lines apart to create new rhythms and cadences, thereby imparting her own emphasis to individual words and images. In this regard, Raab's translations differ markedly from the translation practices of her contemporaries, particularly those of Goldberg, who also translated Baudelaire. Goldberg's translation of "Spleen," for example, observes greater fidelity to the formal properties of the original French poem, but takes varying degrees of liberty with the poem's content.[106] Raab's translations, on the other hand, are more faithful to the literal meaning of the original text. Lexical fidelity combined with freedom from form results in translations that present Baudelaire's language and imagery more directly, without prosodic adornment, consistent with Raab's poetics of *dalut* (poverty, thinness), a rejection of the maximalist style that continued to dominate the work of her (mostly male) contemporaries.[107] Raab alluded to the gender politics of Hebrew prosody in her interview with Shamir when she remarked: "I'm not ashamed to say that I was jealous of (Shlonsky's) virtuosity. I didn't have this quality. I was heavy and very slow … The short poetic line also marks (my) speech. I am a staccato. Of course, also a legato but that's only when I am sad."[108] It is important to note, though, that Raab's break with classical prosody and the quatrain would have been at odds with Baudelaire's own attention to form and meter.

A closer comparative reading of Raab's translation of Baudelaire's "Spleen," titled "Mara shechora" ("Black Bitterness"), and the French original illustrates how Raab's own writing shaped her choices as a translator. The differences between Baudelaire's original and Raab's translation are apparent from the onset:

Quand le ciel bas et lourd pèse comme un couvercle
Sur l'esprit gémissant en proie aux longs ennuis,
Et que de l'horizon embrassant tout le cercle
Il nous verse un jour noir plus triste que les nuits;

When the sky, low and heavy, weighs like a lid on the groaning
spirit, prey to long ennui; when from the full encircling horizon it
sheds on us a dark day, sadder than our nights;

(Translated by Keith Waldrop)[109]

וְעֵת שָׁמַיִם נְמוּכִים
וּכְבֵדִים יָנֻחוּ כְּנֶטֶל
עַל הַנְּשָׁמָה הַמְיַלֶּלֶת
טְרוּפַת-שִׁמָּמוֹן אָרֹךְ,
וְעֵת הָאֹפֶק יָעוּג מִסָּבִיב חוּגוֹ
וְשָׁפַךְ עָלֵינוּ יוֹם עָצוּב;

Ve-'et shamayim nemukhim
u-khvadim yunchu ke-netel
'al ha-neshema ha-meyalelet
trufat shimamon arokh,
ve-'et ha-ofek ya'ug mi-saviv chugo
ve-shafakh 'aleinu yom 'atsuv;

When skies low
and heavy are rested like a weight
over the wailing spirit
gripped by a long boredom,
and when the horizon traces its full circle
it pours over us a sad day;

Raab begins her translation by doubling Baudelaire's initial two lines. The result is a significantly longer first stanza, one that ultimately includes the second quatrain of Baudelaire's poem (Raab's translation is five stanzas to Baudelaire's four). This results in a decisive cleaving of the quatrain, a classic building block of early modern Hebrew poetry. The principle of compression, or *staccato* effect, which guides Raab's own poetry, is at work in this translation, where Raab typically breaks the Baudelairean alexandrine into uneven hemistiches, thereby calling attention to the prosodic differences between the original and translation. Baudelaire's poem opens with a long monosyllabic sequence that Raab does not reproduce in her translation, opting rather for the plural and *legato* "shamayim nemukhim u-khvadim" in place of Baudelaire's "ciel bas et lourd." But Raab also inserts an enjambment at "bas et lourd" (low and heavy), which results in a shifting of "lourd" to the next line, in effect, "lightening" the load of the first line. Her rendering of the second line observes a more even breaking of the hemistich at gémissant/*meyalelet* (wailing, groaning). In the Hebrew translation, the third line consists of twelve syllables, more closely approximating the alexandrine. Her rendering of the fourth line, on the other hand, not only compresses the number of syllables of the original, but also alters the lexical meaning of the final line considerably. In Raab's translation, "il nous verse un jour noir plus triste que les nuits" becomes "ve-shafakh 'aleynu yom 'atsuv" (literally: and poured over us a sad day). The line shortens and simplifies Baudelaire's language and imagery, distilling it into one clear, direct statement. Furthermore, Raab renders this final line in iambs, producing a straightforward, steady tempo that contrasts notably with the slower, melancholic cadence of Baudelaire's line. In other words, in her translation of the first stanza, Raab simultaneously enforces her poetic preferences on Baudelaire's poem while demonstrating her own prosodic abilities (when she desires to).

Goldberg's Hebrew translation of the same poem, for example, preserves, to a far greater extent, Baudelaire's prosody, often by adding elements that are not present in the original.[110] Compare Raab's translation of the first stanza to Goldberg's:

שְׁמֵי-קַדְרוּת נְמוּכִים כְּגוֹלָל כִּי נִסְתַּמּוּ
עֲלֵי נֶפֶשׁ טְרוּפַת יְגוֹנִים אֲרֻכִּים
וּמֵאֹפֶק עַד אֹפֶק עָבִים שֶׁלֹּא תַּמּוּ
כִּי יִשְׂאוּ יוֹם עָגוּם מִלֵּילוֹת מַחְשַׁכִּים;

Shemei-kadrut nemukhim ke-golal ki nistamu
'alei nefesh trufat yegonim arukim
u-me-ofek 'ad ofek 'avim she-lo tamu
ki yis'u yom 'agum mi-leilot machshakim;

Low skies of gloom that were blocked like a tombstone
over a spirit prey to long sorrows
and from horizon to horizon [skies] thick without end
raised a sorrowful day from darkening nights;

Note Goldberg's fidelity to the original prosody of Baudelaire's poem. The rhyme structure remains intact, as does the alexandrine; Goldberg even measures her hemistiches according to Baudelaire's own line. Nevertheless, Goldberg achieves this proximity to the original's prosody by and large through lexical infidelity. In his reading of Goldberg's translation of "Spleen," Itamar Even-Zohar observes that Goldberg opts consistently for less "concrete" language where Baudelaire offers very specific and descriptive language. The decision to translate "low and heavy sky" as "shmei kadrut nemukhim" (low skies of gloom), for example, replaces a specific image with an abstraction, but also introduces an additional metaphor to the line, in effect, neutralizing Baudelaire's simile "comme un courvercle." Additionally, Goldberg's "like a tombstone" strains the semantic range of the original simile.[111] In other words, what emerges in Goldberg's translation is a fidelity to the idea and form of the poem rather than to Baudelaire's specific images and language. To a degree, Goldberg adheres more closely to prosodic convention than Baudelaire, whose own alexandrine exhibits some flexibility. In this respect, Goldberg's translation preferences are consistent with the classically prosodic features of her own poetry, as well as with the early twentieth-century Russian practices of poetic translation that Raab was categorically rejecting.

Citing J. C. Catford, a translation theorist and linguist, Even-Zohar characterizes Goldberg's translation as an "equivalent translation" that renders the poem according to the "dominant norms" of the target language:

> The code of modern Hebrew poetry was to a very great extent developed under Russian impact, and when the poetess [*sic*], who knew French language and literature perfectly, had to translate, she adhered automatically to that code rather than trying to cope with the original and violate it. The result is a Hebrew poem highly compatible with Goldberg's own poetry but very remote from Baudelaire.[112]

A 1919 essay titled "O stikhotvornykh perevodakh" ("On Verse Translations") by the acmeist poet Nikolay Gumilyov elucidates the "Russian impact" on Goldberg's translation. Gumilyov outlines nine "commandments" that a translator of poetry must observe: "the number of lines, the meter, the alternation of feminine and masculine rhymes, the character of enjambments, the rhyme structure, the vocabulary, the type of comparisons, 'special effects' (*osobye priemy*), and transitions in tone."[113] In other words, the kind of translation that Gumilyov advocated was "equivalent," and yet also acknowledged the unspecified "special effects" of poetry. Even-Zohar also points out that what makes Goldberg's poem a study in equivalency is that by the time Goldberg's translation was published in 1947, Hebrew poetry was already shifting away from these early twentieth-century conventions. Abiding by these conventions (i.e., the rhyming quatrain) in 1947 would have produced a formal "equivalent" for Baudelaire, but by the time Goldberg's translation was republished in 1975, *vers libre* had become the preferred form for Hebrew poetry.

Even-Zohar's reference to "violation" also hints at ways that translation has been used, and continues to be used in the Hebrew context, to reinforce certain poetic models (Goldberg), as well as to advance new ones (Raab).[114] Indeed, Raab's rejection of early twentieth-century modern Hebrew poetic

norms is on full display in her translation of the fifth and final stanza of
"Spleen":

—Et de longs corbillards, sans tambours ni musique,
Défilent lentement dans mon âme; l'Espoir,
Vaincu, pleure, et l'Angoisse atroce, despotique,
Sur mon crâne incliné plante son drapeau noir.

—And the long hearses, without drums or music,
march slowly through my soul; Hope
vanquished, cries, and terrible, despotic Anguish
drapes a black flag over my bent head.

וּלְוָיוֹת אֲרֻכּוֹת בְּלִי תֹּף וְשִׁיר
נִמְשָׁכוֹת אַט תּוֹךְ נִשְׁמָתִי
הַתִּקְוָה כּוֹרַעַת, בּוֹכִיָּה.
עַז וְאַכְזָר הַמַּכְאוֹב—
עַל קָדְקֳדִי הַשָּׁחוּחַ
דִּגְלוֹ הַשָּׁחוֹר נוֹטֵעַ.

Ulvayot arukot bli tof ve-shir
nimshakhot at tokh nishmati
ha-tikva kora'at, bokhiya.
'Az ve-akhzar ha-makhov—
'Al kodkodi ha-shachu'ach
diglo ha-shachor note'a.

And long [funeral] processions without drum or song
continue slowly inside my soul
Hope kneeling, weeping.
The pain is intense and cruel—
on [the top of] my bent head
it plants its black flag.

In her translation, which becomes a six-line stanza, Raab takes "l'Espoir"
from the second line of the fifth stanza of Baudelaire's poem and creates a separate, shorter line with the third line's "vaincu, pleure." Whereas
Baudelaire's line exhibits both a caesura ("mon âme; l'Espoir) and an
enjambment ("l'Espoir/vaincu), Raab curiously creates a more grammatical
unit with her line "ha-tikva kora'at, bokhiya" ("Hope kneeling, weeping").

By removing the punctuation of the original line, Raab loses the effect of suspended hope that Baudelaire's original line and syntax creates, but at the same time, as is common in her work, Raab's choice reflects a tendency to compress the poetic line in order to give added emphasis to the image. As a result, Raab's single line "Hope kneeling, weeping" intensifies the personification that is delayed in Baudelaire's original. In this final stanza, Baudelaire's increased use of commas slows down the rhythm of the lines to correspond with the "longs corbillards ... /Défilent lentement dans mon âme" (l.17–18), and creates a tension with the heavy lines that structure the poem, a tension that Raab consistently alleviates in her translation, in ways that are, again, consistent with a poetics of *dalut*. The compactness of Hebrew in general, and Raab's Hebrew in particular, results in the compressed, *staccato* lines that were characteristic of Raab's poetry.[115] Unlike Goldberg, who is intent on preserving the prosody of the original, Raab leans towards translation strategies of compression and subtraction. Aside from a few changes in word order, most of Raab's final decisions regarding her translation of this poem rest on keeping a word in or opting for a shorter alternative. Usually, the option that results in greater compression prevails.[116]

The poems of Baudelaire's *Les Fleurs du mal*, particularly when read in Raab's translation, share an affinity with Raab's own dynamic, active, personified landscapes. One can draw a relation, for example, between the opening poem of *Kimshonim*, "'Al ma'arumaykh chogeg yom lavan" ("White day celebrates over your nakedness") and a poem like "Tristesses de la lune" ("Sorrows of the Moon"), where the lunar landscape is personified as a reclining woman, her eyes fixed on "les visions blanches/que montent dans l'azur comme des floraisons" ("white visions/that rise into the blue like a flowering"). Raab's translations of Baudelaire, nevertheless, raise the question of influence. Is Raab imposing her own poetic preferences on Baudelaire or can we trace an influence of Baudelaire on her original Hebrew poems? The answer is somewhere in between, as is often the case for poet-translators. Observing the placement of these poems in her manuscript, it becomes clear that Raab worked on them alongside her original poems, although they did not seem to undergo the same protracted and rigorous editing process that went into her own writing. Rather, Raab's first drafts often differed very little from their final versions, raising the possibility that Raab applied a more instinctive approach to translation or simply preferred to focus her energy on her own poetry—although the later diacritical versions imply that she had a sense of when a translation was finished, and perhaps publishable. It is also crucial to underscore that in the period of *Kimshonim*'s composition, Raab also translated works by Calé (German) and Schatz (Yiddish). Her translations of Baudelaire are only one facet of her translation activity in this period.

Wanner offers a quote by the Russian poet Valery Bryusov that may articulate the appeal of translation for a poet like Raab:

> Pushkin, Tyutchev, Fet, of course, did not engage in translations out of philanthropic desire, out of indulgence for insufficiently educated people who did not study or did not study enough German, English, or Latin. Poets are attracted to the translation of verses by a purely artistic problem: to render in their own language what captivated them in a foreign tongue; they are attracted by the wish to "feel what is foreign as one's own for a moment," the wish to possess this foreign treasure. Beautiful verses are like a challenge to the poets of other nations: to show that their language too is capable of accommodating the same creative idea.[117]

It is possible that Raab translated Baudelaire as a way of experimenting with poetic language, in order to develop her own way of writing against emerging trends in Hebrew poetry. As Ben-Ezer notes, "the translations of Calé, Baudelaire, and Březina were part of an internal workshop (*sadna pnimit*) through which [Raab] honed her singular and characteristic style throughout her life."[118] As Raab explains in the essay "Milim ke-tsiporim nedirot," she turned to writers with whom she identified as she developed her early poetry, eschewing any obligation to trends and schools of writing and even to the demands imposed on Hebrew poetry in Palestine. Although she held several Hebrew poets in high esteem, including Bialik, Shaul Tchernichovsky, Uri Zvi Greenberg, and her contemporaries Shlonsky and Alterman, Raab never considered herself a part of any coterie. "Of course there's a linguistic influence at the very least and indirectly—but with respect to content—I was far removed from them," she related to Shoham.[119] This stance extended even to the kinds of non-Hebrew writers that she publicly admired, for example, Calé and Baudelaire—so it is entirely possible that the decompositional effects (subtraction, contraction) that she performs on Baudelaire are one way of asserting her own authority over the original author and text, but in so doing, also breaking down and breaking away from the poetic conventions in which modern Hebrew poetry remained, in her characterization, "stuck" (*taku'a*). On the other hand, translation offered Raab a solution to the "artistic problem" of developing a native poetry in an emerging national literary culture that privileged the immigrant status of its poets. The process of translation requires that a translator break down a text and then rebuild it—indeed, rewrite it—in another language. In that respect, decomposition is a precondition for translation *and* original writing.

For Raab, translating Baudelaire reflected her commitment to assert new affiliations and potentially map a new trajectory in Hebrew literature, at the same time that she was working on the poems that would make her the first "native" Hebrew poet. Raab's translations of Baudelaire articulate, arguably even more emphatically than the poems of *Kimshonim*, the creation of a new model for Hebrew poetry. Blatantly breaking apart traditional poetic forms and prosody, Raab does not hesitate to reinvent the original text against the terms of equivalency. In that respect, these early translations of Baudelaire emerge as a link between Raab's cosmopolitan, multilingual background and the native frame in which she situated her work, and also further elaborate the extent to which French culture and literature shaped Raab's own literary output.

The relation between this work of translation and the composition of *Kimshonim* is evident in specific poems in the collection, for example, the poems "Kahira! Kahira!" ("Cairo! Cairo!") and "Tso'anim—hungarim" ("Gypsies—Hungarian"), which will be the focus of the reading that follows. A number of the *Kimshonim* poems were composed during the Cairo years, but "Kahira! Kahira!" is the only poem that specifically addresses the city. In the otherwise pastoral *Kimshonim*, it stands out as an urban poem, but as a poem set in Egypt, it also stands out amid the *eretsyisre'eli* spaces in which many of the *Kimshonim* poems are located:

קָהִירָה, קָהִירָה!

זוֹנָה בָּלָה וּפְרוּמָה,

שָׁוְא יְקַטְּרוּ שֵׁיכַיִךְ מֹר,

וּמִמַּחֲבוֹאַיִךְ הָאֲפֵלִים

רֵיחַ הַקַּהֲוָה הַטוֹבָה

תַּעֲלִי,

בְּצֵל מִסְגָּדַיִךְ-הוֹד

אַלְלָה עָצֵל

קְפוּל-רַגְלָיו יֵשֶׁב,

כְּתַבַת-זִמְרָה שְׁחוּקָה

חַזָנֵךְ מֵרָאשֵׁי מִגְדָלִים יְגַעְגֵעַ
וּתְפִלָתוֹ עִם כָּרוֹזִים
בַּשׁוּק תִתְעָרֵב.

תַרְבּוּשִׁים, תַרְבּוּשִׁים,
בַּרְבָּרִים, כּוּשִׁים,
הָךְ, תַרָרַח, לִילִי!
תֻפִּים, חֲלִילִם
אוּלִי אוּלִי, יְלָלוֹת וּצְוָחוֹת
הַמְקוֹנְנוֹת הַשְּׁחוֹרוֹת:
הַךְ חָזֶה וִילֵל;
חֲתֻבּוֹת וּמֵתִים בַּסָךְ יַעַבְרוּ
בְּחוּצוֹת קָהִירָה הַמְקֻשָּׁטָה,
צְוָחוֹת וְהַעֲוָיוֹת
וּשְׁלַל גְוָנִים
וְרֵיחַ מוּשָׁק מַקְהֶה חוּשִׁים...
וְהָיָה כִּי יָצוּפוּ פְּנֵי אָדָם:
עֵינַיִם, מֵצַח—
וְנִשְׂאָה הָעַיִן לֵאָה, שְׁכּוֹרָה
חוֹתֶרֶת לַשָׁוְא בֵּין אֵדִים חַמִים.

Cairo! Cairo!
Worn and tattered whore
in vain her sheikhs puff out myrrh,
and from your dark recesses
aroma of the good coffee
rises,
in the shade of your mosques' splendor
Allah sits,
lazy, cross-legged,
like a ragged music box
your chanter yearns from tower-tops
and his prayer blends
in the souk with criers.

Tarbooshes, tarbooshes,
Berbers, blacks,
beat, tarrarum, trilli!
Bass-drum, reed-flute

ouli ouli, wails and screeches
black female keeners:
breast-beat and wail;
weddings and the dead pass in procession
on streets of decked-out Cairo,
screams and grimaces
and myriad shades,
a whiff of musk stupefies the senses....
and sometimes a face floats:
eyes, forehead—
and the eye wanders exhausted, drunk
striving in vain among hot vapors

(Translated by Harold Schimmel)[120]

The poem betrays an orientalizing outlook in the way that it emphasizes the city's (stereotypically) eastern details (souk, muezzin, sheiks), but how it activates Cairo's multilingualism is striking in this particular collection. As Schimmel rightly notes in his introduction, "Cairo lends depth and difference ... to her Middle-Eastern-Mediterranean-ancestral landscapes."[121] It is worth noting here that Raab uses the Arabic name of the city and not the Hebrew "Kahir," which she uses in the essay "Be-kahir." In Hebrew, the final "heh" in "Kahira" could serve as a suffix indicating movement towards that location—"to Cairo"—but Raab repeats it later in the poem, where it is clearly used as a place name. Raab's Cairo is a dissolute woman ("Cairo! Cairo!/Worn and tattered whore!"), a city where death and putrescence merge with an intense, erotic vitality ("from your dark recesses/aroma of the good coffee/rises") that both repels and attracts the speaker.[122] Compare these lines with the following, lush description of Cairo that opens Raab's essay "Be-kahir":

ברחוב היה שפע של מוכרים, ותנובת הסביבה השמנה של הנילוס זרמה ברחובות,
וזה בשיר ובחרוז שרובו לא הבינותי, אבל היה רך ומרגיע. [פירות] מנגו גדולים
ונהדרים בסלי-קש מעלי-תמר קלועים ויפים – תמרים טריים שחורים ונוצצים על
עגלות-יד, מנדרינות קטנטנות כגודל אגוזים, ריחניות ומתוקות כדבש, ונרקיסים
מהגדות השמנות של הנהר ...

An abundance of vendors filled the street, and the produce of the Nile's wide, surrounding girth flowed through the streets, with a tune and rhyme I did not understand but which was tender and soothing. Large and impressive mangoes filled straw baskets made of beautiful, braided palm fronds—and fresh, black dates shine from push-wagons, teeny mandarins the size of nuts, fragrant and sweet as honey, and narcissus from the wide banks of the river…[123]

These sensual prose observations complement the imagery of "Kahira, Kahira!" and call attention to the relation between the city and its language(s) through prosodic effects, particularly in the first lines of the second stanza, which I have transliterated below for the non-Hebrew reader. Note here how Raab combines rhyme, repetition, and onomatopoeia to reproduce Cairo's urban soundscape:

Tarbushim, tarbushim,
barbarim barbarim,
hakh, tararach, lili!
Tupim, chalilim
uli uli, yelalot u-tsvachot
ha-mekonenot ha-shechorot

(l.14–19)

Schimmel's English translation likewise relies on assonance, repetition, onomatopoeia (his translation of *hakh, tararach, lili!* combines interlingual translation as well as transliteration), and internal rhyme, but my transliteration of Raab's Hebrew illustrates how, in addition to these poetic devices and effects, Raab applies a more conventional prosody in utilizing rhyming couplets in the first six lines of the second stanza (AABACC). The rhythm of the Hebrew original is percussive, onomatopoeic, and incantatory, and also contained and controlled. In contrast to the essay "Be-Kahir," where Cairo's Arabic soundscape is experienced as inaccessible, the poem "Kahira! Kahira!" engages with the language from a place of intimacy, even creating doubling effects between Hebrew and Arabic. For example, the lines that Schimmel translates as "and from your dark recesses/aroma of the good coffee/rises" could be rendered more literally as "and from your hiding places/the aroma of the good coffee/you will raise up." Here, the Hebrew "ta'ali" (you will raise up, which Schimmel translates as a present tense verb) could also be read as the Arabic feminine imperative "taali," come. The word "kahava," an Arabic loanword (*qahwah*, coffee) that appears in early modern Hebrew literature, is yet another reminder of the cultural and linguistic relations between Hebrew and Arabic.[124] The ululation *ouli ouli* (for the Arabic *waylī*, a cry of woe comparable to the Yiddish *oy vey iz mir*) also marks an interesting moment of cultural and linguistic mediation, where Raab assumes the role of translator to convey a scene of Arab mourning in a Hebrew poem. In Egyptian Arabic, *ouli* is also the feminine form of the imperative, "say," and when read alongside "ta'ali," gestures to the ways in which the city is called forth by the poem itself.[125] While "Be-kahir" portrays Cairo as a dissonant, modern Babel, the poem "Kahira! Kahira!" addresses the city directly in its languages and opens a multilingual and translational space in which Hebrew and Arabic are brought together. The face that emerges at the end of the poem "among hot vapors" (*bein edim chamim*) may even be a reference to Genesis 2 and the creation of Adam, whose formation is preceded by a "mist" (*ed*) that covers the earth, preparing it for growth—thereby underscoring the extent to which Cairo lays the foundation for the act of linguistic rebirth that Raab later dramatizes in "Be-kahir."

In the poem "Tso'anim—hungarim" ("Gypsies—Hungarians"), also dated 1926, Raab again activates a relation between immigration, composition, and translation. While the poem addresses her immigrant Jewish Hungarian forebears, it also acknowledges, albeit enigmatically, a more universal experience of transience and uprootedness:

צוֹעֲנִים—הוּנְגְרִים—
מִי זֶה הָפַךְ דָּמִי לְיַיִן,
וְדֶרֶךְ לֵילוֹת
כְּבְתוֹךְ מְעָרוֹת
בְּיָד כְּבֵדָה יוֹבִילוּנִי.
כָּבְדוּ רַגְלַי נְסוּכוֹת-שֵׁנָה,
רַק קַרְבַּי בִּי יָרֹנּוּ,
שׁוֹטְפִים כִּנְהַר רָחָב,
שׁוֹקְקִים מִיץ חַיִּים
וּמְגַשְׁשִׁים כְּפִצּוּלֵי מַעְיָנוֹת
בְּאִישׁוֹן לַיִל
פְּנֵי תֵּבֵל עֲזוּבָה...

Gypsies—Hungarians—
who is it turned my blood to wine,
and through nights
as within caves,
will lead me with a heavy hand.
My feet have grown heavy, veiled with sleep,

only my innards sing in me,
flooding like a wide river,
swarming with life
and groping like branching springs
in the dead of night
across an abandoned world…

(Translated by Harold Schimmel)[126]

Unlike "Kahira, Kahira!" which imagines a Middle Eastern diaspora rich in sensory experience, "Tso'anim—hungarim" emphasizes the empty desolation of an "abandoned world" that could be, though not exclusively, a diasporic space.[127] Raab's father was Hungarian-born and an immigrant to Palestine, but the unidentified space in which the "gypsies" wander leaves open the possibility that the poem also refers to the internal migrations of immigrants within the Yishuv (in Yehuda Raab's case, from Jerusalem to Petach Tikva). The poem, on the other hand, is dated 1926, a year after Raab returned to Palestine from Egypt, thereby suggesting a self-referential reading. The Hebrew word gypsy, tso'ani, derives from the root for wandering and travel and is also related to Tso'an (Tanis), a major port city in ancient Egypt that is mentioned several times in the Hebrew Bible. These resonances persist in the poem's translation into English, where the word "gypsy" is etymologically related to the Middle English gypcian, a contraction of egypcien (Egyptian). These relations, I argue, are not incidental but rather become visible when this poem, as well as others in Kimshonim, is read as a translingual text.

Raab's time in Egypt, as I described earlier, was a period of translation—from native to immigrant, from Hebrew to French—which this poem thematizes. The question that opens the poem—"who turned my blood into wine"—is posed rhetorically but alludes to the Last Supper, the last meal, according to Christian tradition, that Jesus shared with his disciples before his crucifixion. The New Testament contains a few retellings of this event, and, in particular, of the famed scene of transubstantiation, where Jesus likens the bread and wine they are consuming to his own body and blood (Catholic tradition holds that this transformation takes place in actual fact during the sacrament of the Eucharist). Raab's poem notably reverses the metaphor, returning it, as it were, to a Jewish origin. Bread and wine are key elements of many Jewish meals, blessings, and holidays; indeed, the Last Supper itself may have been a Jewish Passover meal. Furthermore, it is hardly incidental that wine was one of the major industries of the Yishuv.

Raab's rewriting advances a metaphor for migration that is physical
and figurative, material and creative. As in the poem "La-av," Raab's speaker
inherits the transformative and translational potential of this migration,
which the poem realizes as a compositional act ("my innards sing in me, /
flooding like a wide river, / swarming with life [*mits chayim*]/and groping
like branching springs"). In Raab's Hebrew, the phrase *mits chayim*, the juice
of life, connects this line with the image of wine in the second as metaphors
for the ink that brings a new text/landscape into figurative and literal fruition (in an earlier draft of the English translation, Schimmel suggested the
line "fermenting life juice").[128] This relation between wine and creativity is
unmistakably Baudelairean and recalls, in particular, the poems "L'Âme du
vin" ("The Soul of the Wine") and "Les Vin des chiffoniers" ("The Ragpickers'
Wine") from *Les Fleurs du mal*. In both poems, Baudelaire draws a correlation between intoxication, imagination, and poetic creation that Raab's
poem arguably enacts through the transmutation of "blood into wine."[129]
Here, Raab is also in conversation with Baudelaire's ideas on originality and
influence, as well as his understanding of the reciprocal relation between
originals and translations.[130]

Raab's imagery of transformation and composition in "Tso'anim—
hungarim" also reveals an intertextual relation between her poem and
Baudelaire's "Bohémiens en voyage":

Bohémiens en voyage

La tribu prophétique aux prunelles ardentes
Hier s'est mise en route, emportant ses petits
Sur son dos, ou livrant à leurs fiers appétits
Le trésor toujours prêt des mamelles pendantes.

Les hommes vont à pied sous leurs armes luisantes
Le long des chariots où les leurs sont blottis,
Promenant sur le ciel des yeux appesantis
Par le morne regret des chimères absentes.

Du fond de son réduit sablonneux, le grillon,
Les regardant passer, redouble sa chanson;
Cybèle, qui les aime, augmente ses verdures,

Fait couler le rocher et fleurir le désert
Devant ces voyageurs, pour lesquels est ouvert
L'empire familier des ténèbres futures.[131]

Gypsies Traveling

The prophetic tribe with burning eyes
Set off yesterday, carrying their babies
On their backs, or giving to their proud appetites
The treasure of hanging breasts always ready.

The men go on foot under their shining weapons
Beside the carts where their people are huddled,
Running their burdened eyes over the sky,
With a gloomy regret for absent chimeras.

From the bottom of its sandy hole, the cricket,
watching them pass, redoubles its song;
Cybele, who loves them, increases her greenery,

Makes the rock run and the desert bloom
Before these travelers for whom the familiar
Empire of future shadows is open.

(Translated by J. Kates)

The first two stanzas of Baudelaire's sonnet include ekphrastic descriptions of "Les Bohémiens," also referred to as "La Vie des Egyptiens," a series of four etchings by the seventeenth-century printmaker Jacques Callot (1592–1635). Details of the print "Bohémiens en March II," the second print in the series, reveal, as Baudelaire's poem relates, a woman on horseback nursing a child and another woman carrying a child on her back, while holding the arm of the child seated in front of her.

Callot also included lines of verse on each print that, taken together, comprise a short poem, with this particular print bearing the words "Ne voila pas de braves messagers/Qui vont errants par pays estrangers?" [Are these not the brave messengers/who wander through foreign lands?][132] While the band of travelers see only "future shadows" ahead, the lands they cross undergo a transformation: as they pass by, the cricket intensifies its song, and Cybele, an ancient earth goddess whom the Greeks and Romans worshipped, extends her reach, turning the landscape green. These "verdures," however, do not lie ahead of the wanderers. In this compositional moment, Baudelaire's poem acknowledges, even critiques, Romanticism's appropriation and representation of the migrant, but in Raab's poem, this critique is leveled at Zionism's privileging of the immigrant status.[133] It is not difficult to draw a comparison, reading Raab's poem alongside Baudelaire's, between

Figure 2.5. Jacques Callot (1592–1635), "Bohémiens en marche II," from the series *Les Bohémiens* (1621–1625). The Inscription reads "Ne voila pas de braves messagers / Qui vont errants par pays estrangers?" ("Are these not the brave messengers / who wander through foreign lands").

Source: Bibliothèque nationale de France, http://gallica.bnf.fr

Zionism, the "absent chimeras" of Baudelaire's wanderers, and the renewal the earth undergoes as this itinerant band walks through (Baudelaire's "fleurir le désert" clearly alludes here to Isaiah 35). In her reading of Baudelaire's poem, Ana Fernandes notes how Baudelaire's prosody suggests this relation: "Already in the first hemistich [*la tribu prophétique*] there is an analogy, implicit in the second tercet, between the Israelites' sojourn to the Promised Land (as if Jeremiah or Ezekiel had been charged with communicating the divine message) and the wandering of the gypsies, who are depicted as ideal pilgrims."[134] In Raab's poem, the transformative and translational experience of immigrant wandering is transferred to the speaker as well, "with a heavy hand." This synecdoche recalls the father's hands in "La-av" but, as in that poem, it also relates to an act of creation/composition that occurs a short while later in the poem. Against the weight of the ancestors' migrations, a diasporic burden that also weighs the speaker down ("my feet have grown heavy"), the interior (Hebrew) song remains unfettered, vital, and mobile.

Poems such as "Kahira, Kahira!" and "Tso'anim—hungarim" in a predominantly "native" Hebrew poetry collection provide a vantage point for reconsidering Raab's cultural and linguistic affiliations and how she revises and blurs the line between foreign and native in her own writing. Take, for example, her response to Shamir's question, "Was Hebrew your first language?" "No," Raab replied, "We spoke Yiddish—Hungarian Yiddish, I am from Hungary. Later Lithuanian Jews came to the *moshava* [Petach Tikva] and the entire house welcomed that wonderful Yiddish from Białystock. And even today, when I speak Yiddish, people ask if I am from Białystock. I answer—Yes."[135] Raab's response discredits the assumption that Hebrew was her first language and shows that from an early age her background was multilingual; indeed, even her Yiddish was polyphonic.

On the other hand, in his description of Raab's linguistic background and the relation of Hebrew to the other languages that she encountered as a child, Ben-Ezer relies on a somatic metaphor of growth and composition, imagining Raab as a plant or flower nurtured by the development of Hebrew:

אסתר צומחת עם צמיחה העברית כשפה חיה, מדוברת. עברית היא הפריזמה היחידה שלה להבין את עצמה ואת נוף ילודתה. שאר המשוררים בני-דורה באים אל העברית משפה אחרת, מאופקי תרבות ומנופים אחרים, ולכן העוני וגם העושר שלהם נובע ממקורות אחרים ומתהליכים שונים.

Esther grew (*tsomachat*) with the burgeoning (*tsmicha*) of Hebrew as a living, spoken language. Hebrew was the sole prism through which she understood herself and her childhood landscape. The poets of her generation came to Hebrew from another language, from other cultural horizons and landscapes, and therefore their [artistic] poverty and wealth flow from other sources and different processes.[136]

The repetition of the shared root צ-מ-ח, from which the word "plant" derives, emphasizes the organic and symbiotic relationship between Hebrew and the Yishuv, the lens through which Ben-Ezer filters most of his analysis of Raab's work. But this observation, in particular, invites further scrutiny because it follows rapidly on the heels of this statement (which echoes Raab's response to Shamir): "It is true that in her childhood there were still those in the *moshava* who spoke a great deal of Yiddish and a bit of Arabic. And in her home: Hungarian Yiddish, which then stepped aside for Lithuanian-Białystockian Yiddish."[137] Yet, the sections I have extracted from Ben-Ezer's biography and Raab's own writings (poetry and prose) reveal that the composition of *Kimshonim* hardly emerged through the "sole prism" of Hebrew monolingualism, but rather as a result of more complex and varied linguistic and cultural contexts.

For Raab, one of the great paradoxes of the early twentieth-century modern Hebrew literary canon was the primacy it gave to non-native writers while marginalizing native Hebrew speakers; however, in asserting her native status as a mark of difference, Raab arguably consigned her own work to the native reading and further compounded this with her tendency to camouflage or rewrite key elements of her own background. For instance, her comment on Shlonsky's and Alterman's cultural burdens glossed over her own multicultural and multilingual background. The presence of translation in the *Kimshonim* manuscript, particularly translations of Baudelaire, suggests that Raab was conscious that her poetry was shaped by and emerged from a more multicultural and multilingual background, one that broke with Hebrew poetic conventions of the period to introduce a new poetic model. An inquiry into the implications of translation and multilingualism on Raab's oeuvre not only exposes the shortcomings of native readings of her work, and, in particular, of *Kimshonim*, but also contributes to ongoing scholarship that problematizes the terms of her native status within the modern Hebrew canon. The publication of *Kimshonim* may have marked, for some, the first appearance of a native, modern Hebrew poetry, but a closer look at Raab's own background and influences reveal the *shlal gevanim*, myriad shades, underlying many of its poems.[138]

CHAPTER 3

Twice Planted

Leah Goldberg's Poetics of Translation

Almost all of my creative output is foreign or inspired by the foreign; despite this, all of it is mine.

—VASILY ANDREYEVICH ZHUKOVSKY[1]

In a journal entry dated May 28, 1937, just two years after she had immigrated to Mandatory Palestine, the poet Leah Goldberg recounted the terms of an invitation to participate in a lecture series organized by the publishing house Ha-kibbuts ha-me'uchad.[2] She had proposed a talk on Fyodor Dostoevsky, but the organizers rejected the idea and suggested that she address instead the work of Maxim Gorky or Leo Tolstoy, "something affiliated with 'the movement.'"[3] Goldberg took offense at their request. "The farmer has it good in this country," she wrote, "he belongs to a *kibbutz* of people who want the very things that he wants.[4] And there are *so many* kibbutzim. But here a writer is obliged to live among people who want the very opposite of what he wants."[5] The 1935 publication of Goldberg's first poetry collection *Taba'ot 'ashan* (*Smoke Rings*) provided the young poet with a passport into Palestine's Hebrew literary elite.[6] Goldberg, who began writing Hebrew poetry as a child in Lithuania, became a prominent member of Shlonsky's *moderna*, her own background aligning well with their interest in European and Russian poetry of the fin-de-siècle and the early twentieth century.[7] As Chana Kronfeld has shown in her work on Hebrew modernism, these early poets were instrumental in advancing their own version of international modernism that placed the construction of a national literary canon at its center.[8] To this end, the ethos of "the rejection of exile" (*shlilat ha-galut*) became a central tenet of their public poetic discourse, though their own poetic practices and translation activity often articulated a more complex engagement with diasporic models and languages. Goldberg was acutely aware of how such a rejection conflicted with her own, and the group's own, affiliation and dialogues with European, and particularly Russian, writing and translation. Her conviction that poetry served both the national, public, and the inner, individual life guided her work as a writer, as well as her career as a translator and professor of literature.[9] In this journal entry, Goldberg also remarks that although Shlonsky regards himself as the organizer of a large, cohesive literary and cultural movement, Goldberg suspects that no such coalition exists among modern Hebrew writers in Palestine, a feeling that the Dostoevsky incident corroborated. As she is recounting this incident, she interrupts her thoughts on this matter with the observation, "In Italy, perhaps, I will be able to write."[10]

Goldberg's published journals, which date back to 1921, contain no entries between November 1932 and May 1937, thereby bypassing her preparations for immigration to Palestine, the move itself, as well as the first couple of years of her new life in Palestine.[11] The consistent pace of her writing from 1921 to 1932 suggests that the break from journal writing may have been deliberate.[12] The journals resume, notably, at the precise moment when Goldberg, prompted by feelings of professional discontent, begins to prepare for a long trip to Europe. In an entry dated May 15 of that year, in fact, the second entry after her long break, Goldberg writes: "If I don't go to Paris, I don't know how I'll get out of this."[13] Two weeks later, Italy has replaced Paris as her chosen destination, and Goldberg sets off on a month-long journey that will take her through Rome, Florence, Venice, and Trieste.

Goldberg's conviction that her ability to write will return once she leaves Palestine is notable, and even provocative, in the context of Zionism's investment in Hebrew literature as a constitutive component of Jewish territorial nationalism. By this time, the European centers of Hebrew literary production had shifted primarily to Palestine, and to Tel Aviv, in particular, but for Goldberg, this consolidation of the Hebrew literary economy had the effect of limiting options for the Hebrew writer.[14] Nevertheless, in choosing Italy as her eventual destination, Goldberg was also participating in a long tradition—particularly in Russian literature as far back as the work of the Romantics Mikhail Lermontov (1814–1841) and Alexandr Pushkin—that imagined Italy as a source for creative inspiration. At the time, Goldberg was also reading the poems of the German-language poet Rainer Maria Rilke (1875–1926), whose writing reflected his deep attachment to Italian culture and Italy's landscapes.

While this chapter addresses in particular the relation between Goldberg's poetry and her translation practices, I open this chapter with this Italian trip in order to consider a broader formulation of translation in Goldberg's work, in other words, "translation" as both an interlingual movement and a practice that was closely aligned with the desire for the kind of cultural and geographic mobility that Goldberg expresses in this journal entry. Travel is a major theme and trope in Goldberg's oeuvre, and one through which Goldberg often articulated her ambivalence toward Hebrew national culture in Palestine, and later, Israel. But travel, like translation, also develops in her work as a mode for articulating a complex relation between memory, language, and writing, and for breaking down the binaries of past/present, Israel/Diaspora, and Hebrew/foreign languages that shaped literary and national identity in Palestine in the early to mid-twentieth century. Goldberg's narrative of her trip to Italy, which I pieced together through a close reading of her journal entries and poems from that period, articulates her sense of being "in-between," a position that Goldberg would reassert and rework throughout her literary career. Although nostalgia partly motivates the trope of travel in Goldberg's work, I also show, in the next section, how the relation between travel and translation allowed Goldberg to position herself as an international, cosmopolitan, and even diasporic figure in the Palestinian, and later, Israeli, literary scene, all the while remaining committed to the development of modern Hebrew literary culture. For Goldberg, these relations were not incompatible. In her 1944 essay "Ha-meshorer ha-le'umi" ("The National Poet"), which I introduced in chapter 1, Goldberg asserts a reciprocal relation between national and world literatures, observing that the same qualities that make Goethe, Bialik, and Pushkin great national poets also account for their international stature: "The national poet is always a citizen, even when he is a 'citizen of the world.' Contrary to expectation, this large middle position turns national poets of great nations into great international poets, for the 'common denominator' of the people of a certain nation is always, and forever will be—their humanity."[15] Following the section on travel and translation, I will examine Goldberg's thematization of translation in seminal poems like "Oren" ("Pine") and "Ahavata shel Tereza di Mon" ("The Love of Teresa de Meun"), both published in her 1955 collection *Barak ba-boker* (*Lightning in the Morning*). These poems underscore how Goldberg ultimately came to use translation as a mode of writing that allowed her to engage simultaneously a range of cultural and linguistic frames, and to move, indeed translate, between her diasporic past and Israeli present, between world and nation.

In fact, Goldberg's return to Europe, so soon after her "return" to Palestine, rejects the one-way journey that was meant to culminate with a full and final transformation as a national figure. Instead, as Sidra Ezrahi has noted with regard to narratives that eschewed that model (and a number of early twentieth-century Hebrew texts did), Goldberg's return is "a form of critical thinking that refuses to take refuge in the promise of collective social or religious redemption."[16] Goldberg asserts the round trip as her constant mode, as exemplified in the poem "Oren" and its iconic imagery of in-betweenness: "[O]nly birds of travel know/as they are suspended between earth and sky/*this* pain of the two homelands." But this movement, as I will demonstrate later in my readings of "Oren" and "Ahavata shel Tereza di Mon," blurs the lines between the native and the foreign and between related binaries. At the same time, as these are the alleged lost works of a medieval French poet, it also enacts a slippage between original Hebrew writing and translation that I trace back to a series of "Italian" poems that Goldberg composed during the aforementioned 1937 trip to Italy. As was also the case for Esther Raab, translation emerges as a vital component of Goldberg's own poetry, at times synonymous with writing itself, and constituted a practice that allowed the poet to develop her own "poetic map" in and against prevailing lines of influence in modern Hebrew poetry.[17]

GOLDBERG'S ITALIAN POEM

Goldberg set off for Italy from the port of Haifa on June 17, and after a traumatic boat journey and a few lackluster days in Rome ("the espresso is bitter"), she reached Florence on June 29, nine days after her arrival.[18] She writes: "Everything assures me that I will feel better here than in Rome."[19] Goldberg's affection for the Florentine landscape and the city's cultural life was rooted in a long attachment to and interest in Italian Renaissance literature, particularly the works of Francesco Petrarca and Dante Alighieri. But Italy also serves, as Salzburg does for Raab's protagonist in "Ahava be-Zaltsburg," as a site that connects Goldberg to both a Russian and a European cultural sensibility that she remained attached to throughout her life. In "Eiropa shelachem" ("Your Europe"), an essay published in 1945, Goldberg offers a "best of" list of European culture, which opens, not too surprisingly, with the Italians:

מה הייתה אירופה בשבילנו? – דנטה, וג'וטו, ומיכלאנג'לו, גתה, ופלובר, ומוצרט,
וסטנדהאל, וורלן, ורילקה ורודן, סזאן, וסטרבינסקי וג'ימס ג'ויס...שמות, שמות,
שמות...ואנחנו לא נשכח, אותך, את פצעי האוהב ואת פצעי השונא לא נשכח.
ועד יום מותנו נישא אותה בקרבנו, את הכאב הגדול הזה ששמו אירופה – "אירופה
שלכם", "אירופה שלהם" וכנראה...לא "אירופה שלנו", – אף כי אנחנו היינו שלה,
מאוד שלה.

What did Europe mean for us?—Dante, Giotto, Michelangelo, Goethe and Flaubert, Mozart, Stendhal, Verlaine, Rilke, Rodin, Cézanne, Stravinsky, James Joyce ... names, names, names... We won't forget you, *we won't forget the wounds of the lover, the wounds of the enemy* [Proverbs 26:6].[20] Until our dying day we will hold it close to us, that deep pain called Europe—"your Europe," "their Europe".... and not, it seems, "our Europe"—even though we were hers, very much hers.[21]

As A. B. Yoffe aptly noted, "the center of gravity of this attraction, of this fascination that Europe exerted over her was Italy."[22] Her published oeuvre attests to this deep interest in Italian culture. In 1953, Goldberg completed a substantial Hebrew translation of the sonnets of Petrarca, which she published with an extensive biographical and historical introduction.[23] In fact, the completion of this collection coincided with the composition of many of the poems that formed the 1955 collection *Barak ba-boker*, which includes the cycle "Ahavata shel Tereza di Mon" (a relation that I will address later in this chapter). Her lectures on Dante, part of a course at the Hebrew University of Jerusalem, were also gathered in two separate volumes in 1956 and 1957, respectively.[24]

That being noted, as Natasha Gordinsky has discussed in a recent book on Goldberg's early poetry, this interest in Italy also came to Goldberg via her readings of German and Russian literature, and Rilke in particular.[25] Russia may not form an explicit part of Goldberg's "Eiropa" but it remains present in, and vital to, that model through her work of cultural and literary translation. In fact, Goldberg's first encounters with Petrarca and Dante were in Russian and German translation, a detail that proves particularly relevant in light of the influence of Italian culture on nineteenth- and early twentieth-century Russian and German literatures.[26]

By way of illustration, comparing Goldberg's account of her trip to Italy with the trip that the Russian poet Aleksandr Blok (1880–1921)—also translated by Goldberg into Hebrew—undertook in 1909, reveals a number of affinities.[27] Like Goldberg, in the year preceding his travels, Blok was experiencing difficulties in his writing life and, in Jenifer Presto's words, "a growing sense of the discordance of modern life."[28] In a letter to his mother, he writes: "There are still no new poems but I think in Venice, Florence, Ravenna, and Rome there will be."[29] In a subsequent letter, dispatched from Venice, he refers to Italy as his *drugaia rodina*, other homeland, and remarks that these separations from the native land are vital to the creative development of the Russian artist. The trip ultimately gave shape to Blok's series of twenty-three poems titled *Ital'ianskie stikhi* (*The Italian Verses*), which were published that same year.

Goldberg's frequent references to Rilke in her Italian journal entries are also notable, given Rilke's extensive interest in Italian culture. On this trip, Goldberg brought with her a collection of Rilke's poems, and if we go by the lines that she quotes in her entries, it was likely his 1905 collection *Das Stunden-Buch* (*The Book of Hours*). This collection, which took its name from the medieval book of hours (illuminated Christian devotional book), was in part inspired by his late nineteenth-century travels through Russia and Italy.[30] On the recommendation of his friend and lover Lou Andreas-Salomé, Rilke had traveled to Florence to study Renaissance art, and from April to May 1898, he recorded his thoughts on art, and the relation of the artist and work of art to the world, in his travel journal.[31] It is highly unlikely that Goldberg would have been familiar with Rilke's diaries at the time that she undertook her Italian trip—they would not be edited and prepared for publication for another five years—yet, Rilke's conviction that artists create their own homeland resonates in Goldberg's own assessment of her work and life in Palestine in this period. On May 17, Rilke writes:

> National art! And every honest art is national. The roots of its innermost substance draw warmth from their native ground and receive their courage from it. But already the trunk rises up in solitude, and the region where the crown spreads out is no one's kingdom. And it may be that the dull root does not know when the branches are in blossom....
>
> Art at its high points cannot be national. Why? Every artist is born in an alien country; he has a homeland nowhere but within his

own borders. And those of his works that proclaim the language of this homeland are his most deeply organic.

Indeed, I would consider this one of the most profound characteristics of any artist: everyday-man walks away from his homeland into an alien world; he ages, as it were, into the uncertain.[32]

Rilke's words offer a possible explanation for Goldberg's disenchantment with the cultural and political climate of the literary scene in Palestine. For Goldberg, the trip to Italy becomes a way to challenge and release herself, if only temporarily, from the constraints imposed on Hebrew writers in Palestine in this period, particularly the demand to address and write material that was single-mindedly invested in the national project. Goldberg was committed to nurturing a viable Hebrew literary culture in Palestine, but being in Italy offers Goldberg, as it did for Blok, an opportunity to relax those constraints by returning to familiar geographic and cultural landscapes that constitute her "other homeland," and perhaps to reclaim the possibility of being a Hebrew writer in Europe.[33] Her writing in this period attests to this possibility. For instance, in her unpublished 1937 novel *Avedot*, Goldberg speculates on the fate of the Hebrew writer in Europe and the possibility of European Hebrew literature.[34] Her protagonist Elhanan Yehuda Kron, a Hebrew poet and Orientalist scholar of Russian origin, immigrates to Palestine to give the kibbutz life a try, but decides to return to Europe to conduct research in Berlin, where he falls in love with a non-Jewish German woman. After a number of setbacks, including the loss of a Hebrew manuscript, he eventually returns to Palestine. But this return may not be definitive. In an unpublished version of the last chapter of Goldberg's 1937 epistolary novella *Mikhtavim mi-nesi'a meduma* (*Letters from an Imaginary Journey*), Goldberg's protagonist, L., suggests that one day, she may even leave "the white city" (a sobriquet for Tel Aviv).[35]

What Goldberg is invested in—and remained so throughout her career—is the possibility integrating both the diasporic and the national in her Hebrew writing. In her 1957 essay "Gefen ha-yayin she-be-karmei zarim" ("A Vintage from a Foreign Vineyard"), Goldberg poses the question "What can Baudelaire offer us?" as a way of framing her argument that relations between European literature and Hebrew writing in Palestine cannot be filtered solely through Jewish values, Jewish nationalism, and Jewish identity. To prove her point, Goldberg extracts various examples of non-Jewish foreign influences on Hebrew literature's long history, including the Arabic-inspired poetry of Al-Andalus, the development of the Hebrew sonnet in Italy, and the Haskala's engagements with German Romanticism.[36] Central to her argument is the role of translation in these cross-pollinations. Nevertheless, like Raab's protagonist in "Ahava be-Zaltsburg," Goldberg is

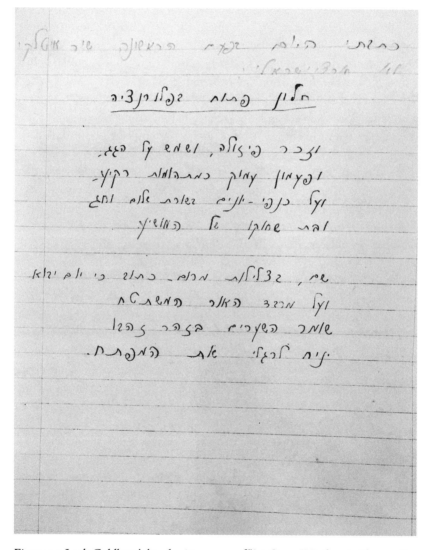

Figure 3.1. Leah Goldberg's handwritten copy of "An Open Window in Florence," with the sentence "Today, I wrote for the first time, an Italian, not *eretsyisre'eli*, poem" written above the poem.

Source: Gnazim-Hebrew Writers Archive, File 274/33357

aware of the difficulty of belonging, as a Jew, to European culture of the 1930s—as she will later lament in "Eiropa shelachem"—and, rather than choose sides, Goldberg instead places herself between these affiliations, ultimately settling into the in-between position that became a defining characteristic of her oeuvre.

In the entry dated June 25, 1937, Goldberg comments on the fact that she has managed to write "three, not bad poems in one sitting," thereby fulfilling objective of the trip: to resume writing poetry.[37] Then, a few days into her Florentine stay, on July 1, following a visit to a monastery in Fiesole,[38] she writes "for the first time, an Italian, not *eretsyisre'eli*, poem."[39] This "Italian" poem later became the second poem of a four-part cycle that Goldberg eventually published under the title "Mi-shirei Italiya" ("From the Poems of Italy"):[40]

חַלּוֹן פָּתוּחַ בִּפְלוֹרֶנְצִיָּה

וְזֵכֶר פְיֶזוֹלֶה, וְשֶׁמֶשׁ עַל הַגַּג,
וּפַעֲמוֹן עָמֹק כְּמִתְהוֹמוֹת רָקִיעַ,
וְעַל כַּנְפֵי יוֹנִים בְּשׂוֹרַת שָׁלוֹם וָחַג
וּבַת שְׂחוֹקוֹ שֶׁל הַמּוֹשִׁיעַ.

וּבְשַׁלְוַת מָרוֹם כָּתוּב כִּי יוֹם יָבוֹא
וְעַל מַרְבַד הָאוֹר הַמִּשְׁתַּטֵּחַ
שׁוֹמֵר הַשְּׁעָרִים בְּזֹהַר זְהָבוֹ
יַנִּיחַ לְרַגְלַי אֶת הַמַּפְתֵּחַ.

An Open Window in Florence

And the memory of Fiesole, and sun on the roof,
And a bell as deep as heaven's depths
And on the wings of doves good wishes and tidings
And the light laughter of the redeemer.

There, against the sky's tranquility,[41] it is written *that a day will come*
And on the extending carpet of light
The gatekeeper in his golden radiance
Will rest the key on my legs.

In her journals, Goldberg does not delve into the distinction between an Italian and *eretsyisre'eli* poem, leaving the reader to deduce what makes this particular poem "Italian." What characteristics does an Italian poem by Goldberg have that are not shared by one her *eretsyisre'eli* poems? Is it

location—where the poem is written rather than the residence of the author?
Is it language? By situating this poem in Florence—and by making specific
reference to Fiesole, where she toured a monastery—Goldberg turned again
to the very landscapes and imagery that raised debate and controversy in
her earlier work, specifically the Christian iconography and locations that
featured prominently in her first book.[42] These relations are most explicit in
the draft of a poem titled "Ha-katedrala" ("The Cathedral"), which appears
in these journals but remained unpublished. The idea that a Hebrew poem
could still be written in Italy and qualify as "Italian" challenges Hebrew literature's affiliation with territorial nationalism in this period. Instead, this
poem, and Goldberg's characterization of it, argues that Hebrew poetry need
not exist only within the borders of a monolithic and territorial national
identity, and that the demand for locally engaged Hebrew literature could
expand to include a broader, more fluid idea of the local.

The "open window," a frequent trope in Goldberg's work, also frames
the speaker of the poem as an insider/outsider. In fact, the image of the
window in the poem "Peticha" ("Opening") literally opens Goldberg's
second collection *Shibolet yerukat ha-ʿayin* (*The Green-Eyed Stalk*), which
includes the poems "Mi-shirei Italiya." "Peticha" belongs to the cycle
"Yaldut" ("Childhood"), a series of poems that situate the diasporic
past, and nostalgia for this past, as central concerns of the collection.[43]
In Goldberg's oeuvre, the window also serves as a complex metaphor for
poetic perspective, but it also generally involves some form of mediation
between the internal world of the speaker and an outside reality. In the
cycle "Slichot" ("Prayers of Atonement"), which also appears in *Shibolet
yerukat ha-ʿayin*, the window transports the speaker into a heightened state
of creative vision:

בָּאתָ אֵלַי אֶת עֵינַי לִפְקֹחַ,
וְגוּפְךָ לִי מַבָּט וְחַלּוֹן וּרְאִי,
בָּאתָ כְּלַיְלָה הַבָּא אֶל הָאֹחַ
לְהַרְאוֹת לוֹ בַּחֹשֶׁךְ אֶת כָּל הַדְּבָרִים.

You came to me to open my eyes,
your body was for me a glance a window and a mirror,
you came like night comes to the owl
to show him all things in the dark.

(l.1–4)[44]

Ruth Kartun-Blum notes that the window is a ubiquitous image in the works of Hebrew women writers of the early twentieth century, particularly in the poetry of Rachel (Bluwstein). But whereas windows serve in Rachel's poem to mark the speaker's detachment from the outside world, in Goldberg's poetry, the relationship between outside and inside, external and internal worlds that the window frames, is often far more active and porous.[45] In the case of "An Open Window in Florence," the pointedly "open" window allows the memory of the Italian landscape (*zekher Fiezole*) to move into the personal space of the speaker. In this sense, the Hebrew poem also functions as an "open window," as a porous mode of transport, or translation, for these Italian memories, experiences, and landscapes.

A couple of months after concluding her Italian travels, Goldberg published "Ba-derekh" ("On the Road"), the first poem of the Italian cycle, in the periodical *Davar*.[46] Of the four poems that comprise "Mi-shirei Italiya," it is the only poem that is not located expressly in Italy.

בַּדֶּרֶךְ

שָׁעוֹת מִתְנוֹדְדוֹת. פַּסִּים וּמִנְהָרוֹת.
וּבְשׁוּלֵי הַזְּמָן כָּתוּב: מִכָּאן עַד רוֹמִי.
הָאוֹר הָרַךְ צוֹלֵל בְּיָרֹק הַבְּאֵרוֹת.
תְּפִלַּת דַּרְכֵּךְ אִתָּךְ. אִמְרִי שְׁאוֹתָהּ וָדֹמִּי.

גְּשָׁרִים וּכְנֵסִיּוֹת רוֹקְדִים מוּל הַשַּׁחֲרִית
גְּבָעוֹת מְסֻלְסָלוֹת רוֹעוֹת בְּכַר-רָקִיעַ
וְקֶרֶן מֶרְחַקִּים קַלָּה כּוֹרֶתֶת בְּרִית
עִם לַהַט נוֹף הַיּוֹם אֲשֶׁר יַגִּיעַ.

אֶל עֲבָרֵךְ צוֹפָה תִּפְאֶרֶת נָכְרִיָּה,
וְזֶמֶר הַדְּרָכִים בְּשֶׁקֶט אֱלֹהִי:
כָּל אַגָּדָה פּוֹתַחַת בְּ"הָיֹה הָיָה",
אַךְ כָּל שִׁירָה נוֹלֶדֶת בְּ"וַיְהִי".

On the Road
Fluctuating hours. Rails and tunnels.
And at Time's edges it is written: from here to Rome.
The tender light sinks into the green wells.
Your travel prayer accompanies you. Recite it and be silent.

Bridges and churches dance before the dawn.
Curling hills take pasture in heaven's field.
And a soft ray of distances severs a covenant
With the blaze of the coming day's landscape.

A foreign splendor gazes towards your past,
And a song of roads in divine silence:
Every fable opens with "once upon a time,"
But all poetry is born from "let there be."

"Ba-derekh" thematizes travel through a series of varied but connected images, beginning with the *sha'ot mitnodedot* (fluctuating hours) of the first line to the *zemer ha-drakhim* (song of roads) in the last stanza.[47] Aside from an allusion to the idiom "all roads lead to Rome," the poem does not designate a clear destination; rather, the speaker celebrates a mode of travel that is intimately connected to the creation of poetry, and may even be necessary for it. The speaker is located in intermediary, transitory sites, "rails and tunnels," and in a non-linear, kinetic temporality. Although the poem acknowledges that "a foreign splendor gazes upon your past," it also understands the past as part of a forward-moving continuum, an orientation that distinguishes it from the fable. In the space of the poem, the past is not a static landscape, frozen in time; rather, the "bridges and churches dance," an image that may refer to the approaching Florentine landscape and also recalls the closing lines of a later poem, "Tel Aviv 1935": "And it seems—if you just turn your head, in the sea/your city's church is sailing."[48] In Goldberg's work, the past moves and transforms in the space of the poem, becoming present, as it does from poem to poem. What emerges, in Goldberg's work, are landscapes that conflate temporal and geographic frames of references. For example, the absence of a clear referent in the line "a foreign splendor gazes toward your past" creates a deliberate confusion. Where is the "foreign" located in this poem? Is it Italy? Palestine? Or is it an imagined landscape? In this respect, the landscapes that emerge in "Mi-shirei Italiya" are more "vicarious," to use Barbara Mann's term, than real.[49] In fact, Goldberg's Italian journal entries frequently describe mundane quotidian movements that translate, literally, between the past and present. As she crosses the Arno, for example, she notes that it is covered in quotations from Dante—"He crossed here," she writes.[50]

In "Ba-derekh," Goldberg also advances the image of the poet as a *helekh*, or wanderer, a prominent (male) archetype in Hebrew literature of the period, and a figure that would take a major place in her own work.[51] In Golderg's "Ba-derekh," however, this traveler is explicitly female (the line "Your travel prayer accompanies you" is addressed to a female addressee). What these poems written in Italy demonstrate, particularly when read in the context of her journal entries, is Goldberg's resistance to a local or territorial poetics or to any framework that restrains or limits the poem to a particular place, time, and subject. Instead, as a poem like "Ba-derekh" shows, Goldberg favors imagery that emphasizes movement, transit, and transformation. Kartun-Blum has observed, "Leah Goldberg is a traveling poet ... who sees the world as though through a train window."[52] The Italian poems that Goldberg composed in 1937 while in Italy reflect what Gordinsky refers to as Goldberg's work of "cultural translation," but they also articulate the poetics of translation that Goldberg consistently developed in her later work. Alongside her Italian journal entries, these poems contextualize for us the ambivalent, fluid, and translational exchanges between here and there, past and present, and native and foreign that pervade Goldberg's subsequent work, and specifically the poems that the remainder of this chapter will address: "Oren" and "Ahavata shel Tereza di Mon."

TRANSLATING THE TWO HOMELANDS: GOLDBERG'S "OREN"

I turn now to a reading of Goldberg's poem "Oren," from the three-poem cycle "Ilanot" ("Trees").[53] This poem—a sonnet—is arguably Goldberg's most canonical poem, and it has become a touchstone text in readings of Goldberg's oeuvre. Scholarly discussions of this poem often focus on the deliberately unresolved binary condition between "native" and "adopted" homelands in Goldberg's poem. The "two homelands" to which the poetic speaker claims to belong in the poem articulate the double-bind of exile that characterized the experiences of many Jewish immigrants in early twentieth-century Palestine and finds expression, in particular, in the works of the artists and intellectuals of this period.[54] My reading of the poem will engage the unresolved nature of the home/exile binary—as elaborated by Gluzman and Gordinsky—through the prism of translation.[55] As I read it, this poem not only aestheticizes an ambivalent exilic condition, but also proposes the poem itself as a site of translation. In other words, the poem emerges through the crossing over of languages, landscapes, and memories, and also places these movements in a state of suspension. As in "Mi-shirei Italiya," the state of being in between both opens and closes the poem. In the process, the speaker/poet asserts poetic language as the language that uniquely can articulate acts and sites of translation.

The poem famously begins by acknowledging the absence of a past land-scape through the anaphora "kan lo" (here not):

כָּאן לֹא אֶשְׁמַע אֶת קוֹל הַקּוּקִיָּה.
כָּאן לֹא יַחְבֹּשׁ הָעֵץ מִצְנֶפֶת שֶׁלֶג,
אֲבָל בְּצֵל הָאֳרָנִים הָאֵלֶּה
כָּל יַלְדוּתִי שֶׁקָּמָה לִתְחִיָּה.

Here I will **not** hear the cuckoo's voice.
Here the tree will **not** wear a turban of snow,
But in the shade of these pines
My entire childhood comes back to life.

(My emphasis)

In this poem, Goldberg engages but also rewrites the terms of Jewish exile—famously set forth by Psalm 137—by replacing the classic marker of the exilic position, *sham*, there, with *kan*, here. Gluzman argues, "[W]hile contemporary theory advances the idea that 'there is an essential virtue and gain in escaping the singularity of one culture into the multiplicity of all, or of all that are available,' Goldberg stresses her inability to feel fully at home in either of her homelands. The multiplicity is experienced as loss."[56] Although the poem opens with a double negation—*kan lo*—that under-scores what is missing and absent, these negations are immediately followed by a transformation that brings these absent elements to life, albeit in a different form. Lines three and four—"[B]ut in the shade of these pines/ my entire childhood comes back to life"—establish a site of translation that permits the past to cross over into the space of *kan* and the present. That this crossing over or translation occurs specifically in the "shade of the pines" is significant given the status of pine trees as European transplants. The reforestation of the Palestinian landscape was a project actively promoted by the Jewish National Fund, which financed the planting of European pines, a project that lasted for a good part of the twentieth century. The pine was brought over explicitly for the purpose of transforming the dis-puted *tabula rasa* of this landscape into the image of the European forests

Ashkenazi Jewish immigrants had left behind. Ultimately, the pine became a distinctive and normative element of the national landscape. The Hebrew "techiya" (revival, resurrection), alludes to the *Techiya*, the Hebrew literary renaissance of the late nineteenth century, and also suggests a Proustian restoration of the past in the space of the poem, just as the pine forests in Palestine were an attempt to restore the native European landscapes of the new immigrants.

The figure of the pine tree also situates Goldberg's poem in the topography of nineteenth-century Russian and Lithuanian literature, as well as in the immediate landscapes of her childhood. In his comprehensive study of the landscapes of Russian Romanticism, Otto Boele compiles a literary taxonomy of trees, including the pine, which he draws from Russian poetry and prose of the nineteenth century.[57] Among the texts he cites is Lermontov's poem "Сосна" ("Pine"), to which Goldberg's poem very likely gestures.[58] In Lermontov's poem, a snow-covered, northern pine tree imagines its southern counterpart, the palm, also standing alone in its landscape:

> На севере диком стоит одиноко
> На голой вершине сосна,
> И дремлет, качаясь, и снегом сыпучим
> Одета, как ризой, она.
>
> И снится ей всё, что в пустыне далекой,
> В том крае, где солнца восход,
> Одна и грустна на утесе горючем
> Прекрасная пальма растет.[59]

> In the wild north stands alone
> a pine tree on a bare mountain peak,
> and she slumbers, swaying, covered
> by flowing snow, like a mantle.
>
> And she dreams always that in a distant desert
> in that land where the sun rises,
> Alone and melancholy on a fiery crag
> a beautiful palm tree grows.

In Russian Romanticism, the pine tree often served as metonym for "northern" Russia, usually in opposition to the "south" (i.e., the Caucasus).[60]

In this north/south binary, the gloom, severity, and starkness of the north contrasts sharply with the verdant south (figured in Lermontov's poem by the "Прекрасная пальма," beautiful palm). "With his roots planted in the North, in Russia, the lyric subject contemplates and responds to a world which is not his own," Boele observes.[61] He further notes, in his reading of a poem by Fyodor Tyutchev, that this northern position that the poetic speaker assumes becomes a way of "underscoring [one's] status of an outsider."[62] "At the same time," Boele writes, "[the speaker] reduces his native land to a limited set of elements which can be regarded as an extremely concise index of the northern world: cold, snow, blizzards, mist, etc."[63] Echoes of this binary can be found in Hebrew and Yiddish poetry as well, for example, in Bialik's 1891 poem "El ha-tsipor" ("To the Bird"), which relates the visit of a bird from "warm" Zion to a wintery diaspora, and in Itzik Manger's "Oyfn veg shteyt a boym" ("On the Road Stands a Tree"), which features a tree that has been deserted by its birds, who have "turned to the west—to the east/and the rest—to the south."[64] In Goldberg's poem, the landscape that is not (*lo*) here (*kan*) is drawn from such a "concise index"—a cuckoo's voice, a snow-covered tree—but like Proust's famous madeleine, these images, in the space and language of the poem, unpack far more expansive geographic, cultural, and psychological associations.

Lermontov's poem, however, is also a reworking of "Ein Fichtenbaum steht einsam" ("A Pine Tree Stands Alone"), a poem by the nineteenth-century Jewish-born German poet Heinrich Heine (1797–1856) from his 1827 collection *Buch der Lieder* (*Book of Songs*), reproduced here alongside Emma Lazarus's English translation.[65]

> Ein Fichtenbaum steht einsam
> Im Norden auf kahler Höh.
> Ihn schläfert; mit weißer Decke
> Umhüllen ihn Eis und Schnee.
>
> Er träumt von einer Palme,
> Die, fern im Morgenland,
> Einsam und schweigend trauert
> Auf brennender Felsenwand.
>
> There stands a lonely pine-tree
> In the north, on a barren height;
> He sleeps while the ice and snow flakes
> Swathe him in folds of white.

He dreameth of a palm-tree
Far in the sunrise-land,
Lonely and silent longing
On her burning bank of sand.

(translation by Emma Lazarus)[66]

In fact, Chaim Shoham reads Goldberg's poem as both a *chikui* (imitation) and continuation of Heine's poem, noting that the arrangement of Goldberg's imagery in the octet appears to follow, at least initially, the binary structure of Heine's poem.[67] Furthermore, he also suggests that Heine's poem is a "broad, metaphorical paraphrasing" of Yehuda Halevi's twelfth-century Hebrew poem "Libi ba-mizrach" ("My Heart Is in the East").[68] What these versions, including Goldberg's poem, show is how the figure of the pine is transplanted—indeed, translated—over time, and ultimately read as a native element within the new linguistic and cultural contexts in which it is received. In this respect, the pine tree becomes a figure for, and of, translation.

In Goldberg's poem, the pine tree offers a space for recalling the childhood landscape that is *lo kan*, participating actively in constructing a language for this crossing over. If the "voice of the cuckoo" evokes a European lyric tradition that has been left behind, the "chiming" of the pine tree needles in the following stanza suggests the presence of a lyric voice that can mediate and translate between the past and present:

צִלְצוּל הַמְּחָטִים: הָיֹה הָיָה—
אֶקְרָא מוֹלֶדֶת לְמֶרְחַב-הַשֶּׁלֶג,
לְקֶרַח יְרַקְרַק כּוֹבֵל הַפֶּלֶג,
לִלְשׁוֹן הַשִּׁיר בְּאֶרֶץ נָכְרִיָּה.

The chiming of the needles: Once upon a time—
I will call the distance of snow a homeland,
The greenish ice that fetters the brook,
The poem's language [also, *tongue*] in a foreign land.

The relation between the sound or voice of the needles and the fairy-tale utterance "once upon the time" underscores, Gordinsky argues, the fictive quality of the emerging homeland: "Homeland as a fiction does not always have to obey biographical or geographical rules."[69] The Hebrew *hayo haya*—once upon a time—marks this moment as an imagined moment, *histoire*, and not history. In this mode, memory can be retold, revised, and retranslated.[70] Locating the homeland in historical space and time requires that the reader pay close attention to textual clues; at the same time, however, Goldberg deliberately conflates these past/present and native/foreign landscapes to assert what Gluzman refers to as a "simultaneous affiliation."[71] Goldberg invokes "here" and "homeland" as deixes; rather than distinguish between these terms, the poet attempts to capture their "simultaneous affiliation" through language and imagery that complicates, rather than disambiguates, any distinction between the "two homelands." Gluzman argues that "a simple sense of home is untenable for Goldberg, for she perceives her two home-lands as mutually exclusive."[72] While it is the case in this poem, and in others by Goldberg, that absence and loss characterize the relation between the two homelands, my reading suggests that Goldberg nonetheless attempts to arrest these landscapes simultaneously and inclusively in the space and language of the poem. Echoes of John Keats's "In drear nighted December" in the line "the greenish ice that fetters the brook" support Goldberg's understanding of time past as continuously present.[73] In Keats's poem, "frozen time" carries the assurance of a renewal that winter "cannot undo." Likewise, Goldberg's "greenish ice" suggests that time past remains vital and present. In "Oren," the poem itself frames and encases the moment when these landscapes meet, and it is in this state of translation—in fact, in the moment of translation—that they become "mutually inclusive."

At the end of her essay on "Oren," Gordinsky attributes to Goldberg a "nomadic poetic mode" that resolves the problem of this double affiliation.[74] She characterizes "Oren" as "a poetic performative act" that makes present what is missing, lost, or absent through the language of the poem. "The rem-edy lies in the recognition of the duality of homeland and double roots," Gordinsky observes, citing the traditional argument model of the sonnet, where the last stanza represents a resolution, albeit in this case a "painful" one, of the binary condition.[75] As Gluzman notes in his reading of the poem, Goldberg worked and reworked this binary throughout her career; it is present as early on as the poem "Galut" ("Exile"), which Goldberg wrote when she was twelve.[76] In his reading of "Galut," Gluzman observes that even at a young age, Goldberg already could assert that "exile" was a "difficult word" (*mila kasha*) while at the same time comparing the exilic state to a field "filled with oats and flax (*ha-mele'im shibolei shu'al u-pishta*)."[77] Also, in this early poem, many of the images that Goldberg employs reflect states of change or transit: "the season which is neither summer nor autumn," "green turning to gold," and "the melting snow."[78] As Gluzman points out, later in life, Goldberg's articulation of the home/exile binary would become more complex and ambivalent, but it is worth considering that even in this early poem Goldberg not only challenges the conventional language of exile but also sees it as a site of creation.

For Goldberg, I argue, what is ultimately at stake is not how poetry heals or resolves the "pain of two homelands," but rather the ways in which poetry and poetic language can further elaborate and problematize notions of home and exile from an in-between position. If the pine trees mediate the past and present, they do so through the creation of a site of translation that is temporal, impermanent, and transformative. The language of the poem, as stated in the fourth line of the second stanza, is pointedly left unnamed. Is it Russian? Hebrew? German? Or is Goldberg asserting, rather, the non-territoriality of poetic language? It is possible that Goldberg's line refers to Hebrew writing in the diaspora (e.g., the Hebrew poems she wrote in Lithuania and Germany), but given the translations that underlie the poem—and the state of translation that it thematizes—one can read this line as an evocation of the Hebrew poem that transports the "language(s) of the poem"—Russian and German, for example—to Palestine, a foreign land. The line gestures at once to a general condition of poetry as homeless or foreign and self-reflexively to Goldberg's own poem. If homeland is a concept that the artist, following Rilke and Lermontov, continuously reworks and recreates, then the language of the poem is always already in a foreign state.[79]

The third stanza underscores the uprooted and unsettled condition of the speaker with its (now) iconic image of the "tsiporei mas'a," birds of travel, that functions as a metaphor of the in-between and the poet's state of translation:

אוּלַי רַק צִפֳּרֵי-מַסָּע יוֹדְעוֹת—
כְּשֶׁהֵן תְּלוּיוֹת בֵּין אֶרֶץ וְשָׁמַיִם—
אֶת זֶה הַכְּאֵב שֶׁל שְׁתֵּי הַמּוֹלָדוֹת.

Perhaps only birds of travel know—
when they are suspended between land and sky—
This pain of the two homelands.

The poem's volta, signaled by the word "perhaps," prepares the reader for some kind of resolution between these landscapes. But this resolution is complicated by the word "mas'a," travel. English translations of "Oren" differ in significant and revealing ways in their rendering of the phrase "tsiporei masá." "Migrating birds" and "passing birds" are among the possibilities that various translations have suggested.[80] However, these translations of "tisporei masá" attenuate the intertextual relations that the literal meaning of Goldberg's phrase invokes. Goldberg's deliberate use of the word "travel," rather than migration (in Hebrew, *tsipor nodedet* is a "migratory bird"), connects this poem to other works in her oeuvre, particularly the novella *Mikhtavim mi-nesiá meduma* and the cycle "Ha-masá ha-katsar be-yoter" ("The Shortest Journey"), which includes the aforementioned poem "Tel Aviv 1935."[81]

Whereas migrating birds move between two opposing points (more commonly, north/south), the "birds of travel" exist in a state of suspended movement, between places (interestingly, the critic Y. Saaroni even referred to the poet as a "caged bird" in his 1935 review of her first book). This in-between position may provoke the pain of double affiliation—of the two homelands—but it becomes a productive site for Goldberg. It is the hovering between homelands that the poet chooses to frame; not only is the poem written from this in-between space, but the "bird of travel" also replaces the absent cuckoo as the lyric voice.

This in-between position emerges more explicitly in the final stanza with its images of doubling—the twice-uprooted poetic speaker whose roots now lie simultaneously in "two different landscapes":

אִתְּכֶם אֲנִי נִשְׁתַּלְתִּי פַּעֲמַיִם,
אִתְּכֶם אֲנִי צָמַחְתִּי, אֲרָנִים,
וְשָׁרָשַׁי בִּשְׁנֵי נוֹפִים שׁוֹנִים.

> With you I was planted twice,
> With you I grew, pines,
> And my roots are in two different landscapes.

The constant translational movement that Goldberg performs between the past and present in "Oren," as in other poems, assures that the binary of "the two homelands" remains unsettled. Read biographically, the two major uprootings to which Goldberg may be referring are, first, the expulsion from her childhood home, and later, her move from Europe to Palestine.[82] Gluzman also reads this stanza in relation to modern Hebrew literature's figure of the *talush* (uprooted individual), and thereby as an expression of her "inability to feel fully at home in either of her homelands." (In Hebrew, the verb *le-hishta'el*, to be planted, also recalls the verb *le-hitalesh*, to be uprooted.)[83] But Goldberg is also very likely invoking in this line a long-standing relation, particularly in Hebrew literary tradition, between poetry and exile. In Ezrahi's words:[84]

> The modern, not unlike the romantic, discourse on home, exile, and return captures the intensified longing for a place of origin as ultimate reference or antecedent—the presumption of a paradise whose loss or absence preserves it in a kind of negative space. The categories and strategies of reading may have changed radically, but the theme of exile and homecoming is as old as literature itself—and has become nearly synonymous with our understanding of the psychogenesis of literary practice. As the source of a long intertextual journey, Psalm 137 generates the poetic vocabulary of exile ... Being elsewhere, being far from Zion, is the pre-text for poetry.

What Goldberg's poem argues is that even in Zion, one is elsewhere. In the final two tercets, Goldberg's refusal to give a proper name to these home-lands means that one cannot decide between them. The resolution to the problem—or pain—of the two homelands does not rest in choosing one over the other. Although the landscapes remain "shonim" (different) and apart, Goldberg positions the poetic speaker simultaneously between them. The title's singular "oren," a metonym for both landscapes, is doubled—in fact multiplied—in the last stanza, producing a space for and of translation ("the shade of these pines"). In the process, the poem advances the possibil-ity of a relation between poetry and translation that allows these "different" landscapes to come—even momentarily—into contact. It is this in-between space of translation that generates the poem, arguably more so than the exilic position—indeed, it becomes a precondition for poetry.

POETRY AS TRANSLATION: THE LOVE OF TERESA DE MEUN

In the 1955 collection *Barak ba-boker*, Goldberg further elaborates a rela-tion between translation and poetry in her famed poetic cycle "Ahavata shel Tereza di Mon" ("The Love of Teresa de Meun"), which consists of twelve Petrarcan sonnets.[85] The speaker of these poems is an older woman in love with a younger man, but the individual poems provide very little historical and cultural information that would identify more specifically the speaker's time, place, and circumstances. When *Barak ba-boker* was first published, Goldberg provided a note of explanation for these poems at the end of the volume. In later editions, this note was moved to the beginning of the poem[86]:

תרזה די מון הייתה אישה מן האצולה הצרפתית, שחיתה בסוף המאה הט"ז בסביבות
אביניון שבפרובאנס. בהיותה בת ארבעים בערך התאהבה באיטלקי צעיר, ששימש
מחנך לבניה, והקדישה לו כארבעים ואחת סונטות. כאשר עזב האיטלקי הצעיר את
ביתה, שרפה את כל שיריה והיא עצמה פרשה למנזר. זכר שיריה נשאר רק כאגדה
בפי בני דורה.

Teresa de Meun was a woman born into the French aristocracy, who lived at the end of the sixteenth century in the environs of Avignon, in Provence. At around the age of forty, she fell in love with a young Italian man, who worked as her children's tutor, and she dedicated to him about forty-one sonnets. When the young Italian man left her home, she burned all of the poems and retreated to a convent. The memory of her poems remained only as a tale told by later generations.[87]

In a discussion of Goldberg's translation work in the 1940s, Gordinsky notes, "Goldberg regarded the craft of translation as one of the main channels of the work of memory."[88] Indeed, a relation between memory and translation is evident in the preface above when Goldberg pointedly states that it is the memory of the poems, and not the poems themselves, that has survived. In the absence of the original texts, the Bialikian veil between poetry and translation collapses and the translations of these lost poems take the place of original texts. But these "translations" of Teresa's poems also constitute a material memory of these works.

In these poems, as is the case with "Oren," translation is a multi-faceted operation. This section will address three interconnected types of translation that shape the poems. The first is the revival of the poems out of the ashes, from the sixteenth century into Goldberg's present day, which recalls the "techiya" (revival) of the childhood landscape in "Oren" and hints at a relation with the Christian resurrection of the dead. The fact that these are Hebrew texts suggests a second, possibly interlingual translation. One deduces from the context provided by Goldberg that Teresa de Meun was most likely not Jewish (her Christian name and flight to a monastery seem to cancel out that possibility). It is improbable, though not impossible, that a sixteenth-century noblewoman from Avignon would have composed these poems in Hebrew.[89] If "Tereza di Mon" was a real figure, in what language did she write?[90] What is the relation of the poems that Goldberg offers to those that were reportedly destroyed?[91] Are the poems fictive Hebrew translations of poems originally written in Latin, French, or (possibly) Italian? The phrase "a tale told by later generations" signals a third mode of translation from an oral to written tradition, from the past to the present.[92]

In these poems, the word "translation" never appears, and yet, it implicitly serves as a guise for Goldberg's own writing (as it did for Elizabeth Barrett Browning's *Sonnets from the Portuguese*, a text I will return to). Nevertheless, the historical prologue successfully tricked some of Goldberg's readers into thinking that these were indeed Hebrew poems by the sixteenth-century French poet Teresa de Meun.[93] But not everyone remained convinced. Upon the publication of these poems in *Molad*, Mina Landau, an old friend from Lithuania, contacted Goldberg "and although she didn't say anything about them, it was entirely clear to me that she knew that 'Terez [*sic*] di Mon' was my invention."[94]

As Tuvia Ruebner noted in his monograph on Goldberg, when these poems began to appear in 1952, she was making steady progress on her manuscript of translations of Petrarca's sonnets, a project that took her several years to complete but was in its final stages by the time the "Tereza" poems appeared, and it is likely that this project shaped the composition of these poems.[95] The decision to locate Teresa de Meun in Avignon is one of the more explicit connections between Petrarca and these poems.[96] It is also possible that hints of this project appeared earlier in *Avedot*. After a disappointing attempt to settle in Palestine, the novel's protagonist Kron returns to Berlin and, after a few unproductive months, resumes work on his magnus opus, a poetic cycle titled "Brichat elohim" ("God's Escape"), a work that he transcribes onto parchment in the style of thirteenth-century Hebrew script. The poems are dedicated to Kron's new love but are subsequently lost during a lecture Kron attends; with their disappearance, the possibility of being a Hebrew writer in Europe is cast into doubt. Following the Nazi rise to power, Kron learns that a former colleague had stolen his poems and published them in an academic journal as evidence of the purported long history of anti-Christian attitudes among German Jews—and did so despite knowing that Kron was the actual author of the poems. In other words, the conceit of thirteenth-century authorship is intentionally taken at face value. The recovery of his poems prompts Kron to finalize his plans to return to Palestine, a move that signals a more decisive break from the dream of Hebrew writing in Europe. His only recourse, he determines, is to return to Palestine and publish the poems there.[97]

Goldberg's entries from 1952, a very productive and creative period for the poet, also suggest correlations between these poems and events in Goldberg's personal life. In that year, Goldberg was forty-one years old (the number of sonnets that Tereza, also "around forty," purportedly composed) and in love with a younger man, a teacher by the name of Jacques Adout, who specialized in Latin language instruction and French literature.[98] Adout was only three years younger than Goldberg, but in her journals she frequently referred to him as *ha-na'ar*, the young man.[99] Adout seems to have harbored no long-term plans to stay in Israel, although Goldberg repeatedly encouraged him to continue his study of Hebrew and attempted to draw him into her social milieu. Eventually, Adout returned to France and, in effect, became her "Laura." This autobiographical context underscores the extent to which the guise of translation allowed Goldberg to address—but also distance herself from—the very personal narrative underlying these poems.

The guise of translation also frames Barrett Browning's *Sonnets from the Portuguese* (1850), a series of forty-four Petrarcan love sonnets dedicated to Barrett Browning's husband, the English poet Robert Browning.[100] According to one version, Barrett Browning had planned to title the collection *Sonnets from the Bosnian* until Browning persuaded her to rename them "from the Portuguese," a title that alluded to a group of sonnets by the poet Luís de Camões and also may have referred to Browning's term of endearment for the poet. In a letter to her sister, Barrett Browning remarked that the title "did not mean (as we understood the double meaning) 'from the Portuguese language' ... though the public (who are very little versed in Portuguese literature) might take it as they pleased."[101] Eventually, Barrett Browning dropped the mask and included the sonnets in a later collection of her works, thereby claiming her authorship of the poems, but the poetic speaker of these poems—an older woman in love—may have been a model for Goldberg's Teresa. Goldberg only began to study Italian seriously in the late 1940s, so her early readings on the history of the sonnet were primarily via German and Russian translations. Ofra Yeglin even suggests that Goldberg may have encountered Barrett Browning's *Sonnets* for the first time in Rilke's German translation, which was published in 1908.[102] On the other hand, in a September 1939 entry, Goldberg remarks that she is bedridden with a fever and taking advantage of the illness to read up on English literature, and includes Barrett Browning in her reading list. There is no mention of reading Barrett Browning, or any other English writer, in translation—and Goldberg consistently credited translators by name—so it is possible that Goldberg read Barrett Browning's sonnets in English.[103]

As I argue in my chapter on Raab, and throughout this study, modern Hebrew poets have engaged translation, as both a poetics and a practice, in order to reclaim as well as invent personal narratives and affiliations that do not accord with the demands imposed on Hebrew literature as the nation-building project progressed. Even outside of the political realm, writers are often working within and against the internal politics of their literary milieu. The poems of "Ahavata shel Tereza di Mon" are no exception. Goldberg's poems camouflage a personal narrative to assert, create, and continue alternative lines of influence and circulation in modern Hebrew poetry through a highly charged intertextuality—much of it mediated in and through translation. Unlike Barrett Browning, who later removed the mask of translation and acknowledged her authorship of the *Sonnets*, Goldberg gave increased visibility to the imaginary history of "Ahavata shel Tereza di Mon." By foregrounding this fictive historical context, Goldberg further blurred the relation between the poems' author and the poetic speaker. In so doing, Goldberg deliberately complicated the question of the work's origins.

Scholarship on these poems has focused by and large on untangling their rich intertextuality, in part in an effort to unveil this mask. Yeglin, for instance, cites a few possible, and likely, female historical influences for the figure of Teresa, namely the French Renaissance poet Louise Labé (c. 1520–1566), the Italian poet Gaspara Stampa (1523–1554), and, of course, Barrett Browning.[104] Interestingly, the work of Stampa and Labé also draws Rilke into this network. Stampa appears in the first of his *Duino Elegies* and a collection of his German translations of Labé's poems appeared in 1918. María Encarnación Varela also cites Labé as a "hypotextual" influence on Goldberg, but also attempts to establish what she refers to as "circulation relations" between Goldberg's Teresa and various authors and literary texts, among them the twelfth-century *trobairitz* (female troubadour) Comtessa de Día, Gustave Flaubert's *Madame Bovary* (1856), Leo Tolstoy's *Anna Karenina* (1873–1877) and Leopoldo "Clarín" Alas y Ureña's realist novel *La Regenta* (1884/1885).[105] Giddon Ticotsky even explores the possibility of an intertextual relation between "Ahavata shel Tereza di Mon" and the French medieval chantefable *Aucassin et Nicolette*, which Goldberg translated into Hebrew and published in 1966.[106] The surname "Di Mon" suggests a strong relation to Jean de Meun (c. 1260–1305), the thirteenth-century French author best known for his continuation of Guillame de Lorris's *Roman de la Rose* (1230/1275).[107] De Meun was also a translator, and his French translations of the letters of Abelard and Héloïse were well known to Petrarca.[108] The de Meun connection also brings to the foreground the relation between writing and translation that similarly frames the poems of "Ahavata shel Tereza di Mon." Since de Meun's translation of the letters of Abelard and Héloïse came to light in the thirteenth century, various scholars have tried to claim the letters as forgeries concocted by de Meun.[109] These assertions have emerged in part because of the dual composition of the *Roman de la Rose* and the difficulty of establishing the extent of de Meun's continuation, which has cast doubt on his other works. Finally, Ticotsky suggests a link between the name "Tereza" and the sixteenth-century Spanish mystic and poet Santa Teresa de Ávila (1515–1582).[110] While these historical, literary, and critical relations offer a rich intertextual mapping of the sources that may have shaped these poems, I will focus in particular on those that pivot around the figure and works of Petrarca, whose poems Goldberg was translating during the composition of these poems, and especially on an explicit intertextual moment in "Ahavata shel Tereza di Mon"—mediated by translation—that situates these poems in a specifically Petrarcan network, from which Goldberg drew the observations that shaped her own theory of translation.

In 1964, Goldberg participated in the IVe Congrès de l'Association Internationale de Littérature Comparée, which took place that year in Fribourg, Switzerland. The overarching theme of the event was "nationalisme et cosmopolitisme en littérature," with a panel devoted to "Le problème de la traduction."[111] Goldberg's presentation "Certain Aspects of Imitation and Translation in Poetry" focused primarily on sixteenth-century French and Italian imitations of Petrarca.[112] Although Goldberg had written and lectured extensively on Petrarca, what makes this particular document so interesting and important is that it is one of a handful of substantive accounts—in English, no less—by Goldberg on the subject of translation.[113] Here, Goldberg illuminates aspects of her own approach to translation and translation's relation to original writing.

The essay opens with the following observation:

> Though there are almost as many ways of translating poetry as there are individual translators, we must assume for the purpose of this argument that a translator of poetry is a person who intends to reproduce in another language all the characteristics of the poem translated: i.e., the form, the contents [sic], the atmosphere, the particular poetic personality of the original author and the style and spirit of his time.[114]

These comments open Goldberg's discussion on sixteenth-century imitations of Petrarca, where she distinguishes between translation and imitation (poetic adaptation or rewriting), and between free and close imitations. Of particular interest to Goldberg is the "border line" between them. Goldberg observes that some imitators of Petrarca achieve what she terms "a creative identification" with the work they have chosen to imitate. This kind of imitator begins by "[taking] only what he thinks essential for the enrichment of his own poetry and dismisses freely everything which might have an effect of a foreign body, or of remoteness." In the process, the imitator develops an attachment to the "poetic achievement" of the original text that a translator, who is more concerned with remaining faithful to the original author, rarely does. The result is a poem that reflects "the style of the original as if it were [the imitators'] natural idiom": "They always considered the result as part of their personal creative activity and the foreign poem became immanent to their own literature."[115]

By way of example, Goldberg cites two sixteenth-century French imitations of Petrarca's "Pace non trovo": Labé's "Je vis, je meurs" and Pierre de Ronsard's "J'espere et crain."[116] There are similarities between Ronsard's and Labé's imitations that suggest that, to the extent that they were engaging Petrarca's poem, they were also in conversation with each other. These movements, between and within literary cultures, demonstrate what Goldberg refers to as the ways by which the "foreign poem [becomes] immanent" in the target literary culture through an imitation that stands on its own literary merits. The part of the imitation that contains traces of the original text and its foreignness is what Goldberg regards as translation.

Goldberg demonstrates how Labé's "Je vis, je meurs" reveals "the under-current of Italian verse," specifically allusions to Dante, that were not present in the original poem.[117] In other words, in her imitations of Petrarca, Labé demonstrates a fluency with the Italian literary canon as though it were part of her own native literary patrimony. What Labé's poem calls into question, however, is to what extent one needs to be born into and inhabit particular literary borders in order to claim an affiliation or sense of belonging to them, an issue that also preoccupied Rilke in his Italian journals. Through imitation, Labé seized an opportunity to engage texts outside of her time, place, and language, and make them her own, resulting in the creation of an intertextual family tree in which Goldberg later inscribed herself. Labé succeeds in doing so in ways that, Goldberg suggests, would not be possible for a more faithful translator, who would stick closely to what is written in the poem and to the time, place, and circumstances of the original author. A faithful translation can still influence a foreign literary culture, but works that lie on "the border of imitation and translation" can wield this influence internally.

"Ahavata shel Tereza di Mon" contains at least one poem that belongs to this family of Petrarcan imitations, and specifically the branch of "Pace non trovo":

Sonnet 8, "Nimei ha-geshem ke-meitrei kinor" ("The strands of rain like violin strings"):

נִימֵי הַגֶּשֶׁם כְּמֵיתָרֵי כִּנּוֹר
תְּלוּיִים עַל הַחַלּוֹן. רֵעִי, הַדְלֶק-נָא
הָאֵשׁ בָּאָח. נֵשֵׁב בֵּין אוֹר וְאוֹר
וּבְבוּאוֹת בְּנֵינוּ תְּשַׂחֵקְנָה.

הוֹלֵם אוֹתְךָ הָרֶקַע הָאָפֹר
שֶׁל יוֹם גָּשׁוּם. וְשַׁחֲרוּתְךָ נִלְבֶּבֶת
בְּאוֹר כָּפוּל שֶׁל סְתָו וְשֶׁל **שַׁלְהֶבֶת**—
לִבִּי הַלַּהַט וְשִׂכְלִי **הַכְּפוֹר**.

עַד מָה מָתְקָה לִי הַמִּרְמָה הַזֹּאת:
הַסְתֵּר אֶת תְּשׁוּקָתִי וּתְמִימוּתְךָ
לְשִׁבּוֹת בְּקֶסֶם אִמָּהוֹת נִזְהָרֶת.

וְלֹא יָעִיב חָשָׁד אֶת מִצְחֲךָ,
כִּי פֹה, מוּל גֶּחָלִים מְפַזְּזוֹת,
שְׁעַת-אַהֲבָה גָּנַבְתִּי לְמַזְכֶּרֶת.

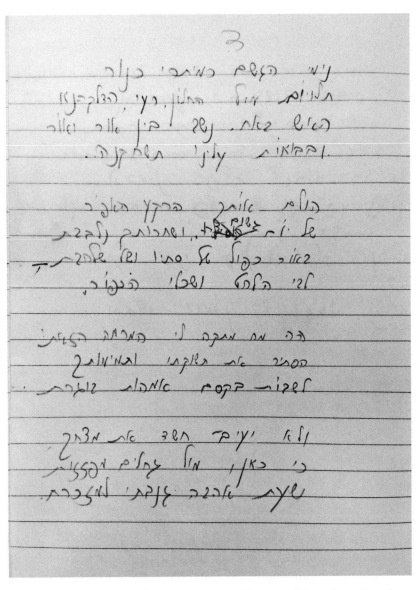

Figure 3.2. Leah Goldberg's handwritten copy of Sonnet 8, "Nimei ha-geshem ke-meitrei kinor" ("The strands of rain like violin strings") from "Ahavata shel Tereza di Mon."

Source: Gnazim-Hebrew Writers Archive, File 274/13263

The strands of rain like violin strings
are suspended over the window. My friend, please light
the fire in the hearth. We will sit between the sparks
and in these reflections [the fire] will play between us.

It suits you, the gray backdrop
of a rainy day. Your lovely youth
in the doubled light of autumn and flame—(*be-or kaful shel stav*
ve-shel **shalhevet**)
my heart the blaze, my mind the frost. (*libi ha-lahat ve-sikhli ha-***kefor**)

How much it delighted me this deception:
concealing my passion and your innocence
held captive by the charm of a maternal glow.

But no suspicion will cloud your brow,
for here, facing these dancing coals,
I stole an hour of love as a souvenir.[118]

The last two lines of the second stanza of Goldberg's poem clearly invoke
Petrarca's "Pace non trovo." For comparison, I have included the relevant
stanzas, beginning with Petrarca's original and followed by the imitations
by Labé and Ronsard:

Petrarca's "Pace non trovo" (Sonnet CXXXIV):[119]

Pace non trovo, et non ò da far guerra;
e temo, et spero; et **ardo**, et son un **ghiaccio**;
et volo sopra 'l cielo, et giaccio in terra;
et nulla stringo, et tutto 'l mondo abbraccio.

I find no peace, and all my war is done:
I fear, and hope; I burn, and freeze like ice;
I fly above the wind, yet I can not arise;
And nought I have, and all the world I seize on.

(translation by Robert M. Durling)

Labé's "Je vis, je meurs" (Sonnet VIII):[120]

Je vis, je meurs; je me brûle et me noie;
J'ai **chaud** extrême en endurant **froidure**:
La vie m'est et trop molle et trop dure.
J'ai grands ennuis entremêlés de joie.

I live, I die: I burn and I also drown.
I'm utterly hot and all I feel is cold.
Life is too soft and too hard for me to hold;
my joy and my heavy burden are mixed in one.

                                  (translation by Annie Finch)

Ronsard's "I'Espere et crains" (Sonnet XII):[121]

I'Espere et crain, ie me tais et supplie,
Or' ie suis **glace**, et ores un feu **chaut**,
I'admire tout, et de rien ne me chaut,
Ie me délace, et puis ie me relie.

I hope and fear, I grow quiet and implore,
Now I am ice, and already a hot fire,
I admire everything, and care for nothing,
I come undone, and then bind myself again.[122]

In her own translation of Petrarca's "Pace non trovo," Goldberg translates
the first two lines as follows:[123]

אֵין בְּלִבִּי שָׁלוֹם, אַךְ אֵין לִבִּי נִלְחָם,
בִּי פַּחַד גַּם תִּקְוָה, **בִּי כְּפוֹר וְגַם שַׁלְהֶבֶת**

Eyn be-libi shalom, akh eyn libi nilcham,
Bi pachad gam tikva, *bi kefor ve-gam-shalhevet.*

What Goldberg's translation reveals is that Sonnet 8 of "Ahavata shel
Tereza di Mon" rewrites Petrarca's "et ardo, et son un ghiaccio" as "libi ha-
lahat ve-sikhli ha-kefor" (my heart the blaze and my mind the frost), which
also shares a strong intertextual relation with Goldberg's own translation
of the poem. In other words, Goldberg's poem activates two translation
operations simultaneously: the first is her imitation of Petrarca's line ("libi
ha-lahat ve-sikhli ha-kefor") in sonnet 8, and the second is the breaking
apart and subsequent grafting of a line from her own Hebrew translation
of "Pace non trovo." In sonnet 8, the "double light"—or *kaful*—gestures to
the linguistic doublings or reflections that shape the poem. The words *shalhevet* and *kefor* may come into Hebrew via Petrarca, but the moment that
Goldberg brings these words into "Ahavata Tereza di Mon," she is asserting
them as her own poetic language. In this respect, they are both translation
and original.

In her conference presentation, Goldberg argues that expressions and words that are "hackneyed" in one language—for example, Petrarca's "fire and ice"—"molded ... in another language ... still might have had the freshness of a new metaphor."[124] Although her subject is sixteenth-century French and Italian Renaissance poetry, Goldberg's argument touches on one of the important and primary motivations for translation in early modern Hebrew literature. The Pléiade poets, like Ronsard and Joachim du Bellay, pursued their imitations of ancient texts, as well as Italian poetry, as a way to invigorate and expand the vernacular possibilities of their French. Likewise, modern Hebrew translations in the late nineteenth and early twentieth centuries were part of the essential rebuilding and vernacularization of the Hebrew language as a modern, and later, national language. Yiddish-to-Hebrew translations, for instance, were undertaken partly with this aim. Yiddish, unlike Hebrew, had a vibrant, rich, and contemporary vernacular, and in translating from one language to another exposed what Hebrew was lacking, thereby compelling Hebrew translators to create equivalents, that is, to create a language.

According to Bialik, poets, more so than prose writers, are invested in what is, in his words, "vital and mobile in language":

> ...הם עצמם מחויבים להכניס בה כל רגע – על פי מפתחות מסורות בידיהם –
> תנועה בלתי פוסקת, הרכבות וצרופים חדשים. המלים מפרפרות תחת ידיהם: כבות
> ונדלקות...בחמר הלשון בא על ידי כך חלופי משמרות והעתק מקומות. תג אחד,
> קוצו של יו"ד – והמלה הישנה זורחת באור חדש.

> ... using their unique keys, they are obliged themselves to introduce into language at every opportunity—never-ending motion, new combinations and associations. The words writhe in their hands; they are extinguished and lit again ... By this process there takes place, in the material of language, exchanges (he'etek) of posts and locations: one mark, a change in the point of one idea, and the old world shines with a new light.[125]

By adopting, that is, translating, Petrarcan clichés in their own languages, these imitators were "creating the poetic dictions of their time."[126] Goldberg highlights this process through various examples of how the Petrarcan expression "fire and ice" undergoes various imitations in the works of different writers. In a Benjaminian turn, Goldberg observes that the "freshness" that the cliché displays in a new language suggests that "it was not as stereotyped before as to lose all original beauty or meaning"; on the contrary, the multiple translations that it generates testify to the strength of the original's translatability, that is, to its "aura."[127]

By the end of Goldberg's talk, it becomes clear that what she means by imitation is a kind of translation that is more creative and personal than faithful. For Goldberg, "ideal translation"—translation as a perfect, seamless reproduction of a poem from one language to another—"scarcely exists in reality"[128]:

> If a translator is not a poet, he would almost certainly be guilty of unnatural language, of forced rhymes and flatness, which is seldom to be found in imitation, because the imitator is free in everything but the self-imposed poetic rules, and only some of these rules are borrowed from the model. On the other hand, if the translator *is* a good and inspired poet, he would, for all his intended subordination to the poem translated, hardly manage to refrain from imposing on it his own manner and style, and sometimes his own ideas. So, his final achievement would turn out to be much nearer imitation than translation.[129]

This closing paragraph from Goldberg's talk opens a window into how she approached her own translation activity, and how she understood translation—that is, good translation—as a generative, creative act, and advanced "imitation" as the term that best encompassed both interlingual translation and creative rewriting of source material. As Even-Zohar demonstrated in his analysis of Goldberg's translation of Baudelaire's "Spleen," which I discussed in the previous chapter, although Goldberg was often very pedantic with regard to prosody and form, her translations on the whole reflected her own poetic preferences.[130] In this respect, they were creative, despite their careful attention to the prosody of the original poem. Though Goldberg was committed to translation as an essential component of a developing and original Hebrew literature, she also understood translation as an art. In an essay on Shlonsky, Goldberg wrote: "The problem of translating poetry has been and will remain for all of the literatures of the world as one of the most difficult problems. The solution to it can be found only in occasional moments, in the unique personality of the translator-creator (*ha-metargem ha-yotser*)."[131] Only in the hands of this translator-creator, Goldberg argued, could the translated poem become part of "our poetry."

Ruebner observes in his afterword to *Kolot rechokim u-krovim*, a post-humous 1975 collection of Goldberg's translations, that "those well-versed in Goldberg's poetry will discern a similarity between the language of translation and the language of her original poetry, a relation that her publication history corroborates."[132] With its emphasis on the "language" of translation and original poetry, Ruebner's comment suggests a relation of mutual reciprocity between translation and writing in Goldberg's oeuvre.[133] If the poem "Oren" reflects a process by which Goldberg uses poetic language and the space of the poem itself to generate a site of translation (as a movement between places, histories, and languages), the poems of "Ahavata shel Tereza di Mon" take this process a step further and assert the poetic text itself as a translation, and translation as its own original.

CODA

In the 1960s, Goldberg undertook the project of editing an anthology of love poetry in Hebrew translation. In the course of gathering materials for the volume, Goldberg observed that folk poetry was underrepresented.[134] According to the poet and translator T. Carmi, Goldberg ultimately presented her own poem as a Hebrew translation of "a French folk poem" (*shir-'am tsarfati*). Carmi does not name the poem in question, but the 1966 anthology *Lu'ach ha-ohavim* (*A Calendar of Lovers*) includes only one "French folk poem," a poem titled "Tereza tsachat ha-panim" ("Teresa of Fair Complexion").[135] The poem relates the story of a young woman courted by three men with distinct attributes. One is lame, the other blind, and the third "old and very short." Each suitor offers Teresa a good marriage by making the best of their respective disadvantages ("The lame one said: / … 'I'll be faithful/and never leave you!'" [l.9–12]). But Teresa is swayed by the dashing Jean-Baptiste, a soldier who makes no promises.

Perhaps it is not incidental that the protagonist of this poem is named Teresa or that Goldberg is said to have composed this poem between 1955 and 1956, around the time that *Barak ba-boker* was published. In "Tereza tsachat ha-panim," the guise of translation is camouflaged to a greater extent than in "Ahavata shel Tereza di Mon"—although admittedly, we have to take Carmi at his word that this is the poem's history.[136] What Carmi's account corroborates, if we take it at face value, is how Goldberg consistently negotiated the "border line" between translation and original writing to situate her own work in alternative historical, linguistic, and cultural frames of reference. The line that closes Sonnet VIII of "Ahavata shel Tereza di Mon"—"I stole an hour of love as a souvenir"—articulates the kind of intertextual translation that Goldberg is engaging. Although the speaker is referring ostensibly to stolen hours with her lover, Goldberg's *mazkeret* (souvenir) also functions here as a metaphor for intertextuality, for the words and images that one poet borrows or steals from another. To the extent that Teresa's account of her love affair is made up of such "souvenirs," so is the poem composed of a rich gathering of translated or otherwise transported text and language.

Goldberg's translation and graft of Petrarca's "Pace non trovo" inscribes her poem in a Petrarcan network, while it arguably creates an entirely new female lineage within modern Hebrew poetry (the Teresas of Yona Wallach, Dahlia Ravikovitch, and Agi Mishol may attest to that).[137] Wendy Zierler, in fact, reads the poems of "Ahavata shel Tereza di Mon" as a feminist revision of literary history: "Like Virginia Woolf's Judith Shakespeare, Goldberg's Teresa de Meun attests to the desire to lend a voice to the lost women writers of the past … Goldberg's 'Ahavata shel Teresa de Meun' might, therefore, be seen as a feminist companion to [her Petrarca translations], offering a glimpse of the unknown contributions women poets might have made to the European sonnet genre."[138] In this respect, they are a response to Barrett Browning's observation, "I look everywhere for grandmothers and see none."[139] The guise of translation allows Goldberg to write personal poems that ultimately transcend her own biography, while they also create their own lineage and history through this imagined translation.

In the final sonnet of the Teresa cycle, Goldberg "returns to the metapoetic mode," as the speaker reflects precisely on this textual afterlife[140]:

מַה יִשָּׁאֵר? מִלִּים מִלִּים, כָּאֵפֶר
מֵאֵשׁ הַזֹּאת לְבִּי אָכַל,
מַחְרְפָתִי, מִכָּל אָשְׁרִי הַדַּל
רַק אוֹתִיּוֹת הַחֲתוּמוֹת בַּסֵּפֶר.

What will remain? Words, words like the ash
of this fire that consumed my heart
of my shame, of my meager happiness
only words sealed in the book.

(l.1–4)[141]

The speaker's figurative heartburn alludes here to the burning of the poems that the prologue recounts, but stanzas like this one have prompted Ariel Hirschfeld to read these poems as Goldberg's articulation of the problem or impossibility of writing poetry after the Holocaust.[142] As Gordinsky has noted, after the Holocaust, Goldberg went through a period when she wrote very little poetry, and instead, she focused her energies on prose, as well as translation.[143] Supporting Hirschfeld's reading is a possible allusion in this cycle to "The Horseshoe Finder" (Нашедший подкову) by the Russian Jewish poet Osip Mandelstam (1891–1938), whose preoccupation with the future, or afterlife, of poetry was central to this poem, as is the case for Goldberg's. Diana Myers describes "The Horseshoe Finder" as a poem that articulates "the rift between the poet and the time and space in which he lives." The poet's language, she writes, is "like wheat, preserved but unable to germinate."[144] Likewise, while writing offers Teresa a way of archiving—or sealing, as Goldberg puts it—the memory of her love, the words that survive the burning of the poems nonetheless remain "sealed," that is, confined and immobile. This is, initially, the fate of poetic language in Mandelstam's poem:

Так
Нашедший подкову
Сдувает с нее пыль
И растирает ее шерстью, пока она не заблестит;
Тогда
Он вешает ее на пороге,
Чтобы она отдохнула,
И больше уж ей не придется высекать искры из кремня.

(l.72–79)

So,
The finder of a horseshoe
Blows off the dust
And burnishes it with wool, until it shines
Then
He hangs it over the threshold,
To take a rest,
So it no longer needs to strike out sparks from flint.

(l.80–87; translation by Steven J. Willett)[145]

The horseshoe that once threw sparks across long distances may now hang idly over a doorframe, but Mandelstam's imagery of dead or immobile poetic language is fundamentally ironic—the poem's rich intertextuality, which combines various classical and contemporary sources, bring once idle words back into circulation. Likewise, Goldberg's speaker also envisions a time when her words will be taken (even out of context) and subject to interpretation and translation. Such movements are necessary for poetry to unmoor itself from its time and place, and even from its own language. The final stanzas of "Ahavata shel Tereza di Mon" declare that the future of poetry, and its afterlife, relies on this possibility[146]:

פָּלְטָה אַהֲבָתִי אֶת אַלְמֻגֶּיהָ,
וְדַיָּגִים שֶׁנִּזְדַּמְּנוּ בַּחוֹף
אָסְפוּ אוֹתָם וַיִּשָּׂאוּם הַרְחֵק,

וְזָר מִשְׁתַּעֲמֵם בָּהֶם נוֹגֵעַ,
וּבְעוֹלָם חוֹפֵז וּבֶן-חֲלוֹף
הַזְּמָן בָּהֶם כְּיֶלֶד יְשַׂחֵק.

My love cast out its corals
And fishermen who happened along the shore
gathered them and carried them far away.

And a bored stranger touches them,
And in a hurried, fleeting world
Time will play with them like a child.

Compare these stanzas with the following lines from Mandelstam's poem:

Шорох пробегает по деревьям зеленой лаптой,
Дети играют в бабки позвонками умерших животных.
Хрупкое летоисчисление нашей эры подходит к концу.

(l.53–55)

A rustle runs along the trees like some green ball.
Children play at knucklebones with vertebra of dead animals.
The fragile chronology of our era is drawing to its close.

(l.58–60; translation by Steven J. Willett)[147]

With its imagery of coins, broken and whole, and language of economy, Mandelstam's "The Horseshoe Finder" examines the limits of poetry's currency in a bankrupt age. But taken more broadly, both poems also ask how poetry can remain current. Do the children playing with the broken vertebrae of the past represent a rewriting and remembering of this history in a new form, or its irreparable shattering? The discarded corals in "Ahavata shel Tereza di Mon" may very well include the nineteen poems that Goldberg does not recover, but like Mandelstam's knucklebones, these poems are not irrevocably lost. Instead, they are recast into a space from which "later generations" can revive, that is, translate, Teresa's poetry, which is to say, Goldberg's poetry, in other times, places, and languages.

CHAPTER 4

The Missing Element
Prosthetic Translation in *Thirty Pages*
of Avot Yeshurun

אדם שמאבד את שפת אמו הוא בעל מום בכל חייו.

A person who loses his mother tongue is handicapped for the rest of his life.
—AHARON APPELFELD[1]

A few days after Avot Yeshurun's death, the *New York Times* published a short obituary for the Israeli poet under the odd and laconic headline "Poet in Unusual Idiom."[2] It is not clear, at first reading, if this characterization applies to the language in which Yeshurun (1904–1992) wrote his poems—that is, Hebrew—or to some quality of Yeshurun's poetic language. At any rate, by framing Yeshurun's poetic output as "unusual," the *Times* participated in a pervasive reading of Yeshurun as an eccentric poet who wrote against the existing norms and trends of Hebrew poetry and in a poetic language that was somehow uncommon and even exceptional.[3] Yeshurun's career spanned the greater part of the twentieth century, and incorporated the various subjects, themes, questions, and debates that preoccupied Hebrew poetry throughout the twentieth century, particularly with regard to language politics.[4] Like many writers of his generation, Yeshurun was not a native Hebrew speaker, and his poetry, like theirs, maps the linguistic shifts and transformations that shaped the twentieth-century development of vernacular modern Hebrew. The *Times'* characterization of Yeshurun as "an Israeli poet who wove Arabic and Yiddish idiom (sic) into a unique and influential form of Hebrew verse" is an understated acknowledgment of the extent to which Yeshurun challenged and redressed Israel's ethos of monolingualism, negation of the diaspora, and denial of the Nakba (Arabic for "catastrophe," referring to the 1948 displacement of Palestinian Arabs) through the development of a radically experimental, multilingual, and translational poetic language. These practices account, in part, for the far-reaching influence of Yeshurun's work on Hebrew literature, both in the ways that it shaped the Israeli cultural discourse in the years following Statehood and in its continued dialogue with contemporary Israeli poetry.

Born Yechiel Perlmutter in 1904 and raised in an observant Jewish home in Krasnystaw, Poland, Yeshurun immigrated in 1925 against his family's wishes to Mandatory Palestine, where he held a variety of jobs, including land laborer and night watchman, for many years.[5] His early poems were largely invested in acknowledging and articulating Palestine's "exuberant multilingualism," with a particular and personal focus on Yiddish.[6] The poems that he wrote in this period formed his first collection 'Al chakhmot drakhim (On the Wisdom of Roads), which he published under his birth name in 1942. According to Benjamin Harshav, the Yiddish "hokhmes"—"clever insights, anecdotes (of the roads)"—underlies the title 'Al chakhmot drakhim.[7] After the Holocaust and the establishment of the State of Israel, an intensified sense of loss, guilt, and betrayal shaped the poet's use of Yiddish and motivated its increased visibility in his poems.[8] His later work thematized the desire to recover, remember, and repair Yiddish, and in his own broken, fragmented, and hybrid poetic language, enacted the tensions and ruptures that had come to characterize the Hebrew–Yiddish relation. The speaker of the poem "Safa Telavivrit" (a fusion of 'ivrit [Hebrew] and Tel Aviv), for example, rejects the demand for Hebrew monolingualism: "Don't cleave the language (lashon, lit. tongue) of Tel Aviv, Tel-avivrew,/into two languages (safot) ... Since I came to Tel Aviv I wander toward Krasnystaw."[9]

Yeshurun's 1937 poem "Balada shel Miriyam ha-magdalit u-vena ha-lavan," ("The Ballad of Mary Magdalene and Her White Son"), one of his first major Hebrew poems, featured Yiddish, Russian, and Polish words in Hebrew transliteration. A quotation from the Book of Revelations, which Yeshurun included in Hebrew translation, brought Greek into this picture.[10] Yeshurun consistently grafted foreign words into the Hebrew text of his poems with varying degrees of visibility, alternating between Hebrew transliteration and transcription in the foreign alphabet. Another common multilingual strategy in his poetry was the creation of multilingual portmanteaux. In this period, multilingual writing in modern Hebrew was hardly exceptional. Many of the canonical writers who emerged in the pre-Statehood period and would later become major national poetic figures—poets such as Avraham Shlonsky, Natan Alterman, and Leah Goldberg—frequently incorporated foreign words, to varying degrees, in their own texts, which were discernibly influenced by their native literary cultures (predominantly European and Russian). The linguistic acrobatics that Yeshurun executed in his poems—multilingualism, neologism, and formal hybridity, to name a few—were also characteristic of international modernism and notably present in Yiddish modernism, a strand that influenced Yeshurun's own work.[11] Harshav cites the Yiddish and Hebrew poet Uri Zvi Greenberg as one of two major influences on the development of Hebrew modernism in the 1920s, and later on Yeshurun's early poetry. According to Harshav, "when Grinberg suddenly left Europe for Eretz Israel in 1924 and resumed writing in Hebrew, he brought Whitmanesque rhythms, Futurist metaphors, Expressionist rhetoric, and the syntax of a spoken language saturated with political, journalistic, and 'International' diction from Yiddish to Hebrew poetry, which did not permit these elements before."[12] But what distinguished Yeshurun from other Hebrew poets in this period was the extent to which he engaged in these practices, resulting in what some early critics regarded as the "deformation" of the language and forms of Hebrew poetry, a feature of his work that became more pronounced after the publication of *'Al chakhmot drakhim*, the most conventionally prosodic of Yeshurun's works.[13]

Translation, and specifically the translation of Yiddish into Hebrew, was one of the more prominent of Yeshurun's multilingual strategies. In the poet's own words: "'From my mother I brought a word into Hebrew,' I wrote once. Everyone brings a word from his mother ... to the world, to literature."[14] Explorations of the linguistic and cultural traffic between the past and the present pervade his poetry and prose, but Yeshurun's remarks also address one of the central complications of Israeli literature's entangled relationship with its diasporic past: the fact that Hebrew was not the native language of many of its early writers. And in that respect, all writing in Hebrew in this period—and even later, as my chapter on Harold Schimmel shows—was translational.

For writers like Yeshurun, bringing the "mother's word" (in his case, Yiddish) into Hebrew involved acts of translation that alternated between interlingual translation and latent or implicit translation, practices that the lexical and scriptural proximity of Hebrew and Yiddish further complicated. While Hebrew and Yiddish are historically intertwined, the persistence of a "border-crossing language" like Yiddish in Hebrew also compromised the national desire for (linguistic) settlement.[15] In his famous 1912 address on the Yiddish language, Franz Kafka noted, "[T]he migration of peoples runs through Yiddish from one end to the other."[16] This mobility of Yiddish is evident in the acts and forms of translation that Yeshurun engaged to destabilize the Hebrew *bayit* (home) as a material and figurative space, and as formal and prosodic unit (*bayit* as stanza).[17] The plural "peoples" allows for translational movements that are non-linear, open-ended, ongoing, and, to use Harshav's term, "plurisignifying," thereby challenging traditional formulations of translation as a movement between one language and another and acknowledging, rather, the Derridean possibility of "more than two" languages on the move within a text.[18]

Hebrew translations of Yiddish, as well as other languages, arguably served a prosthetic function in Yeshurun's work as well. In several contexts, which this chapter explores, Yeshurun described modern Hebrew as a linguistic body disabled by hegemonic monolingualism, the rejection of the Jewish diasporic past, and the denial of Palestine's other cultures and languages. And while this chapter offers a rereading of the Hebrew–Yiddish relation through the lens of prosthetic translation, it is important to note and explore the relations that Yeshurun drew between Hebrew and Arabic in his work, which he did, beginning with his earliest poems, in ways that accord with his engagement with Yiddish. In the process, Yeshurun exposed the erroneous perception of Palestine as an empty place, absent of culture, a *tabula rasa* onto which Zionism inscribed a new history in a Hebrew vernacular that rejected its diasporic origins, as well as the Arab population, which extended to Jews from Arab lands and native Jewish Palestinians.[19]

The 1952 long poem "Pesach 'al kukhim" ("Passover on Caves") made these relations explicit and provoked a range of criticism when it first appeared in *Haaretz*.[20] In this multilingual poem, Yeshurun challenges the Zionist myth of the empty land and underscores, through a complex series of similes and intertextual moments, the relation between this myth and diasporic negation.[21] The following stanza, for example, draws from the story of Yeshurun's own arrival in Palestine:

שֶׁהִגִּיעָנוּ אֶל הַחוֹף בְּגִ׳יאַנִיקוֹלוֹ
וְהֵקִימָנוּ עַל הַסַּף סַפָּן עַרְבִי—
אָזְרְעוֹתָיו שְׁלוּחָנִיּוֹת וְקַנְצֵי קוֹל לוֹ,
וְהַיָּדַיִם—מִבֵּית אָבִי ...

Which brought us to the shore on the *Gianicolo*[22]
and placed us on the threshold, an Arab sailor—
with outstretched arms and ensnared words
and the hands—from my father's house

(l.25–28)[23]

The Arab sailor features in Yeshurun's own account of his arrival in Palestine and is a figure that recurs in other texts, notably in "Hanmaka" ("Reasoning"), a short prose essay that concludes the poem "Huna machatetat" ("Here Is the Station").[24] In "Pesach 'al kukhim," the phrase "from my father's house" applies to both the Arab sailor and the Jewish immigrant and signals one of many moments in the poem when Yeshurun, as Hever observes, "blurs the distinction between Jewish and Palestinian narratives."[25] But Yeshurun also addresses the issue of Jewish responsibility for the Arab refugees by drawing a comparison between Jewish and Arab displacements:

וְאַבָּא-אִמָּא מִן מַלְקֹחַ,
אֶש-אֶל-רַבְּרַבָּא מִלְקֵחַ—
צִוּוּנוּ יַהְנְדֶס לֹא לְשְׁכֹּחַ.
וְעַל פּוֹילִין לֹא לְשָׁכַח.

And father-mother, from where they were taken,
in the extraordinary fire, taken—
commanded us not to forget *Yahndes*
and not to forget *Poylin*

(l.93–96; my emphasis)

A classic entry from Yeshurun's multilingual lexicon, *Yahndes* (יַהְנְדֶס), which appears in this poem for the first time, invokes *yandes* (יאנדעס), Yiddish for conscience and specifically the idea of a Jewish conscience (from the Hebrew, *yahadut*, Judaism). Amos Noy, in his extensive reading of the word, locates Yeshurun's *Yahndes* in the Yiddish dialect of Greater Poland but notes that Yeshurun's unique rendering of the word alters and adds to its various understandings.[26] The appearance of *Yahndes* in a poem that redresses the negation of the Nakba meant that it would continue to carry this relation in much later poems— in other words, the rich etymology and permutations of the Yiddish *yandes* and its relations to ideas of Jewish compassion and conscience become inextricably bound to Palestinian

Arab memory. In "Ru'ach ba-arbe" ("Wind in the Locusts"), a follow-up poem to "Pesach 'al kukhim," Yeshurun defines *Yahndes* as "compassion for the property of the barren."[27] The Hebrew for barren, *'ariri*, can refer to a state of solitude but also describe someone who has no descendants. By expanding the range of meaning of *Yahndes*, Yeshurun creates a space where Jewish and Palestinian narratives of displacement can be compared. Thereby, a word that Jonathan Boyarin characterized as "untranslatable" is charged by these relations.[28]

For Yeshurun, translation offered Yiddish a form of textual afterlife, while it simultaneously and deliberately disabled the Hebrew language and text against Zionism's desire for settlement and monolingualism, thereby destabilizing the binary structure that gave Hebrew authority over Yiddish.[29] As Riki Traum-Avidan has argued, this prosthetic relation is also evident in Zionism itself, "an allegedly monolithic construct that is built on stumps, in a way, of nations, cultural groups, and also languages.... Yeshurun's poetry never attempts to repair [this construct] but rather to present, convey, remain committed to the 'wound.'"[30] Against monolingual "wholeness," Yeshurun proposed the *tsrif* (shack) as a metonym for Israeli culture, which comprises fragments and erasures of the Jewish diasporic past and its languages, as well as the remains of broken Palestinian homes and their histories.[31] The *tsrif* also represents here the multilingual and transnational twentieth-century Hebrew *bayit* or stanza, also shaped by Yiddish and Arabic (where *beyt* refers to a line of verse).[32] In his introduction to his translations of Yeshurun, Schimmel characterized Yeshurun's break with the conventions of early twentieth-century modern Hebrew prosody as a multilingual, destabilizing act: "The quatrain spills, opens, takes in prose, dialogue, grows asymmetrical—top-heavy, or sagging. It is undermined, extended ... As do the city's signs and billboards, newspapers and libraries and theaters, speak in all languages ... so does Yeshurun's quatrain."[33]

To the extent that operations of breakage and reconstruction come to define the Hebrew and Yiddish in Yeshurun's work, they are also fundamental to the way Yeshurun thought about poetic language in general. In a 1974 essay titled "Shnei nofim" ("Two Landscapes"), Yeshurun explicitly describes the relation between writing and breakage as a productive one. "For a writer," he writes, "language is like a child's toy. Language is in the hand of the creator—he doesn't feel it until he breaks it; when he throws it down—he hears the voice of language, the language that is his.[34] In the prevailing discourse of the early twentieth-century Hebrew–Yiddish language war (*milchemet ha-leshonot*), Yiddish was often cast as a disease, a weakness, a burden holding back the possibility of a new, transformative national life.[35] However, as far as Yeshurun was concerned, the absence of Yiddish also disabled Hebrew. Through strategies of breakage—translation among them—by which Yeshurun paradoxically reconstructs the Hebrew poem, a visible or concealed Yiddish surfaces and attempts to reintegrate the Hebrew poetic text. However, in the process, this translation creates and marks sites of relentless linguistic discomfort and phantom pain that persist in the body of the Hebrew text.[36]

THE MISSING ELEMENT

Yeshurun's characterization of his native Yiddish as a "missing element" in his Hebrew writing accords with the discourse of loss and rupture that continues to frame discussions of Yiddish in Israel, but it also interrogates the very idea of normative, naturalized, able-bodied Hebrew writing. On the one hand, the strategies—and specifically translation strategies—that Yeshurun employed to account and compensate for this absent Yiddish could be understood as operations of replacement that sustain the mobility and afterlife of Yiddish in the Hebrew textual body, while bearing in mind, as Sarah S. Jain has observed, that "replacements are never neat and tidy; they do not simply reiterate the very same body that was before."[37] It is in this respect that Hebrew translation is prosthetic—and yet, the trope of the prosthesis, like translation itself, calls attention to how perceptions of wholeness and integrity are contrived, and in what kinds of textual bodies ideas of wholeness and able-bodiedness are privileged and naturalized.[38]

Shlonsky's description of Yiddish–Hebrew bilingualism as "tuberculosis, gnawing away at the lungs of the nation" is a classic example of the embodied metaphors that shaped language debates in early twentieth-century Jewish nation-building.[39] Tuberculosis was largely perceived as a diasporic disease that threatened the collective health of the Jewish national body in Palestine, which in 1927, when Shlonsky made these remarks, already privileged Hebrew.[40] Extending the metaphor further, and further sharpening the relation between text and nation, Shlonsky proclaims, "[W]e want Israeli breathing to be completely (in) Hebrew, with both lungs." This formulation literally excises the possibility of (literary) multilingualism, but this operation is also a disabling act. If Yiddish both occupies and infects one lung, and Hebrew the other, what happens to this linguistic body when the Yiddish lung is removed (at the time, tuberculosis was largely incurable)? In this scenario, breathing with one lung is not improbable, but, following this kind of surgery, Israeli breathing with *two* Hebrew lungs would require a prosthetic and thereby "form an ensemble, a physical or metaphysical whole, the existence or idea of one being included in the existence or idea of another."[41] One possible candidate for this prosthetic operation is Hebrew translation.

The movements of Yiddish and other languages in Yeshurun's Hebrew, particularly in Hebrew translation, mark and create sites of rupture at the expense of a seamless national linguistic body.[42] This prosthetic translation allows Yeshurun to fashion a new Hebrew body that accommodates both its immigrant baggage and its relations and encounters with other languages and cultures.[43] In this respect, David Wills writes, "[T]ranslation is precisely such a prosthetic economy, a matter of making things fit." The understanding here is that "making" is both—and often simultaneously—a creative act and an application of force, or as Yeshurun put it succinctly, "in poetry you must go by force."[44]

A textual relation inheres in the very etymology of *prosthesis*, which was first introduced in the mid-sixteenth century as a rhetorical term for the addition of a letter or syllable at the beginning of a word (a usage that remains current). In the early eighteenth century, the application of prosthesis shifted from rhetoric to medicine, where it referred to the craft of making artificial limbs. By the twentieth century, it had taken on its more common meaning: "a device, either external or implanted, that substitutes for or supplements a missing or defective part of the body."[45] While the term circulates in a variety of disciplines, particularly in the interface of digital and new media studies and disability studies,[46] Wills argues for an understanding of the prosthetic *as* translation:

> ... prosthesis seeks to describe precisely the differential transfer or articulation by means of which the body is disturbed or problematised in its supposed self-intactness; it refers to that transfer-out-of-itself that is the becoming translation of the original, supposedly intact "first" body. As the experience of language shows, it is as if one carries or transfers one's detachable bodily effects into a relation with the outside. From this point of view prosthesis is before anything else a matter of *translation*. (Wills, "Two Words *Pro*-Derrida")

Following Wills, the contemporary poets Joyelle McSweeney and Johannes Göransson propose a translation paradigm that radically acknowledges that translations, in their words, "give the lie to the supposed centeredness, completeness, originariness of able, enabled, or 'original' bodies and texts."[47] They propose that we think of translation as a "deformation zone," a space where the border between original and translation blurs and erases, and from which the poem takes shape.[48] What is central to both formulations of prosthetic translation is how prosthesis interrogates, problematizes, and exposes the perceived wholeness of the original body/text. Critiques of literary translation, going back centuries, often emphasize failures and losses, but in doing so, they call into question the completeness or wholeness that is attributed to an original text and the criterion by which certain textual bodies are privileged as whole and untranslatable.[49] Prosthetic translation acknowledges, rather, what is already broken, maimed, and scarred in the original. In this respect, Yeshurun's fragmented, deformed, polyglot, and translational *safa shel smartutim*, language of rags, *is* the lingua franca of immigrant daily life in Tel Aviv.[50] "Thus, prosthesis falters," writes Jain, "between two renditions of meaning; a prosthesis can fill a gap, but it can also diminish the body and create the need for itself."[51] A prosthetic reading of Yeshurun's poetry and its translations calls attention to the ways in which a multilingual Hebrew *bayit* is fashioned, in both its literal and prosodic meanings. Furthermore, it acknowledges, as Yeshurun did, that if broken Yiddish could move and translate in and through a Hebrew poem, it was because the poet could turn to a Yiddish home that remained "whole" at the threshold of memory and translation.[52]

The question of precisely how, and how precisely, Hebrew translation "fits" Yiddish in Yeshurun's Hebrew poems, and what meanings and relations emerge when it attempts to do so, shapes my reading of his 1964 collection *Shloshim 'amud shel Avot Yeshurun* (*Thirty Pages of Avot Yeshurun*) as a work of prosthetic translation.[53] In this cycle of thirty poems, Yeshurun incorporates Hebrew translations of private Yiddish letters in ways that alternately camouflage and reveal their presence in the Hebrew text. The Yiddish originals are sometimes quoted directly, as they are in other poems, but their translation into Hebrew is also performed thematically, syntactically, and formally. Yeshurun was not a literary translator in the conventional sense of the term. Of the four poets in this study, Yeshurun is the only one who did not engage in "translation proper," which is to say that we do not have evidence that he translated other poets into Hebrew or any other language. While he employed, as this chapter examines, various translation strategies in his writing and had close ties with his own translators, his views on translation remain opaque. According to his daughter Helit Yeshurun, after reading some of her translations from French, he pulled her aside and encouraged her to keep writing, but voiced his resistance to her dedication to translation, "Only Proust can write like Proust!"[54] Nevertheless, instances of translation in his oeuvre reveal a very creative, foreignizing, and transgressive understanding of translation. As Daphna Erdinast-Vulcan notes, in a too-brief commentary on *Shloshim 'amud*, "if the aim of the translator is to smooth out the differences, to make the translated text sound as though it were written in the target language, Yeshurun does the very opposite of that, transposing the Yiddish syntax and idiomaticity [of the mother's letters] onto the Hebrew text, foregrounding its foreignness."[55] In this collection, Yeshurun continuously makes reference to the original Yiddish letters and postcards to which his Hebrew poems respond in a decomposed, translational, and fragmentary poetic language. In these instances, as in many others in Yeshurun's work, the translation of Yiddish into Hebrew is a creative process, but one that also breaks down the "organizing binaries" that characterized the relations between these languages for most of the twentieth century.[56]

In my reading of prosthetic translation in Yeshurun's work, I am also attentive to distinct modes of translation, which are particularly germane to the collection *Shloshim 'amud*. The forms that these poems address—the letter, postcard, and telegraph, as well as the scrap and bundle—relate to specific technologies of writing, archiving, and translating, which give shape to a desire for intimacy, presence, revival, and memory. Taken together, Yeshurun's poem-missives constitute an alternative, personal archive of twentieth-century Jewish history that encompasses Jewish nation-building in Palestine, World War II and the Holocaust, and Israel's public and private reckoning with the aftermath of the Holocaust. In these poems, the epistolary mode allows the poet to thematize translational acts and movements, while framing the poem itself as a translational space—mediating, revising, and transforming trauma, memory, and language.

HEBREW REMEMBERS YIDDISH

In an intimate 1982 interview with his daughter, Yeshurun described the relation between his Hebrew writing and Yiddish, his native language, as a constant and complicated negotiation between absence and presence:

העברית שלי היא אדם שחי כאן, בארץ, ובזמן הזה, לפי שהוא מוכרח לחיות, לפי
שהוא חי את ההכרח הזה. זה לא עברית, זה יידיש, זה פולנית, זה גם עברית, כל
מה שצברתי בדרך. אלמנט היידיש חסר לי מאוד. יש חור בנשמה, בגלל זה שאני
לא כותב יידיש, בגלל זה שאין לי היידיש. זה מתמלא בכל מיני חלקי דברים ואורחי
ביטוי, נקודות, סימנים, כדי להרגיע את התביעה הזאת של חוסר ביטוי.

My Hebrew is a person who lives here, in the land, right now ...
It's not Hebrew, it's Yiddish, Polish, and it's also Hebrew, everything
that I accumulated on the way. The Yiddish element is missing for
me. There is a hole in the soul because of the fact that I don't write
in Yiddish, because I have no Yiddish. This is fulfilled in all sorts of
bits of words and expressions, markings, signs, in order to relax that
demand of the missing expression.[57]

Although Yeshurun articulates in this passage a binary between "present" and
"living" Hebrew and absent Yiddish, a closer reading of his comments suggests that the relationship between the two languages is not as dichotomous
and antagonistic as he initially frames it. For Yeshurun, Hebrew—or rather,
"his" Hebrew—is not a monolithic language; rather, it is an amalgamation
of other languages, with Yiddish occupying a prominent place among them.
At the same time, the poet acknowledges the absence of Yiddish as a persistent "hole in the soul" of his Hebrew (and modern Hebrew in general) that
the act of Hebrew writing both addresses and attempts to repair. The "bits
of words and expressions, markings, signs" that replace this absent Yiddish
in Yeshurun's Hebrew results in the radical linguistic heterogeneity and
experimentalism of his poetry. Years of attempting to "relax that demand" of
Yiddish, as well as other repressed and suppressed languages, resulted in a
way of writing in Hebrew that ultimately made these tensions and fissures
more visible, insistent, and extreme. This way of writing, on the other hand,
was also prosthetic. The "bits" of language that Yeshurun employs attempt
to impart a new integrity to his Hebrew, but like a prosthetic limb that can
be removed, replaced, and changed, they do so in a variety of ways, none
guaranteeing Hebrew's stability, nor can they ameliorate the phantom pain
that the absent element leaves behind.

Shortly after the publication of *'Al chakhmot drakhim*, Yeshurun received
confirmation that most of his family, including his mother, had been killed
in the Holocaust.[58] During that eighteen-year gap between *'Al chakhmot
drakhim* and his second collection *Re'em* (1960), he officially changed his
name to Avot Yeshurun, which in Hebrew translates as "the watching

fathers" or "the fathers of Israel."[59] Although he adopted an ostensibly masculine, paternalistic Hebraic name, Yeshurun was—by his own admission—
very attached to his mother, who came from a family of rabbinic scholars; it
was primarily through her influence that he became interested in literature
and languages at an early age. And in fact, a maternal, Yiddish association
underlies the very name "Avot Yeshurun," as the following anecdote reveals:

> I remembered my mother singing beautiful lullabies to my brothers
> in her beautiful voice. Once, she bent over the cradle and sang to the
> youngest one in Yiddish and Ukrainian. But the children wouldn't
> fall asleep, and my mother stopped singing and instead called out
> excitedly, "tatelekh, tatelekh" [little fathers, little fathers]. And then the
> child understood that she wasn't going to sing and he went to sleep
> himself. From this I took the name Avot...[60]

According to Yeshurun, he adopted his Hebrew name in 1948 as part of
his army swearing-in ceremony, a context that aligns this name with the
project of Jewish nation-building.[61] However, in the account offered here,
the Yiddish mother tongue or mame-loshn nevertheless remains present in
the new, masculine national culture and language. The translation of the
Yiddish term of endearment tatelekh into Hebrew allows for its survival but
also undermines the narrative of Hebrew triumphalism.[62] Naomi Seidman
has observed that "the disappearance of the diminutive in the move to
Hebrew might signal the process of replacing a Yiddish childhood with a
Hebrew adulthood, but it might also be a clever concealment of the continuing existence of the Yiddish boy."[63] Indeed, the word tatelekh (little fathers)
functions as a metonym for the Yiddish language itself. Nevertheless, in the
story, as was the case with Yiddish in Israel, the mother's song is cut off and
this disruption also underlies the relation between the two languages.

The loss and recovery of the Yiddish mother tongue are the prevailing
themes of Shloshim 'amud shel Avot Yeshurun, which attempts to reconstruct
an epistolary exchange between the poet and his family, particularly his
mother Rikl.[64] These letters are a recurrent motif in his work, and in this
collection, Yeshurun's terse quotations, excerpts, and Hebrew translations
of the Yiddish missives underscore the emotional, geographical, and temporal ruptures that underlie this correspondence (including his own failure to
respond to some letters).[65] These epistolary poems attempt to repair what
is ultimately an irrevocably broken connection, all the while articulating its
broken quality. The very title of the collection invokes this relation between

mourning and writing: *shloshim* (thirty) refers to the number of poems in the cycle and the thirty days of mourning that follow burial in Jewish tradition.[66] The first poems describe the "burial" of the mother's letters inside the poet's desk, mixed with other letters and papers and "put to the side" (poem #5). Instead of writing letters home, the son writes poems (in Hebrew) on the very desk that contains these letters, thereby writing on the textual grave of Yiddish, but also indicating how Yiddish remains integral to Hebrew writing. These scenes conflate the son's abandonment of the family with his abandonment of the Yiddish mother tongue in favor of Hebrew in his writing, as well as the turn to poetry as a form of writing back to the past. The cycle begins with the following, untitled poem:

יוֹם יָבוֹא וְאִישׁ לֹא יִקְרָא מִכְתָּבִים שֶׁל אִמִּי.
יֵשׁ לִי מֵהֶם חֲבִילָה.
לֹא שֶׁל מִי
וְלֹא מִלָּה.

יוֹם יָבוֹא וְאִישׁ לֹא יִקַּח אוֹתָם לַיָּד.
יֵשׁ מֵהֶם צְרוֹר וְהוֹתֵר.
יֹאמְרוּ: נְיָר פְּסַת
וְלֹא יוֹתֵר.

בַּיּוֹם הַהוּא אֲבִיאֵם אֶל מְעָרַת בַּר-כּוֹכְבָא
לְהַעֲלוֹתָם בָּאָבָק. הָעוֹלָם הַקּוֹדֵם
לֹא יַחְקֹר בָּהּ
שְׂפַת אֵם.

The day will come and no one will read my mother's letters.
I have a pack of them.
No one's
no one word.

The day will come and no one will take them by the hand.
There's a bundle of them and more.
They will say: paper scrap
and nothing more.

On that day I will take them to Bar Kokhva's cave
to send them into the dust. The ancient world
will not search there
mother tongue.

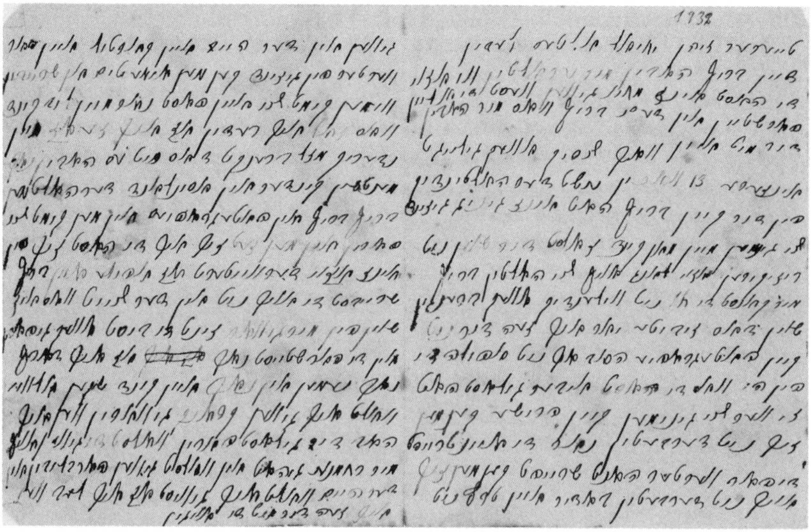

Figure 4.1. "My dear son, Yechiel…": Letter from Rikl Perlmutter
Source: Helit Yeshurun, Personal Archive

The line "The day will come and no one will read my mother's letters" which opens the first poem in the cycle, encapsulates the fundamental irony of these poems: the mother's letters, though unread in the Yiddish mother tongue (*sfat em*) are being read, and continuously reread, through the Hebrew poems. As the cycle progresses, the mother's voice is further uncovered—indeed, exhumed—but the fragmentary and grammatically disjointed quotations that comprise her voice underscore the incompleteness and impossibility of repair. One could also draw an analogy between the image of the "paper scraps" and the Jewish practice of *kria* (tearing), the rending of garments by mourners before burial.[67] This tear marks the state of mourning and also serves as an open wound, which is usually located over the heart if the deceased is a parent. When a parent has died, Jewish tradition prohibits surviving children from fully repairing the torn garment, a proscription that arguably informs Yeshurun's cycle. Quotation and translation work together to grant the mother tongue a degree of mobility that it no longer has in its original, native state, but as Maurice Lamm has observed, Jewish law acknowledges that parents occupy "a special case": they cannot be replicated or substituted, there is no compensation for their absence, and, therefore, the tear/wound remains.[68] Though the fragmented family letters

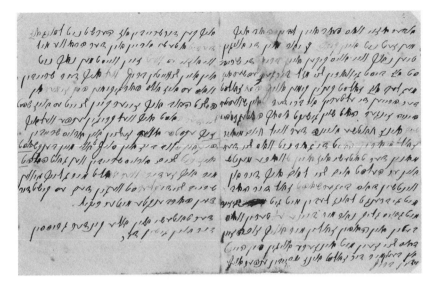

Figure 4.1. Continued

are recomposed in the Hebrew texts, the rends remain visible, ultimately expanding the range of meaning of these displaced and translated texts.[69]

The poem's reference to the caves of Bar Kokhva points to a form of survival for these fragments, a way that they may be preserved for the future. It also addresses the politics of memory, and specifically Holocaust memory, in the Israeli context. Between 1960 and 1961, the famed Israeli archeologist Yigael Yadin led two intensive, official explorations of the Cave of Letters (מערת האיגרות), located along Nahal Hever in the Judean desert. Several years prior to Yadin's expedition, Bedouin had discovered in this area fragmentary papyri attributed to the second-century Jewish leader Shimeon Bar Kokhva, who commanded a rebellion of Jews against the Roman Empire and briefly presided over an independent Jewish state in the Roman-held province of Judaea. Yadin's expedition turned up additional bundles of letters dating to the Bar Kokhva revolt (c. 131–136), some authored by Bar Kokhva himself, documents that provided additional insights on multilingualism in classical antiquity and, in particular, on the cultural and political status of the Hebrew language in a multilingual milieu.[70] Yadin's expedition suggests a historical framework for the burial of the mother's letters, but Yeshurun also invokes it as a context for exploring and problematizing the relation between national and personal memory.[71] In this poem, the juxtaposition of the mother's letters and the contents of the Cave of Letters situates the burial of Yeshurun's mother tongue in an ongoing discourse of recovery and memory in Israeli culture that privileges and politicizes the Hebrew language.[72] Yadin himself surmised that the shift from Aramaic to Hebrew in documents from the Cave of Letters indicated Bar Kokhva's intention to "restore Hebrew as the official language of the state."[73]

While the Bar Kokhva letters further legitimized for the Jewish Israeli public the territorial continuity of Hebrew, in Yeshurun's cycle, the buried Yiddish missives replace the Bar Kokhva letters, representing a deterritorialized history that "no one will search for." The rejection of Yiddish in Israel, in this regard, can be understood as such a burial, and yet, the act of burying the letters in the cave also suggests a precarious mode of preservation. The moment the letters are brought out of the desk/cave and into the present day, processes of decomposition accelerate; it is this activity that Yeshurun's speaker initially attempts to delay through the act of reburial. And yet, this attempt to preserve the letters and arrest their decomposition removes them from any dialogue with the present and future, and in the context of these poems, to be unread is synonymous with being forgotten. In Amir Gilboa's well-known poem, "Ve-achi shotek" ("And My Brother Is Silent), the speaker removes several belongings from the body of his soldier-brother including "a worn postcard with her name/under a sketch of flowers."[74] This act reactivates the postal exchange, but also ensures that the letter will not be buried and forgotten. Instead, it becomes, with the other souvenirs he gathers and "unbundles," material for a kind of afterlife in poetry ("I shall proudly sing your name!"). In Yeshurun's poem, the speaker decides to bring the letters out, to reread—that is, remember—them, and through acts of composition and translation salvage these remains in a new textual body/ home.[75] And yet, as Todd S. Presner has observed, "something happens or will happen to remains; the potential for their disposal or removal is always imminent."[76] Rather than evade the possibility of their neglect, the poems in this cycle address thematically, formally, and linguistically the inevitable breakdown of this relation with the past.

The very form of the poems also suggests this breakdown. With few exceptions, Yeshurun's quatrain begins with a long line that tapers off by the end, usually following a pattern of 5-4-3-2 words or lexical units.[77] This telegraphic pattern offers a visual representation of the increasing compression and restraint of the poem's language, and the language of these correspondences, into "paper scrap" (also ungrammatical in the Hebrew), an aesthetic that reproduces the compact language of the telegraph.[78] But this fragmentary language also recalls the post-Holocaust poetry of the German poet Paul Celan (1920–1970), as well as Dan Pagis's famous epistolary poem "Katuv be-'iparon ba-karon he-chatum" ("Written on a Sealed Railcar").[79] In the first poem, for example, the concluding lines of each stanza—"no one word" (*ve-lo mila*), "and nothing more" (*ve-lo yoter*), and "mother tongue" (*sfat em*)—underscore the absence of a Yiddish mother tongue that can only be recalled in a translated and fragmented Hebrew.[80]

The exchange of letters grows increasingly sporadic until the day "from there, from home, suddenly there's no letter" and a postcard arrives in its place, "with bluish ink/words like a telegram/via Red Cross Mail" (poem #24). The phrase, "milim ke-telegram" ("words like a telegram"), indicates that this formal shift also gives shape to new constraints in the correspondence, but this postcard also provides the cycle's most concrete, historical details. The brothers, we are told, have moved to a different city (most likely Kovel), but the mother, father, and sister have relocated to an "ayara mashchezet" ("grindstone town"), possibly a euphemism for the Krasnystaw Ghetto, to which most of Krasnystaw's Jewish population was relocated.[81] In early 1942, most of its Jewish inhabitants, including the remaining members of Yeshurun's family, were transferred to the Sobibor and Bełżec extermination camps.[82] While mail services between Allied and Axis nations were suspended during World War II, the International Red Cross was able to provide limited service.[83] These missives were restricted to twenty-five words that, by requirement, had to remain personal in content but were subject to censorship.[84] In fact, the detail "be-tsev'a yod" (*yod*, iodine) could refer to the color of the ink used to write the letter, but may also refer to the chemical solution that German censors brushed across these messages to test for invisible messages, leaving bluish traces.[85] In poem #26, the line "there's flimsy news from there" is a direct reference to the way these constraints limited what could be communicated, constraints that also shape the very language of Yeshurun's poem. This line also resonates in the previous poem/letters, which addresses the desire for news, the withholding of bad news, and questions that remain, even many years later, unanswered, leaving these voices in a suspended state.[86]

Yeshurun's references to the postcard raise questions concerning mobility and translatability that are both historically contingent and also related to a problematics of translation that these texts explore. The introduction of the postcard in the late nineteenth century provoked debates around issues of privacy and authenticity that continue to resonate in contemporary anxieties about new platforms and technologies of communication (e.g., texting,

Twitter, Snapchat).[87] What meaningful messages could be communicated in just a few lines? How could people remain authentically present despite the material constraints of the postcard and the public nature of this writing? And yet, the introduction of this form, combined with developments in the postal system that allowed for more rapid and expansive exchanges, undeniably conferred a new mobility to these texts.

Galit Hasan-Rokem, in a lucid examination of Jewish picture postcards, advances the postcard as a metaphor for Jewish mobility, specifically in the ways that the production and circulation of picture postcards interfaced with the modern history of Jewish migration and wandering, in her words, "quite naturally [serving] to mark routes of traveling and migration."[88] Though the precise details of the Perlmutter family's displacement remain muted, Yeshurun is relying on the Hebrew reader's ability to infer the historical context, thereby creating a tension between the historical circumstances that determine the movements (and, later, immobility) of the family (and this correspondence) and the mobility of the postcard, which carries associations with travel and tourism. "The irreversibility of the migratory move," argues Hasan-Rokem, "is thus metonymically alleviated by the counter movement of the postcard in the opposite direction."[89] In the poems of *Shloshim 'amud*, Yeshurun invokes this irony of postcard mobility; indeed, it is unlikely that any of the postcards in Yeshurun's collection are picture postcards, though the word *gluyia* places the Red Cross postcards in the same semantic field. Instead, these poems highlight the paradox of the poem-postcard that confers translatability to the Perlmutter family, while the very form is necessitated because of conditions of immobility and displacement. In his 1932 essay *Berlin Chronicle*, Walter Benjamin observes that the picture postcards of his youth place him in proximity to vistas that are, in reality, remote, and allow for a continuous return to these spaces—"for I was there ... when I gazed."[90] The spaces that the Perlmutter family occupied in the last years of their life were not typically memorialized by the picture postcard, but Yeshurun nevertheless harnesses the return mode that Benjamin describes through his rewriting and translating of the family's correspondence. As Esther Milne has pointed out, postcards include no space for the sender's address. The impossibility of a "return to sender" opens up, then, opportunities to create and imagine spaces for proximity and presence, and it is through this "affective geography," framed by the poem, that the Yeshurun/Perlmutter correspondence now circulates.[91]

The epistolary movement of these poems also reveals the shifting borders of a Jewish diasporic space in the Israeli present.[92] Letters, postcards, and telegrams can be continuously reread, which is to say that the very act of reading these poems allows for a revisiting and revising of a Jewish diasporic space within an Israeli present (i.e., the desk drawer), with all of the attendant tensions these moves activate. In the 2013 series "Shirim le-megira" ("Poems for a Drawer"), the Israeli artist Noa Osterreicher combines found materials to create new archival contexts for Hebrew literary texts.[93] One notable example is the collage that she creates out of Yeshurun's poem "Eikh nikra" ("How Shall We Read"/"What Is It Called"), which she places in a drawer that had been discarded on a Tel Aviv street.[94] Text from Yeshurun's poem overlays a collage of epistolary material: letters in Yiddish and Hebrew, envelopes sent from Canada and the United States, and an unaddressed postcard covered in Israeli stamps that feature Theodor Herzl, gazelles, and palm trees. And while the drawer frames and contains this material, it is also representative of the Israeli home in an unsettled and fragmented state.

In poem #7, the son's enviable description of the fertile Palestinian landscape—"beautiful things to envy"— contrasts with the "no good word from home" in the mother's letter, invoking a longstanding binary between Erets Yisrael and the diaspora that privileges the former and casts the latter in a negative light (e.g., see Bialik's "To the Bird" and Tchernikhovsky's "Oh My Land, My Country").[95] Melissa Jane Hardie argues about "one crucial aspect of the postcard, which was that it enfranchised readers, writers, and collectors across social classes, generations, and fixed geographical locations."[96] But while Hardie is referring specifically to the availability and accessibility of the picture postcard, Yeshurun's poems indicate rather how the social and geographic constraints imposed on his family shaped their diasporic communication, and how sharply it contrasted with his agency and mobility in the Yishuv. But what use does this binary serve now that the family is gone, now that the Israeli pastoral has given way to "baronic houses and domestic cedar"?[97] Removed from the drawer, the borders between diaspora and Israel, between Hebrew and Yiddish, blur, as they do between the living and the dead in Wallace Stevens's "A Postcard from the Volcano," whose departed speaker acknowledges continuity where the living only see rupture: "We left much more, left what still is/The look of things" (l.8–9).[98] While Yeshurun transposes the formal constraints of the epistolary mode, and the postcard in particular, to create both a frame and, thereby, an enclosure for the circulation and traffic of these movements, these same constraints shape a prosody that enforces productive fragmentation, openness, and indeterminacy (activated, in large part, by the translation of the Yiddish fragments).

In poem #5, the speaker professes a desire to forget the mother's letters; he gathers up the pieces of paper and files them "one by one … even the stamps." Susan Stewart notes that when it comes to collections, arrangement is as meaningful as the material souvenir.[99] Objects in a collection can be remixed to tell different stories, which is the case for these letters. This attempt to put the letters in some kind of order sparks an ambivalent temptation to read them—"read or don't read"—but ultimately the speaker concludes that "there is interest even/in the letters of the dead," an allusion to the Israeli public's interest in the Bar Kokhva letters. The Hebrew *'inyan* (interest) can also refer to the content of the letters, suggesting that the "letters of the dead" still have something to say. As the speaker bides his time, the voices of the dead begin to insist on a response. In poem #7, this demand takes the form of a letter from home urging the son to write back:

קִבַּלְתִּי מִכְתַּבְכֶם וּבוֹ עֲנֵה עֲנֵה.
עַד נוֹשֵׂא הַפּוֹסְט בִּגְבוּרָתוֹ
עוֹבֵר הַטַּל עֵינַיִם.
עֲנֵה עֲנֵה.

עָנִיתִי בְּמִכְתָּב וּבוֹ יָפִים לְקַנֵּא
עֲצֵי שִׁטִּים וַעֲצֵי שַׁמוּטִי.
אֲנִי הָיִיתִי מְעַנֶּה.
עֲנֵה עֲנֵה.

אֵין לִי בַּבַּיִת מִלָּה טוֹבָה.
בְּמִכְתָּבְךָ אֵין זֵכֶר לִי.
כְּהָעֵת עָבַד הַשֶּׁמֶשׁ.
עֲנֵה עֲנֵה.

I received your (*pl*) letter and in it Answer Answer
Until the postman goes forth in his might[100]
the dew passes over eyes.
Answer Answer.

I replied with a letter and in it beautiful things to envy
Acacia and shamouti orange trees.[101]
I would torture.
Answer Answer.

I have no good word from home.
In your letter there's no mention [literally, memory] of me.
Just now the sun passed over.
Answer Answer.[102]

Yeshurun's biographer Eda Zoritte notes that many letters from Rikl Perlmutter included the exhortation "Write! Write!"[103] In this poem, the command to "write" becomes *'ane*, Hebrew for "reply," a verb that also shares a root with the verbs "to torture" and "to sing." In this case, the translation of the Yiddish into Hebrew creates a more expansive and vexed series of associations. In this poem, the son recalls his end of the correspondence as a form of affliction (directed at both his mother and himself), but the association with "singing" that the root ע-נ-ה carries further elaborates the idea of poetry as a continuous response. "What is the meaning of 'to answer'?," Yeshurun reflected in an interview with Zoritte, "to write, to erase, to make a stylistic change, to add, to alter until the letter bursts."[104] The "answer" that the poem comes to represent revises, but cannot resolve, the failure or belatedness of the reply in historical time.[105] This particular poem also addresses the power relations—between mother and son and between these recipients and the postal authority—that underlie this correspondence. The line "the postman in his might" contains a key biblical reference to the Song of Deborah, and also acknowledges the postal worker as an agent that determines how, where, and what kind of communication circulates. "The 'posts' are always posts of power," writes Derrida in *La Carte Postale*. "And power is exercised according to the network of posts."[106] In Mahmoud Darwish's "A Letter from Exile," the letter from an exiled Palestinian son to his mother cannot circulate through official postal channels, thereby assigning this postal authority to the poem itself.[107]

The intertextual relations that the translation of Yiddish into Hebrew generates continue to develop in the second stanza of poem #18, which opens with the aporia "she'ei mize matayhu pa'am erekha?" ("For where at what time will I see you again?"). As Harshav and Helit Yeshurun point out, this is one of several lines from family letters that reappear in other poems, one of which I will turn to shortly.[108] The translation of this question into Hebrew, as opposed to a direct quotation from the Yiddish, allows the poet to alter the original language of the quotation, to "make it fit" in various ways in the Hebrew text. The movements of this line from one poem to another span several decades of Yeshurun's oeuvre and creates a relation between these poems, generating a textual genealogy for which the Yiddish material serves as an unsettled or restless point of origin.

The 1989 poem "Zichronot hem bayit" ("Memories Are a House"), which appeared in the 1990 collection *Adon menucha* (*Master of Rest*), emerges as a companion text to the poems of *Shloshim ʿamud* precisely through these acts of (self) translation and quotation. The last three stanzas, in particular, exemplify this interweaving of (mis)quotation and translation. In this poem, the translation of Yiddish is not transparent, as it is in *Shloshim ʿamud*; rather, Yeshurun transcribes Yiddish and also offers multiple, explicit translations into Hebrew:

אֵינֶנִּי מַכְחִישׁ, שֶׁאָדָם הַמַּגִּיעַ לְגִיל,
אֵינוֹ יָכֹל לְקַוּוֹת
שֶׁאֵלֶּה שֶׁמֵּהֶם יָצָא יִשָּׂרְדֵ
עַד חַיִּים עִמּוֹ, כְּפִי שֶׁכָּתְבָה לִי

אִמִּי פַּעַם בְּאַחַד מִמִּכְתְּבֵי
הַדִּמְדֻּמִים שֶׁלָּהּ. מִדִּמְדֻּמֵי מִכְתָּבֶיהָ
בְּגֹרָלִית אֱנֹשׁ: וְכִי מָתַי יְהֵ
יְכֹלִים הֵן. הֲלֹא אֵין סִכּוּי לִרְאוֹת אוֹתָךְ.

וּפַעַם בְּמִכְתָּב נִדָּח וְנִשְׁכָּח:
"לַיְלָה טֹב לְךָ, יְחִיאַל אַלְטֶער לֵעִיבֶּן. נָפְלָה עָלַי תַּרְדֵּמָה.
אָחַז בִּי חֶבְלֵי שֵׁנָה. כְ'בִּין
שְׁלֶעיֶפֶעריק גֶעוואָרֶן." נֶאֱמַר בְּמִכְתָּב שֶׁלֹּא קוֹרְאִים. שֶׁלֹּא קָרָא.

I can't deny that a man who reaches a ripe old age
cannot hope
that those he came from will live on
with him, these were the words

my mother wrote in one of the letters
of her twilight. From the twilight of her letters
to a human fate: for when
will they be able. There is no chance of seeing you.

And once, in a forgotten and cast-off letter:
"Good night, Yechiel alter leiben. A slumber has fallen over me.
Sleep's grip has a hold on me." "Kh'bin
shlayferik gevoren." It was said in a letter that no one reads. That no
one read.[109]

The question that the mother poses in poem #18 of *Shloshim 'amud*—"for where at what time will I see you again?"—reappears in "Zichronot hem bayit" in the last two lines of the second stanza excerpted above. Here, the mother's question is broken apart and reconstructed as a statement of fact, now expressed by the son: "[F]or when/will they be able: There is no chance of seeing you." The question has become its own reply. Translation, then, not only mediates between the past and the present in Yeshurun's work, but also, as this example shows, can be used to displace language and bring it into new frames of reference.[110]

Whereas the poems of *Shloshim 'amud* do not include Yiddish-language quotations, the poem "Zichronot hem bayit" juxtaposes Hebrew translations of Yiddish and Yiddish-language quotation.[111] Because of the scriptural relation between Hebrew and Yiddish, the presence of Yiddish words in this poem is less intrusive when compared to the appearance of other alphabets—Cyrillic, for example—in Yeshurun's work.[112] Nevertheless, the inclusion of the Yiddish is not seamless. A Hebrew reader would immediately grasp the linguistic shift. Closer scrutiny of the language Yeshurun employs reveals the word play and intralingual translation occurring in the Yiddish that he transcribes. The phrase "Yechiel alter lebn" could be read in Yiddish as "Yechiel, dear eldest (son/brother)" or "Yechiel, long life (to you)," the latter carrying an allusion to the Hebrew meaning of the name Yechiel ("may God live").

Another example is the Yiddish phrase "kh'bin shlayferik gevoren," which translates literally as "I have become sleepy," and which is prefaced by two Hebrew phrases that can be read either as translations of the Yiddish or as the source material for the Yiddish words. The first, *nafla 'alai tardema*, translates literally as "a deep sleep fell over me," but idiomatically means "I am falling asleep." The second, *achazu bi chevlei shena*, translates as "the pains of sleep grasped/held me," but *chevlei shena* bears a very close similarity to the more idiomatic phrase *chavlei shena*, the cords of sleep.[113] In the Hebrew, the relation between sleep and death is further intensified by language that imagines sleep/death as an aggressor, locking the mother in its grip.[114] The Hebrew *tardema* literally means "deep sleep," but also refers to the period of dormancy or hibernation between fall and spring, thereby underscoring the relation between sleep and death that Yeshurun thematizes in this poem. *Chevlei shena* also recalls the expressions *chevlei leida* (labor pains) and *chevlei lashon* (inarticulateness; literally, "language pains"), the latter also the title of a seminal essay by Bialik.[115]

Additionally, the relation between sleep and death touches on an anxiety that pervades Yeshurun's work, specifically the fear that language and memory are so interwoven that to lose one means the inevitable loss of the other.[116] The very title of the poem also underscores these relations. In Hebrew, *bayit* is both house and home, a crucial distinction in the context of Yeshurun's work, which resisted Zionism's demand to replace the home of the past with the Israeli national home. The speaker's memories encompass a personal and private space that "houses" him and his dead, but *bayit* also highlights a critical correlation between memory and writing, and poetic composition in particular. The speaker of "Zichronot hem bayit" constructs the poem as a space of constant mourning and recollection, where the letter "that nobody read" is continuously recalled and even partially revived.

Although the process of creating a modern Hebrew vernacular in the late nineteenth century required extricating its Yiddish and diasporic influences, the vast corpus of Yiddish vernacular texts provided a vital foundation for Hebrew.[117] Indeed, the translation of Yiddish texts into Hebrew in the late nineteenth century proved instrumental in creating a modern Hebrew vernacular. For example, calques and adaptations of Yiddish words and phrases frequently crept into Hebrew writing of the early twentieth century.[118] Even when Hebrew successfully asserted its hegemony over Yiddish and other diasporic languages, they remained inextricably bound to the personal histories, memories, and identities of new immigrants, even the most staunchly Zionist among them. In a 1918 essay titled "Nidudei lashon" (literally, "language wanderings," but also a play on *nidudei shena*, insomnia), Rachel Katznelson, who was active in the Labor Zionist movement (and whose husband Zalman Rubashov-Shazar later served as the third President of Israel), recounts her first-hand experience with the language debates in this period, and the way in which Yiddish, in particular, was supplanted by Hebrew. Although she describes the move from Yiddish to Hebrew as a "betrayal," Katznelson also acknowledges that the desire for a radically new life, within a national context, required that pioneers abandon Yiddish for Hebrew. In her description of the personal transformation that occurs in the process of language switching, Katznelson draws, as did Raab in the essay "Be-Kahir" (see chapter 2), on the familiar relation between language, memory, and identity: "Every language has its own magic circle, and he who enters it surrenders to the influence that every word breathes on him. Anyone who has learned a few languages knows that every time he changes a language, he changes himself as well."[119]

In his autobiography *Ha-chalom ve-shivro* (*The Dream Fulfilled*), the Hebraicist Eliezer Ben-Yehuda (1858–1922), a major figure in the vernacularization of modern Hebrew, vividly acknowledges the multilingual persistence of Yiddish and other diasporic languages:

ואף-על-פי-כן, עלי להודות שוב: פעמים, כשדעתי צוללת במחשבות, בפרט מימים עברו, מימי הילדות והנעורים, והיא משתחררת לרגע, מבלי שאארגיש זאת, מהעול העברי שהרכבתי עליה במשך כל-כך שנים בחזקת היד, אז – יש שאני חש פתאום שחשבתי רגע לא בעברית, שמתחת להמחשבה במלים עבריות צפו למעלה קצת מלים נוכריות, באשכנזית וגם ברוסית וצרפתית! ואז אני חש, כי אפילו אצלי אין הלשון העברית לשון האם, שמילולי הראשונים לא היו בעברית, שלא ינקתי את קולות הלשון הזאת עם חלב שדי אמי, ולא שמעתם אוזני כשיישנתני אמי בעריסתי, ואז אני מרגיש, כי בכל אהבתי להלשון העברית בודאי אין אני יודע אותו הטעם של חיבה להלשון, שחש מי שאוזניו שמעו את קולותיה מיום היוולדו ומי שדיבר בה מרגע מילוליו הראשונים.

In any case, I must confess once more: at times, when my mind dives into thoughts, especially of past days, the days of childhood and youth, and frees itself for a moment, without my feeling it, from the Hebrew yoke that I have mounted on it with a firm grip for so many years, then—I suddenly realize that for a second I was not thinking in Hebrew, that from under this thinking in Hebrew surfaced a few foreign words in Yiddish (*ashkenazit*) and also in Russian and French! And then I understand that even for me Hebrew is not a mother tongue (*lashon ha-em*), that my first words were not in Hebrew, that I didn't suckle the sounds of this language from my mother's milk, and that my ears did not hear them when my mother put me to sleep in my crib, and so I feel that despite my love for Hebrew, I certainly don't feel the same affection for it that someone who has heard it spoken from the moment of birth can feel, someone who spoke it from the moment he said his first words.[120]

Ben-Yehuda is often credited with accelerating the development of modern Hebrew as a spoken language, thereby making his admission even more remarkable. In this passage, it is Hebrew, and not a diasporic language, that is characterized as a burden ("the Hebrew yoke"), forcibly submerging other languages. Ben-Yehuda's choice of words describes the Hebrew speaker as a slave or servant to the language, and it is only during a respite from the effort of "thinking in Hebrew words" that these other languages surface like divers from a wreck. For Ben-Yehuda, as for Yeshurun, the native tongue not only carries strong maternal associations—in fact, both authors employ similar maternal tropes in making this connection—but also represents a state of able-bodiedness that the Hebrew "yoke" compromises. The image of free-floating "foreign words" illustrates a state of fluency and mobility in these languages that contrasts sharply with the exertion and burden of speaking in Hebrew. On the other hand, this is an image that may very well evoke a relation between language and the work of national settlement. Hebrew is grounded and settled, while the foreign words float around in a diasporic sea of languages. And yet, in this passage, the mobility of these repressed diasporic languages is undeniable.

Consider the linguistic situation described by Russian poet Joseph Brodsky in his essay "In a Room and a Half," where he elegizes his Russian parents in English, his adopted language, one that neither of them knew. In this work, he describes their translation into English in terms of mobility and freedom, in ways that recall Yeshurun's reflections on the relation between memory and language, between Yiddish and Hebrew:

> I write this in English because I want to grant them a margin of freedom: the margin whose width depends on the number of those who may be willing to read this … this won't resurrect them, but English grammar may at least prove to be a better escape route from the chimneys of the state crematorium than the Russian … May English then *house* my dead. In Russian I am prepared to read, write verses or letters. For Maria Volpert and Alexander Brodsky, though, English offers a better semblance of afterlife, maybe the only one there is, save my very self.[121]

As signposts for English and Russian, the distance between Mount Holyoke and St. Petersburg allows Brodsky to remember his parents in an unencumbered space, outside of national or ideological frames.[122] Their translation from Russian to English allows his parents Alexandr Brodsky and Maria Volpert to inhabit a transnational house more capacious than the room and a half of Brodsky's Soviet childhood. In Yeshurun's case, the Hebrew poems in which the letters of Rikl Perlmutter are remembered and rewritten grant her words "a margin of freedom" and afterlife in Hebrew that Yiddish

can no longer offer.[123] At the same time, however, Hebrew is also continuously made present and alive in Yeshurun's work by the other languages,
particularly Yiddish, that move through it, by the memories and histories
archived in these other languages that translation unseals. Yeshurun's multilingual and translational Hebrew shaped a poetic language that exposed
and amplified—through an increasing disregard for conventional syntax,
grammar, and orthography—the fragmented and broken, but also productive and active, presence of these other languages.[124]

A YIDDISH POEM REMAINS

In 1964, Aharon Megged, the editor of the journal *Massa*, invited a number
of Hebrew writers to submit recollections of their first creative work for
publication in a special issue. In his contribution, a poetic prose piece titled
"Ad hena ve-sham nishar" ("Hither and There It Remained"), Yeshurun
reveals that his first poem was, in fact, a Yiddish poem lost during World
War II:[125]

> יום אחד חיברתי שיר ארוך ביידיש: "די נבואה אין געזאנג." נביאים מתנבאים
> בשירה וזמרה. נפלי עיני על קופסת הקרטון המרושלת וחסרת המכסה של סבי, בה
> נתונים בערבוביה חוזים של ריבית, של מכירה ושאר ניירות—והשיר נבלע עמהם.
> השיר נשאר שם.

One day I composed a long poem in Yiddish: "Di nevue in gezang."
Prophets prophecy in poetry and song. My eye fell on a ragged, lid-
less cardboard box belonging to my grandfather, inside a muddle of
receipts, sale contracts, and other papers—the poem was swallowed
up with them. The poem remained there.[126]

Yeshurun first provides the name of the poem in Yiddish and follows it
with a non-literal Hebrew translation. The Yiddish line "di nevue in gezang"
translates literally as "prophecy in song," whereas Yeshurun's Hebrew translation, "nevi'im mitnabim be-shira ve-zimra," translates as "prophets prophecy in poetry and song." The provenance of this poem cannot be verified;
no copy of it exists, which means that its claims of Yiddish originality, in
this essay and in the few other poems where it is mentioned, cannot be
ascertained.[127] Unlike the letters of *Shloshim 'amud*, which the poet is able to

recover, the poem is packed away with other scraps of paper and later left behind, presumably lost.[128] The title "Di nevue in gezang" is all that remains of this poem, opening the possibility, as in Goldberg's "Ahavata shel Tereza di Mon," for rewriting this lost poem in Hebrew translation. In her work on pseudotranslations, Emily Apter considers the implications of translating without originals, and describes this kind of translation as a form of reproduction that is not unlike cloning. In this respect, the Yiddish fragment can be likened to a minuscule splice of genetic code from which the Hebrew poems that follow are reproduced, in Apter's words, "[growing] ... anew from the cells of a morbid or long-lost original."[129]

Although the poem highlights the displacement of the Yiddish poem, it also gestures to the relation between Hebrew and Yiddish in the poet's own upbringing. The poem "Tovland" ("Goodland," a pun on the title of Theodor Herzl's Zionist novel *Altneuland*), written in 1975, makes reference to the *Mikra'ei Tsiyon* (*Readings of Zion*), a series of pamphlets of Hebrew poetry that were part of Yeshurun's Hebrew-language instruction as a youth.[130] The poems in these pamphlets spanned a long tradition of Hebrew poetry, beginning with the poetry of Al-Andalus (a relation that I return to later). According to Zoritte, the Yiddish translations that accompanied these poems revealed "the beauty of Yiddish" to the poet and inspired his own writing in the language.[131] "Before I returned to Hebrew, I returned to Yiddish," the poet writes in the poem "Tovland." The description of the grandfather's "cardboard box" suggests that this writing is neglected, even disregarded. The cardboard box, in this regard, corresponds to the cave, desk, and briefcases in *Shloshim 'amud* that bury the "scraps" of the mother tongue. Here, it keeps company with documents that testify to an active (cultural) economy of which the Yiddish poem was a part. In the poet's personal *geniza* (repository), these texts take on sacred meaning—indeed, the Hebrew *chozim*, "contracts," also translates as "prophets."

Poem #28 in *Shloshim 'amud shel Avot Yeshurun* arguably alludes to this "cardboard box" and articulates the poet's attempt to reconstruct its contents in a broken-down Hebrew:

הַמְּכֻתָּבִים, הָאֲרֻכִּים וְהַקְּצָרִים, נִתְרַשְׁרְשׁוּ לְבָסוֹף:
יָשׁוּבוּ, קְרָא לָהֶם דְּרוֹר,
עִם הַיִּידִישׁ הַזֹּאת,
אֶל הַצְּרוֹר.

נִתְקַפְּלוּ כְּקִלְפַּת הַתַּפּוּז בְּשׁוּלֵי הַתַּמּוּז.
וְאֵצֵא מֵהַצְּרִיף. הַקְּצָרִים נֶחְבָּאִים.
מִי חָשַׁב עֲלֵיהֶם?
חָשַׁבְתִּי עִבְרִית.

אַבָּא וְאִמָּה שְׁלֵמִים וְהַבַּיִת שָׁלֵם.
הָאֲרֻכִּים הָאֲרֻכִּים הַקְּצָרִים הַקְּצָרִים
מִי חָשַׁב עֲלֵיהֶם?
חָשַׁבְתִּי הַצְּרִיף.

The letters, the long and the short, rustled in the end:
They would return, released [*kora la-hem dror*],
with that Yiddish,
to the bundle.

They folded like orange rind at the edge of Tammuz
And I'll leave the shack. The short ones are hidden.
Who gave them a thought?
I thought Hebrew.

Father and mother are whole and the house is whole.
The long the long the short the short
Who thought about them?
I thought the shack.[132]

The letters that "rustle" and "fold like orange rind" (recalling the orange trees in poem #7) represent the quotations, translations, and fragments in Yiddish that the poet has collected and left in the shack, possibly an iteration of the cave in which the mother's letters are buried. The question "who gave them a thought?," echoing the suggestion that no one will search for the mother tongue, is immediately followed by the reply "I thought Hebrew." The hegemonic reading of the poem would insist that the speaker now thinks in Hebrew and not in Yiddish, but Yeshurun pointedly distorts the rules of Hebrew grammar. The speaker does not "think *in* Hebrew" (be-'ivrit) but rather "thinks Hebrew," suggesting a Hebrew that remembers but also embodies the short, hidden, and abandoned letters.[133] In the last stanza, Yeshurun moves between *bayit*—house—and *tsrif*—shack, suggesting a relation between the abandoned Yiddish home and the poetic text that now houses its memory.[134] The shack is representative of the home that was left behind with the short, hidden letters. But it also the home that Hebrew builds in a *safa shel smartutim*, a Hebrew made of scraps, fragments, and remains.

The return to the bundle may be a euphemism for entombment, an allusion to the acronym inscribed on Jewish tombstones תנצב"ה, *tehe nafsho/ nafsha tsrura bitsror ha-chayim*, which translates into English as "may her/his soul be bound in the bundle of life."[135] But the expression "kora la-hem dror" ("a sparrow called out"), which appears in the second line of the first stanza, is also a Hebrew idiom—*kara dror*— meaning "to free or release." "Kara dror" also alludes to "Dror yikra," a *piyyut* authored by the ninth-century Andalusian poet Dunash Ben Labrat, who was credited with, but also vilified for, adopting Arabic's quantitative prosody in place of the qualitative metric system on which Hebrew poetry had relied.[136] Despite this criticism, the new prosodic paradigm that Ben Labrat proposed ushered in a long period of dynamic poetry in Hebrew that combined liturgical writing with a wide array of secular themes. In this context, the "long" and the "short" letters in Yeshurun's poem may very well refer to the "long" and "short" syllables of Arabic prosody.[137] But the expression "kora la-hem dror" may also allude to the poems of Al-Andalus that Yeshurun first encountered in Hebrew and Yiddish translation as a child, and which inspired his own forays into poetry.

Returning briefly to "Ad hena ve-sham nishar," the description of the grandfather's cardboard box precedes Yeshurun's recollection of an incident concerning a Jewish National Fund stamp that he and his younger brother coveted, an event that he references in other poems.[138] In his version, Yeshurun steals the stamp in the middle of the night and by doing so instigates a tug-of-war, each brother conspiring to steal the stamp from the other.[139] For the poet, a relation emerges between this stamp and the Yiddish poem:

יום אחד אחי הצעיר החזיק בול קרן קיימת לישראל. בחשאי בלילה לקחתיו אני.
בבוקר החזירו אליו. בחשאי בלילה לקחתיו אני. ולקחנו והחזרנו ולקחנו והחזרנו
פעמים הרבה, ולא אמרנו דבר.

יום אחד עליתי לארץ-ישראל.
הבול נשאר שם.

כתבתי הביתה שבחי הארץ.
השיר נשאר שם.

One day my younger brother took hold of a Jewish National Fund
stamp. At night I secretly took it. In the morning it returned to him.
In secret at night I took it. And we took and returned and took and
returned many times, and didn't say a word.

One day I immigrated to the Land of Israel
The stamp remained there.

I wrote homeward in praise of the land.
The poem remained there.[140]

The tug-of-war between Yechiel and his brother represents the struggle
between *sham*—the land over there, the Diaspora—and the Yishuv and the
vexed relation between Yiddish and Hebrew in Mandatory Palestine. In fact,
the conflation of the Yiddish poem and the Jewish National Fund stamp—
which Yeshurun underscores in their mutual "remain[ing] there"—invites
this comparison. Rather than share the riches of the stamp, the promises
of renewal that it offers, the brothers instigate numerous betrayals on its
behalf. We do not know who ultimately comes into full and final possession
of the stamp, but we learn that the poet's immigration to Palestine renders
the stamp useless in some way. For what need does he have of the bucolic
images of the land featured on many of these stamps now that he is there,
in the land? But one could also read the stamp as a ticket or passage for the
poet's literal and poetic *'aliya*, the price of translation. The Yiddish poem,
like the stamp, is a loss that has to be incurred, the price that the poet must
pay in order to write Hebrew poems. Nevertheless, the expression "nishar
sham" leaves open the possibility of recovery.

In 1967, Yeshurun received the Brenner Prize for lifetime achievement
in Hebrew poetry. In his acceptance speech, later published under the title
"Ha-sifrut ha-'ivrit ta'arokh et ha-tefila" (Hebrew Literature Will Arrange
the Prayer), he describes the return of Yiddish in his work like the return of
a repressed memory: "And if you dreamt or spoke it while you slept … you
quickly had to translate all you had said into Hebrew, and only then could
you fall asleep again."[141] The Yiddish letters are never entirely free from the
encumbrances of their original context; rather, their movements within the
Hebrew language mimic the stealthy tug-of-war between Yeshurun and his
younger brother and the ongoing conflict between Israelis and Palestinians,
between Hebrew, Arabic, and other languages. The challenge of finding
sites of concealment in a home both sides know intimately creates dramatic

ruptures, provoking a linguistic back-and-forth that often takes place in Yeshurun's work between Hebrew, Yiddish, and Arabic, a struggle in which there are no clear victors. Rather, the wear and tear that occurs at their sites of contact continuously generates poetic language itself. This is the paradox of breakage that the English words "hole" and "whole" cleverly articulate. Ultimately, translation serves for Yeshurun as a crucial mode of retrieval, albeit one that is fragmentary and partial. In and through translation, the stamp and the lost Yiddish poem, the mother's letters "that no one will read," and the "ensnared words" of the Arab sailor reemerge in the space of the Hebrew poem—and in the highly personal Hebrew of scraps and remnants that the poet reconstructs, the Hebrew that is his, these languages are continuously remembered.

CHAPTER 5

Like a Centipede, Multiple Voices
Harold Schimmel and the Poetry of Translation

Poetry is not only Hebrew; it is inclusive. When one says "Hebrew" there is also another which stands to its side and also precedes and follows it.

—HAROLD SCHIMMEL[1]

Harold Schimmel's foreword to his English translations of Avot Yeshurun's *The Syrian-African Rift and Other Poems* includes the following reflection on the polyphony of poetic language:

> The poet will neither relinquish what his hands once grasped nor cease to hold on to what his hands now grasp. He speaks in the language of his youth, the language of his father, and the language of his manhood, himself at his father's age then. He also appropriates the language of his children, for he must speak to them.
>
> This tenterhook hold on words (for every poet is his own historical dictionary") often results in a non-"spoken language." The lingua franca of the poet is the product of a multiple vision…[2]

For many twentieth-century Hebrew poets, the "language of youth, the language of [the] father" was not modern Hebrew, and often, underlying the poet's language were various, ongoing processes of translation that allowed the father—and mother—tongue to remain in the Hebrew text. "Yeshurun carries over the feel of Yiddish into his Hebrew," Schimmel observes. "He doesn't ask, he takes the new language in his hands. The mouth is pried open, as the mouth of a child at the hands of a doctor who knows what's good for the child more than the child can."[3] The poetic language that emerges in Yeshurun's oeuvre is a *safa shel smartutim*, a language of rags, a way of writing that acknowledges, and also performs, the cultural, linguistic, and psychological rifts and schisms that shaped Hebrew literature throughout the twentieth century.[4] With regard to translating Yeshurun's complete poetic "idiom," Schimmel comments that he "felt inclined to take it whole … I have never glossed the odd or excised the difficult. I have tried to keep the difficulty (a closeness of thinking, or poetic argument, I have discovered) in."[5] Schimmel's commitment to this kind of fidelity is impressive given the challenges Yeshurun's poetic language presents even to a native Hebrew speaker, but it is also possible, he assures us, because of developments in the Anglo-American poetry of his time:

> But can one defend his Hebrew through English? Ten years ago it would have been wild even to consider the notion of translation. But what has happened in English poetry these last years has made the way somewhat easier.
>
> Beyond that, the reader of translated poetry today approaches it much the way the translator himself approaches his work. One reads to find what is new, what is advanced in poetic thinking—much the way Robert Lowell approached his first Montale versions about 1959 in Boston, or the way Michel Deguy went further back, to Gongora, during his sojourn in Spain about the same time.
>
> For poetic technique is poetic wisdom, and Avoth Yeshurun would be delighted at the idea of young New Yorkers, Californians or graduate-student poets in walled Chester reading him to get smart.
>
> "Tel Aviv is the holy city," he writes, placing it on the poetic map.[6]

For Schimmel, translation participates in the expansion of a "poetic map" that reflects varied, and sometimes incongruous, lines of influence and affiliation, and this results in a complex and rich reciprocity between target (English) and source (Hebrew) languages. On the one hand, Schimmel's fidelity to Yeshurun's language brings the older poet closer to an English-language readership. On the other, his references to Robert Lowell and Lowell's translations of Montale, as well as to "nineteenth-century English poets clinging to the soil of Italy," formulate a view of translation as a transformative practice of reading and rewriting, as well as a laboratory or workshop for testing out new ways of writing poetry.

Through the course of the introduction, Schimmel brings Yeshurun's work into continuous relation with Anglo-American poets and artists, like himself, who thrive creatively in states of translation, and who have developed an aesthetic that privileges the foreign, while at the same time imposing their own styles and forms on the works they translate. "'Volveran' of Lowell's *Notebook* transforms and overtakes its antecedent Bécquer," he contends.[7] "Or, to put it differently, Lowell consciously inhabits the local Spanish grammar of Bécquer's magical word the way Merce Cunningham teases the gravitational pull under the singular stones of Piazza Grande."[8] Schimmel is referring here to Cunningham's performance Event No. 45, which took place in Piazza San Marco in Venice on September 14, 1972, as part of the 35th International Festival of Contemporary Music, which ran alongside the Venice Biennale. Cunningham went on to develop over eight hundred events throughout his career, each one a site-specific choreography that drew from previous performances, activating a poetics of recycling and recontextualizing that nonetheless produced works that felt new and current. With this analogy, Schimmel opens his own translation to the question of what footprints or marks he has left in rendering Yeshurun into English, and conversely, the ways in which Yeshurun's poetry has exerted a "gravitational pull" in his own work, which encompasses both English and Hebrew.

It is not incidental that Schimmel invokes Lowell in particular or that he exclusively refers to poet-translators in his introduction. As a poet and translator, Schimmel situates himself, through his translations of Yeshurun, in a tradition of poetic translation that is transhistorical, transnational, multicultural, and fundamentally multilingual and creative. Even the decision to translate Yeshurun into English is an acknowledgment of a shared translational poetics, between Yiddish and Hebrew in Yeshurun's case and between Hebrew and English in Schimmel's. Schimmel's observation that this relation is translated and archived in Yeshurun's name also applies in the case of his own name.[9] "Two Views of Jerusalem," a poem dated January 8, 1963, a year after his immigration, includes the lines, "The sun is here./All my handkerchiefs have my name/in hebrew" (l.6–8).[10] The replacement of the English letters of the poet's name with the Hebrew alphabet prefigures Schimmel's switch from English to Hebrew in his writing, but the lower case "h" in "Hebrew" is nevertheless a nod to the influence of the American modernist E. E. Cummings, a relation that cannot be transcribed by the Hebrew letters, which make no distinction between lowercase and uppercase letters.

In the 1970s and the 1980s, Schimmel actively translated and published Hebrew poetry in English. Recalling Ehud Ben-Ezer's characterization of Esther Raab's interest in literary translation as a *sadna*, workshop, for her own creative output,[11] Schimmel initially invested in literary translation as a kind of preparation for writing poetry in Hebrew, and chose the poets whom he translated—Raab and Yehuda Amichai, among others—in order to intimately study their poetic language as a basis for his own. His efforts were also part of a larger project by Anglo-American poets living in Israel to bring Israeli Hebrew poetry to a global stage via English translation.[12] While Schimmel's literary translation activity eventually gave way to a substantive output of original Hebrew poetry, his practices of translation nevertheless continued to shape his own Hebrew writing.[13]

Schimmel's translations of Yeshurun coincided with the publication of *Ar'a* (אַרְעָה), the first part of a long poem project that has occupied Schimmel for most of his literary career.[14] Louis Zukofsky's "A," a twenty-four-part long poem that the American poet composed between 1928 and 1974, is arguably one of the sources for Schimmel's work.[15] As is the case for "A," an exuberant range of subjects, themes, and forms shapes *Ar'a*, using the poem as a space for blending, in Zukofsky's words, the poet's "historic and contemporary particulars."[16] *Ar'a*— Aramaic for "earth"— initially advanced a pioneer self-mythology that rejected the poet's American diasporic past and languages. In this respect, Schimmel's translation of *The Syrian-African Rift* and his composition of *Ar'a* marked a crucial juncture between English and Hebrew composition—the point when translation gave way to writing in Hebrew. Through *Ar'a*'s act of revision, Schimmel claimed an imagined native status in modern Hebrew literature. Nevertheless, Schimmel's plotting of this narrative relied on a range of contiguities and acts of translation that unsettled the project from the outset, as this chapter explores.

As *Ar'a* has developed, across six collections, Schimmel has moved continuously back and forth between English and Hebrew, generating a rich traffic from their respective histories, literatures, and landscapes.[17] By the time he published *Lo'el* (Lowell, 1986), also part of the *Ar'a* project, the line between translation and writing had blurred entirely, as it does in Lowell's own work, notably in *Notebook* (1970) and *History* (1973).[18] In *Lo'el*, Boston, New York, and Jerusalem are indeed "real" places, but how Schimmel moves between them—and how he links them together— produces texts that are, in Schimmel's words, "polyphonic, shifting, fickle."[19]

Jahan Ramazani's exposition on "traveling poetries," briefly mentioned in the introduction, elucidates the implications of Schimmel's poetics in a national context:

> Although national labels impute singularity and coherence, poets make and remake their often-interstitial citizenship, as we have seen, through formal and ideological rewritings, through sonic mutations and tropological reinscriptions that can span multiple nationalities and ethnicities…a concept of poetic transnationalism—perhaps even poetic citizenship of a kind—allows for the complex tessellations of modern and contemporary writing, poems formed by both unwilled imaginative inheritances and elective identifications across national borders. When living poets face the hard political boundaries of nation-states at airports and checkpoints, it may not count for much that they practice traveling poetries, that they are citizens of imaginative webs formed by cross-national reading and rewriting.[20]

Schimmel's mapping of Hebrew poetry, and where he locates himself within it, may explain in part why his work did not enjoy a wider readership in Israel for many decades, though journals like *Chadarim* and *Helikon* have championed his work consistently over the years.[21] Despite the personal relationships that he forged with writers such as Amichai, Natan Zach, and Aharon Shabtai, for the most part, Schimmel elected to remain outside of the public sphere of Hebrew literature, which, in a recent appraisal of his oeuvre, bestowed on him the dubious sobriquet of "poet's poet."[22] His earliest forays into Hebrew writing advanced a hybrid, translingual, and translational poetry that resisted prevailing trends, an "American blend" that proved unassimilable (possibly because of Schimmel's proximity to it) despite Israeli literature's engagements with American culture in the 1970s and the 1980s.[23] In part, this is because Schimmel's "blend" has made considerable, sometimes impossible, demands on the Hebrew reader, who must possess considerable knowledge of "the Jewish echo chamber" and a command of nineteenth- and twentieth-century American poetry and translation, to be able to identify references and allusions to poets like Ezra Pound, Zukofsky, and Emily Dickinson, to name a few, in Schimmel's non-vernacular Hebrew. In an early review of his work, Hanan Hever noted Schimmel's penchant for slight—*avririm*—associations around which the poem forms.[24] This results

in a poetry that excels at blending together a variety of cultural and historical materials, but may have been less successful, in the Israeli context, at
"blending in."

In the section that follows, I examine how translation has mediated relations between Hebrew and English, and Israel and the United States, in
Schimmel's oeuvre, forming a constitutive part of his poetic language, which
shapes my reading of *Lo'el* later in the chapter. As in Lowell's own work,
the convergence of translation and writing creates a hybrid, multilingual
poetic language for the real and imagined languages, histories, and geographies of the poet. In other words, the very translation activity that activated
Schimmel's self-fashioning as a Hebrew poet in the 1970s also found its way
into his own Hebrew writing. Here, the line between translation and original blurred, and productive points of contact and continuation emerged
between his Hebrew and American English that developed into a translational and multilingual poetics.

BECOMING שימל

In its Fall 1965 issue, the editors of *Epoch*, a literary journal published
out of Cornell University, included the following biographical statement
for Schimmel, a regular contributor: "Harold Schimmel is, according to
our frequent re-assertions, one of the most powerful voices in contemporary poetry in English; his continued residence in Jerusalem removes him
from the American scene."[25] Though he would continue to publish in other
American journals over the next several years, what stands out here is the
clarification "in English," as if the editors felt it necessary to explain something that may no longer be obvious in light of Schimmel's current place of
residence "in Jerusalem." This editorial comment would mark Schimmel's
last appearance in *Epoch*.[26] His trajectory from "the American scene" to
Jerusalem began with a two-year stint in the U.S. army that took the New
Jersey native (b. 1935) to Italy, where he was assigned to a unit that included
the American artist George Schneeman (to whom he dedicated some early
English poems) and the American poet Charles Wright, who became a good
friend.[27] In Verona in 1959, Schimmel borrowed Wright's (still unread) copy
of *Selected Poems of Ezra Pound*, a book that would profoundly shape his
later Hebrew poetry. In 1962, he published the collection *First Poems* in Italy,
his first and only collection in English.[28]

Soon after Schimmel relocated to Israel, where he befriended many important writers and artists of the period, notably Amichai, Dennis Silk, Shabtai, and Aryeh Sachs.[29] They informally referred to themselves as *Ha-mishpacha* (the family), and congregated at Silk's home in Abu Tor, a neighborhood in southeastern Jerusalem.[30] Between 1948 and 1967, the Israel–Jordan border ran through Abu Tor and the area became a "bohemian outpost" for young artists, writers, and filmmakers who were energized by the tension of living on the Arab–Jewish borderline.[31] In the 1967 Six-Day War, Israeli forces secured Abu Tor, which resulted in a remapping of southern Jerusalem and with it the dynamic of this creative milieu. "A different city perhaps/is now being cut in two; two lovers/separated," wrote Amichai in his long poem "Jerusalem, 1967," which he dedicated "to my friends Dennis, Arieh, and Harold."[32]

Schimmel's participation in Israel's literary scene initially centered on writers affiliated with the journal *Akhshav* (*Now*), which Amichai had edited between 1959 and 1960, and he was also an active collaborator in Silk's efforts to increase the visibility of Israeli poetry in English translation as well as the work of English-language Israeli poets.[33] Several of his English poems appeared in 1964 in *Now*, a collection published under the aegis of *Akhshav*, which also included poems by Silk and Robert Friend, an Anglo-Israeli poet and translator.[34] This publication is notable because it suggests an attempt (however short-lived) to expand the scope of *Akhshav* to include Israeli writing in other languages, and is also evidence of the way poets like Schimmel were able to integrate practices of (English and Hebrew) translation and writing in this period. And yet, in his introduction, editor Maxim Ghilan validates this writing by calling attention to the transformative effects of foreign literature on Hebrew writing in the early twentieth century: "The effect of foreign literature on Hebrew letters," he writes, "[which was] restricted by ideological considerations and the lack of a modern tradition, was invigorating. It is the editor's conviction that the influence of non-Hebrew writing, published here, may also be beneficial."[35] The question that Ghilan's assertion raises, however, is what these other languages stood to gain from Hebrew. Were composition and translation mutually reciprocal activities or was this writing in English—or in any other language, for that matter—peripheral to the more central project of developing modern Hebrew literature? Some of these English poems made their way into Schimmel's first Hebrew chapbook, *Ha-shirim* (*The Poems*), published in 1968, and their inclusion suggests that translation and original writing were interrelated practices for Schimmel in this period.[36] But these poems were also translated by Amichai and Zach, thereby giving them the authoritative stamp of approval by Israel's Hebrew literary center.

Shirei malon tsiyon (*Hotel Zion Poems*), published in 1974, was the poet's first full-length publication of original works in Hebrew. More precisely, it was with this publication that Schimmel entered the Israeli literary scene as an "original," and not a translated, Hebrew poet. While many writers have assumed new literary languages later in life to great success—for instance, Vladimir Nabokov, with whom Schimmel studied at Cornell—Schimmel's switch from English to Hebrew was notable because he was moving from a major global language to a language with a much smaller readership and circulation, which is the subtext of the *Epoch* bio that I cited earlier. While these shifts were common in the lives of modern Hebrew writers of the early twentieth century and carried high stakes within the nation-building project, they were less so by the time Schimmel immigrated to Israel in the mid-1960s.

From the outside, the poets of the post-1948 generation (Amichai, Dahlia Ravikovitch, David Avidan, et al.) represented a fully realized national Hebrew literary culture. And by the time Schimmel came onto the Israeli literary scene in the late 1960s, poets such as Amichai and Zach (both German-born), as well as Meir Wieseltier (b. Moscow) and Shabtai, actively and insistently brought more cosmopolitan and international perspectives into Israeli literature and could do so without undermining their status as Israeli writers or calling into question their commitment to a national literature.[37] Indeed, poetry remained a site where alternatives to the demand for *sifrut meguyeset* (socially engaged literature) could continue to be created and performed *within* the national frame. But the poet Peter Cole, who has translated Schimmel's Hebrew poetry into English, has also argued that the "cultural refraction" that this linguistic shift involved allowed Schimmel to recalibrate his affiliation with Anglo-American modernism, which was a visible influence on his English poetry, and frames Schimmel's language shift as a vital aesthetic choice: "For some poets this might be a death sentence; for Schimmel, the longer incubation period and the increased resistance presented by Hebrew seems to have brought about a quantum leap in linguistic consciousness, even a kind of *gilgul*, or poetic transmigration of the soul. The result is something utterly singular and marvelous in Hebrew."[38]

Shirei malon tsiyon emerges in this context as a portrait of the poet in a state of translation. Although the "hotel" of the title positions the poet as a

Figure 5.1. Cover of Harold Schimmel's *Hotel Zion Poems* (Tel Aviv: Ha-kibbuts ha-me'uchad, 1974), Image by Yaakov Rozenblatt

temporary resident, a passer-by, the drawing on the cover features an open glass bottle of locally produced milk. The words inscribed on the bottle, "Tnuva-Yisrael," refer to Tnuva, Israel's largest dairy manufacturer, which has been in operation since 1926. But in Hebrew *tnuva* also means fruit or produce, suggesting that Schimmel's poems are part of, and nourished by, the land's yield. The inclusion of three poems originally written in English and translated into Hebrew by Amichai and Sachs, could be construed as a move to replace the American poet with an Israeli one, a translation for which the two Hebrew poets serve as go-betweens, like Amichai's *turgemanim*.[39] Schimmel, nevertheless, pointedly remarks at the end of the collection that these are translations of poems originally written in English *ba-arets*, in Israel, thereby labeling them as local products, a qualification that recalls Leah Goldberg's assertion in 1937 that the Hebrew poems she had written in Italy were "Italian, not *eretsyisre'eli*, poems."[40]

In his review of *Shirei malon tsiyon*, Hever discerned a "synthetic" quality to Schimmel's work that worked on behalf of this self-fashioning: "In [Schimmel's] mind a person absorbs a meager association, a thin but above all personal echo. The existence of slight facts like these becomes ... a sufficient and also essential reason for their inclusion in a poem."[41] For Hever, the "meagerness" of these associations gave Schimmel's work a disparate, sometimes unfocused quality, which contributed to a level of almost insurmountable hermeneutical difficulty. But how Schimmel gathers and assembles these "associations" *in* and *as* the poem owes much to the second-wave modernism of Zukofsky and Charles Reznikoff, and in particular to the former's expansive, playful, and political description of the poem's particulars: "[that is], an Egyptian pulled-glass bottle in the shape of a fish or oak leaves, as well as the performance of Bach's *Matthew Passion* in Leipzig, or the Russian revolution and the rise of metallurgical plants in Siberia."[42] Zukofsky's juxtapositions break down the authority and hegemony of official histories, allowing "things" and "events" on a personal, individual scale to assume a historical status equivalent to the Russian Revolution, for example. Schimmel's own poetic language, in Hebrew, reflects an arrangement that privileges the mundane as much as the sacred. Take, for example, his account of learning Israeli Hebrew: "At Machane Yehuda [a market in west Jerusalem], I would buy stacks of *Ha-'olam ha-ze* (*This World*), cheap dailies and children's magazines, like *'Olameinu* (*Our World*), and bring them home. I deliberately borrowed from them expressions and sentences, so as to feel the language, the same language a high-end prostitute in Tel Aviv uses to talk about her life."[43] As he does in other contexts, Schimmel reasserts here a commitment to poetic language that draws from the local, that is, the immediate environment and location of the poet. But this idea of the local also derives from an American articulation of local poetry, which is fluid and relational, and is in conversation with American modernism, and particularly the work of William Carlos Williams, as well as the work of the nineteenth-century poets Walt Whitman and Dickinson.[44]

The participation of Amichai and Sachs as translators also situates these poems in an active period of Hebrew–English poetry translation in Israel, specifically the translation of Hebrew poetry into English, the area where Schimmel was most involved. In fact, one major project of cultural translation between these Israeli poets and Anglo-American poets pivoted around the translation of Amichai into English. In the early 1960s, the English poet Ted Hughes and translator Daniel Weissbort approached Silk with their idea for a new publishing venture and requested that he provide translations of poems "by the best living Israeli poet."[45] In response, Silk sent over several poems by Amichai, which appeared on the cover page of the 1965 inaugural issue of *Modern Poetry in Translation*. The successful reception of Amichai's poems encouraged Hughes to pursue the possibility of publishing a collection of Amichai's work in English, a project that Hughes's partner Assia Wevill would undertake under Hughes's supervision.[46] Wevill's death in 1969 threatened to cut this project short, but Schimmel's contribution allowed a long-desired Penguin edition of Amichai's translations to materialize in 1971.[47] Indeed, after Yeshurun, Amichai was the poet whom Schimmel translated most extensively.[48] For Schimmel, translating Amichai reaffirmed a commitment to placing Israeli poets on an international poetic map, while allowing Schimmel, who by now was writing primarily in Hebrew, to remain present and active in the contemporary Anglo-American literary scene (a letter from Harper & Row editor Frances McCullough suggests that Schimmel may have hoped to publish a collection of his own in English).[49] Schimmel's selections in the Penguin edition are also notable because they include poems that touch on the friendship between the poets (e.g., an epithalamium dedicated to Schimmel and his wife Varda).[50] His side of the collection underscores his friendship with Amichai and demonstrates a desire to present Amichai as a local, private, Jerusalem poet, and not exclusively as a "national" or international figure. In this context, the inclusion of Amichai's translation in *Shirei malon tsiyon* is a crucial validation of Schimmel's efforts on the part of Amichai, but also a form of reciprocation.

A poem dedicated to Raab in *Shirei malon tsiyon* also brings this work into relation with Schimmel's own translation practices. In a 1985 interview with Helit Yeshurun, Schimmel acknowledges that Raab was responsible for his first forays into Hebrew-to-English translation:

מצאתי בין ספרים משומשים את ספרה של אסתר ראב, "קמשונים", ומשך אותי
עניין בהירות עין. רק לשים את הדבר ולא יותר. לא ללכת מעבר. כאילו להגיד את
המלה שאתה יודע, כאילו להגיד שחסרה לי המלה. היא לא היתה מחפשת שם של
עץ או צמח ואז מכניסה את המלה...היא השתמשה במילון שלה, מילון מצומצם,
ועם זאת עשתה המון. וזה היה שונה לגמרי מהבתים של לאה גולדברג, שלונסקי או
אלתרמן...

I found Esther Raab's *Kimshonim* among some used books, and was attracted to its visual clarity: to set down nothing more than the "thing" itself—and not to go any further. As if you're saying only the word you know, as if you're saying that you lack the word. She would never look for the name of a tree or plant and then insert the word … She used her own dictionary, a condensed dictionary, and with it expressed a great deal. This differed entirely from the stanzas of Leah Goldberg, [Avraham] Shlonsky or [Natan] Alterman…[51]

In addition to staking a place in this modern Hebrew literary genealogy (the collection also includes poems dedicated to Yosef Chaim Brenner and Chaim Nachman Bialik), Schimmel was attracted to a poet's "way of thinking" and attentive to how certain poets and their work could shape and advance his own poetics, concerns that outweighed considerations of canonicity.[52] What Schimmel appears to have taken from Raab is a penchant for syntactical convolutions, unexpected punctuation, fragmented words, and disruptions of normative grammar (characteristics that Yeshurun's poetry also shares). In "Hedim (le-Ester Rab)" ("Echoes"), Schimmel applies the formal and lexical compactness of Raab's poetry to his own poem, as the first seven lines show:[53]

שְׁלֹשֶׁת הָ-
עֵצִים
שֶׁל אֶסְתֵּר
דַּקִּים כָּ-
לְבָנִים
אוֹ אֶקְ-
לִיפְּטִים...

Trio of
Esther's
trees
lean like
styrax
or euca—
lyptus

But leanness of expression, lexical fragmentation, and ungrammatical constructions are also features found in Schimmel's earlier English poetry, where one can trace them to Pound, Cummings, and Zukofsky, and also further back to Dickinson. In his introduction to his translations of Raab, Schimmel makes this link explicit: "[Raab] stands outside of her contemporaries much in the way that Emily Dickinson stood outside mainstream New England poetry in the sixties of the former century."[54] In this respect, then, one could read Schimmel's *Shirei malon tsiyon*, and his later work, as a continuation *in* Hebrew of iconoclastic turns in American poetry that Schimmel activates in relation to comparable trends in modern Hebrew poetry.

In the same interview, Schimmel explained that the translator's responsibility was to give the reader a poem as close in meaning to its original as could be achieved: "If I'm reading a poet, the translation I want is the one that is the most literal ... I say to the translator: don't worry if you seem to stutter, give me the closest thing possible. As a reader of poetry, I'll find a way, I'll read beyond the translation."[55] Schimmel proposes an idea of translation as an act of radical fidelity, one that allows a reader to experience the poem as it might read in the original. In attempting to mimic the original as closely as possible—in fact, he invokes the parrot as a figure for the translator in his foreword to Yeshurun's *The Syrian-African Rift*—the translator produces a text that, in its fidelity to the source, has a foreignizing effect in the target language. On the other hand, Schimmel's remarks imply that if the translation "stutters" it may be because it is reproducing a quality of the original text, or what Johannes Göransson has termed "the unfaithful translation ambience."[56] This strategy also shapes Schimmel's own writing; indeed, the poem that he writes in his "original" Hebrew contains these translational echoes of Raab. As he explained to Helit Yeshurun, "You fall in love with a new language and follow it. It grabs you. At the same time, that which is yours—your language—sort of breaks apart. You can't take a step forward without this opposing disintegration."[57] The poem dedicated to Raab demonstrates how this "disintegration" carries over into the new language and responds to the echoes, stutters, and fractures that already inhabit it.

Take, for example, the English poem "His Commitment," which was published in *Epoch* in 1964:[58]

> I have taken down
> the map of Italy and put, in its stead, the Ordnance
> survey map (1924 revised) of Jeru—
> salem. Jeru—
>
> salem. Jerusalem the golden—
> into your corners I have driven
> four brass tacks, of local,
> and inferior, make.

The dislocation of "Jeru-salem" (ירו-שלם), which occurs and repeats in lines 3 and 4, coincides with the moment when the new map replaces the old one, and may also represent a city divided, like the poet, between ancient and modern namings and their respective contested histories (e.g., the city's non-Hebraic origins and the 1924 Mandatory map), as well as the real location of Schimmel and his peers in Abu Tor, on the Jewish/Arab borderline.[59] This site of dislocation is violent (the hyphens seem to literalize the "driving" of the tacks), exposing the non-Hebraic etymology of the name ("Shalem" was an Ugaritic deity) and then bringing both sides of Jerusalem together in a moment of creative, but also politicized, repair (in Hebrew, "peace" and "wholeness" share an etymological root). Although the map-switch in "His Commitment" prefigures Schimmel's English-to-Hebrew translation by several years, the brass tacks that hold this new map in place also refer, in nautical terms, to a change in position or direction. If we read this shift as a linguistic one, we can infer that its "inferior make" is a reference to its, as of yet, unpolished state, but this local position nevertheless constitutes the speaker's "commitment." And yet, the expression "Jerusalem the golden" is also the title of Reznikoff's 1934 long poem, which brings Jewish tropes of exile and diaspora to bear on Depression-era New York City.[60] As a poem that, in Norman Finkelstein's words, "continually [rehearses] themes of linguistic difference, geographic displacement, and historical rupture," this possible allusion to Reznikoff's poem in Schimmel's text suggests that the dislocations of "His Commitment" are a continuation of an American, and specifically Jewish-American, modernist poetics.[61]

"His Commitment" was reprinted in Silk's anthology *Retrievements*, which gathered selections of art and writing about Jerusalem, spanning almost 1500 years, as imagined and documented by its residents and passers-by.[62] Here, Schimmel's poem shares the page with a Claude Reignier Conder (1848–1910) engraving of a British-financed exploration party in Palestine.[63] In this illustration, a man gazes into the desert through a theodolite while, at his feet, another man takes down measurements in a notebook. The first man stands holding an umbrella that casts shade they both can share, creating a mutual space that, next to Schimmel's poem, encapsulates dual representations of the poet: one is the active observer, measuring and mapping his world, and the other, the writer, rooted to his location, where he is absorbed in the task of taking into account what has been seen. The rifle resting next to them, however, conveys an understanding of the politics of their position—indeed, imposition. The 1865 Ordnance Survey of Jerusalem was commissioned, in part, to assess Jerusalem's water supply, but it also constituted the most comprehensive cartographic and archeological survey of the city, and of Ottoman Palestine, of its time.[64] In meticulously rendered and multilingual detail, these maps asserted the authority of modern, science-based cartography over the "sacred geography" that had shaped encounters with the region well into the nineteenth century, not to mention British imperial authority over Ottoman rule.

It is the 1924 map, in particular, that becomes a point of reference for Schimmel's speaker. The 1920s were a period of heightened cartographic activity in Jerusalem, a rapidly urbanizing city. Despite numerous revisions, as Dov Gavish has explained, "these maps became obsolete faster than they could be updated."[65] Switching the Italy and Jerusalem maps is part of the performance of immigration, but it is also telling that Schimmel's speaker does not choose a contemporary map of the city. Rather, going back to the Ordnance map, as he does to the pre-1948 generation of Hebrew poets in *Shirei malon tsiyon*, allows, in Cole's words, for "a deceleration in the move from landscape to language" to take place, from which the poet can begin to rewrite his own origins just outside of the national frame.[66]

By the time Schimmel immigrated, the Hebraization of the Israeli map was a fait accompli, with the exception of Jerusalem and its ambivalent borderlines, but for the most part, pre-Statehood locations, which appear on Ordnance maps in Hebrew and Arabic transliteration, as well as in English translation, were renamed and translated to erase all traces of non-Jewish settlement.[67] That the multilingual Ordnance map would represent the poet's "commitment" reveals the kind of ironies at play in the forging of modern Israeli identity and the extent to which the mapping of Israeli identity continuously implicates both territory and language. It illustrates their "revival" and recuperation in the twentieth century as a simultaneous and integrated process.[68] "As personal history merged with state history, with geography, with topography, with botany, a change of address became synonymous with national growth," Schimmel argued.[69] This merging was also the case for the American poet who could not sneeze into his handkerchief "without feeling Jewish."

The publication of *Ar'a* in 1979 signaled the beginning of Schimmel's decades-long project to write a Hebrew epic "as though I had had no past before Hebrew and before this land."[70] In contrast to Schimmel's early work in English and his early Hebrew poems, the poems of *Ar'a* dazzle in their length—the first Canto runs to thirty-eight pages—and innovative formal and linguistic range. In fact, the poems of *Ar'a* eschew any obvious semblance of poetic formal conventions; indeed, they seem to openly defy them.[71] Yet, each "canto"—a term Schimmel himself uses and clearly takes from Pound—represents an intricate and dense intertextual network, which Gabriel Levin has described as "a fine orchestration of myriad minutely perceived details."[72]

Ar'a takes its name from the biblical Book of Daniel, where the word appears repeatedly. Written in Hebrew and Aramaic, the Book of Daniel is set during the time of the Babylonian exile, a period that marked the rise of Aramaic as a Jewish vernacular and introduced exile as a major trope of Jewish literature. Here, the Babylonian narrative of exile and return serves as a critical context for Schimmel's engagement with a distinctly Jewish Israeli problematics of language and territorial belonging. In this respect, Schimmel's use of the Aramaic can be read in its more literal relation to Daniel and his reworking of its key scene, and also as part of a claim to an autochthonous Semitic relation to the region. The place of Aramaic in Jewish textual tradition is not restricted to biblical texts and the Targumim (Aramaic translations of the Bible)—it circulates widely, and in a variety of dialects, in talmudic literature, particularly the Gemara, as well as liturgical texts like the *Kaddish* and *Kol Nidre*.[73] And though it is today considered an endangered language, modern varieties of Aramaic remained in use through the twentieth century in small Jewish and Christian communities of Western Asia and the Middle East. These contexts have conferred on Aramaic the status of both a classical and a diasporic language vis-à-vis Hebrew.[74] In contrast to its former status as a cultural and economic lingua franca in ancient Judea, the presence of Aramaic in contemporary Israeli Hebrew texts often signals a shift to a higher, more poetic diction.[75] In fact, Aramaic features meaningfully in Amichai's oeuvre, including the poem "Bekhol chumrat ha-rachamin" ("To the Full Severity of Compassion") which also interweaves language from the Book of Daniel.[76] Schimmel's Aramaic title may draw on all of these associations, but Wilhelm Gesenius's entry for *Ar'a* also indicates that the difference between the Aramaic *Ar'a* (ארעה) and the Hebrew *erets* (ארץ) attests to a "frequent interchange of the letters *tsade* and *'ayin*," between the languages, with the Aramaic preserving one of the earlier pronunciations of *tsade*.[77] In Rabbinic and modern Hebrew, there is also a relation between *Ar'a* and *ara'i* (ארעי), which means temporary and transitory, meanings that accord with the transformative mobility and translatability of languages and places in Schimmel's work, even in this reworking of his own history.

In one of the book's most famous scenes, King Belshazzar, son of King Nebuchadnezzar, observes a hand emerging from a wall and inscribing on its surface a cryptic message.[78] When the wisest men of his court fail to decipher this code, his wife counsels him to seek the hermeneutic skills of Daniel, who had won great fame in King Nebuchadnezzar's court as an interpreter of dreams. Canto I of *Ar'a* recasts Belshazzar's vision within the local landscape of Bat Shlomo, a Jewish settlement founded in 1899 (located in the northern Israeli coastal plain). The entire book is set in bold, square Ashkenazi letters (comparable to the FrankRuehl typeface), which Levin describes as the kind of script commonly found in Hebrew grammar books, though it is also characteristic of biblical texts.[79]

סִימְקִין עַצְמוֹ הָיָה

כּוֹתֵב עַל הַקִּירוֹת: "אֱלֹהִים חָכָם"

תְּרָאוּ

אָפְלוּ הָעוֹרְבִים עַל הָרְעָפִים

מְקַרְקְרִים:

"אֵיזֶה מִין דְּבָרִים שׁוֹנִים

מִתְאַחֲדִים?" וְ-

"אֵיךְ

נִהְיֶה מֵעַתָּה וָהָלְאָה?"

Symkin himself used
to write on the walls: "God is wise"

                                                            Look

Even the crows on the roof-tiles
are cackling:
            "What kind of different things
            come together?" and—
"How
    will we be from here on out?"[80]

In Schimmel's reworking of this scene, the hand on the wall belongs to the pioneer Symkin, thereby resolving the question of agency that the biblical text leaves open. And yet, the allusion to the biblical "writing on the wall" nonetheless unsettles this question. The crows' query—how do these lines come together?—imposes a hermeneutical responsibility on the reader. We are not meant to take these things at face value. Levin endeavors to trace these associations back to some origin that may explain more fully what this writing means, and does so largely through translation. He points out that the crows' question "What kind of different/things come together?" is a translation of an epigram by the Greek poet Callimachus, a voice that Schimmel channels through Pound.[81] This move—indeed, all the movements and translations (and retranslations) that bring Callimachus into Ar'a—unsettle the very origin that Symkin is trying to claim. Quoting from Pound's "Homage to Sextus Propertius"—"Shades of Callimachus, Coan ghosts of Philetas/It is in your grove I would walk"[82]—Levin wonders, "Are these Pound's lines? Propertius's? Such distinctions are no longer significant, Pound would insist, for the modern poem's surface had become above all a medium or mask through which a polyphony of voices were to be heard."[83] In this respect, Schimmel's dense intertextuality, which he mediates primarily through Hebrew translation, challenges Walter Benjamin's claim that translations are untranslatable.[84] Rather, Schimmel's retranslation of an epigram by a Greek poet—that, in turn, has been transmitted through Latin (Propertius) and English (Pound)—revives this material and rewrites it as part of his "native" poem. In so doing, Schimmel is also participating in a rich tradition of Hebrew engagements with Ancient Greek literature, which have been, and continue to be, activated in large part in translation.[85] Ar'a may, on the surface, advance Schimmel's self-mythology as a Hebrew "pioneer" through an outmoded reenactment of the classic Zionist repudiation of the diaspora and its replacement with a local, indigenous Jewish

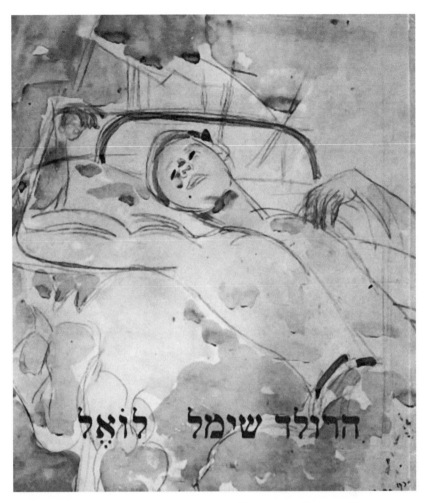

Figure 5.2. Cover of Harold Schimmel's *Lowell* (Tel Aviv: Chadarim/Galeria Gordon, 1986), featuring Joseph Zaritsky's "Man Resting" (Watercolor, 1930)

identity, but it is ultimately and fundamentally, to invoke Jacques Derrida once more, "indebted, taxed, obligated by another text, and a priori translating."[86]

לואל/LOWELL

Helit Yeshurun's 1985 interview with Schimmel, which I have cited earlier, serves as an apt preface for my reading of *Loˀel* (in fact, a selection from *Loˀel* accompanied the interview). In the 1980s, Schimmel was a frequent contributor to her journal *Chadarim*, and in this interview he explicitly frames his work in an American tradition and in relation to an American local poetry:

מה משך אותך בשירה האמריקנית?

שימל: בשנות הלימודים שלי מה שמשך אותי היתה היתה העובדה, שזו לא היתה שירה אנגלית. שזו היתה אחרת. כמו הדוגמאות הקרובות ביותר, וולט ויטמן ואמילי דיקנסון. הם זרקו את המסורת והיו משונים כלשהו וקצת פרועים בכל הנוגע למה זה שיר, ואיך שיר צריך להיות, וזה היה ביטוי מקומי, משכנע. פראנק או׳האָרה אפשרי רק בניו יורק, למרות שבא מבלטימור ולמד בהארווארד. יש בו משהו משחרר. אני צמחתי מזה, או אולי אני בחרתי להגיד לעצמי שאני צומח מזה.

Yeshurun: What attracted you to American poetry?

Schimmel: When I was in school, what attracted me was the fact that this wasn't "English" poetry. It was different, the most obvious examples being Walt Whitman and Emily Dickinson. They threw tradition out the window. They were completely strange and a bit wild in their poetics and in their understanding of what a poem should be; [theirs] was a convincing, local expression. Frank O'Hara was possible only in New York, even though he came from Baltimore and had studied at Harvard. There's something liberating about this. I grew out of this, or perhaps I just decided to tell myself that I was growing out of this.[87]

This particular exchange highlights the preoccupation with literary tradition and inheritance that runs through Schimmel's poetry, but also suggests that his self-inscription in the Israeli narrative (recalling Symkin's writing on the wall) may have been informed by iconoclastic tendencies and motivations that inhere in American literature. Helit Yeshurun's line of inquiry in the *Chadarim* interview suggests that she also discerns a continuous thread between Schimmel's Anglo-American modernist influences and his Hebrew/Israeli poetry. Schimmel's response is notable for his simultaneous assertion and revision of origins, his attraction to the iconoclastic turn in American poetry in the late nineteenth century—a rejection of literary inheritance and tradition that becomes, alternatively, a dominant tradition and inheritance in its own right—as well as his argument that a "convincing, local expression" does not necessarily limit a poet to a particular (native) locality, thereby reframing poetic language as transnational.

Where a poet is born does not ultimately determine where a poet belongs—as in the case of O'Hara, who is born in Baltimore but is "possible only in New York"—or where a poet chooses to locate him or herself, for as Schimmel observes, "[P]erhaps I just decided to tell myself that I was growing out of this." In *Paris France*, Gertrude Stein remarks, "Writers have to have two countries, the one where they belong, and the one in which they live really. The second one is romantic, it is separate from themselves, it is not real but it is really there."[88] Stein's perception of belonging accounts for imaginary affiliations to place and the imaginary places where writers may choose to reside, a possibility that resonates in Schimmel's response. What he observes, and what Stein also implies in her formulation of belonging, is that what remains "convincingly local" about poetry lies in poetic language itself, that is, in its "expression"— and it is to this language, with its possibilities for translation, that a poet belongs.

According to Schimmel, *Lo'el* marked the introduction of American landscapes in his Hebrew poetry:

כשכתבתי את לואל, כתבתי פעם ראשונה על נופים לא ארץ-ישראליים; לראשונה השתמשתי בחומרים נוכריים בעברית. רציתי לתפוס את ניו-יורק והארכיטקטורה שלה, ואת זה להעביר לעברית. לקחתי את הערך "ניו-יורק" באינציקלופדיה העברית ורציתי לראות אם יש איזה טעם של ניו-יורק. ניסיתי להתחרות עם הכישלון של האינציקלופדיה. זה היה ריכוז נכון כדי לכתוב על חלקים מסוימים מהעבר שלי.

המחזור "לואל" בנוי שלושה פרקים: בוסטון, ניו-יורק וירושלים. ניסיתי לתת אווירה של חוג חברים ונוף מקומי בקטעי בוסטון. נופים ואנשים שווים בעיני. זה תמיד אותו עולם. זה בא לי מאהבתי לשירה הפאסטוראלית, שם אין הבדל בין הנושא לבין הרקע. לעומת זה, חשוב לי לתפוס את המקום המסוים. כשאני עובר מבוסטון לניו-יורק, אני רוצה שהקורא ירגיש עיר אחרת וטעם אחר. אני איש שאוהב את המקומי ושומר את המקומי, ולא כל כך מוכן להגיע למשהו כללי.

Writing *Lo'el* was the first time that I wrote about non-Israeli landscapes; for the first time, I used materials that were foreign to [my] Hebrew. I wanted to seize New York and her architecture and bring all of that into Hebrew. So, I consulted the *Encyclopaedia Hebraica* entry for New York to see if it conveyed the flavor of the city. I tried to compete with the failure of the encyclopedia. This kind of concentration proved right for writing about certain parts of my past.

The cycle "Lowell" is built out of three chapters: Boston, New York, and Jerusalem. I tried to capture a certain social milieu and local landscape in the Boston sections ... When I move from Boston to New York, I want the reader to feel another city and another ambiance. I am someone who loves the local and preserves the local and is not quite prepared to settle on generalities.[89]

In his preface to *Lo'el*, Schimmel confesses, "[W]ith the publication of this poem, I am correcting a mistake that I have made: namely, writing in Hebrew only about the land (*ha-arets*)—not as if I had been born into Hebrew or in this land, but rather as if I had had no past before Hebrew and before this land. The *Encyclopaedia Hebraica* includes entries for Boston and New York, now so do I."[90] The one hundred sonnets of *Lo'el* also comprise a detailed, personal homage to Lowell, whose 1959 collection *Life Studies* positioned him as a paragon for American poets of the 1960s. Lowell's *Life Studies* was notable for its break from the strict adherence to form and prosody that had marked his earlier work and for its overt autobiographical material and preoccupation with personal history, which many critics marked as the "confessional" turn in American poetry. The confessional appeal notwithstanding, what made *Life Studies* a radical work in its time was how its combination of realist conventions with a less constrained or less formal mode of writing foregrounded a private mythology.[91] "There's a good deal of tinkering with fact [but] the reader was to believe he was getting the *real* Robert Lowell," Lowell conceded.[92] Even poems that present autobiographical facts are constructed out of a "nexus of images," to use Marjorie Perloff's term, that are kinetic, mutable, and unsettled, thereby allowing the autobiographical to give way to the fictive.[93]

Despite the claims of the preface, the poems of *Lo'el* do not move seamlessly from one locality to the next. Even though the table of contents clearly demarcates Boston, New York, and Jerusalem as separate geographies, Schimmel also constructs a comparable intertextual "nexus of images" that migrates from one section to the other, often with the effect of confusing these locations and their corresponding histories. Even the formal properties of the sonnet cannot hold these texts in place. Frequently, lines stretch into the gutter of the page (e.g., #90) or sudden gaps appear between words, creating considerable white space within the poem (e.g., #31).[94] The effect of this mix and conflation of places and histories is the construction of an imagined, heterogeneous, and multilingual poetic map. In *Lo'el*, Boston,

New York, and Jerusalem are indeed "real" places, but how Schimmel moves between them—and how he links them together (to answer Callimachus's crows)—results in a textual landscape and poetic language that attenuates and blurs their borders, allowing them to move, change, and translate. This is a characteristic that his earlier work shares; in fact, Hever, in his review of *Shirei malon tsiyon*, avoided using the terms "Israeli" or "American" as categories for Schimmel's work. Instead of relying on a national category, Hever characterized it as a poetry "shel 'al-yad," a poetry of adjacency.[95] This adjacency is central to Schimmel's personal literary map—the proximities that result when Israel and the United States meet.

Take, for example, #47, which begins with the following lines:[96]

קוֹרֵא "לְיַד הָאוֹקֵיָנוֹס" טָרִי מְנִיוּ
יוֹרְק שֶׁהֱבִיא-לִי אָבִי   יוֹשְׁבִים בִּשְׁנֵי
כִּסְאוֹת-סָלוֹף מְפַסְפָּסִים מִתַּחַת אֵיקָלִיפְּטוּסֵי-עֲנָק עַל-שְׂפַת
יָם-כִּנֶּרֶת.

Reading *Near the Ocean* fresh from New
York which my father sent to me   sitting in two
striped reclining chairs under giant eucalypti on the shore
of the Kinneret...

(l.1–4)

"Le-yad ha-okeyanus" is Schimmel's Hebrew rendering of Lowell's *Near the Ocean*, a collection published in 1967. Schimmel's poem appears in the New York section of *Lo'el*, but is situated in Israel, a location that is clear from the speaker's point of reference, the Kinneret (or Sea of Galilee, as it is most commonly known in English), which is located in northern Israel and was the site of the earliest Jewish collective settlements. New York nonetheless remains present through the transaction the poem describes, which includes a reference to Schimmel's American father. Indeed, the dislocation of "nyu/york" in the first two lines also results in a clever bilingual and translational word play between the Hebrew "tari" (fresh) and the English "nyu"/new, each word, in effect, translating the other. Indeed, the liminal language in both the title of Lowell's book "Le-yad ha-okeyanus" and the speaker's location "'al sfat ha-kineret" ("on the shore of the Kinneret") articulate the edges where two distinct geographies, albeit of a very different scale, come into contact. These sites are mediated by the father, who functions here as a go-between, bringing Lowell, the literary father-figure, to his son. The *sfat* in "sfat ha-kineret" and its connection to *safa* (lip) is also suggestive of a relation between linguistic and geographic borders.

This exchange implicates translation both in the literal Hebrew translation of *Near the Ocean* and in the choice of this text. Translations—or what Lowell called imitations—of Juvenal, Dante, Horace, and Quevedo comprise the majority of the poems of *Near the Ocean*.[97] "How one jumps from Rome to the America of my own poems is something of a mystery to me," Lowell muses in his prefatory note to the collection.[98] Schimmel's *Lo'el* adds northern Israel to this trajectory through acts of translation, which is precisely how Lowell brings Rome to his America. Although Schimmel adds a note at the end of *Lo'el* that lists the poems he has translated,[99] his self-described "adaptations" (*'ibudim*) nonetheless advance an understanding of translation as a revisionary and transcreative act, and one that allows him to inhabit the work of his literary "father figure," all the while rewriting Lowell in his own terms, place, and language. Shahar Bram, in his reading of *Lo'el*, goes so far as to suggest that Schimmel resolves his "anxiety of influence" by "translating Lowell into the space of his work and his physical and cultural surroundings ... simply put, Schimmel rewrites Lowell in Hebrew. And in this respect, he turns Lowell into 'Schimmel.'"[100]

By way of example, I turn to #21, a sonnet from the Boston section, which illustrates the different and revisionary acts of translation that a reader encounters in Schimmel's *Lo'el*:[101]

"הַמַּגְנוֹלְיָה הַיַּפָּנִית"   שֶׁל מוֹנטָלֶה הִשְׁתַּנְּבַת
בְּתַרְגּוּמְךָ לְ"מַגְנוֹלְיָה נַכְסִית"—וְהַסֵּפֶר הִגִּיעַ
בְּסוֹף יָנוּאָר מִבּוֹלוֹנְיָה עִם תוֹסָפַת
צִיּוּר הַשַּׁעַר : צֶבַע-מַיִם שֶׁל מוֹרַנְדִי
מֵאֹסֶף בַּקְבּוּקִים וְקַפְסָאוֹת פְּרָטִי שֶׁשָּׁמֶשׁ-לוֹ
בְּעַרְבּוּבְיָה) בְּנֶאֱמָנוּת בִּלְתִּי-נִלְאֵית כְּטֶבַע-דּוֹמֵם   שְׁנוֹת-חַיִּים)
תְּמוּנוֹת-דְּמֻיּוֹת-וּמַרְאוֹת שֶׁל מְשׁוֹרֵר   שֶׁטֶף דַּק
סָגֹל בִּצְלָלִית רְגִישָׁה כְּתַרְשִׁים בִּנְיָנֵי
עִיר-מֶכֶרֶת אֲהוּבָה   חֲתִימָתוֹ קִמְעָה מִתַּחַת
בְּגָדוֹל וּבְעָפְרוֹן בְּמֶרְכַּז-הַלֹּבֶן הִיא כְּתִיבָה-בַּשָּׁמַיִם
לְתִרְכֹּבֶת הַשֵּׁמוֹת הַמְּתוּקָה-לָאֹזֶן יֵשׁ נִימָה-שְׁקֵטָה
שֶׁל תַּלְמִידָה-לְמוּסִיקָה שֶׁפָּגַשְׁתָּ בְּזַלְצְבּוּרְג וּלְאַחַר-זְמָן
הִתְכַּוַּנְתָּ לָשֵׂאת-לְאִשָּׁה: ג'וֹבָנָּה מָדוֹנִיָּה   "אַךְ
הָרוּחַ בְּעֵינֶיךָ אֵלֵץ אוֹתְךָ לַחֲזֹר"

Montale's "magnolia giapponese" became
in your translation "the dwarf magnolia"   the book arrived
at the end of January from Bologna with
a cover image : a Morandi water-color
a private stash of bottles and cartons rendered
(in a muddle) unfailingly like a still-life   a life-time
a poet's pictures-figures-and-views   a delicate
violet flow in a tender silhouette like a blueprint
for the buildings of a familiar, beloved city   his signature a bit below
writ large in pencil in the whitespace sky-lettering
for a formula of names sweet to the ear there the hushed note
of the music student you met in Salzburg and later
intended to make your wife: Giovanna Madonia   "But
the wind in your eyes obliged you to return"

First, the "biographical" particulars: Lowell's translations of Eugenio Montale (1896–1981) appeared in 1960 in a bilingual collection titled *Poesie di Montale*, which, in fact, was published in Bologna by Edizioni della Lanterna (a detail that connects this volume to Schimmel's *First Poems*, published in Italy).[102] Montale's magnolia is a reference to the poem "L'ombra della magnolia" ("The Shadow of the Magnolia"), which is included in this volume. A blue-grey watercolor by Giorgio Morandi (1890–1964) graces the frontispiece, with his signature, indeed, "hovering below" a still-life of "bottles and cartons." Giovanna Madonia refers to a young, Sicilian music student with whom Lowell had an affair. She attended his 1952 seminars on American literature at the Salzburg Seminar in American Civilization. According to his biographer Paul Mariani, Lowell apparently did express—during one of his manic episodes—an intention to marry her.[103]

What the poem highlights, however, is the extent to which it gathers these biographical details through and around an act of translation. In the Bologna edition of his Montale translations, which were published in 1960, Lowell renders Montale's "magnolia giapponese" as "the Japanese magnolia." The "change" that Schimmel identifies—"the dwarf magnolia"—appears a year later in Lowell's *Imitations*, but Schimmel's poem insists that the mistranslation occurs in the book from Bologna. Furthermore, although my translation of Schimmel's poem reinstates Montale's original Italian, thereby suggesting a direct correlation between Montale and Schimmel, Schimmel's poem actually quotes Montale via his Hebrew translation ("ha-magnolia ha-yapanit") of Lowell's English translation. In this respect, as is the case throughout Schimmel's oeuvre, sources and origins mix and "muddle" in the poem.

In fact, in #47, the speaker relates how "without a dictionary I / translate Montale's poems and insolently (be-chutspa) switch/(to the names of my beloveds) the not-so-traditional names-of-Jewish-women" (l.7–8). In other words, Schimmel takes the Jewish female names that appear in Montale—most notably in the 1939 collection *Le Occasioni* (*The Occasions*)—and retranslates/rewrites them as the names of his own lovers.[104] But the reference to these "insolent" translations calls the reader's attention back to Lowell's own translations of Montale, some from *Le Occasioni*.[105] Montale's "Dora Markus," for example, one of his most acclaimed poems, centers on a figure of a Jewish woman. The speaker observes the Jewish Dora on the beach, remarking: "[Y]our restlessness makes me think/of migratory birds diving at a lighthouse/on an ugly night" (Lowell's translation).[106] Both Montale and Lowell invoke the tropes of Jewish wandering and exile in their respective renderings of the Jewish Dora to highlight her liminal position: "with a toss/of your thumb, you point out the other shore,/invisible, your true country" (Lowell). She serves, in this respect, as a foil for the (male) poets and their reflections on tradition, history, and place. But through his retranslation, Schimmel, the Jewish American poet in Israel, intervenes to bring these Jewish women, with "not-so-traditional names," like Dora Markus, to "this other shore," into a Jewish space and language. This "switch" allows him to adapt the Montale poems, and, by extension, Lowell's translations, to his own personal and local narrative, space, and language, a practice that is consistent with Lowell's own translation practices, as well as Schimmel's "adaptations" of Lowell.

Poem #15, for example, is both a translation and a rewriting of one of Lowell's signature sonnets from *History*, "For Ann Adden I. 1958," of which an early version, titled "1958," appears in *Near the Ocean*.[107] Schimmel draws from both versions in his translation:[108]

אַתְּ זוֹכֶרֶת שֶׁעָמַדְתְּ אִתִּי בַּחוֹשֶׁךְ

אָן אָדֶן? בְּבֵית הַפְּרוּעִים? הַכֹּל—

אֲנִי-מְשֻׁגָּע אַתְּ מְשֻׁגַּעַת-עָלַי? וְהֵבֵאתִי טַבַּעְתִּי

אוֹתָהּ-חֲתִיכַת-זָהָב שֶׁל שְׁנֵי-עָשָׂר-קָרָט...ג'וֹן מֵאַרְק

עֲדַיִן לְלֹא סָטִיָּה מֵהַמַּטָּרָה הָאֲמִתִּית?

בְּרִיאָה אַה שַׁתְקָנִית! זוֹכֶרֶת-אֶת-עַצְמֵךְ מַשְׁמִיעָה
מָרִיאַן אַנְדֶרסוֹן "הַמֶּלֶךְ-הָרוֹעֶה" שֶׁל מוֹצַרְט
אִיל רֵי פַּסְטוֹרֶי? הוֹ כְּרִישַׁת-פַּטִּישׁ
הוֹ סַלְמוֹן-הַקֶּשֶׁת שֶׁל הָעוֹלָם—יָדֵךְ
שׁוֹשָׁן! אַתְּ זוֹכֶרֶת בַּמִּיטֶרסִיל הֶחְלַשְׁנוּ
אֶת קִלְפָּתוֹ הַפְּגוּמָה שֶׁל הַכַּדּוּר-הַמַּפְחִיד
לִקְלִפּוֹת-בֵּיצִים—ג'וֹן מַאַרְק עוֹמֶדֶת אַתְּ
עוֹמֵד אֲנִי אִם אֶשְׁכָּחֵךְ צִיּוֹן
תִּשְׁכַּח יְמִינִי מָרָה הוֹ תָּפְתִּי!

Do you remember that you were standing with me in the dark
Ann Adden? In the house of the wild ones? Everything—
I'm mad you mad-about-me? And I brought my ring
that-gold-chunk of twelve carats…. Joan of Arc
still unswerving from the true target?
Healthy ah reticent! Remember-that-you played
Marian Anderson in Mozart's "The Shepherd King"
Il re pastore? O hammerhead shark
O rainbow salmon of the world—your hand
A rose! Remember in Mittersill we glided down
the defective shell of the-fearful-sphere
like eggshells—Joan of Arc you are standing
I am standing if I forget you Zion
let my right hand forget bitter oh hell!

#15 is not a full translation of Lowell's poem; lines 10–12, for instance, incorporate language from Lowell but ultimately constitute a total reworking of the poem. Schimmel also offers a crucial rewriting of the poem's last line, where Lowell invokes Psalm 137: "[I]f I forget you, Ann, let my right hand forget its cunning." In Schimmel's translation, the addressee of the biblical text is reinstated, but the line is nonetheless modified: "[I]f I forget you Zion/let my right hand forget bitter oh hell!" The exclamation "oh hell!" may signal some frustration or failure to translate Lowell—indeed, perfectly timed with the description of skiing in Mittersill, the translation begins to veer off course—but it may be a reaction as well to how "Zion" has slipped—or slid—into the translation. The replacement of "Ann" with "Zion" not only brings this translation closer to Schimmel's own (Jewish) sources but also highlights the dislocations that create the conditions for writing a Hebrew translation of Lowell's English poem.

Lowell traveled to Israel in March 1969 for a two-week literary tour that took him around the country, including Nazareth and the Golan Heights. Through Schimmel, he made the acquaintance of Amichai and Silk, and also—if Schimmel's poem on the matter is to be trusted (poem #81)— managed to insult Goldberg.[109] Lowell's visit to Israel becomes a major point—but not the only point—of departure for Schimmel, who uses this encounter with his mentor to revisit and revise his own literary biography; however, as Schimmel himself admits, throughout these poems, autobiographically "real" events are confused with "reimaginings" of what could have taken place. Translation is central to this reimagining; as observed earlier, throughout Lo'el, one encounters Lowell's own poetry in Schimmel's translation, as well as numerous references to and quotations of American English poetry, including Schimmel's own English poems, in Hebrew translation. While the first books of Ar'a were primarily invested in a poetry of settlement, through which Schimmel staked a claim in Hebrew culture (tarbut 'ivrit), in Lo'el, Schimmel exposes what Motti Regev and Edwin Seroussi have described as "the invention of a locally specific, native Jewish culture" (my emphasis) and turns this critique toward his own previous Hebrew writing.[110]

The date also provides a critical vantage point for Schimmel, who had written his first Hebrew poem in 1968, a poem titled "Ha-alfabeita ha-mevurekhet," which Zach proofread.[111] In other words, Lo'el serves the purpose of plotting a literary lineage at the moment when points of origin and affiliation began to shift, in other words, at the moment when this historical narrative is about to revised and reframed. As Cole observes:

> Lowell—within or just beyond the frame of the page—becomes a point of stimulation (or irritation) around which a poem takes shape, but the real subject of the book is a commitment to the tradition of poetry that brings both the developing, always "raw" poet (Schimmel) and the master ... (Lowell) beyond the features of either's style or school.[112]

One of Lo'el's major historical markers is 1973, the publication date of Lowell's History, a major collection of sonnets that begins its "history" with the Greeks and Romans and progresses to Lowell's present day life.[113] History, which reworks poems from earlier collections, opens with the pronouncement: "History has to live with what was here, / clutching and close to fumbling all we had— / it is so dull and gruesome how we die, / unlike writing, life never finishes."[114] The phrase "unlike writing, life never finishes" carries a shade of irony in the context of Lowell's own habit of rewriting and revising poems (sometimes to the consternation of his editors).[115] In fact, Schimmel's *Lo'el* very much relies on the possibility, and promise, of unfinished writing, on revision, rewriting, and translation. A case in point is a poem like #15, one of several texts that originate with Lowell but become, in Schimmel's translation, part of *Lo'el's* expanded history.[116] The fact that Schimmel does not indicate directly when these appropriations have taken place simultaneously affirms the continuity of a (patrilineal) model and asserts a "cannibalistic logic" in its reauthoring of this source material.[117]

#90, for example, sets out to reconstruct an informal poetry reading that took place on the occasion of Lowell's visit to Israel and included the participation of Amichai, Silk, and Schimmel (even the Russian poet Osip Mandelstam has a cameo of sorts). Here, Schimmel once again appropriates and retranslates one of Lowell's translations:

"תִּשְׁמֹר אֶת מִלּוֹתַי לָעַד בְּעַד
טַעְמָן הַשׁוֹהֶה שֶׁל מִסְכֵּנוּת וְעָשָׁן
בְּעַד הַזֶּפֶת שֶׁבָּן שֶׁל סַבְלָנוּת
מְשֻׁתֶּפֶת וְעָמָל נֶאֱמָן   מַיִם בִּבְאֵרוֹת
נוֹבְגוֹרוֹד חַיָּבִים לִהְיוֹת שְׁחוֹרִים וּמְמֻתָּקִים
כְּדֵי לְשַׁקֵּף כּוֹכָב עִם שִׁבְעָה
סַנְפִּירִים בְּחַג הַמּוֹלָד" הַקְרֵאתָ-לָנוּ-אֶת-תַּרְגוּמְךָ-לְמַנְדֶלְשְׁטָם
מֵאוֹתָם-"דַּפִּים-מַצְהִיבִים".
"הוֹ אֶרֶץ אֲבוֹת רֵעִי עוֹזְרִי-הַגֵּס
זְכֹר-נָא אָחִיךָ הַבַּלְתִּי-מְזֹהֶה הַכּוֹפֵר מִמִּשְׁפַּחַת-הָעָם..."
וּכְשֶׁדָנִיס לְאַחַר-מִכֵּן הַקְרִיא אֶת שִׁירוֹ-שֶׁל-עַמִּיחַי: "חֲבָל
הָיִינוּ אַמְצָאָה טוֹבָה" אָמַרְתָּ "סְלִיחָה
פָּשׁוּט-אֵינִי-מֵבִין עַל-מַה-מְדֻבָּר כָּאן" ("רוֹפְאִים כֻּלָּם
הֵם פָּרְקוּ אוֹתָנוּ זוֹ מְזוֹל???")
וְדָנִיס בְּסַבְלָנוּת-הֵשִׁיב "זֶה-שִׁיר-עַל-סוֹף-הָאַהֲבָה!" וִיהוּדָה הִסְמִיק

"Guard my words forever for
their lingering taste of wretchedness and smoke
for their tar of shared patience
and faithful toil   water in the wells
of Novgorod must be black and sweetened

in order to reflect a star with seven
fins on Christmas" you read-us-your-translation-of-Mandelshtam
    from-those same-"yellowing-pages"
"Oh land of the fathers my friend my rough helper
Remember your unidentified brother the heretic from the people's
    family…"
And when Dennis afterwards read the-poem-by-Yehuda: "Too Bad
We Were a Good Invention" you said "Sorry
I-just-don't-understand what-is-being-said here" ("all the doctors
unloaded us one by one???")
And Dennis patiently-replied "it's-a-poem-about-the-end-of-a-love-
    affair!" And Yehuda blushed.

#90 begins with several lines from one of Lowell's translations of an unti-
tled poem by Mandelstam (1891–1938).[118] The untitled poem, which opens
with the line, "Сохрани мою речь навсегда" ("Keep safe my words forever"), is dated 1931 and is addressed to the poet Anna Akhmatova. In
Schimmel's poem, these lines are recited by Lowell, followed by Silk's
reading of an Amichai poem, presumably in English translation for
Lowell's benefit. Given the date of Lowell's visit, it is very possible that
he is reading one of Assia Wevill's translations (which were published
in 1968), but also likely that Silk, a capable translator himself, provides
his own. The poem "Chaval, hayinu amtsa'a tova" ("A Pity, We Were a
Good Invention") appeared a year earlier in the collection *Akhshav ba-
ra'ash: 1963–1968* (*Now in the Storm*).[119] Rewriting my translation of #90,
with the inclusion of Lowell's English translation of Mandelstam's poem,
as well as Wevill's Amichai (assuming that her translation was read),
produces the following text[120]:

"Preserve my words forever for
    their aftertaste of misfortune and smoke,
for their tar of collective patience
and conscientious work—water in the wells
of Novgorod must be black and sweetened
to reflect a star with seven
fins at Christmas" you read-to-us-your-translation-of-Mandelshtam
    from-those-same-"yellowing-pages"

"Oh my Fatherland, my friend, my rough helper,
remember your unrecognized brother, the apostate from the
    people's family..."
And when Dennis afterwards read the-poem-by-Yehuda: "A Pity.
We were a Good Invention" you said "Sorry
I-just-don't-understand what-is-being-said here" ("surgeons. All
    of them they dismantled us each from the other???")
And Dennis patiently-replied "it's-a-poem-about-the-end-of-a-love-
affair!" And Yehuda blushed.

Inserting Lowell's and Wevill's words—rather than retranslating these passages from poem—reveals an interesting modification of Amichai's poem, which suggests either that Lowell is incorrectly paraphrasing what he has heard or that it has been mistranslated for him. The original line in Hebrew "Rofim. kulam. / Hem perku otanu / ze mi-zo" translates more or less literally as "Doctors. All of them. / They took us apart from one another." This further informs the reader that Wevill takes some liberty in rendering "rofim" as "surgeons," most likely with the understanding of "taking apart" as a kind of surgery. What Schimmel has Lowell say, however, is "they unloaded us from one another," modifying Amichai's *perku* (they broke apart) so that it reads as *parku* (they unloaded). This slight change in vocalization completely alters the meaning of the poem's key line. Whereas the Hebrew poem expresses the end of a romance as an amputation, Lowell's words characterize the end of the love affair as the release of a burden. This rewritten/retranslated line must also be read in the context of *Lo'el* and its preoccupation with tradition and influence. With this mistranslation, Schimmel in effect projects his own desire to unload his predecessor and to rewrite him, an act that also allows him to unload the self-mythologizing revisions of his earlier Hebrew collections.

Finally, I return these lines to their "source":

"Сохрани мою речь навсегда за
привкус несчастья и дыма
За смолу кругового терпенья
за совестный деготь труда   Как вода в
новгородских колодцах должна быть черна и сладима
отразилась семью плавниками звезда

הִקְרֵאתָ-לָנוּ-אֶת-תַּרְגּוּמְךָ-לְמַנְדֶלְשְׁטָם "Чтобы в ней к Рождеству
מֵאוֹתָם-דַּפִּים-מַצְהִיבִים

"И за это, отец мой, мой друг и помощник мой грубый
Я—непризнанный брат, отщепенец в народной семье..."

וּכְשֶׁדָּנִים לְאַחַר-מִכֵּן הַקְרִיא אֶת-שִׁירוֹ-שֶׁל-עֲמִיחַי: "חֲבָל
"Sorry   הָיִינוּ אַמְצָאָה טוֹבָה" אָמְרְתְּ
I-just-don't-understand what-is-being-said here" ("all the doctors
unloaded us one by one???")
וְדָנִים בְּסַבְלָנוּת-הֵשִׁיב "it's-a-poem-about-the-end-of-a-love-affair!"
וִיהוּדָה הִסְמִיק

Isolating the English dialogue in this fashion has the effect of casting Lowell as a clueless bystander. What is more, his inability to understand Amichai's love poem deflates his status, now he is the student patiently educated by the younger poets for whom he has served as a mentor and paragon. In fact, this deflation is hinted at in the very title of the book—in Hebrew, *lo el* means "not a god." Moreover, recomposing the poem with the original source texts materializes the considerable space that Mandelstam's poem—and specifically Lowell's translation of the poem—takes up in Schimmel's poem, a space that Schimmel then claims for himself in his Hebrew retranslations of this material. Indeed, the line "preserve my words forever" lies at the heart of the translations and retranslations that both Lowell and Schimmel engage. Through translation, Mandelstam is carried from Russia to Boston/New York to Israel, from Russian to English to Hebrew. The "collective patience" (кругового терпенья, "all-encompassing patience") in Mandelstam's poem echoes in Silk's "patient" explanation of Amichai's poem. Now it is the father who receives instruction, who is asked, through Schimmel's retranslation, to "guard my words."

It is through such acts of translation and retranslation, that is, writing and rewriting, that Schimmel's *Lo'el* advances its own "partly self-sufficient" narrative, all the while marking the traces of its predecessors.[121] But the injunction *tishmor et milotai* (preserve my words) that lies at the heart of the translations that Schimmel engages in *Lo'el* not only is a call to remember the languages of one's predecessors but also can be projected onto the translingual Hebrew poet himself, for whom translating and writing poetry are intertwined modes for "preserving" his many languages. What emerges from these practices, in Schimmel's words (which are also Lowell's), "is one true voice in our poems/a poem that must gather one's contradictions."[122]

Afterword
Every Poem a Translation

In the past fifteen years, translation has emerged as a vital site of cultural, creative, and political engagement for contemporary Hebrew poets.[1] Publishing houses in Israel continue to steadily publish translations from various languages and time periods at increasing rates, but the bulk of translation activity, particularly poetry in translation, happens outside of the book publishing market.[2] The number of Israeli literary journals interested in translation has grown in the past decade, resulting in an active but varied translation activity that often coincides with the aesthetic and political positions and spaces these journals claim. However, journals such as *Ho!*, *Daka*, *Mita'am*, *Dechak*, and many others also embrace translation as an art—that is, as a creative and generative practice—which is given a primary status alongside original Hebrew works and criticism. In fact, these translations are often tied very closely to the original poetry that appears in each journal, engaging in a linguistic, cultural, and transhistoric dialogue that develops from one issue to another.[3]

I want to highlight here the journal *Daka*, which ran between 2007 and 2012 under the editorship of Roni Hirsch, Boaz Yaniv, and Eran Tzelgov. *Daka*, which means "thin" and "light" in Hebrew, offered an economic selection of texts, made even more so by its commitment to publishing non-Hebrew texts; however, the word *daka* also means "a minute"—and, indeed, the editors' commitment to currency was evident in its content of new writing and new translations. *Daka* broke into print with a desire "to find the magic that was lost, buried and shoved into bow-tied basements, sweaty classrooms, and books that no one opened. To return to poetry the energy of a rock concert and carnival spectacle, the language of the street."[4] Though *Daka* went into permanent hiatus several years ago, it remains one of the very few Hebrew literary journals in Israel to include original texts alongside translations (*Ho!* does so as well). This did not apply to its critical essays, but it was consistently applied to poetry, a decision that prompted one literary critic to ask "why waste ... precious pages on foreign poems in their original language?"[5] Implicit in this criticism is the privileging of Hebrew original works over foreign languages, disregarding the fact that contemporary Israeli literature is multilingual; there is no shortage of readers in Israel for poetry in a foreign language, and particularly so for the languages from which *Daka* translated—Spanish, Arabic, Russian, and English. In a preface to his Hebrew translation of Octavio Paz's classic essay "Traducción: literatura y literalidad" ("Translation: Literature and Literality"), Tzelgov cites and translates Paz's assertion that "all writing is translation" in relation to *Daka*'s mission: "In order to awaken and stimulate renewed interest and new tastes, every issue of *Daka* includes new voices in Hebrew literature alongside veteran voices. Voices that were written in Hebrew as well as voices translated into Hebrew."[6] That a journal with modest retail space included texts in foreign languages could be understood as a critique of Israel's economic, housing, and ethnic politics. By giving space to non-Hebrew poems, *Daka* made the space of translation visible and material, even if doing so meant showcasing one less Hebrew poem—a radical, transformative act in a country where space remains so deeply contentious and politicized.

The journal *Ho!*, edited by the poet and translator Dory Manor, recently dedicated its thirteenth issue to "world poetry" in translation, part of its ongoing and polemical commitment to literary translation that began with its 2005 debut issue. For a number of *Ho!*'s regular contributors, translating and writing are reciprocal practices, and it is not unusual to find both translation and original writing by the same contributor in a single issue. One whose work stands out among these poets and translators is Anna Herman, author of three collections of poetry and translator of Sylvia Plath's journals.[7] Herman practices a poetics of remixing, drawing imagery and texts from an array of Hebrew authors as well as the poets she has translated. Her work also participates in the neoformalist turn that has become one of the hallmarks of *Ho!*, with Herman being among its most adroit and inventive practitioners. For Herman, form is a productive constraint; the familiarity and comfort of rhyme and meter provide a meaningful contrast to the unsettling narratives that circulate in her poems. In *Sefer ha-refu'ot ha-peshutot* (*The Book of Simple Remedies*), the poem "Ha-yefefiya ha-nama" ("Sleeping Beauty"), for example, rewrites the familiar, old tale, but sharply turns into a reflection on Plath's suicide, in soothing rhyming couplets that settle on the ear like a dark lullaby. Herman's commitment to prosody and form not only rejects the colloquialism that prevailed in Israeli poetry through the 1990s but also encourages daring and unexpected juxtapositions in her work, establishing formal relations, which she weaves deftly together, between Hebrew and English, Beethoven and George Michael, and medieval myths and the news of the day. This remixing indicates the extent to which prosody is not only an aesthetic choice but also one with social and ideological implications, which also carry into the poems that Herman translates.

Herman closes *Sefer ha-refu'ot ha-peshutot* with a translation of "Mariana," a poem by the English poet Alfred Lord Tennyson (1809–1892).[8] Originally published in his volume *Poems, Chiefly Lyrical* (1830), "Mariana" treats the subject of social isolation from the perspective of a woman waiting in vain for her lover's return, a recurrent figure in several Tennyson poems.[9] The idea for the poem and the figure of Mariana herself came from Shakespeare's play *Measure for Measure*, though Shakespeare's Mariana meets a happier fate.[10] In Tennyson's poem, Mariana acknowledges that "he" will never return, and the reader understands that Mariana's social estrangement will remain unchanged as well. All around her, the physical landscape—very English in Tennyson's poem—shows signs of wear and breakdown but Mariana's isolation remains resolute. Herman's Hebrew translation retains the original poem's prosody (seven twelve-line stanzas in iambic tetrameter following an ababcddcefef rhyme scheme) and remains more or less faithful to the narrative structure of the poem, but images that shape Tennyson's specifically English sense of place take on new relations when recast into Herman's contemporary Hebrew.

The first stanza, for instance, tells us that Mariana can be found "upon the lonely moated grange," a modified, intertextual reference to Shakespeare's play, where one character observes that "there, at the moated/grange, resides this dejected Mariana."[11] In Herman's translation, the line, repeated a few times in the poem, becomes "me'al oto beit-kfar chiger," over the same dilapidated (more literally, "lame," "unstable") village home. In English, the word "moated" means to surround a structure or space with a deep, water-filled ditch, the kind that often surrounded and fortified a medieval town, fortress, or castle against attack. A "grange" is a farm or country house, but in Herman's Hebrew, the "beit-kfar" refers specifically to a village home, a translation that excludes any references to fortifications. To my ear, the Hebrew "me'al oto" is meant to echo the English "moated," a word that is otherwise unavailable in

Hebrew. Herman must work around this, and the inevitable differences in translation result in new relations in rhyme. Herman's "chiger" derives from the Semitic root for "gird," a meaning that carries into its modern usage, but as an adjective—which is how, I argue, it appears in her translation—it can mean "lame" or "handicapped" (and "halting" and "hesitating," when it refers to speech or ways of moving). In Tennyson's poem, "grange" rhymes with "strange," suggesting the image of a "strange grange." But Herman's "chiger" rhymes with the verb "lehishaber," "to be broken." Whereas "moated grange" emphasizes Mariana's isolation, Herman's translation fixes our attention on the state of Mariana's home, a place that, not unlike its inhabitant, is falling apart and decomposing.

Tennyson's "Mariana" concludes as follows: "Then, said she, 'I am very dreary,/He will not come,' she said; / She wept, 'I am aweary, aweary,/ O God, that I were dead!' While Tennyson's final lines echo the poem's refrain, Herman's translation offers a very different closure:[12]

הִיא שָׂחָה: "לֵאוּתִי גּוֹבֶרֶת,
וְהוּא שׁוּב לֹא יַחְזֹר.
הוֹי אֲדֹנָי, אוֹתִי כְּוֶרֶד
בְּחֵיק הַמָּוֶת שְׂזֹר!"

She said: "My weariness grows
But he won't come back again.
Oh Lord, like a rose
wrap me around death's breast!"

(l. 81-84)

Needless to say, there is no rose in Tennyson's "Mariana" though there are many in other poems he composed, notably "Maud," "The Roses on the Terrace," and "The Gardener's Daughter."[13] The rose emerges only in Herman's translation, perhaps as a figure of translation, a souvenir of this encounter with Tennyson's poem and the process of reanimating it in translation.

Tennyson's "Mariana" has inspired numerous works in literature and the visual arts, but most of these interpretations have been by male artists (those by John Everett Millais and W. E. F. Britten are among the most prominent).[14] So what does it mean for Herman to translate this poem, a poem whose very protagonist carries her own name (Mari-ana)? The poem is clear about the state of decomposition in which Mariana finds herself: this is a place where no flowers bloom, where no roses grow. The flowerpots are cracked and covered in moss, and yet, at the end of Herman's "Mariana," there is a rose, a figure of transient beauty and vitality, yet preserved in the translated poem like an offering from the (female) translator.

✦ ✦ ✦

When I first conceived of this project, I brought Esther Raab, Leah Goldberg, Avot Yeshurun, and Harold Schimmel together around translational affinities that I discerned in their work and that offered rich possibilities for a comparative reading. Schimmel had produced substantive translations of Raab and Yeshurun, so bringing these three poets together accorded with a translated-centered reading. The inclusion of Goldberg, one of the more prolific Hebrew translators of the twentieth century, felt appropriate; though (at that early stage) I had not come across any translations by Schimmel of Goldberg's poetry, I had a feeling that Goldberg may have been among the poets that Schimmel had translated. Maybe this was prompted by poem #81 in *Lo'el*, which describes Lowell getting drunk at a party and pinching Goldberg "in the kitchen" (to which she responds, "the nerve of these goyim/who drink themselves into a stupor and 'don't see a thing'").[15] Or maybe it was something in Schimmel's own poetry, particularly the sonnets of *Lo'el*, that suggested that Goldberg was among the poets that he had studied closely, through translation. My answer came in the form of a short essay in *Orot*, a multilingual journal edited by Ada Zemach and published by the World Zionist Organization between 1950 and 1973.[16] A search online had turned up the title of an essay in Hebrew—"Lea Goldberg hameshoreret"—and, as was the practice for *Orot*, the essay also appeared in a facing English version, though the question of which language came first remains open-ended. When I acquired a copy of the journal, I was able to verify that it included a selection of Goldberg's poems in both Hebrew and English.[17] The editor states clearly, "Harold Schimmel translated them."

Schimmel's essay is an elegy for Goldberg, who had died earlier that year, and opens with a Dahlia Ravikovitch poem on Goldberg's funeral, around which Schimmel gathers reflections on Goldberg's legacy in both Hebrew and world literature.[18] "Lea Goldberg's career offered the possibility of a true discipleship," Schimmel writes, "It is the naturalness with which she assumed the role of poet that has allowed others to follow without self-consciousness and without any 'burden' of debt."[19] The essay is a touching mix of astute commentary on the poet's oeuvre as well as references to personal details—Goldberg's "cigarillo" and "the Russian colouring in her Hebrew (highly unShlonskeyesque)"— which, brought together, construct an intimate portrait of the poet. Schimmel is attentive to how much a poet gathers in her work and from how far some of these sources are drawn (the "foreign decorum in her poems").[20]

Of course, translation has something to do with this, as Schimmel observes: "If the Dostoyevskian novel left its mark on the Russian poets of the turn of the century, it can likewise be argued that the influence of prose translations into Hebrew of the '20s and '30s is more to be reckoned with in tracing the development of Hebrew Poetry than any number of Waste Lands, and Twelves."[21] Schimmel acknowledges Goldberg's own role in making this so, making the case that relations between Goldberg's translation activity, and specifically her translations of prose, can be discerned in her descriptive language and imagery. Ruebner, in his introduction to a collection of Goldberg's translations of poetry, makes a similar point when he draws attention to the relation between Goldberg's original poems and the poems she translated.[22] But these translational movements are also fundamental to poetic language, as Goldberg herself acknowledged in the poem "Al atsmi" ("About Myself"), which Schimmel cites and translates in this essay: "[T]hings came up to me/commanded me: sing./They said: we are words/I yielded and sang them."[23] In other words, poetry is translation.

Throughout this book, I have addressed the productive and creative speculations that are activated in the orbit of translation, and I will conclude now with one more example drawn from Schimmel's translation of Goldberg's 1955 poem "Milim achronot" ("Last Words"). In this poem, Goldberg's speaker compares herself to an anonymous eighth-century poet who sat "on the banks of the Yellow River."[24] The speaker is writing "the last line of the poem," but this act appears at the beginning of the poem, which continues for many more lines. The eighth-century poet, on the other hand, "knew the word of closure." But what this word is we are not told—the poem, it becomes clear, is deferring its own ending.[25]

Goldberg does not tell us who this eighth-century poet is, but Li Bai is a strong possibility. This identification is further reinforced by Schimmel's own affiliation with late Anglo-American modernism and his readings of Pound, whose interest in Li Bai (or Li Po in Pound's preferred transliteration) has been well documented in poems like "The River Merchant's Wife" (an adaptation of Li Bai's "Two Letters from Chang Kan") and the following "epitaph": "And Li Po also died drunk. / He tried to embrace a moon/In the Yellow River."[26] The probable cause of death aside, the question remains whether or not Goldberg has a specific poem by Li Bai, or another "8th century poet," in mind. One possibility is Li Bai's "Hard Road," where the speaker faces a psychological impasse or crossroads, illustrated in the poem in terms of natural borders (snow, ice): "Traveling is hard!/Traveling is hard!/ So many forks in the road— / which one to take?"[27] Unable to move forward or back, or rather deciding not to, the speaker sits down, drops a fishing hook in the water, and allows his mind to wander. The poem closes with the line "I hoist my sail into the clouds and cross the mighty ocean." If this closure offers a way out, it does so in a way that remains open-ended and uncertain, which is apt for a poem like Goldberg's, which is concerned with the question, which repeats throughout this cycle, "[W]hat will our end be?"

In poetry of the Tang Dynasty, the Yellow River often represents a border between past and present, youth and old age, and home and exile, themes that run throughout Goldberg's oeuvre. In "Crossing the Yellow River," Wang Wei, another venerated poet of this era, also observes the Yellow River as a space marking the separation between one home and another: "Look back on the old country: wide waters; clouds; and rising mist."[28] This line echoes the lines "haya sheleg be-erets achat/ve-dardar be-erets acheret" in Goldberg's "About Myself" ("snow in one country/thistle in another" in the *Orot* version).[29] The space between two homelands, as I argue in chapter 3, is a space of translation. It represents that space that Anne Carson has described as a "bottomless pit," where the poet/translator faces "that space between the word you're at and the word you can't get to."[30] But this void and chaos is a space of creation, of infinite possibilities. In this space, Goldberg writes, there is the possibility that a "yellow buttercup" (*nurit tsehuba*) will grow on "our grave." This yellow buttercup, which grows abundantly in Israel, represents a creative potential that continues long after the poem has ended. Like the rose in Herman's "Mariana," it is a translational figure, mediating between past and present, between life and death, and between the text and its ending. It is in this respect, as Walter Benjamin famously noted, that translation is afterlife.[31]

Placing translation at the center of a reading of modern Hebrew poetry allows its borders and branches to extend and multiply, like Raab's *gidul pere*, widely and wildly. The poetic map that Schimmel ascribed to Yeshurun stretches to accommodate new coordinates and new languages.

This book extends this map to include Raab, Goldberg, and Schimmel himself, as well as Charles Baudelaire, Germaine Beaumont, Petrarca, Rainer Maria Rilke, Robert Lowell, Emily Dickinson, the poets of Al-Andalus, and a lost Yiddish poem. In *Strange Cocktail*, I propose one constellation. But constellations are not fixed in space. From where you are sitting, many other configurations are possible.

Notes

Introduction

1. Avraham Kariv (1900–1976) was born in Slabodka (then in Lithuania) and studied at the Teacher's Seminary in Odessa, where the poet Chaim Nachman Bialik was among his teachers and an early supporter of his poetry. He was the author of numerous essay collections, poetry books, and works of translation, and also edited the journals *Dvar* and *Moznayim* for a number of years. He was one of the recipients of the Bialik Prize for Literature in 1973.

2. Leah Goldberg, *Yomanei Leah Goldberg* [Diaries], ed. Rachel and Arieh Aharoni. Bnei-Brak: Sifriyat po'alim -Ha-kibbuts ha-me'uchad, 2005, 318.

3. In this book, I employ the following three terms when referring to the years before the establishment of the State of Israel: Ottoman Palestine (until 1917, the region under control of the Ottoman Empire), Mandatory Palestine (1917–1948, the region under control of the British Mandate of Palestine) and *Yishuv* (the Hebrew term that broadly refers to Jewish settlement in the region until 1948). Occasionally, I use the term "pre-Statehood period" to refer to the years preceding 1948, the year when the Jewish Agency of Israel declared independence, thereby establishing the State of Israel. In this book, I generally refer to the poets featured in the chapters that follow as "modern Hebrew" poets as the term spans both the pre-State and Statehood periods. The term "Israeli literature" refers specifically to post-1948 literature and also includes texts that are not written in Hebrew.

4. Kariv's translation was based on the version that appeared in Tolstoy's collected works.

5. Karen Grumberg addresses this episode in her reading of Goldberg's play "Ba'alat ha-armon" [The Lady of the Castle] and in the context of the tension between aestheticism and realism in modern Hebrew literature of this period. Grumberg, "Gothic Temporalities and Insecure Sanctuaries in Lea Goldberg's *The Lady of the Castle* and Edgar Allan Poe's 'Masque of the Red Death,'" *Comparative Literature*, vol. 68, no. 4 (2016): 408–426.

6. See Rachel Seelig, "The Middleman: Ludwig Strauss's German-Hebrew Bilingualism," *Prooftexts*, vol. 33, no. 1 (Winter 2013): 76−104. Lina Barouch and Galili Shahar recount the story of this friendship in their introduction to a special issue on Strauss, "Arie Ludwig Strauss: Between Hölderlin and Yehuda Halevi," *Naharaim*, vol. 8, no. 2 (2014): 246−252.

7. Aharon Appelfeld, *The Story of a Life*, trans. Aloma Halter (New York: Schocken Books, 2004), 149.

8. "Avraham Kariv," *Leksikon ha-sifrut ha-'ivrit*, https://library.osu.edu/projects/hebrew-lexicon/01261.php.

9. Chana Kronfeld, *On the Margins of Modernism: Decentering Literary Dynamics* (Berkeley: University of California Press, 1996), 59.

10. Most of the examples in the following chapter draw from Western, Central, and Eastern European contexts, but in the Americas, particularly in the United States, translation was also an important practice for modern Hebrew writers. Alan Mintz addresses this fact in his monumental study of American Hebrew literature, and notably in his discussion of Abraham Regelson, who regarded his Hebrew translations (of John Milton and others) as creative works equal to his own original Hebrew writing. Mintz, *Sanctuary in the Wilderness: A Critical Introduction to American Hebrew Poetry* (Stanford: Stanford University Press, 2012), 318.

11. For a fuller discussion on the national status of poetry, see the introduction to Miryam Segal's *A New Sound in Hebrew Poetry: Poetics, Politics, Accent* (Bloomington: Indiana University Press, 2010). Published in *Prooftexts* in Mintz's English translation, Judith Bar-El's "The National Poet: The Emergence of a Concept in Hebrew Literary Criticism (1885–1905)" remains one of the more illuminating accounts of the modern history of Hebrew poetry's national status (*Prooftexts*, vol. 6, no. 3 [September 1986]: 205–220). A Hebrew version of this article was later published in her posthumous collection of essays. Bar-El, "Ha-meshorer ha-le'umi: 'Aliyato shel musag be-bikoret ha-sifrut ha-'ivrit," in *Berakhot shel ketifa: masot u-mekhkarim 'al ha-sifrut ha-'ivrit ha-chadasha* [With Velvet Softness: Studies in Modern Hebrew Literature], ed. Matti Huss and Hannan Hever (Jerusalem: Mossad Bialik, 2009), 158–174.

12. Benjamin Harshav, *The Polyphony of Jewish Culture* (Stanford: Stanford University Press, 2007).

13. Harold Schimmel, "Translator's Foreword," in *The Syrian African-Rift and Other Poems* (Philadelphia: Jewish Publication Society of America, 1980), xx. I discuss these translations in further detail in chapter 4.

14. Matthew Reynolds is also concerned with a tendency in translation studies to read translation within theoretical frameworks that translations either support or disprove, rather than to draw a theory of translation *from* the relations that motivate translation in the first place and are in turn created *by* and *in* translation. Reynolds, *The Poetry of Translation* (Oxford: Oxford University Press, 2011), 38.

15. Ehud Ben-Ezer, *Yamim shel la'ana u-devash* [Days of Gall and Honey] (Tel Aviv:'Am'oved, 1998), 267.

16. Esther Raab, "Milim ke-tsiporim nedirot" ["Words Like Rare Birds"], *Kol ha-proza* [Collected Prose], ed. Ehud Ben-Ezer (Hod ha-sharon: Astrolog, 2001), 419.

17. See Anne-Isabelle François, "The Mother Tongue as Border," in *Minding Borders: Resilient Divisions in Literature, the Body and the Academy*, ed. Nicola Gardini, Adriana X. Jacobs, Ben Morgan, Mohamed-Salah Omri, and Matthew Reynolds (Oxford: Legenda, 2017), 115–134.

18. Zali Gurevitch, "The Double Site of Israel," *Grasping Land: Space and Place in Contemporary Israeli Discourse and Experience*, ed. Eyal Ben-Ari and Yoram Bilu (Albany: State University of New York, 1997), 208.

19. For Goldberg,"Europe" encompassed primarily Western and Central Europe (and Italy and Germany in particular), though her work, as chapter 3 shows, was also closely affiliated with the Russian tradition.

20. See Walter Benjamin,"The Task of the Translator" ["Die Aufgabe des Übersetzers"] *Walter Benjamin: Selected Writings, Vol. 1, 1913–1926*, trans. Harry Zohn, ed. Marcus Bullock and Michael W. Jennings (Cambridge, MA: Belknap Press of Harvard University Press, 2004), 253–263; Theodor W. Adorno,"On the Use of Foreign Words," in *Notes to Literature* [Noten zur Literatur], vol. 2, trans. Shierry Weber Nicholsen, ed. Rolf Tiedmann (New York: Columbia University Press, 1992), 286–291; Jacques Derrida, *Monolingualism of the Other or the Prosthesis of Origin* [Le monolinguisme de l'autre, ou, La prothèse d'origine], trans. Patrick Mensah (Stanford: Stanford University Press, 1998).

21. David Wills, *Prosthesis* (Stanford: Stanford University Press, 1995), 9.

22. Harold Schimmel, *Lo'el* [Lowell] (Tel Aviv: Chadarim, 1986), ii. See also, Yochai Oppenheimer,"Be-makom afus:'al shirat Harold Shimel" [In a Vacant Place: On Harold Schimmel's Poetry], *Chadarim*, vol. 7 (1988): 86–99.

23. Reynolds, *The Poetry of Translation*.

24. Roman Jakobson,"On the Linguistic Aspects of Translation," in *The Translation Studies Reader*, ed. Lawrence Venuti (London: Routledge-Taylor & Francis, 1959/2000), 114.

25. Ibid., 118.

26. Oswald de Andrade,"Manifesto antropófago" ("Cannibal Manifesto"), *Revista de antropofagia*, vol. 1, no. 1 (May 1928): 3, 7.

27. Octavio Paz,"Translation: Literature and Letters," trans. Irene del Corral, *Theories of Translation: An Anthology of Essays from Dryden to Derrida*, ed. Rainer Schulte and John Biguenet (Chicago: University of Chicago Press, 1995), 154.

28. Itamar Even-Zohar,"The Position of Translated Literature within the Literary Polysystem," *The Translation Studies Reader*, 193. In fact, Roman Jakobson delivered the Institute's inaugural lectures in March 1975. See also Even-Zohar,"Polysystem Theory," *Poetics Today*, vol. 1, no. 1–2 (1979): 287–310; and Gideon Toury,"The Nature and Role of Norms in Translation," *The Translation Studies Reader*, 198–211.

29. Along with the poet Tal Nitzán, Dykman was awarded the 2012 Tchernichovsky Prize for translation, one of many accolades he has received for his translation corpus.

30. Shimon Sandbank, *Shtei brekhot ba-ya'ar: kesharim u-makbilot bein ha-shira ha-'ivrit ve-ha-shira ha-eiropit* [Two Pools in the Wood: Hebrew Poetry and the European Tradition] (Tel Aviv: Ha-kibbuts ha-me'uchad, 1976).

31. Walter Benjamin, "The Task of the Translator," *Walter Benjamin: Selected Writings, Vol. 1, 1913–1926*, trans. Harry Zohn, ed. Marcus Bullock and Michael W. Jennings (Cambridge, MA: Belknap Press of Harvard University Press, 2004), 254. The editors significantly modified Zohn's translation of this passage.

32. Gayatri Chakravorty Spivak, "The Politics of Translation," *Outside the Teaching Machine* (New York: Routledge, 1993), 189.

33. Roy Hasan, "Medinat Ashkenaz," *Ha-klavim she-navchu be-yalduteinu hayu chasumei pe* [The Dogs that Barked in Our Childhood Were Muzzled] (Tel Aviv: Tangier Press, 2014), 46–48. This poem first appeared in *Haaretz* (October 31, 2013): http://www.haaretz.co.il/literature/poetry/.premium-1.2151769.

34. For example, Schimmel's Hebrew-reworking of the Arabic *qasida* began to develop in the early 1990s with the publication of his aphoristic essay "Katsida" in *Chadarim*. Harold Schimmel, "Katsida" ["Qasida"], *Chadarim* 10 (1993): 65–80. For an English translation, see Harold Schimmel, *Qasida*, trans. Peter Cole (Jerusalem: Ibis Editions, 1997). Schimmel's 2009 collection *Katsida* (Jerusalem: Carmel Press) gathers this essay as well as several Hebrew *katsidot* composed over the last two decades.

35. See Monique R. Balbuena, *Homeless Tongues: Poetry and Languages of the Sephardic Diaspora* (Stanford: Stanford University Press, 2016); and Lital Levy *Poetic Trespass: Writing between Hebrew and Arabic in Israel and Palestine* (Princeton: Princeton University Press, 2014).

36. Almog Behar, "'Al *Ha-kivun ve-Ho!*: Betokh ha-isre'eliyut u-michuts la" ["Israeliness from the Inside and Beyond"], *Teoria u-vikoret*, vol. 35 (Fall 2009): 264.

37. Reynolds, *The Poetry of Translation*, 6.

38. Jacques Derrida, "Des Tours de Babel," trans. Joseph F. Graham, *Acts of Religion*, ed. Gil Anidjar (New York: Routledge-Taylor & Francis, 2002), 108. Derrida's translator, David Wills, also observed how Derrida's own multilingual, translational prose activated the idea of *a priori* translation. Wills, "Two Words *Pro*-Derrida," Tympanum, vol. 4 (2000), np.

39. Gentzler, "The Poetics of Translation," in *Routledge Encyclopedia of Translation Studies*, ed. Mona Baker (London: Routledge, 1998), 167.

40. In fact, Gentzler calls attention to the "often subjective and eclectic approaches of literary translators," which, he surmises, pose a challenge to advancing a more coherent poetics of translation. (Notably, the 2008 revised edition of this encyclopedia does not include this entry.) Ibid., 168.

41. The term "echo chamber" recurs in many of Alter's writings on Hebrew literature. For an extensive application of the term, see Robert Alter, *Hebrew and Modernity* (Bloomington: Indiana University Press, 1994).

42. For Harshav's definition of "fusion language" and how it applies to Israeli Hebrew, see Benjamin Harshav, "Remarks on the Nature of Israeli Hebrew," *Language in the Time of Revolution* (Berkeley: University of California Press, 1993), 167–172.

43. Kronfeld, *The Full Severity of Compassion: The Poetry of Yehuda Amichai* (Stanford: Stanford University Press, 2016), 175.

44. Jahan Ramazani, "A Transnational Poetics," *American Literary History* (2006): 333.

45. Homi Bhabha, *The Location of Culture* (New York: Routledge, 1994), 6. Emphasis in original.

46. See Lital Levy, "Self-Portraits of the Other: Toward a Palestinian Poetics of Hebrew Verse," in *Transforming Loss into Beauty: Essays in Honor of Magda al-Nowaihi*, ed. Marlé Hammond and Dana Sajdi (Cairo: American University in Cairo Press, 2008), 343–402.

47. Anuradha Dingwaney, "Introduction: Translating 'Third World' Cultures," in *Between Languages and Cultures: Translation and Cross Cultural Texts*, ed. Anuradha Dingwaney and Carol Meier (Pittsburgh: University of Pittsburgh Press, 1998), 8.

48. Maria Tymoczko, "Ideology and the Position of the Translator: In What Sense Is a Translator 'In Between?'" in *Critical Readings in Translation Studies*, ed. Mona Baker (New York: Routledge, 2010), 217.

49. Ibid., 225.

50. Chana Kronfeld, *The Full Severity of Compassion*, 175–178. Kronfeld first presented her reading and translation of this poem at a conference dedicated to the work of Amichai, which took place at Yale University in 2007. Kronfeld, "Making Honey from all the Buzz and Babble: Translation as Metaphor in the Poetry of Yehuda Amichai," Poetics and Politics in Yehuda Amichai's World, Yale University, October 21, 2007. See also Kronfeld, "Ha-meshorer ki-metargem be-shirat Amichai" ["The Poet as Translator in Amichai's Poetry"], *Ot*, vol. 3 (2013): 5–20.

51. Amichai, "Ve-lo nitlahev," in *Shirei Yehuda Amichai*, vol. 1 (Jerusalem: Schocken, 2002), 313; Amichai, *The Poetry of Yehuda Amichai*, ed. Robert Alter (New York: Farrar, Straus and Giroux, 2015), 77.

52. Kronfeld's work on Amichai brought to my attention the scholarship of William W. Hallo, from which I have drawn this summary. William W. Hallo, *Origins: The Ancient Near Eastern Background of Some Modern Western Institutions* (New York: Brill Academic, 1996).

53. Kronfeld, "Translation as Metaphor in the Poetry of Yehuda Amichai."

54. The relation between writing, translating, and recycling is prominent in the poem "Conferences, Conferences: Malignant Words, Benign Speech," which contains the line "The translators sit and recycle it all to another/recycling plan that has

no end." The following line contains an allusion to Genesis 1:2, thereby suggesting a relation between this labor and the originary act of creation. Yehuda Amichai, *Open Closed Open*, trans. Chana Bloch and Chana Kronfeld (New York: Harcourt Books, 2000), 147.

55. For a feminist critique of this model, see Michael Gluzman "The Exclusion of Women from Hebrew Literary History," *Prooftexts*, vol. 11, no. 3 (1991): 259–278.

56. Babylonian Talmud, *Berakhot* 7a; Rabbi Isidore Epstein, ed., *Halakhah.com: The online Soncino Bablyonian Talmud* (London: Soncino Press, 1938–1961): http://www.halakhah.com.

57. Ibid.

58. Exodus 34:29.

59. Harshav, *The Polyphony of Jewish Culture*, 178.

60. Babylonian Talmud, *Nidda* 31a; Rabbi Isidore Epstein, ed., *Halakhah.com: The online Soncino Bablyonian Talmud* (London: Soncino Press, 1938–1961): http://www.halakhah.com.

61. Babylonian Talmud, *Nidda* 30b.

62. Babylonian Talmud, *Nidda* 31a; emphasis added. I have taken the Hebrew text from *Vikitekst*, an online textual repository of Hebrew texts: https://he.wikisource.org/wiki/תלמוד_בבלי.

63. Nili Scharf Gold uncovered in Amichai's archives a German draft of "Ve-lo nit-lahev" that appears to predate the Hebrew version. Her reading of the Hebrew poem compares both texts, elucidating the persistent influence of German on his Hebrew poetry. Scharf Gold, *Yehuda Amichai: The Making of Israel's National Poet* (Waltham, MA: Brandeis University Press, 2008): 120–121.

64. Gilles Deleuze and Félix Guattari, *Kafka: Toward a Minor Literature*, trans. Dana Polan (Minneapolis: University of Minnesota Press, 1986).

65. This poem appeared in the 1989 collection *Gam ha-egrof haya pa'am yad petucha ve-etsba'ot* [Even a Fist Was Once an Open Palm with Fingers]. Yehuda Amichai, *Shirei Yehuda Amichai*, vol. 5 (Tel Aviv: Schocken, 2004), 30–31; "The Migration of Peoples," trans. Barbara and Benjamin Harshav, in *A Life of Poetry, 1948–1994* (New York: HarperCollins, 1994): 414–415.

66. Amichai's published German–Hebrew translations include Hermann Hesse's *Wanderung* (Nidudim, 1978), poems by Else Lasker-Schuler (Shirim, 1969), Rolf Hochhuth's play *Der Stellvertreter* (Memale ha-makom, 1964), and *Das schönste Ei der Welt* by children's author Helme Heine (Ha-beitsa ha-yafa be-yoter ba-'olam, 1987). He also collaborated with Shlomo Vinner on an English–Hebrew translation of the American poet Howard Schwartz's *Vessels* (Kelim, 1978). In chapter 5, I briefly discuss Amichai's Hebrew translation of an early English poem by Schimmel. Scholars and translators of Amichai's work, notably Nili Scharf Gold and, more recently, Natasha Gordinsky, have shown how translation mediates between Hebrew and German, Amichai's native language (he was born Ludwig Pfeuffer in Würzburg, Germany), in his poetry.

67. I discuss these more recent developments in my article, "Ho! and the Transnational Turn in Contemporary Israeli Poetry," Special Issue on Jewish/World Literature, *Prooftexts*, vol. 36, no. 1–2 (2017): 137–166.

Chapter 1

1. Yaakov Shteinberg, "Hirhurai ('al ha-tirgumim)" ["Reflections: On Translation"], *Ha-arets ve-ha-'avoda*, vol. 5 (January/February, 1919): 45.

2. The Haskala was a European intellectual movement that roughly spanned the late eighteenth century to the late nineteenth century. Inspired in part by the European Enlightenment, modern Hebrew literature began to develop in this period as a secular literature, rapidly expanding its vocabulary and repertoire to incorporate the experiences of modern, urban life.

3. In my chapter on Yeshurun, I discuss this subject with regard to late nineteenth-century Hebrew–Yiddish translations, which included self-translations by several well-known Yiddish writers, such as S. Y. Abramovitch (who went by the pseudonym Mendele Mokher Sforim).

4. My bibliography provides citations for resources that address Hebrew translation from a variety of perspectives and critical frameworks. Much of this work continues to be consolidated as scholars of Hebrew literature are increasingly attentive to matters of translation. In English, Kenneth B. Moss's work on the Yiddish and Hebrew translation economies of the early twentieth century is one of the more comprehensive treatments on the topic. Robert Singerman's *Jewish Translation: A Bibliography of Bibliographies and Studies* (Amsterdam/Philadelphia: John Benjamins, 2002) opens with an essay by Toury that offers a historical introduction to Jewish translation history, including Hebrew. Dykman's essay on Leah Goldberg's translation practices offers such a taxonomy of translation terms and approaches, but with a focus on the Russian influence on twentieth-century Hebrew translation. The work of Even-Zohar and Toury also engages case studies of this history, one of which I address in the following chapter, but a fuller list of these works is available in Singerman's bibliography. Ronen Sonis's unpublished dissertation addresses the role of translation in twentieth-century Hebrew literature, with particular attention to the influence of modernism. Finally, Sandbank's *Shtei brekhot ba-ya'ar* (*Two Pools in the Woods*), which I reference in the Introduction, is also a valuable resource for scholars interested in the relation between poetry and translation. Each chapter of his book pairs a Hebrew poet with his/her non-Hebrew European counterpart, a structure that highlights the translational relation between these poets. Moss, "Not the *Dybbuk* but *Don Quixote*: Translation, Deparochialization, and Nationalism in Jewish Culture, 1917–1919," *Culture Front: Representing Jews in Eastern Europe*, ed. Benjamin Nathans and Gabriella Safran (Philadelphia: University of Pennsylvania Press, 2008), 196–240; Dykman, "'Al Leah Goldberg ke-metargemet shira" ["Leah Goldberg as a Translator"] in *Pegishot 'im meshoreret* [*Encounters with a Poet*],

ed. Ruth Kartun-Blum and Anat Weisman (Tel Aviv: Sifriyat po'alim, 2000), 218–248; Sonis, "Make It New: Magamot chadashot be-tirgumei ha-shira ha-'ivriyim mi-anglit u-mi-rusit bishnot ha-shiv'im ve-ha-shmonim" ("New Trends in Poetic Translation from English and Russian into Hebrew in the 1970s and 1980s"), unpublished dissertation (Jerusalem: Hebrew University of Jerusalem, 2013).

5. H. W. F. Gesenius, *Hebrew and Chaldee Lexicon to the Old Testament Scriptures* (Grand Rapids, MI: Baker Book House, 1979 [7th ed.]), 663.

6. Ibid.

7. Marcus Jastrow, *Dictionary of the Targumim, the Talmud Babli and Yerushalmi, and the Midrashic Literature*, vol. 2 (New York: G. P. Putnam and Sons, 1903), 1130.

8. The Hebrew University of Jerusalem's Historical Jewish Press digital archive was an indispensable resource for tracking the circulation of these terms.

9. E.g., Nimrod Matan's poetry collection *'Al pi* (*As per*), which explores themes and practices of translation (Jerusalem: Mossad Bialik, 2013).

10. Daniel Weissbort and Astradur Eysteinsson, eds, *Translation—Theory and Practice: A Historical Reader* (Oxford: Oxford University Press, 2006), 241.

11. Weissbort and Eysteinsson, 202. The translation is by André Lefevere from his *Translating Literature: The German Tradition from Luther to Rosenzweig* (Assen/Amsterdam: Van Gorcum, 1977), 37.

12. Weissbort and Eysteinsson, *Translation*, 212.

13. Schleiermacher presented this as a series of lectures at the Prussian Academy of Sciences. The published version appeared in 1815. Friedrich Schleiermacher, "On the Different Methods of Translating," trans. Susan Bernofsky, *The Translation Studies Reader*, ed. Lawrence Venuti (New York: Routledge, 2012 [3rd ed.]), 51.

14. Susan Bernofsky, "Friedrich Schleiermacher," *Translationista* (February 4, 2011), http://translationista.net/2011/02/friedrich-schleiermacher.html.

15. Moshe Pelli's work on the Haskala has been instrumental to my study, though it focuses by and large on the German context. For English-language readers, I recommend Pelli's *The Age of Haskala: Studies in Hebrew Literature of the Enlightenment in Germany* (Leiden: Brill, 1979), and particularly the chapter "Revival of Hebrew and Revival of the People: The Attitude of the First Maskilim toward the Hebrew Language" (73–90). Pelli also addresses early maskilic translations of German literature in *Haskala and Beyond: The Reception of the Hebrew Enlightenment and the Emergence of Haskala Judaism* (Lanham, MD: Rowman & Littlefield, 2010), 110–113.

16. Letteris's German collection *Sagen aus dem Orient* (*Speak from the East*, 1947) included several reworkings of Jewish *aggadot* (folk tales). For a more comprehensive list of his translations and publications, which include Goethe's *Faust* and Racine, see "Meïr Halevi (Max) Letteris," *Jewish Encyclopedia* (1906), http://www.jewishencyclopedia.com/articles/9791-letteris-meir-halevi-max.

17. Meir Letteris, *Divrei shir* (Zolkiev: G. Letteris, 1822); *Ayelet ha-shachar* [*Morning Star*] (Zolkiev: G. Letteris, 1824).

18. Meir Letteris, *Tofes kinor ve-ugav* [*The Harp and Organ Player*] (Vienna: Druck und Typografisch-literarisch-artistische Anstalt, L. C. Zamarski & C. Dittmarsch, 1860). According to Letteris, the poem "Galei ha-mayim" ("Waves"), was first written in German (*lashon askhenazi*). "[I composed] its translation (*ha'atakatav*) into Hebrew in rhyme and meter, as if it its origins (*bereshit tseto le-or*) were in a foreign language." Letteris, *Tofes kinor ve-ugav*, 7.

19. Gideon Toury, "Translation and Reflection on Translation: A Skeletal History for the Uninitiated," in *Jewish Translation*, ed. Singerman, xxii.

20. Reynolds, *The Poetry of Translation*, 8.

21. Ibid., 19.

22. Pelli, *Haskala and Beyond*, 110.

23. I return to this relation in the "Afterword."

24. Letteris, *Ayelet ha-shachar*, n.p.

25. This is not to be confused with the Hebrew annual *Otsar ha-sifrut* edited by Isaac Shaltiel Gräber, which published works in the areas of Jewish literature, science, and belles-lettres, and was supportive of young Hebrew writers. It appeared in five volumes between 1887 and 1896, and reemerged as a single issue in 1902. *Hibbat Zion*—Love of Zion—was a pre-Zionist Jewish nationalist movement founded in the early 1880s. *Hovevei Zion*, as its supporters were called, were committed to territorial nationalism and to Hebrew as the lingua franca of a Jewish national culture. (In this instance, I have opted for the more standard transliteration of the names of these movements.) The term *Techiya* (revival, renaissance) generally designates Zionist Hebrew literature written in the 1890s and the early twentieth century, with Bialik as one of its most prominent representatives. The term is problematic, as Harshav has argued persuasively, because it suggests that until then Hebrew literature was in a state of dormancy, and thereby the term asserts a break with the Haskala in order to reinstate modern Hebrew literature within a selectively continuous Zionist historiography. See Harshav, "Theses on the Historical Context of the Modern Jewish Revolution," *Jewish Studies Quarterly*, vol. 10 (2003): 300–319.

26. Natan Shapira, "Tochelet nikhzava" ["Hope Deceived"], *Ha-asif*, vol. 2 (Warsaw: Isaac Goldman, 1885), 565–568.

27. Editorial, "Natan Shapira eineno!" ("Natan Shapira is Gone!"), *Ha-tsefira* (November 11, 1897): 2–3.

28. K. A. Shapira, "Amarti yesh-li tikva" ["I Said, I Have Hope"], *Ha-asif*, 3 (Warsaw: Isaac Goldman, 1887), 706–713. Those wishing to compare the two versions of Schiller's poem may consult the following resource: Friedrich Schiller, *Werke und Briefe* [*Writings and Letters*], vol. 1, ed. Georg Kurscheidt (Frankfurt: Deutscher Klassiker Verlag, 1992), 168–171, 417–420.

29. Edward Bulwer Lytton, trans., *The Poems and Ballads of Schiller* (Leipzig: Bernhard Tauchnitz, 1844), 204.

30. Konstantin Abba Shapiro was born in 1839 in Grodno in the Russian Empire and died in 1900 in St. Petersburg. His attraction to the Haskala and secular literature

met with disapproval from his family, and he later converted to Christianity to marry the daughter of a Russian family that had supported him. Jacob Fichman edited a collection of Shapiro's poetry *Shirim nivcharim* (*Selected Poems*, 1911). Avner Holtzman, "Shapiro, Konstantin Abba," *YIVO Encyclopedia of Jews in Eastern Europe* (October 15, 2010), http://www.yivoencyclopedia.org/article.aspx/Shapiro_Konstantin_Abba.

31. I am taking Sokolow at his word here that previous translations of the German poem circulated in the Hebrew press.

32. Nachum Sokolow, "He'arat ha-mul" ("Editorial Comment"), *Ha-asif*, 3 (Warsaw: Isaac Goldman, 1887), 707.

33. In his introduction to his 1844 English translations of Schiller's poetry, Lytton notes, "Schiller's poetry is less in form than in substance—less in subtle elegance of words than in robust healthfulness of thought, which, like man himself, will bear transplanting to every clime." Lytton, *The Poems and Ballads of Schiller*, civ.

34. Lily Kahn, in her introduction to Isaac Edward (Eliezer) Salkinson's translations of Shakespeare's *Othello* (Ithiel) and *Romeo and Juliet* (Ram ve-Ya'el) offers a cogent summary of the Haskala that examines the relation between the Hebrew *maskilim* and their multilingual milieu. Salkinson (1820–1883), had received a traditional Jewish education but later turned to Hebrew literature under the influence of *maskilim* he encountered in his travels through czarist Russia and Western Europe. Like Shapira, he had converted to Christianity, but remained connected to Hebrew maskilic culture primarily through literary translation. Salkinson worked directly from the English, but his translations domesticated the text in a Jewish context. Kahn, *The First Hebrew Shakespeare Translations: A Bilingual Edition and Commentary* (London: University College London, 2017), 1–22.

35. Shapira, "Amarti yesh-li tikva," 706.

36. The clause that follows "if the sun be risen upon it" is from Exodus 22:2 (verse 3 in the KJV). This chapter concerns theft, differentiating between acts of stealing and the restitution or compensation that they require. The verse that follows offers the following formula for compensation: "if a man shall steal an ox, or a sheep, and kill it, or sell it; he shall restore five oxen for an ox, and four sheep for a sheep" (Exodus 22:3; verse 1 in the KJV). The generative formulation in this passage may explain Shapiro's citation.

37. I take the word "enclave" from Shachar Pinsker, who argues that the language of centers and peripheries disregards the fluid spaces that emerged for late nineteenth- and early twentieth-century Hebrew literary production and exchanges (in Europe and the United States in particular). Pinsker, "Deciphering the Hieroglyphics of the Metropolis: Literary Topographies of Berlin in Hebrew and Yiddish Modernism," in *Yiddish in Weimar Berlin*, ed. Gennady Estraikh and Mikhail Krutikov (Oxford: Legenda, 2010), 28–53. Zohar Shavit provides an indispensable literary historiography of translation activity and publishing in early twentieth-century Palestine, and I have drawn some of my examples from her study. Although Shavit focuses on the market of prose translation (as is still the case in Israel and elsewhere, poetry does not generate quite

the same circulation and revenues as prose), the conversations and debates that concerned what and whom to translate into modern Hebrew are relevant in the context of poetry translation as well, a relation that I will address toward the end of this section. Shavit, *Ha-chayim ha-sifrutiyim be-erets yisra'el, 1910–1933* [*Literary Life in Palestine*] (Tel Aviv: Porter Institute for Poetics and Semiotics, 1982), 43. See also David Patterson, "Moving Centers in Modern Hebrew Literature," in *The Great Transition: The Recovery of the Lost Centers of Modern Hebrew Literature*, ed. Glenda Abramson and Tudor Parfitt (Totowa, NJ: Rowman & Allanheld, 1985), 1–10.

38. Zohar Shavit and Yaakov Shavit, "Lemale et ha-arets sefarim" ["To Fill the Country with Books: Translated vs. Original Literature in the Creation of the Literary Center in Palestine"], *Ha-sifrut*, vol. 25 (1977): 54.

39. In her article on *Birkat ha-adama* (1921), Nisan Touroff's Hebrew translation of Knut Hamsun's Norwegian novel *Markens grøde* (*Growth of the Soil*, 1917), Karen Grumberg examines the role that Stybel Press, for instance, played in creating a "world literature" in Hebrew translation and the Zionist ideology that underpinned its commitment to translation. Grumberg, "Between the World and the Yishuv: The Translation of Knut Hamsun's *Markens grøde* as a Zionist Sacred Text," *Prooftexts*, vol. 37, no. 1–2 (2017), 111–136.

40. See, e.g., my discussion on late nineteenth-century Hebrew translations of Baudelaire and their circulation in chapter 2. Although beyond the scope of this project, tracking publications of poetry in Hebrew translation across all of the journals, almanacs, and newspapers of the late nineteenth and early twentieth centuries would fill a major gap in Shavit's historiography, which focuses primarily on books.

41. Shteinberg, *Hirhurai*, 42–43.

42. In 1917, Avraham Yosef Stybel, a Polish-Jewish entrepreneur who had made his fortune in the leather trade, founded Stybel Press in Moscow. From the outset, Stybel was committed to publishing only works in Hebrew and also dedicated to Hebrew translation. Many of the translators that the publishing house commissioned were also highly regarded modern Hebrew writers, such as the poets Chaim Nachman Bialik and David Frischmann. It also published the prominent literary journal *Ha-tekufa* as well as a poetry series "Miklat." Eventually, Stybel opened branches in Tel Aviv, Warsaw, and New York, but in the mid-1920s, financial difficulties required a scaling down and consolidation of the branches in Palestine. The press continued to operate in fits and starts until Stybel's death in 1946. Kenneth B. Moss, "Stybel," YIVO Encyclopedia of Jews in Eastern Europe (October 21, 2010), http://www.yivoencyclopedia.org/article.aspx/Stybel. For a full listing of Stybel's publications, see Dania Amichay-Michlin, *Ahavat Aysh: Avraham Yosef Shtibel* (Jerusalem: Mossad Bialik, 2000): 445–455.

43. *Ha-tekufa* 2 (Nissan-Sivan, 1918): back matter.

44. Amichay-Michlin, *Ahavat Aysh*, 48–52.

45. Joseph Klausner (1874–1958), who, like Bialik, was born in czarist Russia, settled in Mandatory Palestine in 1919 and became professor of Hebrew literature at the

Hebrew University of Jerusalem. He published numerous articles and reviews on Bialik, which were instrumental in sealing Bialik's status as the Hebrew national poet. See Klausner, *Ch. N. Bialik ve-shirat hayav: arb'a-'asar ma'amrei-bikoret* [*Bialik and the Poetry of His Life: Fourteen Critical Essays*] (Tel-Aviv: Dvir, 1950). Hamutal Bar-Yosef discusses this status in the context of Zionism's relationship with Romanticism, a reading that problematizes in fascinating ways the urgency to give Bialik this title. Bar-Yosef, "De-Romanticized Zionism in Modern Hebrew Literature," *Modern Judaism*, vol. 16, no. 1 (1996): 67–79.

46. I came across the Ben-Eliezer quote in Kenneth Moss's discussion of the *Onegin* translation project, where Moss translates *nitsotsot* as "traces." I have retranslated the quote but wish to give Moss credit for bringing it to my attention. Moss, "Not the *Dybbuk* but *Don Quixote*," 205. See M. Ben-Eliezer, "'Al ha-targumim" ("On Translations"), in *Kneset*, ed. Ch. N. Bialik (Odessa: Moria, 1916): 320.

47. For a fuller discussion of Pushkin's translation into French and his legacy on late nineteenth-century writers such as Henry James, see Robert Reid and Joe Andrew, eds, *Two Hundred Years of Pushkin: Pushkin's Legacy*, vol. III (Amsterdam and New York: Rodopi, 2004).

48. Indeed, Sara Feldman suggests that Bialik's refusal to undertake this translation may have had something to do with his concern that such a project would seal his status as a "Jewish Pushkin," and argues that this would have "[flown] in the face of his indigenizing aesthetic and project of *kinus* [in-gathering of Jewish texts]." Feldman, *Fine Lines: Hebrew and Yiddish Translations of Alexander Pushkin's Verse Novel* Eugene Onegin, *1899–1937*, unpublished dissertation, University of Michigan (2014), 17.

49. With regard to poetry and translation, what Frost in fact said was "I could define poetry this way: it is that which is lost out of both prose and verse in translation." Cleanth Brooks and Robert Penn Warren, eds, *Conversations of the Craft of Poetry* (New York: Holt, Rinehart and Winston, 1961), 7.

50. See Shmuel Avneri, "Ha-neshika mi-ba'ad la-mitpachat: Bialik ke-metargem" (*Kissing through a Veil: Bialik as Translator*), NRG (May 13, 2013), http://www.nrg.co.il/app/index.php?do=blog&encr_id=7b710fc4596b25648b44472262adc013&id=4490. Materials for the *mechitsa* vary from synagogue to synagogue. It can be made of wood, opaque glass, screens, or semi-transparent curtains, to name a few possibilities.

51. Chaim Nachmin Bialik, "Al 'umah ve-lashon'" ["On Nation and Language"], *Devarim shel be-'al peh* [*Lectures*] (Tel Aviv: Dvir, 1935), 16.

52. Cf. Adam Rubin, "'Like a Necklace of Black Pearls Whose String Has Snapped': Bialik's 'Aron ha-sefarim' and the Sacralization of Zionism," *Prooftexts*, vol. 28, no. 2 (Spring 2008): 157–196.

53. Chaim Nachman Bialik, "Devir u-Moria—sekira ketsara 'al gedolam ve-hitpatchutam" ("A Historical Survey of *Dvir* and *Moria*"), *Proyekt Ben Yehuda*, http://benyehuda.org/bialik/izavon_article_115.html. This essay appears in a collection of Bialik's unpublished writings. Chaim Nachman Bialik, *Ketavim genuzim* [*Unpublished Writings*] (Tel Aviv: Beit Bialik and Dvir, 1970).

54. With regard to the Cervantes quote, these words are placed in the mouth of Don Quixote himself, who in chapter 62 of the novel (part 2) chances upon a translator from the Italian. Miguel de Cervantes, *Don Quijote de la Mancha* (Barcelona: Editorial Juventud, 1998 [1605]), 998.

55. Saul Bellow, "A Jewish Writer in America," *The New York Review of Books* (October 27, 2011), http://www.nybooks.com/articles/2011/10/27/jewish-writer-america.

56. Avraham Levinson, trans. *Yevgeni Onyegin: roman be-charuzim* [*Evgeny Onegin: A Novel in Verse*] (Jerusalem: Vays, 1937). Levinson was born in Lodz, Poland, in 1889 and began publishing Hebrew poems from a young age. He was active in the Hebrew theater community of Lodz and later founded a Hebrew theater company in Warsaw, while also writing for the Zionist press. In 1935, he immigrated to Mandatory Palestine (he had visited briefly in 1914), where he remained active in theater and served as director of the cultural division of the Histadrut. He translated widely from Yiddish and Russian, and also into Yiddish for the theater.

57. Shlonsky first moved to Ottoman Palestine in 1913 to study at the Herziliya Hebrew High School (Ha-gimnasiya ha-'ivrit Hertsiliya) in Tel Aviv. With the outbreak of World War I, he returned to his family's home in Ukraine, but later settled permanently in Mandatory Palestine in 1921. Avraham Shlonsky, trans., *Yevgeni Onyegin (roman be-charuzim)* [*Evgeny Onegin: A Novel in Verse*], by Aleksandr Pushkin (Tel Aviv: Va'ad Ha-yovel, 1937).

58. Hebrew publishing, in general, was hardly a lucrative industry, and many publishing houses ran at a loss or relied on patronage to keep their operations running (Moss, "Not the *Dybbuk* but *Don Quixote*," 221).

59. Michael Gluzman, *The Politics of Canonicity: Lines of Resistance in Modernist Hebrew Poetry* (Stanford: Stanford University Press, 2003), 112–113.

60. Chaim Nachman Bialik, "'Al Shalom Ash ve-Perets Hirshbein," *Proyekt Ben-Yehuda*, http://benyehuda.org/bialik/dvarim_shebeal_peh83.html. Later published in Bialik, *Devarim she-be-'al pe* [*Lectures*] (Tel Aviv: Dvir, 1935). For another description of this episode, see Naomi Seidman, *A Marriage Made in Heaven: The Sexual Politics of Hebrew and Yiddish* (Berkeley: University of California Press, 1997), 124.

61. Ibid.

62. Ibid.

63. Quoted in Seidman, *A Marriage Made in Heaven*, 125 and Yael Chaver, *What Must Be Forgotten: The Survival of Yiddish in Zionist Palestine* (Syracuse, NY: Syracuse University Press, 2004), 106. I return to this episode, and this passage in particular, in my reading of Avot Yeshurun's prosthetic translation (see chapter 4).

64. Naomi Brenner, "A Multilingual Modernist: Avraham Shlonsky between Hebrew and Yiddish," *Comparative Literature*, vol. 61, no. 4 (2009): 369. Emphasis in the original.

65. Although the anthology includes several internationally known Russian poets (e.g., Mandelstam and Akhmatova), it also includes a number of minor poets who were not widely anthologized in that period (or now, for that matter). I am grateful to Alexandar Mihailovic for bringing this contrast to my attention.

66. Nina Segal, "Velimir Khlebnikov in Hebrew," *Partial Answers: Journal of Literature and the History of Ideas*, vol. 6, no. 1 (2008): 83.

67. Ibid., 86.

68. Leah Goldberg and Avraham Shlonsky, "Introduction," *Shirat Rusiya* [*Russian Poetry*], ed. Goldberg and Shlonsky(Tel Aviv: Sifriyat poʻalim, 1983 [1942]), 19. Interestingly, the term "translation" is never mentioned explicitly in the introduction. In his preface to his 2003 anthology of Russian poetry in Hebrew translation, Dykman reflects on the influence of *Shirat Rusiya*: "Never before had there been in Hebrew poetry such a complete and profound accord between original and translation, and never had there been such a bold and clear relation between the two in Russian poetry." Aminadav Dykman, ed. and trans., *Dor sheli, chaya sheli: Mi-shirat Rusiya be-meʻa ha-ʻesrim* [*My Generation, My Beast: Russian Poetry of the 20th Century*] (Tel Aviv: Schocken, 2002): 11.

69. Goldberg and Shlonsky, "Introduction," *Shirat Rusiya*, 7. Segal also discerns here an allusion to the *matan Torah*. Segal, "Velimir Khlebnikov in Hebrew," 84.

70. Hannan Hever, "Our Poetry is Like an Orange Grove: Anthologies of Hebrew Poetry in Erets Israel," *Prooftexts*, vol. 17 (1997): 199. Hever takes the term "imagined national community" from Benedict Anderson.

71. Goldberg and Shlonsky, "Introduction," 19.

72. Gouri recalls that his father used to sing a poem by the Russian poet Mikhail Lermontov but did so when he thought no one else was listening. Haim Gouri, "Noshmim goral ve-adama" ["Breathing Destiny and Earth"], *Haaretz*, vol. 528 (April 9, 2003): 12.

73. Leah Goldberg, "Ha-meshorer ha-leʼumi" ["The National Poet"], *Ha-omets le-chulin* [*The Courage for the Ordinary*], ed. A. B. Yoffe (Tel Aviv: Sifriyat poʻalim, 1976), 186. My emphasis.

74. Goldberg, "Ha-meshorer ha-leʼumi," 186.

Chapter 2

1. Esther Raab, "Ani tachat ha-atad" ["I Am under the Bramble"], *Kol ha-shirim* [*Collected Poems*] (Tel Aviv: Zmora, Bitan, 1988): 31.

2. Petach Tikva was founded in 1878. For a fuller history of the *moshava* and its status among the early Jewish agricultural colonies, see Shaul Katz, "'Ha-telem ha-rishon: ideologiya, hityashvut, ve-chaklaʼut be-Petach Tikva ba-ʻasor ha-shanim ha-rishon le-kiyuma," *Cathedra*, vol. 23 (1982): 57–124. For an English account of this period of Jewish settlement in Ottoman Palestine, see Derek Penslar, *Zionism and Technocracy: The Engineering of Jewish Settlement in Palestine (1870–1918)* (Bloomington: Indiana University Press, 1991).

3. Esther Raab, "Paris o Yerushalayim?" in *Kol ha-proza* [*Collected Prose*], ed. Ehud Ben-Ezer (Hod Ha-Sharon: Astrolog, 2001), 119–122. "Paris or Jerusalem?" first appeared in April 1952 in *Haʼaretz*.

4. Ibid., 119.

5. Ibid., 120. The current Ukrainian national anthem originates from an 1863 arrangement by Mykhailo Verbytsky. Verbytsky, a composer and Catholic priest from Western Ukraine, wrote the original score to accompany a patriotic poem by Pavlo Chubynsky (1839–1884) titled "Sche ne vmerla Ukraina" ("Ukraine, You Have Not Yet Perished"). The poem first appeared in the magazine *Meta* in 1862 and immediately caught the attention of Verbytsky, who felt that it expressed the desire of many Ukrainians for territorial sovereignty. In 1917, the renamed "Hymn to Ukraine" became the anthem of the short-lived Ukrainian National Republic and was officially reinstated in a modified form by Ukraine's Parliament in 2003. See Xing Hang, *Encyclopedia of National Anthems* (Lanham, MD: Scarecrow Press, 2003), 645–647.

6. Raab, "Paris o Yerushalayim?" 120.

7. Raab, "Paris o Yerushalayim?" 120. Avraham Menachem Mendel Ussishkin (1963–1941) was a Zionist leader and an active proponent of the vernacularization of the Hebrew language and Jewish settlement in Palestine, to which he immigrated in 1919. From 1923 to his death he served as president of the Jewish National Fund.

8. Raab, "Paris o Yerushalayim?" 120. Gedera, founded in 1884, is today located in central Israel. In the period that Raab recounts, however, it was one of the more isolated Jewish colonies in the region. Its earliest residents were affiliated with the Bilu movement, which was committed to land labor and Jewish settlement.

9. Liora R. Halperin, *Babel in Zion: Jews, Nationalism, and Language Diversity in Palestine, 1920–1948* (New Haven: Yale University Press, 2014), 39.

10. See Derek J. Penslar, "Hashpa'ot tsorfatiyot 'al ha-hityashvut ha-hakla'it ha-yehudit be-Eretz Yisra'el (1870–1914)," *Cathedra*, vol. 62 (1992): 54–66.

11. Joel Beinin, *The Dispersion of Egyptian Jewry: Culture, Politics, and the Formation of a Modern Diaspora* (Cairo: American University in Cairo Press, 1998), 49–52.

12. Dan Miron, "Neharot me'avshim: Ester Raab ve-shirata" ["Rustling Rivers: Esther Raab's Poetry"], *Ha-adam eino ela … chulshat-ha-ko'ach, 'otsmat-ha-chulsha: 'iyunim be-shira* [Man is Nothing But … The Weakness of Being Strong, The Strength in Weakness: Studies in Modern Hebrew Poetry] (Tel Aviv: Zmora, Bitan, 1999), 259–307.

13. Chana Kronfeld, *On the Margins of Modernism: Decentering Literary Dynamics* (Berkeley: University of California Press, 1996), 59; Adriana X. Tatum (Jacobs), "Paris or Jerusalem: The Multilingualism of Esther Raab," *Prooftexts: A Journal of Jewish Literary History*, vol. 26, no. 1/2 (2006): 6–28.

14. Ibid., 72.

15. The poems that Kronfeld parses closely are "Lo ach ve-esh kirayim" ("Neither a Hearth nor a Stove Fire"), "Ke-tsipor meta 'al ha-zerem" ("Like a Dead Bird on the Stream"), and "Ani tachat ha-atad" ("I under the Bramble Bush"). Kronfeld, *The Margins of Modernism*, 72.

16. Ziva Shamir, "Ne'urei ha-shira be-arets lo zeru'a" ["The Youth of Poetry in an Unsowed Land: An Interview with Esther Raab"], *Chadarim*, vol. 1 (1981): 101–118.

17. Cf. Yael Chaver, *What Must Be Forgotten: The Survival of Yiddish in Zionist Palestine* (Syracuse, NY: Syracuse University Press, 2004), 28–29; Shamir, "Ne'urei ha-shira be-arets lo zeru'a."

18. Ben-Ezer relates that Raab celebrated the publication of *Kimshonim* in Paris. Ben-Ezer, *Yamim shel la'ana u-devash*, 333. For Raab's Hebrew translations of Baudelaire, see Raab, *Kol ha-proza*, 463–468. I discuss these in greater depth later in the chapter.

19. Dana Olmert, *Bitenu'at safa 'ikeshet: ketiva va-ahava be-shirat ha-meshorerot ha-'ivriyot ha-rishonot* [*Predicaments of Writing and Loving: The First Hebrew Women Poets*] (Tel Aviv: University of Haifa, 2012), 93–94.

20. The poet Théophile Gautier, to whom Baudelaire famously dedicated *Les Fleurs du mal*, described Baudelaire's poetic idiom as "a language already marbled by the greenness of decomposition (la langue marbrée déjà les verdeurs de la décomposition)." Gautier, "Charles Baudelaire," in Charles Baudelaire, *Les Fleurs du mal* (Paris: Michel Lévy Frères, 1868), 17.

21. The term *eretsyisre'eli* is the adjectival form of Erets Yisrael, Land of Israel, a contested term in contemporary Israeli politics. It is a phrase that appears several times in the Bible, for the first time in 1 Samuel 13:19 ("Now there was no smith found throughout all the land of Israel: for the Philistines said, Lest the Hebrews make *them* swords or spears"). In this chapter, my use of the term does not align with its contemporary political usage; rather, here it refers to the pre-State period, when such formulations were nonetheless political. For Raab, the term is clearly a marker of authority and ownership of—and *in*—the land. Later, for Leah Goldberg, the term characterizes an idea of cultural belonging that arguably contests an affiliation to territorial nationalism. For more substantive historical treatments of the term, see Anita Shapira, *Land and Power: The Zionist Resort to Force, 1881–1948* (Palo Alto: Stanford University Press, 1992) and Shlomo Sand, *The Invention of the Land of Israel*, trans. Geremy Forman (London: Verso, 2012).

22. Kronfeld, *On the Margins of Modernism*, 59.

23. Raab is referencing here Moshe Kleinman's 1930 review of *Kimshonim*, one of the earliest reviews of her work (emphasis added). Ehud Ben-Ezer, *Yamim shel la'ana u-devash* [*Days of Gall and Honey*] (Tel Aviv: 'Am 'oved, 1998), 396. In my translations of Raab's prose, I have retained, in many instances, the punctuation of the original Hebrew so as to give English-language readers the experience of her style and its characteristic breaks and ruptures.

24. Esther Raab, *Kol ha-shirim* [*Collected Poems*] (Tel Aviv: Zmora, Bitan, 1988), 17.

25. Esther Raab, *Thistles: Selected Poems of Esther Raab*, trans. Harold Schimmel (Jerusalem: Ibis Editions, 2002), 46–47.

26. I thank Liora Halperin for this observation.

27. Genesis 1:11–12.

28. In his account of this event, Yehuda Raab recalls that Yehoshua Stampfer, one of Petach Tikva's founders, wept and gave a short speech that concluded with the *Shehecheyanu* blessing. Yehuda Raab (Ben-Ezer), *Ha-telem ha-rishon: zikhronot*

1862–1930 [The First Furrow: Recollections] (Jerusalem: Ha-sifriya ha-tsiyonit, 1956), 63. I am grateful to one of my anonymous readers for pointing out the relation to Bialik's poem, which opens with the line "Strengthen the hands of all our gifted brothers."

29. For an anthropological reading of the metaphors and symbols that shaped settlement narratives in the Yishuv, see Yael Zerubavel's "Desert and Settlement: Space Metaphors and Symbolic Landscapes in the Yishuv and Early Israeli Culture," in *Jewish Topographies: Visions of Space, Traditions of Place*, ed. Julia Brauch and Anna Lipphardt (Burlington and Hampshire: Ashgate, 2008), 201–222.

30. Gluzman, *The Politics of Canonicity*, 51.

31. Raab, "Sicha be-Tiv'on," 117.

32. Most of its founders, including Raab's father Yehuda Raab, had settled initially in Jerusalem, and for them Petach Tikva also represented a break from the Old Yishuv.

33. Hannan Hever, *Nativism, Zionism and Beyond* (Syracuse, NY: Syracuse University Press, 2014), 5.

34. I am indebted to the translators' footnote for these insights. Giorgio Agamben, *The Idea of Prose*, trans. Michael Sullivan and Sam Whitsitt (Albany: SUNY Press, 1995), 40.

35. In her interview with Shamir, Raab also insists that "La-av" was published in *Haaretz* in the early 1920s, though its actual date of publication in that paper is 1929. Shamir, "Ne'urei ha-shira be-arets lo zeru'a," 111; Ben-Ezer, ed., *Letters of Esther Raab*, vol. 2 (Tel Aviv: Self-published, 1999), 253–260. Dan Miron, *Imahot meyesadot, achayot chorgot* [*Founding Mothers, Step-Sisters*] (Tel Aviv, Israel: Ha-kibbuts ha-me'uchad, 1991), 324–325.

36. Olmert, *Bitenu'at safa 'ikeshet*, 103.

37. Miron, *Imahot meyesadot, achayot chorgot*, 325.

38. Hamutal Tsamir, *Be-shem ha-nof: le'umiut, migdar u-sovyektibiyut ba-shira ha-isre'alit bi-shenot ha-chamishim ve-ha-shishim* [*In the Name of the Land: Nationalism, Gender, and Subjectivity in the Israeli Poetry of the Statehood Generation*] (Jerusalem and Beer Sheva: Keter Books/Heksherim, 2006), 118.

39. Ibid.

40. Olmert, *Bitenu'at safa 'ikeshet*,102. My emphasis.

41. Harold Schimmel, "Introduction," *Thistles*, 30.

42. For a fuller discuss of Raab's "native frame," see Barbara Mann, "Framing the Native: Esther Raab's Visual Poetics," *Israel Studies*, vol. 4, no. 1 (Spring 1999): 234–257.

43. Ben-Ezer, *Yamim shel la'ana u-devash*, 296. "Isaac Grun" is the spelling that appears in Raab's correspondences and other official documents (including his death certificate). Variations of his name include Yitzhak Green and Isaac Grün, among others. I have decided to adhere to the spelling that Raab utilized.

44. For a fuller discussion of Levantinism, see Gil Hochberg, "'Permanent Immigration': Jacqueline Kahanoff, Ronit Matalon, and the Impetus of Levantinism," *Boundary* 2, vol. 31, no. 2 (Summer 2004): 219–243.

45. Jacqueline Kahanoff, "Afterword," in *Mongrels or Marvels: The Levantine Writings of Jacqueline Shohet Kahanoff*, ed. Deborah A. Starr and Sasson Somekh (Stanford: Stanford University Press, 2011): 247.

46. Raab, "Sicha be-Tiv'on," 117. See also Ben-Ezer, *Yamim shel la'ana u-devash*, 82.

47. Ben-Ezer, *Yamim shel la'ana u-devash*, 117–118.

48. The poem "Le-achyotai ha-'aniyot, ha-nis'arot" ("To My Poor, Agitated Sisters") appears in *Kimshonim* with a dedication to Laurette Pascal and Shoshana Bogin, both of whom committed suicide at a young age. Ben-Ezer includes an unpublished poem titled "Le-Loret" ("To Laurette") in *Kol ha-shirim*. See Esther Raab, *Kol ha-shirim*, 35, 248.

49. Ben-Ezer, *Yamim shel la'ana u-devash*, 115–116. For a personal account of the Pascal family history, see Oliver Hazan, "Origines," *Next Journey*, http://nextjourney.org/origines. Hazan is Peretz Pascal's great-great grandson.

50. Ben-Ezer, *Yamim shel la'ana u-devash*, 116.

51. Ibid., 118. In a letter written in the summer of 1913 and addressed to Laurette, an Arab woman figures prominently in the following landscape description: "The olive returns, a branch of pink figs, and an Arab woman calmly lifts a tan arm ringed with bracelets toward the dark fruit—narrow valleys, green like cradles, cling to the black mountain rocks." I mention this figure because Raab's relationship with Arabic, and her views on Arab culture in the Yishuv, remains an area open to further inquiry. In the essay "Milim ke-tsiporim nedirot," Raab relates that "back then there was the influence of Arabic. We used Arabic words, and I sang Arabic songs, and that was meaningful to me, I had a lovely voice. And we ate *lebane*, figs, and sang Arabic songs." Yet, in a letter to her father, written from Paris and dated June 1921, presumably in response to the 1920–1921 Arab-Jewish conflict, and specifically to the May 1921 Arab riots in Petach Tikva, Raab writes, "I think that if I ran into an Arab, I would strangle him." Ben-Ezer, ed., *Letters of Esther Raab*, 45, 63; Esther Raab, *Milim ke-tsiporim nedirot*, 419.

52. Ben-Ezer, *Yamim shel la'ana u-devash*, 118.

53. Ibid., 365.

54. Ibid., 343.

55. Raab, "Be-Kahir," *Kol ha-proza*, 302–308.

56. Ibid., 303. My emphasis.

57. Caroline Bergvall, "Cat in the Throat," in *Meddle English* (Callicoon, NY: Nightboat Books, 2011): 158.

58. Ben-Ezer refers to the Sorbonne period as a "puzzle." The absence of official documentation that could place her at the Sorbonne, and Raab's own tendency to confuse the itinerary and dates of her European travels, means that this detail cannot be confirmed, but numerous letters and postcards in her archive corroborate several extended stays in Paris throughout her life. Ben-Ezer, *Yamim shel la'ana u-devash*, 343–344.

59. Hever, *Nativism, Zionism and Beyond*, 4.

60. Ben-Ezer, *Yamim shel la'ana u-devash*, 384. In her account, Raab writes the name of Louis Jouvet in the Roman alphabet.

61. Many early Modern Hebrew writers, among them Shlonsky, Alterman, Yonatan Ratosh, and Rachel, can claim a "Paris period" that postdates their arrival in Palestine, but in many of these cases, the cultural experience of Paris is also motivated (or perhaps justified) by the need to acquire certain practical skills for the Yishuv's benefit (agronomy was a common field of study).

62. Postcard from Esther Raab to Moshe Stavsky (Stavi), August 31, 1937. Genazim, 6346a. The image on the card is a photographic reproduction of the base of the Eiffel Tower and part of a series celebrating the 1937 Exposition Internationale in Paris. This event, which ran from May to November 1937, was the last of five international expositions that the city hosted. What lies outside of the card's frame are the pavilions for Nazi Germany and the Soviet Union, which were located on opposite sides of the base, spatially "facing off." Pavilions representing other countries were under construction, but on the first day of the festival, only the Soviet and German pavilions were ready.

63. "Ahava be-Zaltzburg" was published in *Haaretz* in 1936. Raab, "Ahava be-Zaltsburg," *Kol ha-proza*, 343–347.

64. Raab, *Kol ha-proza*, 343.

65. Ibid.

66. Raab, "'Olei ha-regel be-Zaltsburg," *Kol ha-proza*, 338–342.

67. Ibid., 344.

68. Ibid, 347.

69. Ibid.

70. Ibid.

71. Ibid.

72. Ibid.

73. Ben-Ezer, *Yamim shel la'ana u-devash*, 241. While this chapter focuses on Raab's affiliation with the French language and French literature, the place of German in her literary development is also significant (and also closely aligned with her French) and worthy of further study. In his postscript to Raab's translations of Calé, Ben-Ezer writes, "Esther knew German from her childhood; her father had been raised in German culture in his Hungarian youth, and for many years had a subscription to a German periodical. He used to exchange books with his friends, German Templar farmers from Wilhelmina." Ben-Ezer, *Kol ha-proza*, 462. For an overview of the intertwined histories of German and Hebrew, see Amir Eshel and Na'ama Rokem, "Berlin and Jerusalem: Toward German-Hebrew Studies," in *The German-Jewish Experience Revisited*, ed. Steven E. Aschheim and Vivian Liska (Berlin/Boston: Walter de Gruyter GmbH, 2015), 265–272.

74. Ben-Ezer, *Kol ha-proza*, 265. Halperin also addresses the circulation of untranslated foreign works in the Zionist home, "even if a [Hebrew] translation existed." Halperin, *Babel in Zion*, 41.

75. Ben-Ezer, *Kol ha-proza*, 265–280. Březina is the pseudonym of the Czech Symbolist poet Václav Jebavy (1868–1929) who was born in the Austro-Hungarian empire in the

Vysocina Region. Raab translated his works into Hebrew from Otto Pick's German translation, which was published in 1913 as *Hymnen* (Leipzig: Kurt Wolff Verlag). According to the poet Elazar Benyoetz, whom Ben-Ezer cites, Březina's work shifted from classical prosody to free verse in his later years. Although the German versions from which Raab retranslated ("tirgum mi-yad shniya") retain Březina's original rhyme and meter, Raab, as was her tendency, eschews this prosody in her Hebrew translations. Raab, *Kol ha-proza*, 469–471. Russian-born Zvi Schatz immigrated to Palestine prior to World War I and befriended Raab during his stay in Degania, a kibbutz in the Galilee. He was killed on May 2, 1921, during the Jaffa Arab riots, alongside the famed Hebrew writer Yosef Chaim Brenner. Raab's translation of his poem "Ke-isha ohevet ve-nikhna'at" ("Like an enamored, submissive woman") appeared in a posthumous collection of his essays and poetry. Zvi Schatz, *'Al gevul ha-demama: ketavim* [*On the Edge of Silence: Collected Writings*] (Tel Aviv: Tarbut ve-chinukh, 1967), 76. The translation is not credited to Raab and differs in a few significant ways from the draft in her journals. According to Ben-Ezer, it is not clear if Raab translated his work from Yiddish or Russian. Ben-Ezer, *Yamim shel la'ana u-devash*, 275.

76. For more on the history of Baudelaire's reception in Hebrew, see Hamutal Bar-Yosef, "Ha-hitkablut shel Bodlir ba-sifrut ha-'ivrit: 'avar ve-hove" ["The Reception of Baudelaire in Hebrew Literature: Past and Present"], *Dimui*, vol. 25 (Spring 2005): 43–49. For a comprehensive discussion of Baudelaire's influence on Russian literature and the history of Russian translations of his work, see Adrian Wanner, *Baudelaire in Russia* (Gainesville: University Press of Florida, 1996).

77. Esther Raab, "Milim ke-tsiporim nedirot," *Kol ha-proza*, 414–420. Germaine Beaumont (née Battendier) was a French novelist, poet, translator, journalist, and a longtime secretary of the French author Colette, who was a close friend of her mother Annie de Pène. Her publications included *Colette par elle-même* (coauthored with André Parinaud; Paris: Éditions du Seuil, 1951) and several novels, including *Piège* (Trap), which won the Prix Théophraste Renaudot in 1930 (the first time it was awarded to a woman). Beaumont's poems have not been collected and are difficult to locate, though a few appeared in *Anthologie de la poésie féminine française de 1900 à nos jours* (1953), edited by the writer and bookseller Marcel Béalu. During her stays in Paris in the 1930s, Raab encountered Beaumont's "chroniques," short texts of poetic prose that appeared regularly in *Les Nouvelles littéraires* and bear a stylistic resemblance to Raab's own prose.

78. Raab, *Kol ha-proza*, 419.

79. Raab's translations of Baudelaire did not appear in print until 2001, with the publication of *Kol ha-proza* [*Collected Prose*], The five Baudelaire translations that Raab produced first appear in a *Kimshonim* notebook that dates to the winter and summer of 1921. Raab, *Kol ha-proza*, 462.

80. Ehud Ben-Ezer, Personal Interview, July 27, 2008, Tel Aviv.

81. Gluzman, *The Politics of Canonicity*, 51.

82. Raab, "Milim ke-tsiporim nedirot," 419.

83. Germaine Beaumont, "De'avon" ["Regret"], trans. Esther Raab, *Moznayim* 28 (1969): n.p. I have not been able to locate this poem in the original French. It is very possible that it is Raab's translation of one of Beaumont's *chroniques*, though extensive searches through the digital archive of *Les Nouvelles littéraires* did not turn up a text that corresponded to Raab's translation.

84. Shamir, "Ne'urei ha-shira be-arets lo zeru'a," 110–111.

85. Esther Raab, "To Avraham Broides," June 17, 1952, TS, Collection of Ehud Ben-Ezer, 1999, Tel Aviv. Broides (1907–1979) published numerous volumes of poetry and also served for many years as the secretary of the *Agudat ha-sofrim ha-'ivriyim be-medinat yisra'el* (Hebrew Writers Association in Israel). Raab's letters are now housed at the Hebrew Writers Archive ("Gnazim").

86. Esther Raab, "To K. A. Bertini," February 2, 1969.

87. Raab, "Letter to K. A. Bertini," February 10, 1969.

88. In the manuscript version of Raab's collected prose, Ben-Ezer includes Hebrew translations of notes and short texts written in French.

89. Charles Baudelaire, *Pirchei ha-r'a: mivchar shirim* [*The Flowers of Evil: Selected Poems*], trans. Eliahu Meitus (Tel Aviv: Yehoshua Chachik, 1962).

90. Jacob Fichman, "Sharl Bodler," *Ha-tekufa* (Warsaw: Avraham Yosef Shteibel, 1924), 509–510. My emphasis.

91. For a closer study of these issues, particularly the making of the Zionist male subject, see Michal Dekel's *The Universal Jew: Masculinty, Modernity and the Zionist Moment* (Evanston, IL: Northwestern University Press, 2010) and Michael Gluzman's *Ha-guf ha-tsiyoni: le'umiyut, migdar u-miniyut ba-sifrut ha-isra'elit ha-chadasha* [*The Zionist Body: Nationalism, Gender and Sexuality in Modern Hebrew Literature*] (Tel Aviv: Ha-kibbuts ha-me'uchad, 2007).

92. Hamutal Bar-Yosef, "Bialik and the Baudelairian Triangle: *Ennui*, Cats and Spider's Webs," *Jewish Studies Quarterly*, vol. 1 (1993/1994): 362–378.

93. For a fuller account of the Russian reception of Baudelaire, see Wanner, *Baudelaire in Russia*.

94. Through the works of Fiodor Solgub, Innokenti Annensky, and Konstantin Balmont, to name a few.

95. Wanner, *Baudelaire in Russia*, 61.

96. Shaul Goldmann (David Frischmann), "Sharl Bodlir (Part 1)," *Ha-dor*, no. 32 (August 15, 1901): 6–8; "Sharl Bodlir (Part 2)," *Ha-dor*, no. 33 (August 22, 1901): 7–9; "Sharl Bodlir (Part 3)," *Ha-dor*, no. 34 (August 29, 1901): 9–11. This essay has been reprinted several times, most recently in 2010, and dispensing with the pseudonym.

97. Frischmann's celebrated Hebrew translation of Nietzsche's *Thus Spoke Zarathustra* (1883–1885)—*Ko amar Sarathustra*—was serialized between 1909 and 1911 in *Reshafim*, a Warsaw-based literary journal that he edited at the time. For a more detailed study of the influence of Nietzsche on late nineteenth-century Zionism, including Nordau's

Degeneration, see Jacob Golomb, *Nietzsche and Zion* (Ithaca, NY: Cornell University Press, 2004).

98. The relation between *yerida* ("descent") and leaving the land of Israel can be traced back to the biblical and rabbinic periods, but it was not until the modern waves of Jewish immigration to Palestine that the term acquired its negative currency. According to Maimonides, Jews may leave the land of Israel only under certain conditions (e.g., to study Torah, get married, in times of famine), and even then only for temporary periods (Mishneh Torah, *Shoftim*). His view, however, represented one position and not a halakhic consensus on the matter.

99. Ronen Sonis, "*Make it New*: Magamot chadashot be-tirgumei hashira ha-'ivri'im me-anglit u-me-rusit bishnot ha-shivi'im ve-ha-shmonim" ["New Trends in Poetic Translation from English and Russian into Hebrew in the 1970s and 1980s"], unpublished dissertation (Hebrew University of Jerusalem, 2013), 19. According to Sonis, who is currently writing an in-depth article on this episode, Frischmann's uncredited translation of Goldmann's article was noticed at the time of its publication (Zweifel), an incredible fact given that modern Hebrew literary scholarship, including my own, has treated it for so long as a Frischmann original (Jacobs, 2006). In 1989, a special section of *Moznayim*, dedicated to Baudelaire, included this essay on Baudelaire, as well as the translations of Baudelaire's "Spleen" that appeared in the essay (in the case of the latter, with the addition of line and stanza breaks) (*Moznayim*, vol. 3, 1989: 41–47). Goldmann, "Baudelaire," *Neue Freie Presse*, no. 13112 (February 24, 1901): 29–33; Y. Zweifel, "Shaul o Paul?" *Ha-melits*, no. 226 (October 28, 1901): 4; and Y. M., "Sichot sifrutiyot" ["Literary Conversations"], *Ha-melits*, no. 272 (December 20, 1901): 3–4.

100. Sonis, *Make It New*, 19.

101. The story of Paul, who was born to a Jewish family in the Mediterranean city of Tarsus (today located in south-central Turkey), is related in the New Testament book Acts of the Apostles, and includes the suggestion that his Hebrew and Latin names were interchangeable (see Acts 13:9).

102. The last two poems cited appeared in the 1868 expanded edition of *Les Fleurs du mal*, quite possibly the edition that Raab consulted. Three editions of Baudelaire's *Les Fleurs du mal* appeared in the nineteenth century. The first edition, published in June 1857, sold out within a year. The French government initially took Baudelaire and his publisher to court on charges of obscenity, which only increased demand for the collection. The book was allowed to continue to be in print with the omission of six poems. Baudelaire composed new poems for the second edition, published in 1861. This edition also added the section "Tableaux parisiens." The posthumous 1868 edition, with an introduction by Gautier, includes all of the poems of the 1861 edition with the addition of several others. The six poems censored from the 1857 edition were still illegal to print. Joanna Richardson, "Introduction," *Selected Poems*, by Charles Baudelaire, ed. and trans. Richardson (London: Penguin Books, 1975), 9–21. According to Ben-Ezer, there are no other translations of Baudelaire in the poet's archives. Ben-Ezer, Personal Interview, July 27, 2008.

103. Raab, *Machberot Kimshonim*, 36–38, 40–41.

104. According to Ben-Ezer, these edited versions are written with diacritical marks "on two large pieces of paper." Poetry published in Hebrew generally includes diacritical marks (*nikkud*), which is not the case with most prose. Interestingly, another poem, also titled "Sicha," appears twice in draft form in the first notebook, but is not a translation of the Baudelaire poem.

105. The first part of this quotation is from an edited version of Raab's letter to Shoham, published in Ben-Ezer, *Yamim shel la'ana u-devash*, 267. The second part of the quotation (following the ellipsis) appears in an unpublished volume of Raab's letters to Shoham. Raab, "Letter to Reuven Shoham, March 8, 1971," *Esther Raab/Reuven Shoham: chalifat mikhtavim, 1971–1981* [Correspondences], 1999, TS, Collection of Ehud Ben-Ezer, Tel Aviv, 15.

106. Aminadav Dykman, "'Al Leah Goldberg ke-metargemet shira" ("Leah Goldberg as a Translator") in *Pegishot 'im meshoreret [Encounters with a Poet]*, ed. Ruth Kartun-Blum and Anat Weisman (Tel Aviv: Sifriyat po'alim, 2000), 218–248.

107. In 1927, the Hebrew poet Rachel Bluwstein (1890–1931) published a short essay titled "'Al ot ha-zman" ("On the Sign of the Times") in which she espoused a poetics of simplicity (*pashtut*) as a challenge to the dominant poetics of the *nusach* and *melitsa* in modern Hebrew poetry (These terms are discussed in the previous chapter.). Bluwstein's emphasis on clear, simple, and direct language was a rejection of the intricate allusions and formulas that characterized much of Hebrew poetry in the nineteenth and early twentieth centuries. Bluwstein, who was born in Saratov, Russia, was deeply influenced by Russian acmeism, particularly the early poetry of Anna Akhmatova, and Hebrew minimalism (Gluzman, *The Politics of Canonicity*, 119–121). Her essay opens with a declaration that is reminiscent of Raab's own observations on poetic inspiration in "Milim ke-tsiporim nedirot": "It's clear to me: The sign of the times in the craft of poetry is simplicity in expression. A simple expression. In other words: an expression of the first flutterings of the lyric emotion (*emotsiya*). A direct expression." Raab takes *pashtut* even further in her rejection of the quatrain and other prosodic conventions of the period. Rachel Bluwstein, "'Al ot ha-zman," *Rachel: shirim, mikhtavim, reshimot, korot chayeiha* [*Rachel: Collected Poems, Letters, Notes, Biography*], ed. Uri Milstein (Tel Aviv: Zmora, Bitan, 1985), 325–326.

108. Raab, "Sicha be-Tiv'on," 118.

109. Charles Baudelaire, "Spleen," in *The Flowers of Evil*, trans. Keith Waldrop (Middletown, CT: Wesleyan University Press, 2006), 100. Waldrop's translation reworks the form of the poem and does not include line breaks, a choice that I have honored here (see "Note on Translation" for an explanation). I much preferred Waldrop's lexical choices over other English translations that I consulted.

110. Even-Zohar offers the following publication history for Goldberg's translation of "Spleen." *'Etim* (March 6, 1947): 2; *'Al ha-mishmar* (May 31, 1957): 1; *Ha-mekulalim: Mishirei Sharl Bodlir, Pal Verlan, Artur Rambod* [*The Damned: From the Poems of Charles Baudelaire, Paul Verlaine, Arthur Rimbaud*], ed. Yonah David (Tel Aviv: Eked, 1961),

30. Itamar Even-Zohar, "'Spleen' le-Bodlir ba-tirgum Leah Goldberg" ["Baudelaire's 'Spleen' in Leah Goldberg's Translation"], *Ha-sifrut*, vol. 6, no. 21 (1975): 2. The translation also appears in Leah Goldberg, *Kolot rechokim u-krovim* [*Voices Far and Near*], ed. Tuvia Reuvner (Tel Aviv: Sifriyat po'alim, 1975), 95.

111. Even-Zohar, "'Spleen' le-Bodlir ba-tirgum Leah Goldberg," 2.

112. Ibid., ii. Cf. J. C. Catford, *A Linguistic Theory of Translation: An Essay in Applied Linguistics* (London: Oxford University Press, 1965). This quotation is taken from the English abstract that accompanied the article.

113. Wanner, *Baudelaire in Russia*, 179.

114. In a brief essay on the translation of Baudelaire into Hebrew, Shamir discusses how translating Baudelaire has shaped contemporary Israeli poetry, particularly the work of Dory Manor and the poets of the contemporary literary journal *Ho!*: "As translators, these young poets struggle with the textual difficulties and restraints of the Baudelairean text, and as a result they offer us crystal-clear poetic lines, with virtuoso unprecedented rhymes … This is one manifestation of a complex phenomenon … how an influential poet like Baudelaire could be absorbed by different poetic schools, each time in a different manner, and how his style markers enhance new and unexpected combinations when they challenge poets who are themselves translators." Ziva Shamir, "Baudelaire's Translations into Hebrew and Modern Hebrew Poetry," *TRANS: Internet-Zeitschrift für Kulturwissenschaften*, vol. 16 (2006), http://www.inst.at/trans/16Nr/09_4/shamir16.htm.

115. Cf. Reuven Shoham, "Ha-ritmos ha-chofshi be-shirat Ester Raab" ["Free Rhythm in the Poetry of Esther Raab"], *Ha-sifrut*, vol. 24 (1977): 84–91.

116. For example, in the last version of "Spleen," Raab removes two words from the twelfth line of her draft. Raab, *Machberot Kimshonim*, 37.

117. Wanner, *Baudelaire in Russia*, 5–6. Translation by Wanner.

118. Ben-Ezer, *Yamim shel la'ana u-devash*, 272.

119. Esther Raab, "Letter to Reuven Shoham," November 1972, *Mikhtavim* 2, 48.

120. Raab, *Kol ha-shirim*, 20–21; Raab, "Cairo, Cairo!," trans. Harold Schimmel, *Thistles*, 50–51.

121. Schimmel, "Introduction," 14.

122. For a brief reading of this poem in the context of Raab's "Orientalist gaze," see Hever, *Nativism, Zionism and Beyond*, 17–20.

123. Raab, "Be-kahir," 303.

124. The word *kahava* entered Hebrew through the Arabic *qahwah* but has been replaced by *kafe*. It typically refers to the Turkish style of coffee preparation, which results in a rich concentrated brew of black coffee commonly referred to today as *kafe turki*. *Kahava* and *beit kahava* (coffee house) appear in Hebrew literary works of the late nineteenth and early twentieth centuries. Reportedly, Eliezer Ben-Yehuda preferred *kahava* over the more European sounding *kafe*.

125. I am grateful to Marina Rustow and Galit Hasan-Rokem for these observations on Raab's use of Arabic.

126. Raab, "Tso'anim—hungarim," *Kol ha-shirim*, 39; "Gypsies—Hungarian," trans. Harold Schimmel, *Thistles*, 63.

127. I am sensitive to the pejorative uses of the term "gypsy," as well as the problematic use of this word to refer broadly to itinerant groups and travelers, but to translate Raab's *tso'anim* as "Romani" would be anachronistic in this context. The etymologies of "gypsy" and *tso'ani* overlap in crucial and meaningful ways, as I explain in this chapter, and in ways that the poem clearly engages.

128. Schimmel, trans. "Gypsies—Hungarians," in *Poems of Esther Raab* (manuscript), 33. This draft manuscript is included among the digital files that Ben-Ezer made available to me.

129. Baudelaire, "L'Âme du vin" and "Les Vin des chiffoniers," *Les Fleurs du mal*, 295–298. Cf. Emily Salines, *Alchemy and Amalgam: Translation in the Works of Charles Baudelaire* (Amsterdam and New York: Rodopi, 2004).

130. Sara Pappas, "Managing Imitation: Translation and Baudelaire's Art Criticism," *Nineteenth-Century French Studies*, vol. 33, no. 3/4 (Spring–Summer, 2005): 325. For a fuller treatment of the role of translation in Baudelaire's oeuvre, see Salines, *Alchemy and Amalgam*.

131. Charles Baudelaire, "Bohémiens en voyage," *Les Fleurs du mal*, 104.

132. The full text of this poem reads as follows:

> Ces pauvres gueux pleins de bonnes aventures (Those poor, fortune-telling
>   beggars)
> Ne portent rien que des choses futures. (Carry nothing but future things)
> Ne voilà pas de braves messagers (Are these not the brave messengers)
> Qui vont errant par pays étrangers? (who wander through foreign lands?)
> Vous qui prenez plaisir en leurs paroles, (You who take pleasure in their words)
> Gardez vos blancs, vos testons, et pistoles. (Watch your blanks, [silver] coins
>   and pistoles [gold coin, firearm].)
> Au bout du compte, ils treuvent pour destin (In the end, they find their way by fate)
> Qu'ils sont venus d'Égypte à ce festin. (For they came from Egypt to this feast.)

There are slight variations in the order of these lines, which is to say, in the order of the etchings. I have followed here the order proposed by Edward J. Sullivan in his short essay on this series. Sullivan, "Jacques Callot's Les Bohémiens," *The Art Bulletin*, vol. 59, no. 2 (June 1977): 217–221.

133. Mohamed Ridha Bougera, "La Permanence de la figure de la bohémien," in *La bohémienne: figure poétique de l'errance aux XVIIIe et XIXe siècles*, ed. Pascale Auraix-Jonchière and Gérard Loubinoux (Clermont-Ferrand: Presses universitaires Blaise Pascal, 2005): 65–83. See also Sarah Houghton-Walker's work on the figure of the

gypsy in English literature, which addresses how and why representations of gypsies shifted in the Victorian period from rogues and vagrants to their depiction as "a symbol of nostalgia and longing." Houghton-Walker, *Representations of the Gypsy in the Romantic Period* (Cambridge: Cambridge University Press, 2014).

134. Ana Fernandes, "Les bohémiens de Baudelaire, une métamorphose possible," *Máthesis*, vol. 12 (2003): 238.

135. Shamir, "Ne'urei ha-shira be-arets lo zeru'a," 109.

136. Ben-Ezer, *Yamim shel la'ana u-devash*, 420.

137. Ibid.

138. This phrase comes from the poem "Kahira! Kahira!" Raab, *Kol ha-shirim*, 21. "Myriad shades" is Schimmel's translation of these words.

Chapter 3

1. Cited in Dykman, "Al Leah Goldberg ke-metargemet shira," 218. I have translated from Dykman's Hebrew translation of the original Russian.

2. Leah Goldberg, *Yomanei Leah Goldberg* (Diaries), ed. Rachel and Arieh Aharoni (Bnei-Brak: Sifriyat po'alim-Ha-kibbuts ha-me'uchad, 2005), 227.

3. Goldberg is referring here to the cultural politics of Labor Zionism (*tsiyonut sotsyalistit*), a major current of the Zionist movement. Its followers promoted the establishment of a strong Jewish proletariat in Palestine founded on agricultural labor. A. D. Gordon (1856–1922), one of the major proponents of Labor Zionism, developed a philosophy of labor shaped largely by the writings of Leo Tolstoy. Gordon encouraged communal living based on collective labor and was an early resident of Degania, the first *kevutsa*. His writings, which included a Hebrew translation of Tolstoy's *What is Art?*, greatly influenced the poet Rachel Bluwstein, among others. Cf. Einat Ramon, *Chayim chadashim: dat, imahut, ve-ahava eliyona be-haguto shel Aharon David Gordon* [*New Life: Religion, Motherhood and Supreme Love in the Works of A. D. Gordon*] (Jerusalem: Karmel Books, 2007).

4. Here Goldberg's *kibbutz* means both a group as well as an agricultural collective.

5. Despite her reservations, Goldberg's scholarship on nineteenth- and early twentieth-century Russian literature included the works of Tolstoy. In 1953, Goldberg published her celebrated translation of Tolstoy's *War and Peace* (Milchama ve-Shalom) in two volumes, which were edited by Avraham Shlonsky (Tel Aviv: Sifriyat po'alim). Her essays on Tolstoy appeared later in *Achdut ha-adam ve-ha-yekum be-yetsirat Tolstoy* [*On the Unity of Man and the Universe in the Writings of Tolstoy*] (Jerusalem: Magnes Press, 1959). Goldberg remained interested in Dostoevsky, and her writings on his work were published posthumously in the collection *Ha-drama shel ha-toda'a—pirkei Dostoevsky* [*The Drama of Consciousness: Chapters on Dostoevsky*] (Tel Aviv: Sifriyat po'alim, 1974).

6. The metaphor of the literary passport is central to Shachar Pinsker's reading of European Hebrew writing. Pinsker, *Literary Passports: The Making of Modernist*

Hebrew Fiction in Europe (Palo Alto: Stanford University Press, 2010). For a fuller discussion of the reception of Goldberg's debut collection, see Dan Miron, "Ha-omets le-chulin u-krisato: 'Al *Taba'ot 'ashan* me'et Leah Goldberg ke-tachanat tsomet be-hitpatchut ha-shira ha-'ivrit ha-modernit" ["The Courage for the Ordinary and Its Collapse: On Leah Goldberg's *Smoke Rings* as a Major Junction in the Development of Modern Hebrew Poetry"], *Ha-adam eyno ela ... chulshat-ha-ko'ach, otsmat-ha-chul-sha: 'iyunim be-shira* [*Man is Nothing But ... The Weakness of Being Strong, The Strength in Weakness: Studies in Modern Hebrew Poetry*] (Tel Aviv: Zmora, Bitan, 1999), 309–388.

7. Goldberg was born in 1911 in Königsberg, Prussia, and raised in Kovno (Kaunas), Lithuania. During World War I, her family sought refuge in Russia. Returning home after the war, they were stopped at the Russian–Lithuanian border where her father was psychologically tortured to the point of madness, an event that Goldberg describes in her autobiographical novel *Ve-hu ha-or* [*And This is the Light*] (Merchavia: Sifriyat po'alim, 1946). At an early age, Goldberg began to write and publish Hebrew poetry, demonstrating a high aptitude for formal poetic techniques and Hebrew poetic conventions.

8. Chana Kronfeld, *On the Margins of Modernism: Decentering Literary Dynamics* (Berkeley: University of California Press, 1996), 59.

9. Leah Goldberg, "'Al oto nose 'atsmo" ["On the Very Same Subject"], *Ha-shomer ha-tsa'ir* (September 8, 1939): 9–10. In this essay, Goldberg advances a sharp critique of socially engaged literature (*sifrut meguyeset*) and its demands, which she categorically rejected.

10. Goldberg, *Yomanei Leah Goldberg*, 227.

11. In these years, Goldberg was completing a PhD in semitic languages at the University of Bonn. Her dissertation *Das samaritanische Pentateuchtargum: Eine Untersuchung seiner handschriftlichen Quellen* [*The Samaritan Translation of the Pentateuch: A Study of Handwritten Sources*] (Stuttgart: Verlag W. Kohlhammer) was published in 1935.

12. Yfaat Weiss speculates that this may be the case. She notes, however, that in this period, Goldberg wrote numerous letters to friends and family, and from these letters we can gather the information that is missing from the journals. Goldberg, *Ne'arot 'ivriyot: Mikhtavei Leah Goldberg min ha-provintsiya 1923–1935* [*Hebrew Youth: Leah Goldberg's Letters from the Province*], ed. Yfaat Weiss and Giddon Ticotsky (Bnei-Brak: Sifriyat po'alim-Ha-kibbuts ha-me'uchad, 2009).

13. Goldberg, "15 May 1937," *Yomanei Leah Goldberg*, 225.

14. Pinsker proposes that we think of these centers more as "enclaves," and to open our considerations of Hebrew literary production in Europe to let in other spaces, like the coffee house, spaces that the term "center" excludes. David Patterson's lucid essay, "Moving Centers in Modern Hebrew Literature," acknowledges the continued production of Hebrew literature outside of Palestine, though the book in which it appears, *The Great Transition*, remains invested in a teleology of diaspora to nation. Pinsker, *Literary Passports*, 33–35; Patterson, "Moving Centers in Modern Hebrew Literature," in *The Great Transition*, 3–10.

15. Goldberg, *Ha-omets le-chulin* [*The Courage of the Ordinary*], ed. A. B. Yoffe (Tel Aviv: Sifriyat po'alim, 1976), 185–186.

16. Sidra Ezrahi, *Booking Passage: Exile and Homecoming in the Modern Jewish Imagination* (Berkeley: University of California Press, 2000), 28.

17. I discuss this idea of the poet's map in the introduction. Schimmel, "Translator's Foreword," xx.

18. Goldberg's journal entry on the boat journey from Haifa to Brindisi contains a long passage that articulates a reversal of the archetypal "boat passage" that brought Jewish immigrants to Palestine, often described in Hebrew and Jewish accounts of the early twentieth century as a passage of conversion, of revival into a new national life. It was on these sea voyages that immigrants cast aside their old identities, often marked by their taking on of new names and professions in the Yishuv. Goldberg's trip to Italy reads as a spiritual expurgation (underscored by scenes of actual vomiting!), but it is unclear what aspects of her Palestinian identity she is casting aside. She describes her feeling of estrangement from the other passengers (predominantly, German, French, English, and Hebrew speakers), whom she describes pejoratively as "berkutim" [Russian for "golden eagles," though Sasha Senderovich suggests that the connotation could be closer to "vultures."] (228–229). For a polyglot like Goldberg, this multilingual situation should not have presented any difficulties, and yet she claims, "[I]t would have been nice if there had been on this trip someone that I could have spoken to aside from myself" (229). Goldberg's arrival in Rome does little to improve her mood: she finds the city's cultural life to be stifling and pedantic. A couple of days into her trip, she encounters some fellow Jewish travelers from Palestine and observes that "they walk about with their tour guide like idiots" and refuses to join their party (238). Goldberg is also rattled by her interactions with other European tourists, particularly Germans (236). Her failure to make connections along expected cultural, national, and linguistic lines becomes a recurrent theme in these entries. Goldberg, *Yomanei Leah Goldberg*.

19. Goldberg, *Yomanei Leah Goldberg*, 243.

20. Proverbs 26:6: "Faithful are the wounds of a friend (*pitsei ohev*); but the kisses of an enemy are deceitful." (KJV). "Pitsei ohev" is also the title of one of Goldberg's poetic cycles.

21. Goldberg, "Eiropa shelakhem" ("Your Europe"), *Mishmar* (April 30, 1945). Republished in A. B. Yoffe, *Pegishot 'im Leah Goldberg* [*Encounters with Leah Goldberg*] (Tel Aviv: Cherikover, 1984), 75–76.

22. Yoffe, *Pegishot 'im Leah Goldberg*, 76.

23. Leah Goldberg, "Franchesko Petrarka: Chayav vi-yetsirato" ["Francesco Petrarca: His Life and Work"], in *Mi-dor u-me'ever: bechinot u-te'amim be-sifrut klalit* [*Contemporary and Beyond: Perspectives and Trends in General Literature*], ed. Orah Koris (Tel Aviv: Sifriyat po'alim, 1977), 123–199.

24. Goldberg, "'Al 'ha-komediya ha-elohit" ["On the Divine Comedy"], *Mi-dor u-me'ever*, 82–122. These lectures were transcribed and published by Goldberg's students with her permission.

25. Natasha Gordinsky also addresses Goldberg's relation to Rilke's poetry in her study of Goldberg's early work. Natasha Gordinsky, *Bi-shelosha nofim: yetsirata ha-mukdemet shel Leah Goldberg* [*In Three Landscapes: Leah Goldberg's Early Writings*] (Jerusalem: Magnes Press, 2016).

26. Ofra Yeglin, *Ulai mabat acher: klasiyut modernit ve-modernizm klasi be-shirat Leah Goldberg* [*Modern Classicism and Classical Modernism in Lea Goldberg's Poetry*] (Tel Aviv: Ha-kibbuts ha-me'uchad, 2002), 52.

27. Leah Goldberg, *Kolot rechokim u-krovim: tirgumei shira* [*Voices Near and Far: Translations of Poetry*], ed. Tuvia Ruebner (Tel Aviv: Sifriyat po'alim, 1975), 200–214. The collection *Shirat Rusiya*, which Goldberg coedited with Avraham Shlonsky, includes one of her translations of Blok ("Ну, что же? Устало заломлены слабые руки" ["Well, then? Tiredly wrung weak hands"]). The remaining ten translations of Blok's poems are by Shlonsky. Leah Goldberg and Avraham Shlonsky, eds, *Shirat Rusiya* [*Russian Poetry*] (Tel Aviv: Sifriyat po'alim, 1942), 49–74.

28. Jenifer Presto, "Reproductive Fantasies: Blok and the Creation of *The Italian Verses*," in *Beyond the Flesh: Alexander Blok, Zinaida Gippius and the Symbolist Sublimation of Sex* (Madison: University of Wisconsin Press, 2008), 71.

29. Quoted in Presto, 71. For a more detailed account of this trip, see Lucy E. Vogel, *Aleksandr Blok: The Journey to Italy* (Ithaca: Cornell University Press, 1973).

30. In two separate entries (January 25 and 30), Goldberg quotes from the first section of the collection "Das Buch vom mönchischen Leben" ["The Book of the Monastic Life"], specifically the poem "Das waren Tage Michelangelo's" ("These Were the Days of Michelangelo"). Goldberg, *Yomanei Leah Goldberg*, 239, 245. For one of many English translations of Rilke's *The Book of Hours*, see Rainer Maria Rilke, *The Book of Hours: Prayers to a Lowly God*, trans. Annemarie S. Kidder (Evanston: Northwestern University Press, 2001). Gordinsky also notes a major intertextual relation between this collection and Goldberg's 1937 epistolary novella *Mikhtavim mi-nesi'a meduma* (*Letters from an Imaginary Journey*). Gordinsky, *Bi-shelosha nofim*, 27–36.

31. Rainer Maria Rilke, "The Florence Diary," *Diaries of a Young Poet*, trans. and ed. Edward Snow and Michael Winkler (New York: W. W. Norton, 1997), 1–78.

32. Rilke, *Diaries of a Young Poet*, 24–25.

33. Weather, in particular, carried for Goldberg strong associations to her diasporic past: "It rained. And I who had already forgotten the taste of the rains in June, was very happy with its approach" (June 29, pg. 243). For a more detailed study of weather in Hebrew poetry, see Ziva Ben-Porat, *Ha-stav ba-shira ha-'ivrit* [*Autumn in Hebrew Poetry*] (Tel Aviv: Matkal/Ketsin rashi, 1991).

34. Leah Goldberg, *Avedot* (Tel Aviv: Sifriyat po'alim, 2010). In his afterword, Ticotsky addresses her attachment to Italy and also reads this novel in relation to her essay "Eiropa shelachem." Giddon Ticotsky, "Boker afel ba-bira: acharit devar" ["Grey Morning in the Capital: Afterword"], *Avedot*, 317–353. See also, Avner Shapira, "Be-Germaniya lifnei ha-milchama: ha-roman ha-ganuz shel Goldberg" ["Germany before the War: Leah Goldberg's Unpublished Novel"], *Akhbar ha-'ir* (January 15, 2010), http://www.mouse.co.il/gallery/1.3322813.

35. Leah Goldberg, *Mikhtavim mi-nesi'a meduma* [*Letters from an Imaginary Journey*] (Bnei-Barak: Sifriyat po'alim-Ha-kibbuts ha-me'uchad, 2007 [1937]), 113. Quoted in Gordinsky, *Bi-shelosha nofim*, 35.

36. Leah Goldberg, "Gefen ha-yayin she-be-karmei zarim" ["A Vintage from a Foreign Vineyard"], *Ha-omets le-chulin*, 220–227.

37. Her journal entries in this period indicate that she was working on a novel, most likely *Avedot* (For a full list of these entries, see Giddon Ticotsky, "Afterword," 349.). Goldberg, *Yomanei Leah Goldberg*, 239.

38. In an entry dated July 1, 1937, Goldberg recounts the details of a day trip to Fiesole, where she toured a local monastery. Goldberg, *Yomanei Leah Goldberg*, 236–237.

39. Goldberg, *Yomanei Leah Goldberg*, 247.

40. The poems include, in order, "Ba-derekh" ("On the Road"), "Chalon patu'ach be-Florentsiya" ("An Open Window in Florence"), "Siena," and "Sharav be-Venetsiya" ("Venetian Heatwave"). Leah Goldberg, *Shibolet yerukat ha-'ayin* [*The Green-Eyed Stalk*], *Shirim* [*Poems*], vol. 1, ed. Tuvia Ruebner (Tel Aviv: Sifriyat po'alim, 1973), 159–162. Drafts of "Chalon patu'ach be-Florentsiya" and "Siena" appear in Goldberg's journal entries of the Italian trip, which include as well the unpublished poem "Ha-katedrala" ("The Cathedral"). Goldberg, *Yomanei Leah Goldberg*, 248–250. *Shibolet yerukat ha-'ayin* also includes an homage to Rilke that makes reference to *Das Stunden-Buch*. Goldberg, "R. M. Rilke," *Shirim*, vol. 1, 154.

41. In the published version, Goldberg replaced "tselilut marom" (clearness of sky) with "be-shalvat marom" (in the sky's tranquility). Goldberg, *Shirim*, vol. 1, 160.

42. Y. (Yosef) Saaroni's review of Goldberg's *Taba'ot 'ashan* (published under the byline Y. Sin) is the most frequently cited in this context. At the time of the book's publication, he wrote, "This poet lives outside of time and place … it's hard to believe that she lives in our times, in a modern city, in a noisy environment, and not in a medieval monastery, in a solitary and dark cell." Y. Sin, "Ba-kele ha-intimiyut: *Taba'ot 'ashan* me'et Leah Goldberg" ["In the Prison of Intimacy: Leah Goldberg's *Smoke Rings*"], *Ha-boker* (October 25, 1935): 3.

43. Leah Goldberg, "Yaldut" [Childhood], *Shirim*, vol. 1, 101–110.

44. Goldberg, *Shirim*, vol. 1, 139.

45. Ruth Kartun-Blum, "Kol ha-isha ba-chalon: degem ha-chalon ha-mehufakh be-shirat Leah Goldberg" ["A Woman's Voice at the Window: The Inverted Window as a Pattern in the Poetry of Leah Goldberg"], in *Pegishot 'im meshoreret: masot u-mechkarim*

'al yetsirata shel Leah Goldberg [*Encounters with a Poet: Essays and Studies on the Work of Leah Goldberg*], ed. Ruth Kartun-Blum and Anat Weisman (Tel Aviv: Sifriyat po'alim, 2000), 32–47. The window also functions in Leah Goldberg's work as an "inverted mirror," to use Kartun-Blum's term. In her reading of the poem "Ba-'erev" ("In the Evening"), Kartun-Blum argues that the expansive perspective that a window offers also serves to call attention to and challenge the speaker's narrow world view (37).

46. Goldberg, "Ba-derekh" ["On the Road"], *Davar* (September 9, 1937).

47. The "travel prayer" to which the poem's first stanza most likely refers is the Jewish prayer "tefilat ha-derekh." It is also worth noting that the verb le-*hitnoded* (fluctuating) shares a root with *nedida* (migration).

48. "Tel Aviv 1935" is the first poem of the cycle "Ha-mas'a ha-katsar be-yoter" ("The Shortest Journey"), published in the 1964 collection *'Im ha-layla ha-ze* ("With This Night"). Goldberg, *Shirim*, vol. 3, 14.

49. Barbara Mann has employed the term "vicarious" (following historian Robert B. Riley) to characterize the landscapes that emerge in early writing about Tel Aviv. Her analysis also offers a way of re-reading Goldberg's writing about Europe: "The vicarious landscape is an expression of one's attitude toward a particular place and often involves a personal narrative of attachment or alienation" (351). Mann, "The Vicarious Landscape of Memory in Tel Aviv Poetry," *Prooftexts: A Journal of Jewish Literary History*, vol. 21, no. 3 (October 2001): 350–378.

50. Goldberg, "30 June 1937," *Yomanei Leah Goldberg*, 243. More work remains to be done on Goldberg's use of the epistolary mode and its relation to her own prodigious practice of letter writing. In her journals, Goldberg makes continuous reference to the constant exchange of letters with her friends and family in Palestine, through which she remains connected to her immigrant life in Palestine. Her epistolary novella *Letters from an Imaginary Journey* was published earlier that year, a text that some scholars read as an imagined correspondence with Arieh Naveh. See, Giddon Ticotsky, "Ha-nishkachot— she-i-efshar lishko'ach" ["The Forgotten Things That One Can't Forget"], in *Mikhtavim mi-nesi'a meduma*, 133–170.

51. "Within the broad exigencies of a Zionist literature of 'return,' the helekh or restless wanderer, animated by personal memory, continued to act as control and reproach. The land envisioned as a haven by prophets, poets, philosophers, and politicians had to make room, if only at the margins, for the yearnings and murmurings of dislocated souls." Ezrahi, *Booking Passage*, 193.

52. Kartun-Blum in *Pegisha 'im meshoreret*, 34.

53. Leah Goldberg, "Oren," *Shirim*, vol. 2, 143. Following her return from Italy, and in the years that preceded the publication of *Barak ba-boker* (1955), Goldberg published several collections of poetry including *Shibolet yerukat ha-'ayin* (*The Green-Eyed Stalk*, 1940), *Mi-beiti ha-yashan* (*From My Old Home*, 1942), and *'Al ha-pricha* (*On the Flowering*, 1948), as well as the autobiographical novel *Ve-hu ha-or* (And This is *the Light*, 1946). She also completed several major translation projects including the collection *Shirat Rusiya*

(1942, coedited with Avraham Shlonsky), the poems of Petrarca, and Leo Tolstoy's *War and Peace* (1953).

54. Gluzman's *The Politics of Canonicity* offers a cogent survey of early twentieth-century modern Hebrew literary engagements with the home/exile binary. Gluzman, "Modernism and Exile," *The Politics of Canonicity*, 36–37.

55. Gluzman, "Modernism and Exile: A View from the Margins," in *The Politics of Canonicity: Lines of Resistance in Modernist Hebrew Poetry* (Stanford: Stanford University Press, 2003), 36–67; Natasha Gordinsky, "Homeland I Will Name the Language of Poetry in a Foreign Country—Modes of Challenging the Home/Exile Binary in Leah Goldberg's Poetry," in *Leipziger Beiträge zur jüdischen Geschichte und Kultur*, vol. 3, ed. Markus Kirchhoff and Monika Heinker (München: K. G. Saur Verlag, 2005), 239–253.

56. Gluzman, *The Politics of Canonicity*, 63. Gluzman is quoting from Seamus Deane's essay "Imperialism/Nationalism," in *Critical Terms for Literary Study*, ed. Frank Lentricchia and Thomas McLaughlin (Chicago, IL: University of Chicago Press, 1995).

57. Otto Boele, "North and South," *The North in Russian Romantic Literature* (Amsterdam: Rodopi, 1996), 117–180. For a discussion of the pine tree in Lithuanian folk literature, see Brone Stundzhiene, "The Depiction of Trees in Lithuanian Folk Songs," *Journal of The Baltic Institute of Folklore*, vol. 1, 1997, n.p., *Baltic Institute of Folklore*, http://www.folklore.ee/rl/pubte/ee/bif/bif1/stund.html.

58. In her reading of "Oren," Gordinsky proposes an intertextual relation with Osip Mandelstam's poem "Воздух пасмурный влажен и гулок" ("The Dull Air Is Wet and Loud"), from his 1913 collection *Kamen* [*Stone*], which also features a pine tree. Gordinsky, "Modes of Challenging the Home/Exile Binary in Leah Goldberg's Poetry," 245–247.

59. Mikhail Lermontov, "Сосна" ["Pine"], *Internet Biblioteka*, http://ilibrary.ru/text/999/p.1/index.html.

60. It is interesting to consider, in the context of Goldberg's European/Israeli double-affiliation, how nineteenth-century Russian writers explored and defined their cultural and national identify vis-à-vis Western Europe through literary representations of the Caucasus. For a fuller treatment of this history, see Susan Layton, *Russian Literature and Empire: Conquest of the Caucasus from Pushkin to Tolstoy* (Cambridge: Cambridge University Press, 1995).

61. Boele, *The North in Russian Romantic Literature*, 117.

62. Ibid., 131.

63. Ibid.

64. I would like to thank here one of my anonymous readers for bringing the Manger poem to my attention. Chaim Nachman Bialik, "El ha-tsipor" ["To the Bird"], *Proyekt Ben Yehuda*, http://benyehuda.org/bialik/bia001.html; Itzik Manger, "Oyfn veg shteyt a boym" ["On the Road Stands a Tree"], Hebrew Songs, http://www.hebrewsongs.com/?song=oyfnvegshteytaboym. According to Manger, he wrote the song in the 1930s. Itzik

Manger, "Destiny of a Poem," trans. Murray Citron, *Pakn-Treger: Magazine of the Yiddish Book Center* (Summer 2016), https://www.yiddishbookcenter.org/destiny-poem.

65. An 1897 anthology of Russian poetry published in Germany refers to Lermontov's poem as a *nachbildung*, a "re-creation" (to use Antoine Berman's translation of Schleiermacher's term). Erich Karl Berneker, ed., *Russisches Lesebuch mit Glossar [Readings in Russian with a Glossary]* (Leipzig: Göschen, 1887), 86. Maurice Friedberg points out that Lermontov's translation deviates pointedly from Heine's original with respect to gender. In Heine's poem, the masculine pine tree (*der Fichtenbaum*) longs for the distant female palm (*die Palme*). Friedberg argues, in his reading of Lermontov's translation, that by opting for the Russian feminine "сосна," Lermontov "desexualizes" the erotic tones of Heine's poem, thereby turning it into "a Romantic poem" about poetic loneliness. Friedberg, *Literary Translation in Russia: A Cultural History* (University Park: The Pennsylvania State University Press, 1997), 135. See also, David Powelstock, "'Fierce Integrity': Inner Freedom and Poetic Potentials," *Becoming Mikhail Lermontov: The Ironies of Romantic Individualism in Nicholas I's Russia* (Evanston: Northwestern University Press, 2005), 398–459.

66. Jeffrey L. Sammons observes that Lazarus was "much drawn to Heine's melancholy and his dichotomy of Hellene and Jew" and first published a collection of her translations of Heine in 1866, at the age of seventeen. Sammons, *Heinrich Heine: Alternative Perspectives 1985–2005* (Würzburg: Verlag Königshausen & Neumann, 2006), 44. Lazarus's translation is also an adaptation to a degree.

67. Chaim Shoham, "Oren ve-nof: Model romanti u-model tsyoni" ["Pine and Landscape: A Romantic Model and a Zionist Model"], *Alei si'ach*, vol. 15/16 (1982): 22–38.

68. For a fuller discussion of the history of Heine's translation into Hebrew and the relation between Heine and Halevi, see Na'ama Rokem, *Prosaic Conditions: Heinrich Heine and the Spaces of Zionist Literature* (Evanston, IL: Northwestern University Press, 2013).

69. Gordinsky, "Modes of Challenging the Home/Exile Binary," 224.

70. Sidra Ezrahi, *Booking Passage*, 9.

71. Gluzman, *The Politics of Canonicity*, 63. Gluzman uses this phrase in relation to Gertrude Stein's proclamation that "writers have to have two countries, the one where they belong and the one in which they live really." Gertrude Stein, *Paris France* (New York: Liveright, 1970), 3.

72. Gluzman, *The Politics of Canonicity*, 63.

73. Keats (1795–1821) wrote the poem in 1817 and published it on September 19, 1829, in *Literary Gazette*. John Keats, "In drear nighted December," in *Selected Poems*, ed. John Barnard (London/New York: Penguin Books, 2007): 97–98.

74. Gordinsky, "Modes of Challenging the Home/Exile Binary," 252.

75. Ibid., 243.

76. For the full text of this poem and its translation, see Gluzman, *The Politics of Canonicity*, 56–57.

77. Ibid., 56.

78. Ibid., 57.

79. The line "lilshon ha-shir be-eretz nokhriya" carries a biblical allusion to the birth of Moses's son Gershom. After killing an Egyptian, Moses takes refuge in the land of Midian in the home of Ruel and marries his daughter Tzippora. She gives birth to a son whom Moses names Gershom (*ger-sham*—he lives over there), "for he said 'I have been a stranger in a strange land'" (*ki-amar—ger hayiti be-erets nokhriya*) (Exodus 2:22). One also discerns here another allusion to Psalm 137 ("How shall we sing the Lord's song in a foreign land [*adamat nekher*]").

80. A few of the variations include: "passing birds" (Gluzman, *The Politics of Canonicity*, 63); "migrating birds" (Rachel Tzvia Back, trans., *Lea Goldberg: Selected Poetry and Drama* [London: Toby Press, 2005], 91); and "migratory birds" (Sharon Kessler). Kessler's translations of Goldberg's poetry remain unpublished, but her translation of "Oren" is available online. Kessler, trans., "Pine" by Lea Goldberg, Fish Eye Press, http://www.fisheyepress.com/Translations.html.

81. This cycle was published in the 1964 collection *'Im ha-layla ha-ze* (*With this Night*). Leah Goldberg, "Ha-mas'a ha-katsar be-yoter" ["The Shortest Journey"], *Shirim*, vol. 3, 14–22.

82. Goldberg writes about this first "exile" in her autobiographical novel *Ve-hu ha-or* (*And This is the Light*).

83. Gluzman, *Politics of Canonicity*, 63. The *talush* was a major archetype in nineteenth-century and early twentieth-century modern Hebrew literature. Often a young male, the *talush* represented young Jewish intellectuals cut off from Jewish tradition, and through this figure, writers examined and articulated the schism between (modern European) secularism and Jewish tradition. In the stories of Yosef Chaim Brenner, the *talush* also came to represent the anxieties of the European Jewish immigrant in face of the realities of Palestine. For a survey of the *talush* in modern Hebrew and Yiddish literature, see Yael Chaver, "The Stranger: Hunters and Wanderers," *What Must Be Forgotten: The Survival of Yiddish in Zionist Palestine* (Syracuse, NY: Syracuse University Press, 2004), 52–61.

84. Ezrahi, *Booking Passage*, 9.

85. Six sonnets were initially published in *Molad* in 1952 without the prologue. Leah Goldberg, "Ahavata shel Tereza di Mon," *Molad*, vol. 9, no. 49 (April–May 1952): 33–35. Throughout this book, I have opted to refer to Francesco Petrarca according to the Italian spelling of his name and not use the anglicized form "Petrarch." Doing so allows me to acknowledge the closer relation between the Italian and Hebrew forms of his name.

86. Tuvia Ruebner, *Leah Goldberg: Monografiya* (Tel Aviv: Sifriyat po'alim, 1980), 219.

87. There are numerous ways one can transliterate Goldberg's "Tereza." The most obvious would be "Thérèse" after the French, but previous scholarship on these poems settled on "Teresa" and this became my preferred transliteration as well. In a journal entry, Goldberg does refer to the speaker of these poems as "Terez" (see note 94), but

this spelling appears nowhere else; therefore, I remain convinced that "Teresa" was the name that Goldberg intended.

88. Gordinsky, *Bi-shelosha nofim*, 155.

89. This is not to say that there was no Jewish presence in Avignon in the sixteenth century. According to historian Esther Benbassa, the Jewish presence in the south of France has remained more or less uninterrupted since the twelfth century. By the seventeenth century, Avignon was one of four official *carrières* (gated districts) in Provence where Jews were permitted to live. Benbassa, *The Jews of France: A History from Antiquity to the Present*, trans. M. B. DeBevoise (Princeton: Princeton University Press, 1999). I am grateful to David Bellos for Benbassa's fascinating study to my attention.

90. The ability of literary protagonists to speak in languages they could not have known is an old literary device, and curiously, there is no succinct term or expression to characterize this particular and widespread literary phenomenon. In Aeschylus' *Agamemnon*, e.g., Cassandra speaks in her own tongue though the reader "hears" her voice in Greek. The only indications that she is speaking a language that those around her do not understand are choral references to her foreign tongue and her nonsensical cry *otototoi apolloi!* See, Heather McHugh, "A Stranger's Way of Looking," *Broken English: Poetry and Partiality* (Middletown, CT: Wesleyan University Press, 1993), 41–67.

91. Ariel Hirschfeld offers a post-Holocaust reading of Goldberg's "Tereza" poems, arguing that the "burned poems" that Goldberg's cycle recovers, as it were, articulate the desire to reclaim a world (i.e., prewar Europe) that has been irretrievably lost. Hirschfeld, "'Al mishmar ha-na'iviyut:'Al tafkida ha-tarbuti shel shirat Leah Goldberg" ["Guarding Naiveté: On the Cultural Role of Leah Goldberg's Poetry"], in *Pegishot 'im meshoreret [Encounters with a Poet]*, ed. Ruth Kartun-Blum and Anat Weisman (Tel Aviv: Sifriyat po'alim, 2000), 148.

92. In Stalinist Russia, the fate of poetry often relied on memory—literally, committing to memory poems that could not be written down without great risk. In her memoir *Hope against Hope*, Nadezhda Mandelstam poignantly describes memorizing large quantities of Osip Mandelstam's poetry with Anna Akhmatova's assistance. It is not incidental that "Ahavata shel Tereza di Mon" does contain a number of allusions to Mandelstam's poetry; in fact, I address one of these later in the chapter. The relation between poetry, memory, and orality may extend to include the oral history and transmission of Jewish sacred and liturgical texts. Nadezhda Mandelstam, *Hope against Hope: A Memoir*, trans. Max Hayward (New York: Modern Library, 1999). See also, David Bethea and Clare Cavanagh, "Remembrance and Invention: Poetry and Memory in Modern Russia," *The Russian Review*, vol. 53 (January 1994): 1–8.

93. Giddon Ticotsky, "Mi-chaloni ve-gam mi-chalonkha: hitkatvut dialektit 'im muskamot sifrutiyot be-shir shel Leah Goldberg" ["From My Window and Also from Yours: A Dialectical Correspondence with Literary Conventions in a Poem by Leah Goldberg"], *Alei si'ach*, vol. 53 (2005): 70.

94. Goldberg, "17 June 1952," *Yomanei Leah Goldberg*, 310.

95. Ruebner, *Monografiya*, 127.

96. Francesco Petrarca (1304–1374) spent part of his childhood in Avignon, where he also encountered Laura ("the primary subject of his Italian poetry," in Goldberg's words) on Good Friday, April 6, 1327, at the Church of Sainte Claire d'Avignon. Leah Goldberg, "Franchesko Petrarka: Chayav vi-yetsirato," 123–199. This essay constitutes the introduction to Goldberg's translations of Petrarca, which were first published in 1953.

97. Goldberg, *Avedot*. For an account of this episode that emphasizes how the figure of the Jew is turned into an Oriental subject, see Schachter, "Orientalism, Secularism, and the Crisis of Hebrew Modernism," 345.

98. During his time in Israel, the Swiss-born Jacques Adout (1914–1989) taught French at the Lycée de l'Alliance israélite universelle in Haifa (1952–1954) and also participated in French-language radio programming (1950). On radio and television, he was known primarily under his pseudonym Jacques Balitzer and also translated Russian films into French. Under his own name he published a survey on French-language radio programming in Switzerland titled *Les raisons de la folie?: une enquête de Radio Suisse Romande* [*Why the Madness? A Survey of Radio Suisse Romande*] (Paris: Flammarion, 1979). In 1967, unable to join the IDF because of his age, he reported on the Six-Day War from the frontline. "Jacques Adout," *Bibliothèque nationale de France*, http://data.bnf.fr/12584887/jacques_adout.

99. In *Mikhtavim mi-nesi'a meduma*, Goldberg refers to the recipient of her letters—arguably, a fictionalization of Arieh Naveh, the man she is trying to forget on her 1937 trip to Italy—as *ha-yeled* (the [male] child).

100. Barrett Browning's *Sonnets from the Portuguese* were written between 1845 and 1846 and published in 1850. For a more detailed reading of the Spanish and Portuguese relations that shape these poems, see Barbara Neri, "*Cobridme de flores*: (Un)Covering Flowers of Portuguese and Spanish Poets in Sonnets from the Portuguese," *Victorian Poetry*, vol. 44, no. 4 (2006): 571–583. See also Dorothy Mermin, *Elizabeth Barrett Browning: The Origins of a New Poetry* (Chicago, IL: University of Chicago Press, 1989) and Dorothy Mermin, "The Female Poet and the Embarrassed Reader: Elizabeth Barrett Browning's Sonnets From the Portuguese," *English Literary History*, vol. 48, no. 2 (1981): 351–367.

101. Quoted in Neri, "Cobridme de flores," 571.

102. Ofra Yeglin, *Ulai mabat acher*, 52–54. Ruebner, *Monografiya*, 127; Elizabeth Barrett Browning, *Sonette aus dem Portugiesischen*, trans. Rainer Maria Rilke (Leipzig: Im Insel-Verlag, 1908).

103. Goldberg, "29 September 1939," *Yomanei Leah Goldberg*, 266.

104. Yeglin, *Ulai mabat acher*, 54; Ruebner, *Monografiya*, 126–127. Labé was born in Lyon and lived her entire life in its environs. Her father was a rope maker, a vital industry in a time of sea trade and exploration, and, against convention, he encouraged his daughter's education. He arranged her marriage to a fellow rope maker (lending her the epithet "la belle cordière"), but Labé appears to have eschewed a traditional

domestic role. She was known to host and correspond with well-known poets, including the Pléiade poets Pierre de Ronsard and Joachim du Bellay. A volume of her poems, including twenty-four sonnets, was published in 1555. Deborah Lesko Baker, "Volume Editor's Introduction," in *Complete Poetry and Prose: A Bilingual Edition*, by Louise Labé, ed. Deborah Lesko Baker, trans. Deborah Lesko Baker and Annie Finch (Chicago, IL: University of Chicago Press, 2006), 1–12. Rilke's German translations of Labé appeared in the volume *Die vierundzwanzig Sonette der Louise Labe, Lyoneserin, 1555* (Leipzig: Insel, 1918). For a reading of Rilke's translations, see Cynthia G. Tucker, "Rilke's Eternal Woman and the Translation of Louise Labé," *MLN*, vol. 89, no. 5, German Issue (October, 1974): 829–839. Stampa was born in Padua but her family relocated to Venice following the death of her father. Her mother ensured that all of her children received an education in the arts, and the Stampa home became a hub for artists and writers. Stampa dedicated many of her 311 poems to her lover and benefactor Count Collatino di Collato, whom she addressed as her "Laura." A collection of her poetry, *Rime*, edited by her sister, was published posthumously in 1554. For more on Stampa, consult Frank J. Warnke, "Aphrodite's Priestess, Love's Martyr," in *Women Writers of the Renaissance and Reformation*, ed. Katharina M. Wilson (Athens: University of Georgia Press, 1987), 3–21.

105. Varela employs Gerard Genette's terminology of hypertextuality, where a "hypotext" refers to source material. In his foreword to the English translation of Genette's *Palimpsestes*, Gerald Prince defines the hypertext/hypotext relation as follows: "Any text is a hyptertext, grafting itself onto a hypotext, an earlier text that it imitates or transforms; any writing is rewriting; and literature is always in the second degree." María Encarnación Varela, "Hypotexts of Lea Goldberg's Sonnets *Ahabata shel Tereza di Mon*," *Jewish Studies at the Turn of the 20th Century, Vol. II: Judaism from the Renaissance to Modern Times*, ed. Judit Targarona Borrás and Ángel Sáenz-Badillos (Leiden: Brill, 1999), 236–243; Gerald Prince, "Foreword," *Palimpsests: Literature in the Second Degree [Palimpsestes]*, by Gérard Genette, trans. Channa Newman and Claude Doubinsky (Lincoln: University of Nebraska Press, 1997), ix.

106. Ticotsky, "Me-chaloni ve-gam me-chalonkha," 77. Leah Goldberg, trans., *Okasen ve-Nikolet [Aucassin and Nicolette]* (Jerusalem and Tel Aviv: Sifrei Tarshish and Dvir, 1966).

107. I am grateful to Daniel Heller-Roazen for bringing this connection to my attention. Heller-Roazen, *Fortune's Faces: The Roman de la Rose and the Poetics of Contingency* (Baltimore: Johns Hopkins University Press, 2003).

108. "Jean de Meun … produced a spirited version, the first in French, of the letters of Abelard and Héloïse. A fourteenth-century [manuscript] of this translation in the Bibliothèque Nationale has annotations by Petrarca." Hugh Chisholm, ed., "Jean de Meun," *The Encyclopaedia Britannica: A Dictionary of Arts, Sciences, Literature and General Information*, vol. 15, 11th ed. (Cambridge: The University Press, 1911), 298.

109. The question of authenticity has been debated in a partially archived and now defunct discussion at Fordham's Internet Medieval Source Book. Peter Halsall, ed., *Medieval Sourcebook: Mediev-l Discussion of Heloise's Letters to Abelard*, Fordham University, December 1997, http://sourcebooks.fordham.edu/source/heloisedisc1.asp. M. T. Clanchy also addresses the charge of forgery, and its implications, that has been leveled at de Meun in his contribution to Radice's English translations of the letters. M. T. Clanchy, "The Letters of Abelard and Heloise in Today's Scholarship," *The Letters of Abelard and Heloise*, lvi–lxxxiv.

110. Ticotsky, "Mi-chaloni ve-gam mi-chalonkha," 70–72.

111. The editor of the volume provides a table breaking down the number of participants, their country and institutional affiliation, and the language of their paper. Goldberg and Tuvia Shlonsky attended as Israeli delegates representing the Hebrew University and both gave their papers in English. Shlonsky delivered a paper on T. S. Eliot and Anglophone writing.

112. Leah Goldberg, "Certain Aspects of Imitation and Translation in Poetry," *Actes du IVe congrès de l'Association internationale de littérature comparée, Fribourg 1964* [*Proceedings of the IVth Congress of the International Comparative Literature Association*], vol. 2, ed. François Jost (The Hague: Mouton, 1966), 837–843.

113. Another comprehensive treatment on the topic of translation is Goldberg's essay "Avraham Shlonsky as a Translator of Poetry." Leah Goldberg, "Avraham Shlonsky ke-metargem shira," *Yevul: Kovets le-divrei sifrut u-machshavah 'im yovel Avraham Shlonsky* [*Harvest: A Collection of Literature and Thought for Avraham Shlonsky's Jubilee*] (Merchavia: Sifriyat po'alim, 1950), 31–37. In 1958, Shimon Gan (Ganz) featured a short interview with Goldberg on the topic of poetry translation, as part of a series of discussions that he curated with writers and academics on that subject. Gan, "Leah Goldberg: Tirgum shira" ("Leah Goldberg: Poetry Translation"), *Moznayim*, vol. 7, no. 1 (June 1958): 41–43.

114. Goldberg, "Certain Aspects of Imitation and Translation in Poetry," 837.

115. Ibid., 840.

116. Ronsard (1524–1585) was a French Renaissance poet and prominent figure of the Pléiade, a group of poets that included Joachim du Bellay and Jean-Antoine de Baïf. The Pléiade called for the renewal of French literature and the development of a vital literary French vernacular.

117. Goldberg, "Certain Aspects of Imitation and Translation in Poetry," 841.

118. Leah Goldberg, *Shirim*, vol. 2, 163. For an alternative English translation of this poem, see Rachel Tzvia Back, trans., *Lea Goldberg: Selected Poetry and Drama*, 101.

119. This poem was included in the *Rime sparse* (Il Canzoniere), a collection of 366 poems. Franceso Petrarca, "Pace non trovo," *Petrarca's Lyric Poems: The Rime Sparse and Other Lyrics*, ed. and trans. Robert M. Durling (Cambridge: Harvard University Press, 1976), 272–273.

120. Louise Labé, *Complete Poetry and Prose: A Bilingual Edition*, ed. Deborah Lesko Baker, trans. Deborah Lesko Baker and Annie Finch (Chicago: University of Chicago Press, 2006), 186–187. Annie Finch translated the poetry in this collection.

121. I have taken the French text of Ronsard's poem from a facsimile of a 1553 edition of his *Amours*. Pierre de Ronsard, *Les Amours nouvellement augmentées et commentées par Marc-Antoine de Muret* (Paris: Veuve Maurice de La Porte, 1553), *Gordon Collection*, University of Virginia, https://explore.lib.virginia.edu/exhibits/show/renaissance-in-print.

122. I am very grateful to Bruce Nathan and Rachel Galvin for helping me navigate Ronsard's French and produce this translation. Galvin points out that in Middle French *chaut* refers to heat but is also the third-person singular of *chaloir*, to matter or be of consequence.

123. Goldberg, *Kolot rechokim u-krovim*, 43.

124. Goldberg, "Certain Aspects of Imitation and Translation in Poetry," 842.

125. Chaim Nachman Bialik, "Gilui ve-kisui ba-lashon," *Proyekt Ben Yehuda*, http://benyehuda.org/bialik/article02.html; "Revealment and Concealment in Language" ["Gilui ve-kisui ba-lashon"], *Revealment and Concealment: Five Essays*, trans. Jacob Sloan, ed. Peter Cole and Adina Hoffman (Jerusalem: Ibis Editions, 2000), 25.

126. Goldberg, "Certain Aspects of Imitation and Translation in Poetry," 842.

127. Ibid., 842.

128. Ibid.

129. Ibid., 842–843.

130. Shimon Sandbank also observed these tendencies in Goldberg's translations of Petrarca. Sandbank, "Leah Goldberg ve-ha-sonet ha-petrarki" ["Leah Goldberg and the Petrarcan Sonnet"], *Ha-sifrut*, vol. 6, no. 1 (1975): 19–31.

131. Goldberg, "Avraham Shlonsky ke-metargem shira," 37.

132. Tuvia Ruebner, ed., *Kolot rechokim u-krovim*, 243. Published posthumously in 1975, this collection comprises translations of poetry from at least eight languages. In his afterword, Ruebner remarks that although most of the poems were translated from their original languages, a few—notably poems from Ancient Egypt and the Far East— were second-hand translations (*targum mi-targum*). Many of the translations were completed in the 1940s and the 1950s, which would correspond with the composition and publication history of the works that this chapter addresses. "[This book's] purpose is to bring before the reader the latent transactions that the poet conducted with poets near and far in time and place, with many different cultures, and to bring as well her voice, which returns like an echo from the poems of others" (244).

133. Neri also raises this point with regard to scholars who cite the influence of Portuguese poetry on Barrett Browning's sonnets but have not sought to substantiate further the connections between these influences and the sonnets themselves. In her reading of *Sonnets from the Portuguese*, Neri finds that the poems are shaped by a far greater number of poets than scholars have mentioned. She also observes that the language of the poems alludes to and borrows from texts by several Portuguese, as well as

Spanish, poets, notably Sor Violante do Ceo and Luis de Góngora y Argote. It could be argued that by removing the guise of translation, readers were no longer compelled to listen for these multilingual cadences and rather approached the poems as monologic, original English works. Neri, *Cobridme de flores*, 572.

134. Amia Lieblich, *El Leah* [*Towards Lea*] (Tel Aviv: Ha-kibbuts ha-me'uchad, 1995), 215.

135. Leah Goldberg, trans. and ed., *Lu'ach ha-ohavim: leket shirei ahava mi-shirat Yisrael ve-'amim le-12 chodshei ha-shana* [*A Calendar of Lovers: An International Anthology of Love Poetry for the Twelve Months of the Year*] (Tel Aviv: Amichai, 1966), 127–128. Also appears in Leah Goldberg, *Kolot rechokim u-krovim*, 91.

136. The poem was set to music for the 1970 album *Nesi'a meduma mi-shirei Leah Goldberg* (Imaginary Voyage Lea Goldberg Songs). Its inclusion suggests that it was understood to be one of Goldberg's original poems.

137. Yonah Wallach, "Tereza" and "Tsaroteyha shel Dona Tereza," ["The Troubles of Donna Teresa"], *Tat hakara niftachat kemo menifa: mivchar shirim 1963–1985* [*Subconscious Opens Like a Fan: Selection of Poems*] (Tel Aviv: Ha-kibbuts ha-me'uchad, 1992), 14, 23; Agi Mishol, "Galop," *Mivchar ve-chadashim* [*New and Selected Poems*] (Jerusalem: Mosad Bialik and Ha-kibbuts ha-me'uchad, 2003), 24–31. In her reading of Wallach's poems "Tereza" and "Dona Tereza," Zafrira Lidovsky Cohen describes Wallach's Teresa as "a new female model," but I would suggest that Wallach is actually participating in and continuing a lineage established by Goldberg. Lidovsky Cohen, like Ticotsky, also cites Saint Teresa de Ávila as a potential model for Wallach's "Dona Tereza." Lidovsky Cohen, *Loosen the Fetters of Thy Tongue, Woman: The Poetry and Poetics of Yona Wallach* (Cincinnati: Hebrew Union College Press, 2003), 115–119.

138. Wendy I. Zierler, *And Rachel Stole the Idols: The Emergence of Modern Hebrew Women's Writing* (Detroit: Wayne State University Press, 2004), 121–122.

139. From Elizabeth Barrett Browning's letter to Henry Fothergill Chorley (January 7, 1984). Quoted in Mermin, "The Female Poet and the Embarrassed Reader," 360.

140. Zierler, *And Rachel Stole the Idols*, 125.

141. Leah Goldberg, "Sonnet XII," *Shirim*, vol. 2, 167.

142. Hirschfeld, "Al mishmar ha-na'iviyut," 148.

143. Gordinsky, *Bi-shelosha nofim*, 154–158.

144. Diana Myers, "The Hum of Metaphor and the Cast of Voice. Observations on Mandel'shtam's 'The Horseshoe Finder,'" *The Slavonic and East European Review*, vol. 69, no. 1 (1991): 37. Myer's article also includes the full Russian text of the poem. See also Clare Cavanagh, *Osip Mandelstam and the Modernist Creation of Tradition* (Princeton: Princeton University Press, 1995).

145. Osip Mandelstam, "The Horseshoe Finder: A Pindaric Fragment," trans. Steven J. Willett, *Arion*, vol. 9, no. 2 (Fall, 2001): 92.

146. According to Hirschfeld, this particular sonnet articulates Goldberg's "open challenge to Israeli perceptions of time and place" and, in particular, to any fixed idea of

Israeli contemporaneity. What is contemporary, Goldberg argues, is always illusory; the Israeli "now" is translatable. In addition to this reading, it is also possible that Goldberg is making a reference here to the work of the poet, and her close friend, Avraham Ben Yitzhak (Sonne) (1883–1950), who left an unpublished Hebrew manuscript with his mother for safe-keeping but later learned that it had been destroyed during the Russian invasion of his hometown Przemysl. Ariel Hirschfeld, "Tereza di Mon," Conference on the Centenary of the Birth of Leah Goldberg, Hebrew University of Jerusalem/Tel Aviv University, Israel, May 29–30, 2011. See also, Hannan Hever, *Prichat ha-dumiya: Shirat Ben Yitzhak* [*The Flowering of Silence: The Poetry of Ben Yitzhak*] (Tel Aviv: Ha-kibbuts ha-me'uchad, 1993).

147. Osip Mandelstam, "The Horseshoe Finder," trans. Steven J. Willett, 91.

Chapter 4

1. Nurith Aviv, *From Language to Language* (Swan Productions, 2004). Film. Tropes of disability and their relation to language and language loss are a common feature of Aharon Appelfeld's prose, where they also connect to Holocaust memory and trauma. For one example, see Aharon Appelfeld, *Sipur chayim* [*The Story of a Life*] (Jerusalem: Keter, 1999).

2. "Avot Yeshurun, 88, Poet in Unusual Idiom," *New York Times*, February 24, 1992, New York ed.: B10.

3. E.g., this bias is evident in the title of Shalom Kramer's review of Yeshurun's 1960 collection *Re'em*. Kramer, "Eccentric Poetry," *Yedioth Achronot*, August 14, 1961.

4. Yeshurun began to publish his Hebrew poems in various journals in the early 1930s. His published collections include the following: *'Al chakhmot drakhim* (*On the Wisdom of Roads*, 1942), *Re'em* (1960), *Shloshim 'amud shel Avot Yeshurun* (*Thirty Pages of Avot Yeshurun*, 1964), *Ze shem ha-sefer* (1970, *This Is the Name of the Book*), *Ha-shever ha-suri afrikani* (*The Syrian-African Rift*, 1974), *Kapela kolot* (*A Capella Voices*, 1977), *Sha'ar kenisa, sha'ar yetsiya* (*Entrance Gate, Exit Gate*, 1981), *Homograf* (*Homograph*, 1985), *Adon menucha* (*Master of Rest*, 1990), and the posthumous collection *Ein li akhshav* (*I Have No Now*, 1992).

5. On his mother's side, he was related to the Tzaddik of Nezkizh (Nesukhoyezhe), a town in (present-day) western Ukraine where Yeshurun was also born. For a biography of the poet, see Eda Zoritte, *Shirat ha-pere he-atsil: biografiya shel ha-meshorer Avot Yeshurun* (*The Poetry of the Noble Savage: A Biography of the Poet Avot Yeshurun*) (Tel Aviv: Ha-kibbuts ha-me'uchad, 1996). "Neskhizh/Niesuchojeze," *Merkaz moreshet yahdut polin*, http://moreshet.pl/he/node/1275.

6. I have taken the term "exuberant multilingualism" from Harshav, who uses this term in relation to pre-Statehood Hebrew writing (Harshav, *The Polyphony of Jewish Culture*, 24).

7. Benjamin Harshav, message to author, October 12, 2009, e-mail.

8. Yeshurun discusses this at length in Amir Harel's documentary on the poet. Amir Harel, dir. *Avot Yeshurun: A Documentary* (Tel Aviv: Eugene Wolf Productions, 1992).

9. Yeshurun, *Kol shirav*, vol. 4, 70–73. This poem was published in the 1990 collection *Adon menucha*.

10. "Balada" was first published in 1937 in the periodical *Davar*. Avot Yeshurun, *Kol shirav*, vol. 1 [*Collected Poems*] (Tel Aviv: Ha-kibbuts ha-me'uchad, 1995), 7–13. Cf. Theodor W. Adorno, "On the Use of Foreign Words," *Notes to Literature*, vol. 2, trans. Shierry Weber Nicholsen, ed. Rolf Tiedmann (New York: Columbia University Press, 1992), 286–291.

11. Chana Kronfeld, *On the Margins of Modernism: Decentering Literary Dynamics* (Berkeley: University of California Press, 1993), 13. The influence of Yiddish and Yiddish modernism on Yeshurun's work is also discussed at length in Gluzman and Oppenheimer.

12. Harshav, *The Meaning of Yiddish* (Stanford: Stanford University Press, 1990), 145. Yael Chaver briefly addresses Greenberg's "linguistic ambivalence" in later years in her study of Yiddish culture in Palestine. Yael Chaver, *What Must Be Forgotten: The Survival of Yiddish in Zionist Palestine* (Syracuse: Syracuse University Press, 2004), 111–113. Gluzman also acknowledges the tense friendship between the poets in his reading of Yeshurun's "Pesach 'al kukhim." Michael Gluzman, *The Politics of Canonicity: Lines of Resistance in Modernist Hebrew Poetry* (Stanford: Stanford University Press, 2003), 164.

13. Over the years, Yeshurun's reception in Israel has raised lively debate among Israeli literary critics. In a review of *Adon menucha* (*Master of Rest*, 1990), the writer Batya Gur remarked with regard to Yeshurun's reception: "It had taken thirty years … to crack the wall that isolated [Yeshurun] from his generation." The critic Dan Miron responded that the marginal reception of Yeshurun was a "banal folk tale." According to Miron, Yeshurun's contemporaries admired his "linguistic deformation" (*deformatsiya leshonit*), as corroborated by Yeshurun's publication history. Other critics weighed in with their own assessments of Yeshurun's reception. The critic and translator Shimon Sandbank, in particular, disagreed with Miron. For a full discussion of this episode, see Zoritte, *Shirat ha-pere he-atsil*, 254–255.

14. Helit Yeshurun, "Ani holekh el ha-kol: re'ayon 'im Avot Yeshurun" ["I Walk towards Everything: An Interview with Avot Yeshurun"], *Chadarim*, vol. 3 (1982): 94. The line that Yeshurun cites appears in the poem "Sinai natan shikhmo" (Sinai lent a shoulder) from *Sha'ar kenisa, sha'ar yetsi'a* (1981).

15. Lara Rabinovitch, Shiri Goren, and Hannah S. Pressman, eds, *Choosing Yiddish: New Frontiers of Language and Culture* (Detroit: Wayne State University Press, 2013), 2.

16. Franz Kafka, "Rede über die jiddische Sprache" ("Speech on the Yiddish Language"), in *Gesammelte Werke*, ed. Max Brod (New York: Schocken, 1953), 421–426. I have taken the English translation from Todd S. Presner, *Mobile Modernity: Germans, Jews, Trains* (New York: Columbia University Press, 2007), 5.

17. For a brief elucidation of the double meaning of *bayit*, with an emphasis on its origins in Arabic prosody, see Vered Karti Shemtov, "Dwelling in the Stanzas of the Text: The Concept of 'Bayit' in Hebrew Poetry," *Shm'a: A Journal of Jewish Responsibility* (June 2012): 4–5.

18. Benjamin Harshav, *The Meaning of Yiddish* (Stanford: Stanford University Press, 1990), 36. Derrida, "Des Tours de Babel," 108.

19. See Salim Tamari, "Ishaq al-Shami and the Predicament of the Arab Jew in Palestine," *Jerusalem Quarterly File*, vol. 21 (August 2004): 10–26.

20. For a fuller account of the poem's reception, see Chaya Shacham, "Be-tsomet meshulash—ha-vikuach sviv 'Pesach 'al kukhim' le-Avot Yeshurun" ["At a Triple Crossroads: The Polemic on Avot Yeshurun's 'Passover on Caves'"], *Dapim le-mechkar ha-sifrut*, vol. 10 (1995–1996): 47–65.

21. For a close reading of this poem, see Michael Gluzman, "The Return of the Politically Repressed: Avot Yeshurun's 'Passover on Caves,'" in *The Politics of Canonicity: Lines of Resistance in Modernist Hebrew Poetry* (Palo Alto: Stanford University Press, 2003), 141–172.

22. The S.S. Gianicolo was an Italian carrier ship that brought Jewish *chalutsim* (pioneers) to Palestine in the 1920s. "Disaster Mars Sea Captain's Centennial Trip to Palestine," *Jewish Telegraphic Agency* (April 4, 1934), http://www.jta.org/1934/04/04/archive/disaster-mars-sea-captains-centennial-trip-to-palestine.

23. The expression *kinstei kol* is not idiomatic but may be related to *kintsei milim* (Job 18: 2, "to put an end to the words"). In his notes to this poem, Harshav remarks that *kintsi* is Aramaic for ends/extremities. According to Gesenius, it may be related through an unused root to *kenets* (snare) (Gesenius, 736), hence my translation, "ensnared words."

24. Yeshurun, *Kol shirav*, I: 104. "Huna machatetat" were the opening words of Kol Yisrael's radio broadcast in Arabic.

25. Hanan Hever, "'The Two Gaze Directly into One Another's Face': Avot Yeshurun between the Nakba and the Shoah—An Israeli Perspective," *Jewish Social Studies*, vol. 18, no. 3 (Spring/Summer 2012): 156.

26. Amos Noy, "Al ha-poschim: 'Yahndes lo-lishkoach'? 'Iyun be-mila achat shel Avot Yeshurun" ["On Those Who Pass Over: Don't Forget Yahndes? A Close Reading of Single Word in Avot Yeshurun's Poetry"], *Teoria u-vikoret*, vol. 41 (Summer 2013): 204.

27. Yeshurun, *Kol shirav*, I: 88. This poem responds to the critics of "Pesach 'al kukhim."

28. Jonathan Boyarin, *Thinking in Jewish* (Chicago: University of Chicago Press, 1996): 196. Quoted in Noy, "Al ha-poschim," 207.

29. Though Zionism aspired to a monologic Hebrew national culture, the reality was that multilingualism was more the norm than the exception, as scholars like Liora Halperin and Ariel Saposnik have shown (see bibliography).

30. Riki Traum-Avidan, e-mail, October 21, 2014.

31. Dan Laor suggests that the shack replaces the Eastern European shtetl, turning it "into a vague and rather unpleasant memory." Laor, "Prodigal Sons: Desertion and

Reconciliation in Contemporary Israeli Writing," *Midstream*, vol. 50, no. 4 (May 1, 2004).

32. In Arabic, the word *beyt* can refer to both a house or a tent. Shmuel Moreh, *Modern Arabic Poetry, 1800–1970* (Leiden: E. J. Brill, 1976).

33. Harold Schimmel, "Translator's Foreword," *The Syrian-African Rift and Other Poems*, by Avot Yeshurun, trans. Schimmel (Philadelphia: Jewish Publication Society, 1980), xv.

34. This essay appears in the collection *Ha-shever ha-suri afrikani* (*The Syrian-African Rift*) in a section titled "Proza devarim kolshehem." Yeshurun, *Kol shirav*, vol. 2, 126–130.

35. Rachel Katznelson also addresses the revolutionary aspect of Hebrew in her essay "Language Insomnia," an essay that I will discuss later in this chapter: "The essential thing was that, even though Yiddish is a living language, the language of the people and of democracy, there is a trend of thought, which for us was revolutionary, that expresses itself in Hebrew; whereas Yiddish literature is resulted by narrow-mindedness, mostly inert and reactionary in our eyes and, at best—only a weak echo of what was revealed in Hebrew." Katznelson, "Language Insomnia," 185.

36. For a more extensive treatment of the relation between translation and phantom pain, see Douglas Robinson, "Proprioception of the Body Politic: 'Translation as Phantom Limb' Revisited," *Translation and Interpreting Studies*, vol. 1, no. 2 (2006): 43–71.

37. Sarah S. Jain, "The Prosthetic Imagination: Enabling and Disabling the Prosthesis Trope," *Science, Technology, & Human Values*, vol. 24, no. 1 (Winter 1999): 50.

38. This argument is central to Vivian Sobchack's critique of "the metaphor of the prosethetic." The need for a prosthetic may be motivated or required by a missing part, but once the prosthetic is incorporated, this absence may no longer be an issue. What needs to be interrogated, rather, is what idea of a "normal" body/text underlies the desire or demand for replacement. Sobchack, "A Leg to Stand On: Prosthetics, Metaphor, and Materiality," in *Carnal Thoughts: Embodiment and Moving Image Culture* (Berkeley: University of California Press, 2004), 205–225.

39. Translated by and quoted in Naomi Brenner, "A Multilingual Modernist: Avraham Shlonsky between Hebrew and Yiddish," *Comparative Literature*, vol. 61, no. 4 (2009): 367. These remarks appeared in the second issue of *Ketuvim*, a weekly literary and arts journal that showcased the work of the Hebrew modernists. Avraham Shlonsky, "'Al ha-shalom" ["On Peace"], *Ketuvim*, vol. 34–35 (May 11, 1927): 1. See also Yochai Oppenheimer, "Mukhrachim hayinu lisno gam et asher ahavnu? Galutiyot ve-evel ba-shirat ha-'aliya ha-shlishit" ["Did We Also Have to Hate What We Loved? Exile and Mourning in the Poetry of the Third Aliyah"], *Teoria u-vikoret* (Spring 2014): 175–206.

40. For more on tuberculosis in Jewish literature, including Hebrew and Yiddish, see Sunny Yudkoff, *Let it Be Consumption!: Modern Jewish Writing and the Literary Capital of Tuberculosis*, dissertation (Harvard University, 2015).

41. Quoted in Sobachack, *Carnal Thoughts*, 214. Sobachack is quoting Paul Ricoeur's *The Rule of Metaphor* (1975; English translation, 1977), though she replaces "or" with

"and"); Ricoeur in turn quotes from Pierre Fontanier's *Les figures du discours* (1830). This chain of quotation is mobilized by translation in a way that is reminiscent of Yeshurun's own intertextual practice, and so in this instance, I too have incorporated it.

42. Gluzman's virtuoso reading of "Pesach 'al kukhim" ("Passover on Caves"), e.g., demonstrates the "deep reading" that Yeshurun's poetry often demands of Hebrew readers (Gluzman, *The Politics of Canonicity*, 173–180, 220–223). The extensive footnotes and glosses that Harshav and Helit Yeshurun provide in *Kol shirav* attest to this demand as well.

43. For examples of how Hebrew poetry addressed this linguistic and cultural baggage, see Avot Yeshurun, "Pekla'ot" ["Packages"] (from the Yiddish *peklakh*, bundle) in *Ha-shever ha-suri afrikani*. Avot Yeshurun, *Kol shirav*, vol. 2 (Tel Aviv: Ha-kibbuts ha-me'uchad, 1997), 33–41, and Leah Goldberg, "Tel Aviv, 1935," in '*Im ha-layla ha-ze* (*With This Night*) (Tel Aviv: Sifriat po'alim, 1964 [1961]), 13.

44. Wills, *Prosthesis*, 309. The line "in poetry you must go by force" appears in "Pekla'ot/ Packages," *The Syrian-African Rift and Other Poems*, trans. Harold Schimmel, 51–52.

45. I have taken part of this summary from Wills's chapter "Cambridge, 1553," where he explores the history of the term. Wills, *Prosthesis*, 214–249.

46. For an overview of this literature, see Jain, "The Prosthetic Imagination." See also Carrie Noland, "Digital Gestures," *New Media Poetics: Contexts, Technotexts and Theories*, ed. Adelaide Morris and Thomas Swiss (2005: MIT Press, 2005): 217–243.

47. Johannes Göransson and Joyelle McSweeney, "Manifesto of the Disabled Text," *Exoskeleton* (June 14, 2008), http://exoskeleton-johannes.blogspot.com/2008/06/manifesto-of-disabled-text.html. A print version of this essay was also published in *New Ohio Review*, vol. 3 (2008): 94–98.

48. Johannes Göransson, "Translation Wounds," in Johannes Göransson and Joyelle McSweeney, *The Deformation Zone* (Brooklyn, NY: Ugly Duckling Presse, 2012), 13. The title comes from a poem ("Deformationszon") by the Swedish poet Aase Berg, whose work Göransson has translated into English.

49. Jain raises the issue of privilege in her critique of the prosthetic trope: "Certain bodies—raced, aged, gendered, classed—are often already dubbed as not fully whole." Jain, "The Prosthetic Imagination," 33. See also Tiffany Funk, "The Prosthetic Aesthetic: An Art of Anxious Extensions," Mid-America College Art Association Conference (2012), http://digitalcommons.wayne.edu/macaa2012scholarship/1.

50. This expression appears in the poem "Shiftach" (Arabic for "opening"). Yeshurun, *Kol shirav*, vol. 2, 170–171.

51. Ibid., 44.

52. The specific line that I have in mind—"mother and father are whole and the house is whole"—appears in poem #28 in *Shloshim 'amud shel Avot Yeshurun*, a poem that I discuss in more detail later in this chapter.

53. In the Hebrew title, Yeshurun uses the contracted form of '*amud*, page, and so a more literal translation of the title would be "Thirty Pgs. of Avot Yeshurun."

54. Quoted in Zoritte, *Ha-pere he-atsil*, 213.

55. Daphna Erdinast-Vulcan, "Language, Identity, and Exile," *Policy Futures in Education*, vol. 8, no. 3/4 (June 2010): 444.

56. Göransson and McSweeney, "Manifesto of the Disabled Text."

57. Yeshurun, "Ani holekh el ha-kol," 98–99.

58. The title *Re'em* (רְעֵם) is one of many portmanteau words in Yeshurun's poetic vocabulary. The title's possible associations and meanings include "wild ox" (רְאֵם), "look at them" (רְאֵה אוֹתָם), and "thunder" (רַעַם). Yeshurun, *Kol shirav*, vol. 1, 286.

59. Isaiah 44:1–2.

60. Translation by Naomi Seidman. Seidman, *A Marriage Made in Heaven: The Sexual Politics of Hebrew and Yiddish* (Berkeley: University of California Press, 1997), 119. Seidman takes this account from Chaim Nagid's 1974 interview with Yeshurun (Chayim Nagid, "An Interview with the Poet Avot Yeshurun" [Hebrew], *Yediyot achronot* [October 11, 1974]). This was a story that Yeshurun often related, "one of the more vital images in his memory," according to his biographer Eda Zoritte. In an interview with the journalist Maya Sela, Helit Yeshurun claims that the words Yeshurun's mother spoke were "avos avos" (the Ashkenazic pronunciation of "Avot"). Zoritte, *Ha-pere he-atsil*, 16; Maya Sela, "Who Touches This Touches a Man," *Haaretz* (October 1, 2009).

61. Seidman, *A Marriage Made in Heaven*. Cf. Naomi Seidman, "Lawless Attachments, One-Night Stands: The Sexual Politics of the Hebrew-Yiddish Language War," *Jews and Other Differences: The New Jewish Cultural Studies*, ed. Jonathan Boyarin and Daniel Boyarin (Minneapolis: University of Minnesota Press, 1997), 279–305. Zoritte highlights Yeshurun's varying accounts of this name change in her biography of the poet. Zoritte, *Ha-pere he-atsil*, 141.

62. The army induction ceremony is a compelling context for Yeshurun's name change, particularly in light of the militarized language that shaped debates on language use in British Mandatory Palestine. This language is implicit in the expression "language wars" (which typically refers to tensions between Hebrew and Yiddish) as well as Max Weinreich's classic definition, "a shprakh iz a diyalekt mit an armey un flot" ("a language is a dialect with an army and navy"). See Anat Helman, "'Even the Dogs in the Street Bark in Hebrew': National Ideology and Everyday Culture in Tel-Aviv," *Jewish Quarterly Review*, vol. 92, no. 3/4 (January–April 2002): 359–382. Max Weinreich, "Der Yivo un ki problemen fun undzer tsayt" ["YIVO and the Problems of Our Time"], *YIVO-Bleter*, vol. 25, no. 1 (1945): 13.

63. Seidman, *A Marriage Made in Heaven*, 119.

64. According to Harshav and Helit Yeshurun, "the poems were written between March 1, 1962 (Adar) and May 15, 1963. The number thirty, as in thirty days of mourning, was determined from the onset. Six poems open the cycle, twenty epistolary poems that are shaped by letters that [Yeshurun] received from his family, and four closing poems." Yeshurun, *Kol shirav*, vol. 1, 299.

65. Yeshurun's family wrote to him regularly, almost every fortnight. For an overview of their contents, see Ruhama Albag, "'Od elef shanim omer shimekh" ["To Speak Your Name for a Thousand Years More"], *Haaretz* (September 27, 2009): http://www.haaretz.co.il/literature/1.1282492.

66. Maimonides cites Deuteronomy 21: 13 (KJV: "[she shall] bewail her father and her mother a full month") as textual evidence for this practice (*Hilchot Avel*, 6:1).

67. *Evel rabbati* (or *Smachot*), one of the minor tractates of the Babylonian Talmud, discusses this practice (and all practices related to mourning) in detail. For an English translation, see *The Tractate 'Mourning': Regulations Relation to Death, Burial, and Mourning*, trans. Dov Zlotnick (New Haven: Yale University Press, 1966).

68. Maurice Lamm, *Consolation: The Spiritual Journey beyond Grief* (Philadelphia: Jewish Publication Society, 2004), 87.

69. Maurice Lamm, "Keriah—The Rending of Garments," in *The Jewish Way in Death and Mourning* (Flushing, NY: John David, 2012), http://www.chabad.org/library/article_cdo/aid/281558/jewish/Keriah-The-Rending-of-Garments.htm.

70. For a full account of this expedition, see Yigael Yadin, *Bar-Kokhba: The Rediscovery of the Legendary Hero of the Last Jewish Revolt against Imperial Rome* (New York: Random House, 1971). See also, Steven D. Fraade, "Language Mix and Multilingualism in Ancient Palestine: Literary and Inscriptional Evidence," *Jewish Studies*, vol. 48 (2012): 1–40.

71. In his reading of the discovery of these letters, Haim Weiss examines their public reception with particular attention to the reburial of these letters in a full military ceremony. Weiss, "Le-fet'a hukam gesher el me'ever le-alpayim shana: mi-arkhi'ologiya mechulenet le-arkhi'ologiya datit: ha-mikre shel Bar-Kosiba, Yigael Yadin u-Shlomo Goren" ("From Secular to Religious Archeology: The Case of Bar-Kosiba, Yigael Yadin and Shlomo Goren"), *Teoria u-vikoret*, vol. 46 (2016): 143–167.

72. For an extensive, and still classic, study on the politics of archeology in Israel, see Yael Zerubavel, *Recovered Roots: Collective Memory and the Making of Israeli National Tradition* (Chicago, IL: University of Chicago Press, 1995), as well as Nadia Abu El-Haj's incisive and polemical *Facts on the Ground: Archeological Practice and Territorial Self-Fashioning in Israeli Society* (Chicago, IL: University of Chicago Press, 2001).

73. Yadin, *Bar-Kokhba*, 181. Michael Owen Wise urges a more "nuanced understanding of language usage" in classical antiquity and, in particular, in the period of the Bar Kokhva revolt. He cites manuscripts that support the possibility that Hebrew had been in official use in Judaea for over a century, thereby implying that its appearance in the Bar Kokhva documents simply accords with general custom rather than serving as a "reflection of concomitant high nationalist feeling." Wise, *Language and Literacy in Roman Judaea: A Study of the Bar Kokhba Documents* (New Haven: Yale University Press, 2015): 130.

74. Amir Gilboa, *Shirim ba-boker ba-boker* [*Songs in the Early Morning*] (Tel Aviv: Hakibbuts ha-me'uchad, 1953): 18. For a reading of this poem and the figure of the living dead, see Hannan Hever, "Gender, Body and the National Subject: Israeli Women's Poetry in

the War of Independence," in *The Military and Militarism in Israeli Society*, ed. Edna Lomsky-Feder, Eyal Ben-Ari (Albany: State University of New York, 1999), 225–260. (For the original Hebrew version, see Hannan Hever, "Shirat ha-guf ha-le'umi: Nashim meshorerot milchemet ha-shichror," *Teoria u-vikoret*, vol. 7 [Winter 1995]: 99–123.)

75. In a comparative reading of the Holocaust poetry of Gilboa and Yeshurun, Laor cites Eda Zoritte's observation that the discovery of the letters in his possession, after so many years, prompted the writing of these poems. Laor, "Prodigal Sons," 33–38.

76. Presner is addressing here the status of the ruins of the Anhalter Bahnhoff, a train station located just outside of Berlin. Presner reflects on the relation between time and ruins, which are material testaments to the past but also subject to processes of decay and commodification. Preserving these ruins in a museum is one way to ensure their persistence and presence in the present and the future, but ultimately these attempts to contain the past prove futile. "One day, these landscapes of ruins will be cleaned up, determined, and assigned meanings. Indeed, in the not too distant future, the last material remains of the Holocaust will be settled." Todd S. Presner, *Mobile Modernity: Germans, Jews, Trains* (New York: Columbia University Press, 2007): 41.

77. E.g., in Hebrew, a single lexical unit like *ve-lo* (and not) contains two words.

78. One may cite here the poetry of the early German expressionist August Stramm (1874–1915), who developed a telegraphic prosody that Bernhard Siegert attributed to his years working in the postal service and his experiences with the telegraph. Siegert, *Relays: Literature as an Epoch of the Postal System*, trans. Kevin Repp (Stanford: Stanford University Press, 1997), 182–185.

79. Dan Pagis, "Katuv be-'iparon ba-karon he-chatum" ("Written on the Sealed Railway Car"), *Gilgul* (Ramat Gan: Masada, 1970), 22.

80. According to Harshav and Helit Yeshurun, Yeshurun devised this pattern before writing the poems. Yeshurun, *Kol shirav*, vol. 1, 299.

81. Robert Kuwalek, "Krasnystaw," *Holocaust Research Project* (2007), http://www.holocaustresearchproject.org/ghettos/kranystaw.html. The last letter that Yeshurun received from his brothers was posted from Kovel in early 1940.

82. It is worth mentioning, though the relation is most likely not relevant to this poem, that the town of Toscek, a word related to the Polish word *toczek* (grindstone), was the location of a civilian internment camp during World War II (the town was renamed Tost during the German occupation). "Toszek," *Wikipedia*, https://en.wikipedia.org/wiki/Toszek. Laor speculates that the Perlmutters may have perished at Majdanek, an extermination camp outside of Lublin, in German-occupied Poland. Laor, "Prodigal Sons."

83. For an overview of the role of the post as a source of news during World War II, see Alexandra Garbarini, *Numbered Days: Diaries and the Holocaust* (New Haven: Yale, 2006), 64–71. Bob Ingraham's online essay on the Red Cross mail service scheme in the German-occupied Channel Islands offers compelling suggestions of how this scheme may have worked in other countries. See Ingraham, "The Channel Islands at War—The

Red Cross Message Scheme," *Ephemeral Treasures* (December 12, 2014), http://www.ephemeraltreasures.net/channel-islands-red-cross-message-scheme.html. For a more general summary of Red Cross activity during World War II, see Elizabeth O. Schafer, "Red Cross," in *World War II in Europe: An Encyclopedia*, ed. David T. Zabecki (New York: Routledge, 1999), 753–754.

84. Yad Vashem's website features such a missive, sent by Stefania Wilczyńska (1886–1942), who worked with children in the Warsaw Ghetto. Wilczyńska accompanied the orphans when they were transferred to the Treblinka extermination camp, from which none survived. Between 1935 and 1939, Wilczyńska was a resident of the kibbutz Ein Harod, located in the Jezreel Valley in what is today northern Israel. Wilczyńska, "Postcard to the members of Ein Harod," *Yad Vashem*, http://www.yadvashem.org/yv/en/exhibitions/women-in-the-holocaust/caring-others/stefania-wilczynska.asp.

85. Advancements were made in invisible ink production in the early twentieth century, but old standbys like lemon juice were still in use. During World War I, the Allies discovered that exposing some of these inks to an iodine solution would reveal the hidden messages, which would appear as blue text. This is due to the reactive properties of iodine, particularly when it comes into contact with starch, which is used in paper production and some ink compounds. Censors continued to rely on iodine solutions and vapors through World War II (the assumption being that the average person would continue to rely on basic home materials to produce invisible ink). Kristie Macrakis, *Prisoners, Lovers and Spies: The Story of Invisible Ink from Herodotus to al-Qaeda* (New Haven: Yale University Press, 2014).

86. "[People] could also clutch at the absence of news to reinforce their hopes, since silence left their loved ones' deaths unconfirmed." Garbarini, *Numbered Days*, 70.

87. For a fascinating illustrated history of the picture postcard, see Frank Staff, *The Picture Postcard and its Origins* (London: Lutterworth Press, 1966). Mark Gobles's *Beautiful Circuits: Modernism and the Mediated Life* (New York: Columbia University Press, 2010) reflects on literary modernism's "medium aesthetic" and its engagement with new practices and technologies of communication. His study prompted me to consider the relation between medium and prosody in *Shloshim 'amud*. Finally, Esther Milne's *Letters, Postcards, Email: Technologies of Presence* (London: Routledge, 2013) offers a comprehensive reading of the development of the epistolary mode from the letter to the blog post.

88. Galit Hasan-Rokem, "Jews as Postcards, or Postcards as Jews: Mobility in a Modern Genre," *Jewish Quarterly Review*, vol. 99, no. 4 (Fall 2009): 510.

89. Ibid., 511.

90. Walter Benjamin, "Berlin Chronicle," trans. Edmund Jephcott, in *Walter Benjamin: Selected Writings 1931–1934*, vol. 2, Pt. 2, ed. Michael W. Jennings, Howard Eiland, and Gary Smith (Boston, MA: Harvard University Press, 1999): 621. Benjamin had an extensive archive of picture postcards and at one point had planned to publish a project on the aesthetics of picture postcards. "Walter Benjamin: His Life in Postcards,"

The Art Newspaper (September 25, 2015), http://theartnewspaper.com/news/walter-benjamin-his-life-in-postcards/.

91. Esther Milne, "Postcards," in *The Routledge Handbook of Mobilities*, ed. Peter Adey et al. (New York: Routledge, 2014): 314. See also, Melissa Jane Hardie, "Late Modern Blog: Affect, Contagion and Flow from the Picture Postcard to the Blogosphere," in *What is the New Rhetoric?* ed. Susan Thomas (Cambridge: Cambridge Scholars, 2007), 140–153.

92. Hasan-Rokem, "Jews as Postcards," 511. A promising point of comparison would be the work of the American-born Hebrew poet Reuven Ben-Yosef and his cycle "Mikhtavim le-America" ("Letters to America"). See Michael Weingrad, ed. and trans., *Letters to America: Selected Poems of Reuven Ben-Yosef* (Syracuse: Syracuse University Press, 2015).

93. Noa Osterreicher, "Shirim le-megira" ("Poems for a Drawer"), *LaMegira*, https://lamegira.wordpress.com.

94. https://lamegira.wordpress.com/2014/04/24/איך-נקראאבות-ישורון/.

95. My reading of Leah Goldberg's "Oren" in chapter 3 offers a fuller account of this binary and its relation to German and Russian Romanticism.

96. Hardie, "Late Modern Blog Blogosphere," 143.

97. Yeshurun, "Shir ʿeres li-shekhunat Nordiya" ["Lullaby for Nordia Quarter"], in *The Syrian-African Rift and Other Poems*, 52–55.

98. Stevens, "A Postcard from the Volcano," 159. "The voices explain that, despite the restrictions of textual space imposed by a postcard and of imaginative space imposed by the passage of years, they are able to express their lost world because their experience was embedded in their language: they have imprinted themselves on the landscape in ways that may be less discernible than bones but that are ultimately more profound. Though children cannot imagine that the bones of these dead ever articulated skeletons like their own, ever hung muscles and walked shoes just as their own bones do, they nevertheless speak the speech of the dead. The experience of the dead has been preserved in their idioms—their vernacular of perception." Allyson Booth, *Postcards from the Trenches: Negotiating the Space Between Modernism and the First World War* (Cary, NC: Oxford University Press, 1996), 16.

99. Stewart, *On Longing: Narratives of the Miniature, the Gigantic, the Souvenir, the Collection* (Durham: Duke University Press, 1993 [1984]), xii.

100. Judges 5:31 (Song of Deborah).

101. The Hebrew Bible contains numerous references to acacia trees, which are used in the construction of the *mishkan* (Tabernacle). The shamouti, a word of Arabic provenance, is more commonly known as the "Jaffa orange." It is a sweet, almost seedless variety of orange that was cultivated in Jaffa, Palestine, in the mid-nineteenth century and became a popular export. Cf. Carol Bardenstein, "Threads of Memory in Discourses of Rootedness: Of Trees, Oranges and Prickly-Pear Cactus in Palestine/Israel," *Edebiyât: A Journal of Middle Eastern Literatures*, vol. 8, no. 1 (1998): 1–36.

102. Yeshurun, *Kol shirav*, vol. 1, 187. Although the third line of the second stanza—"Ani hayiti me'ane"—translates literally as "I would torture," "I would sing" is another possibility. This also may reflect a non-standard conjugation of the verb "answer."

103. Zoritte, *Shirat ha-pere he-atsil*, 90.

104. Ibid., 214.

105. In a comparative reading of Celan and Yeshurun, Sandbank examines the status of the date in both poets' oeuvres and the tension between the poem's date of composition, the event the poem references/addresses, and the present continuous time of the poem's reception. Shimon Sandbank, "Ha-ta'arikh, Celan, Derrida, Yeshurun" ["The Date"], in *Eikh nikra Avot Yeshurun* [*How Shall We Read*], ed. Lilach Lachman (Tel Aviv: Ha-kibbuts ha-me'uchad, 2011), 97–106.

106. Jacques Derrida, *The Post Card: From Socrates to Freud and Beyond* [*La Carte Postale*], trans. Alan Bass (Chicago, IL: University of Chicago Press, 1987). The French original was published by Flammarion in 1980.

107. "Mother!/For whom have I written those letters?/Which mail service will deliver them?/All routes—land, sea, air—are cut!" Mahmoud Darwish, "A Letter from Exile," trans. Ben Bennani, *Boundary* 2, vol. 8, no. 3 (Spring 1980): 203–206. While the late nineteenth-century internationalization of the postal system promised to "enfranchise" readers across various geographies, languages, and social classes, it also emerged out of a desire to regulate communication. Darwish's poem addresses this power of the post but also finds a way to bypass it through the circulation of the poetic text. Hardie, "Late Modern Blog Blogosphere," 143.

108. See Avot Yeshurun, "Habalada shel Berl Shloser" ["The Ballad of Berl Shloser"], in *Kol Shirav*, vol. 2, 152–154; Yeshurun, "Ma she-noge'a" ["That Which Touches"], ibid., 161–162; Yeshurun, "Zichronot hem bayit" ["Memories are a House"], *Kol Shirav*, vol. 4 (Tel Aviv: Ha-kibbuts ha-me'uchad, 2001), 130–131.

109. Avot Yeshurun, *Kol shirav*, vol. 4, 130–131.

110. See Lachman's reading of Yeshurun's "Ha-shir 'al ha-ashma" ["Poem on the Guilt"] and her provocative analysis of the way Yeshurun overlaps personal and collective histories. "The frames unfold through displacements of memory rather than through chronological linking; space is organized through leaps from one frame to another, presenting time as an aberrant movement." Lachman, "I manured the land with my mother's letters," 70.

111. In Leon Wieseltier's fine translation of this poem, the Yiddish text is italicized. Avot Yeshurun, "Memories Are a House," trans. Wieseltier, *Poetry* 192, vol. 1 (2008): 49. In Hebrew, the word *dimdum* can mean fading and twilight (*dimdumim*).

112. See the poem "Спасибо земля" ("Thank You, Land"), which appeared in the 1985 collection *Homograf*. Avot Yeshurun, *Kol shirav*, vol. 3 (Tel Aviv: Ha-kibbuts Ha-me'uchad, 2001), 167.

113. In Hebrew, the words for "pain" and "rope" are virtually the same, *chevel*. Their differences are far more conspicuous in construct form: *chavlei* for "rope" and *chevlei* for "pain."

114. The expression "chavlei shena" appears in the opening of the "Bedtime Shema" (Keri'at shem'a 'al ha-mita), a Jewish prayer that is recited before going to sleep. A comparable image is also present in *Birkot ha-shachar* (*Dawn Blessings*).

115. In "Language Pangs" (1905), Bialik argues in favor a vital and dynamic approach to writing and speaking in Hebrew that resists the constraints of "normative rules," which strip language of its vitality, revealing "the dry bones of its philological skeleton." Chaim Nachman Bialik, "Chevlei lashon" ["Language Pangs"], *Kol kitvei Ch. N. Bialik* (Tel Aviv: Dvir, 1939). For a more extensive analysis of this essay, see Kronfeld, *On the Margins of Modernism*, 83–92.

116. In Nurit Aviv's 2004 documentary, *Mi-safa le-safa* (*From Language to Language*), Appelfeld addresses this anxiety in relation to Yiddish as well as German.

117. When the writer Mendele Mokher Sforim wanted to use the plural "potatoes," he created *bulbusin*, a combination of the Latin *bulbus* and the Yiddish *bulbes* to which he gave an Aramaic plural ending. Later, this word was replaced with *tapuchei adama*, literally "apple of the earth," which is currently in use in Israel. However, as Harshav notes, *tapuchei adama* is, in turn, a calque of the French *pomme de terre*. But the advantage of *tapuchei adama* over *bulbusin* is that it does not sound like Yiddish. For a full account of this transmission, see Benjamin Harshav, *Language in Time of Revolution* (Berkeley: University of California Press, 1993), 83.

118. Chaver provides several examples of Yiddish loan translations in the works of Shmuel Yosef Agnon and Yosef Chaim Brenner. Chaver, *What Must Be Forgotten*, 29–31.

119. Katznelson, "Language Insomnia," 187.

120. Eliezer Ben-Yehuda, *Ha-chalom ve-shivro* [*The Dream Fulfilled*], *Proyekt Ben-Yehuda*, http://benyehuda.org/by/haidan_harishon.html. Although I have translated this quotation into English, I also would like to direct readers to T. Muroaka's full English translation of Ben-Yehuda's biography, *A Dream Come True*, ed. George Mandel (Boulder: Westview Press, 1993).

121. Joseph Brodsky, "In a Room and a Half," *Less Than One: Selected Essays* (New York: Farrar Straus Giroux, 1986), 461. My emphasis.

122. Alexandra Berlina also reads this essay in relation to Brodsky's practices of (English) self-translation. Berlina, *Brodsky Translating Brodsky: Poetry in Self-Translation* (London/New York: Bloomsbury, 2014).

123. Brodsky, "In a Room and a Half," 460.

124. Chaver, *What Must Be Forgotten*, 44. Chaver's research is deeply invested in exploring the ways in which Yiddish literary culture both survived and thrived in a national culture that, at least on the surface, repudiated multilingualism in general and Hebrew–Yiddish bilingualism in particular.

125. Yeshurun, *Kol shirav*, vol. 1, 213–216.

126. Ibid., 215.

127. The poem "Shnei netsachim" ("Two Eternities") in *Sha'ar kenisa, sha'ar yetsiya* also makes reference to this poem: "Studying *lataynish*, writing, (for) the first/time in my life, a poem "Di nevo'a in gezang"/in Yiddish." Yeshurun, *Kol shirav*, vol. 3, 72–73.

128. Zoritte suggests that these documents may have been recovered at some point though there is no archival evidence of this Yiddish poem. Zoritte, *Ha-pere he-atsil*, 28.

129. Emily Apter, "Translation with No Original: Scandals of Textual Reproduction," in *Nation, Language, and the Ethics of Translation*, ed. Sandra Bermann and Michael Wood (Princeton: Princeton University Press, 2005), 162.

130. Yeshurun, *Kol shirav*, vol. 2, 169; Zoritte, *Ha-pere he-atsil*, 28. "Mikra'ei Tsion" is also the title of a poem by Bialik, which he wrote in 1897, following the First Zionist Congress in Basel.

131. Zoritte, *Ha-pere he-atsil*, 28.

132. Yeshurun, *Kol shirav*, vol. 1, 208.

133. Compare this with Salman Masalha's poem "Ani kotev 'ivrit" ("I Write Hebrew"), which also plays with this distinction to assert the agency of the Palestinian Hebrew poet. Masalha, "Ani kotev 'ivrit," in *Echad mi-kan* [*In Place*] (Tel Aviv: 'Am 'oved, 2004), 15–16.

134. See note 31.

135. Samuel 25:29: Yet a man is risen to pursue thee, and to seek thy soul: *but the soul of my lord shall be bound in the bundle of life* (ve-hayta nefesh adoni tsrura bitsror ha-chayim) with the Lord thy God; and the souls of thine enemies, them shall he sling out, as out of the middle of a sling (KJV).

136. For some discussions on the development of Hebrew poetry and prosody in relation to Arabic, see Peter Cole, "Introduction," *The Dream of the Poem: Hebrew Poetry from Muslim and Christian Spain 950–1492*, trans. Peter Cole (Princeton: Princeton University Press, 2007), 1–20; Dan Pagis, *Chidush ve-masoret be-shirat-ha-chol: Sefarad ve-Italiya* [*Innovation and Tradition in the Secular Poetry of Spain and Italy*] (Jerusalem: Keter, 1976); Ross Brann, *The Compunctious Poet: Cultural Ambiguity and Hebrew Poetry in Muslim Spain* (Baltimore, MD: Johns Hopkins University Press, 1991); Ross Brann, "The Arabized Jews," *The Literature of Al-Andalus*, ed. Maria Rosa Menocal, Raymond P. Scheindlin, and Michael Sells (Cambridge: Cambridge University Press, 2000), 435–454.

137. I would like to thank Eran Tzelgov for drawing my attention to this relation.

138. The younger brother in the poem may be Israel Mordechai Perlmutter, who was a year younger than Yechiel and also immigrated to Palestine. The two brothers were the only surviving members of their family. According to his niece Chaya Meroz, their political differences provoked an estrangement that lasted for many years. "Avot Yeshurun, Berdichevsky 8," *Snunit* (January 26, 2010), http://www.snunit.k12.il/shireshet/tel_avot.htm. The brothers later reconciled, an episode that Yeshurun recounted in his poem "'Al ele ani 'atuf," which appeared in the posthumous collection *Ein li akhshav*

(*I Have No Now*): "Many years my brother is here in this country/he didn't come to me. Until I was lying in an isolation ward./He came. I had the chance to say to him: / Didn't we once have *immali, abbali*" (Yeshurun, *Kol shirav*, vol. IV, 210). In the version that Yeshurun related to Zoritte, instead of the Hebrew *immali* (mommy) and *abbali* (daddy)—both words that employ the Yiddish-inspired, though old-fashioned, modern Hebrew diminutive suffix *–li*—Yeshurun uses the Yiddish *mameshi* and *tateshi* (Zoritte, *Ha-pere he-atsil*, 257).

139. This event is also the subject of the poem "Einbul" ("Stampless"), which appeared in the same collection. Yeshurun, *Kol shirav*, vol. 1, 219.

140. Ibid., 215.

141. In the Hebrew title, "Ha-sifrut ha-ʿivrit taʾarokh et ha-tefila" ("Hebrew Literature Will Arrange the Prayer"), the verb *taʾarokh* can be understood in terms of performance, arrangement, and setting (in the musical sense), but also encompasses its more common usage "editing" and "organizing." The essay, dated December 14, 1967, was later published in *Haaretz* on January 5, 1968. Quoted in Roy Greenwald, "Homophony in Multilingual Jewish Cultures," *Dibur*, vol. 1 (2015), http://arcade.stanford.edu/dibur/homophony-multilingual-jewish-cultures. (With his permission, I have slightly modified Roy Greenwald's translation of this essay.) For the full Hebrew text, see Avot Yeshurun, *Milvadata* [*Selected Poems*], ed. Helit Yeshurun and Lilach Lachman (Ha-kibbuts ha-meʿuchad, 2009), 87. For a full English translation, see Yeshurun, "Hebrew Literature Will Set the Prayer," trans. Lilach Lachman and Gabriel Levin, in *PN Review* 174, vol. 33, no. 4 (March–April 2007): 28.

Chapter 5

1. Harold Schimmel, "Katsida," *Chadarim*, vol. 10 (1993): 65.

2. Harold Schimmel, "Translator's Foreword," in *The Syrian-African Rift and Other Poems*, trans. Harold Schimmel, ed. Avot Yeshurun (Philadelphia: Jewish Publication Society, 1980), xi–xxi.

3. Ibid., xiii. In Schimmel's analogy, Yiddish has palliative powers that Hebrew (in this case, the Hebrew readership) initially resists. The idea of Yiddish as a medicine complements the prosthetic reading that I offer in the preceding chapter. Also, it is worth noting that Schimmel refers to Yeshurun as Perlmutter throughout the introduction, thereby acknowledging the Hebrew poet's Yiddish beginnings and the ways in which his English translation of these poems keeps the Yiddish "close" as well.

4. Yeshurun, *Kol shirav*, vol. 2, 170–171.

5. Schimmel, "Translator's Foreword," xx.

6. Ibid. I discuss Robert Lowell's translations of the Italian poet Eugenio Montale later in this chapter. Michel Deguy (b. 1930) is a French poet and author of several collections of poetry. His translations of the Spanish Baroque poet Luis de Góngora can be found in *Revue de Poésie*, No. 60 (September 1966).

7. Schimmel, "Translator's Foreword," xi. Gustavo Adolfo Bécquer (1836–1870) is one of the most celebrated Spanish poets of the nineteenth century. His work is affiliated with post-romanticism and was an influence on a number of twentieth-century poets, including Rubén Darío and Octavio Paz. The poem Schimmel refers to, "Volverán" ("They Will Return"), appeared in his collection *Rimas* (1968). Schimmel's spelling of the title reflects how it appears in Lowell's *Notebook* (1970).

8. Ibid. Merce Cunningham, the famed American dancer and choreographer, developed over eight hundred "Events," dance collages (made up of pieces from previous performances) that were held in unconventional spaces, including the Piazza San Marco in Venice in September 1972. "As Mr. Cunningham defines the term, an 'Event' is a performance lasting about 90 minutes and consisting of bits and pieces from dances in the company's repertory. But instead of being presented as a set of obvious excerpts from longer works, these fragments are so intermingled as to constitute a new entity that is satisfying on its own terms." Jack Anderson, "Dance: Merce Cunningham 'Events,'" *New York Times*, December 2, 1985, http://www.nytimes.com/1985/12/02/arts/dance-merce-cunningham-events.html.

9. Schimmel, "Translator's Foreword," xiv.

10. Harold Schimmel, "Two Views of Jerusalem," *Now*, ed. Maxim Ghilan (Jerusalem: Akhshav, 1964), 31. Reprinted in *Retrievements: A Jerusalem Anthology*, ed. Dennis Silk (Jerusalem: Keter Publishing House Jerusalem, 1977), 163.

11. Ben-Ezer, *Yamim shel la'ana u-dvash*, 272.

12. One notable example is *Fourteen Israeli Poets: A Collection of Modern Hebrew Poetry* (London: Deutsch, 1976), edited by Dennis Silk. Schimmel contributed several translations as well as the introduction. For an overview of Israeli poetry in English translation, see Ruth Whitman, "Motor Car, Bomb, God: Israeli Poetry in Translation," *The Massachusetts Review*, vol. 23, no. 2 (Summer 1982): 309–328. Whitman includes an appraisal of English-language poets like Silk and Robert Friend, whom she regards as Israeli poets writing in English.

13. It is also not clear that he ceased entirely to write in English. For example, the essay "Masekhet 'al zikaron" ("Tract on Memory"), which appeared in 1993 in the journal *Teoria u-vikoret*, is a Hebrew translation of a piece originally written in English. Although the original English text remains unpublished, the Israeli composer Eitan Steinberg incorporated sections from the original in his composition "Dancing Memory Fish" (2012). Harold Schimmel, "Masekhet 'al zikaron" ["Tract on Memory"], trans. Amir Or (with Irit Sela), *Teoria u-vikoret*, vol. 4 (Autumn 1993), 9–22.

14. Louis Zukofsky, "A" (New York: New Directions Books, 2011).

15. The twenty-four parts of "A" correspond to the twenty-four hours of a day. Pieces of the text were published in Zukofsky's lifetime, but the entire collection—which ends on the word "Zion"—only appeared in print in 1978, shortly after the poet's death. The most recent edition, published by New Directions, runs to more than eight hundred pages. Schimmel contributed to a special issue of *Paideuma* which was dedicated to

Zukofsky. His remarks focused on Zukofsky's translations of the Yiddish poet Yehoash (pen name for Solomon Blumgarten), as well as the Hebrew and Yiddish cadences that shape the language of "A." Harold Schimmel, "Zuk. Yehoash David Rex," *Paideuma*, vol. 7, no. 3 (1978): 559–569.

16. See Charles Bernstein, "Introduction," *Louis Zukofsky: Selected Poems* (New York: Library of America, 2006). Reprinted online: http://jacketmagazine.com/30/z-bernstein.html. The phrase "historic and contemporary particulars" comes from Zukofsky's introduction to the 1931 Objectivist issue of *Poetry*, which he guest-edited. Louis Zukofsky, "Program: 'Objectivists' 1931," in *Poetry* (February 1931), 268.

17. The full title is *Ar'a: alef-chet*, 1–8, which is followed by *Lo'el* (Lowell, *Ar'a: yod'alef* [Ar'a: Eleven]; Tel Aviv: Chadarim/Galeria Gordon, 1986), *Sefer midrash tadshe* (The Book of "Let There Be Grass," *Ar'a: yod'bet* [Ar'a: Twelve]; Tel Aviv: 'Am 'oved, 1993), and *Nokhe'ach* (Present, *Ar'a: nun* [Ar'a: 50]; Tel Aviv: Bitan, 1995). Collections that are not explicitly part of *Ar'a* include *Ha-sifriya* (The library; Ra'anana: Even Choshen, 1999), *Kash* (Chaff; Ra'anana: Even Choshen, 2008), *Katsida* (Jerusalem: Karmel, 2009), and *Ha-telefon ha-tsamud le-kir beit ha-knesset: Mivchar shirim* (The Telephone Next to the Synagogue Wall; 2014, special issue of *Helikon* 107 dedicated to Schimmel). Note Schimmel's Zukofsky-inspired serialization in these titles. In Hebrew, the letters of the alphabet represent a numerical value, and it was customary well into the twentieth century to preserve the convention of paginating books according to the *alefbeit*. Schimmel maintains this practice in his own work, a feature which underscores the sensuous and pervasive textuality of his poems and his tendency to delight in "arcane," out-of-date language usage.

18. "By now the echoes are so innumerable that I almost lack the fineness of ear to distinguish them." Lowell, *Notebook* (London: Faber & Faber, 1970), 263.

19. Harold Schimmel, *Qasida*, trans. Peter Cole (Jerusalem: Ibis Editions, 1997), 13. Cole based his translation on an earlier version published in *Chadarim*, vol. 10 (Winter 1993): 66.

20. Jahan Ramazani, "A Transnational Poetics," *American Literary History* (2006): 354.

21. In recent years, Schimmel's work has found the support of the younger generation of editors and poets, including Dror Burstein (editor of *Helikon*), Gali-Dana Singer, and Yehuda Vizen (editor of *Dechak* and translator of Anglo-American modernism). The American poet-translator, Ariel Resnikoff, who is currently translating *Shirei malon tsiyon* into English, has described Schimmel as "a leading figure of contemporary Hebrew avant-garde poetry." Resnikoff, "Fantasy Reading Series No. 12 with Jerome Rothenberg," Bowery Poetry Club, NY (October 4, 2015). A full recording of the reading, which includes work by Schimmel, can be found in the PennSound archive: http://writing.upenn.edu/pennsound/x/Resnikoff.php.

22. David (Neo) Bochbut, "Harold Schimmel, Meshorer shel meshorerim" ["A Poet's Poet"], *Haaretz* (June 7, 2015), http://www.haaretz.co.il/literature/book-week/.premium-1.2648713.

23. Schimmel, *Katsida*, 15. In his introduction to *Anthologie de la poésie en hébreu moderne* (Gallimard, 2001), Dan Miron employs a generational model, with an emphasis on patrilineal relations, to trace a continuous line between Hebrew poets from the late nineteenth century to the present day, a methodology that marginalizes Schimmel. In his discussion on the contemporary "long poem" (*ha-shir ha-arokh*), Miron credits the poet Aharon Shabtai for its development in Hebrew and cites the influence of American poetry on Shabtai's "wide ranging, anthropological lyric" (85–86). Schimmel's extensive contributions to the Hebrew long poem are portrayed as negligible at best. Indeed, reading the introduction, a non-specialist reader would surmise that Schimmel's poetry emerges in the wake of Shabtai, when in fact, Schimmel's long poem has offered the most sustained and radical integration of Anglo-American modernism and the Hebrew *poema* in Israeli poetry. Miron, "La poésie hébraïque de Bialik à nos jours" ["Hebrew Poetry from Bialik to the Present Day"], trans. Laurence Sendrowicz, *Anthologie de la poésie en hébreu moderne*, ed. Emmanuel Moses (Paris: Gallimard, 2001), 9–89.

24. Hanan Hever, "Shirei malon tsiyon le-Harold Shimel" [Harold Schimmel's Hotel Zion Poems], *Akhshav* 33–34 (1976), 199.

25. *Epoch* 15.1 (Ithaca: Cornell University Press, 1965), n.p.

26. Schimmel, however, did continue to publish in other English-language journals over the next several years.

27. George Schneeman (1934–2009) was based in New York City for most of his career and frequently collaborated with poets, particularly those associated with The Poetry Project at St. Mark's Church in-the-Bowery. Though he worked on ceramics, wood, and collage, his primary medium was painting, particularly with egg tempera, a nod to the Italian Renaissance. One of his drawings graces the cover of Schimmel's first collection, *First Poems*, which contains several references to Schneeman and his family, who at the time lived in Tuscany ("George! Quick bring the canvas," 20). For an overview of Schneeman's collaborations with poets, see Timothy Keane, "No Real Assurances: Late Modernist Poetics and George Schneeman's Collaborations with the New York School Poets," *Studies in Visual Arts and Communication: An International Journal*, vol. 1, no. 2 (2014), http://journalonarts.org/previous-issues/vol-1-2-dec2014/timothy-keane-abstract. Schimmel makes an appearance in Wright's poem "Tattoos," where Wright describes Schimmel's practice of Shacharit (Jewish morning prayers) in Positano, Italy (Charles Wright, "Tattoos," *Country Music: Selected Early Poems*, 2nd ed. (Middletown, CT: Wesleyan University Press, 1991), 63, 76; Robert D. Denham, "An Interview by Morgan Lucas Schuldt," *Charles Wright in Conversation: Interviews, 1979–2006* (Jefferson, NC: McFarland, 2008), 131.

28. Harold Schimmel, *First Poems* (Milan: Edizioni Milella, 1962).

29. "I came from Brindisi in Tammuz//1962 without a single/book." Schimmel, *Ha-Sifriya* [The Library] (Ra'anana: Even Choshen, 1999), 18. The London-born poet and playwright Dennis Silk (1928–1999) immigrated to Israel in 1955. He published widely both in Israel and abroad, including three collections of poetry: *The Punished*

Land (New York: Viking, 1980), *Hold Fast* (New York: Viking, 1984) and *Catwalk and Overpass* (New York: Penguin Group, 1991). For a fuller discussion of Silk's poetry, see Gabriel Levin, "Essential Vertigo," *PN Review*, vol. 127 (2000): 42–46. Atira Winchester also offers a portrait of this group of writers in "Abu Tor: Creativity on the Cusp," *Jerusalem Post* (March 27, 2005).

30. Harold Schimmel, selections from "Mishpacha" (Family), *Nekudatayim* (January 27, 2013), https://nekudataim.wordpress.com/2013/01/27/schimmel/.

31. Dion Nissenbaum, "Beatnik Abu Tor," in *A Street Divided: Stories from Jerusalem's Alley of God* (New York: St. Martin's Press, 2015): 46–47. Schimmel's study of the *qasida*, a pre-Islamic ode form, and his composition of Hebrew *qasidas*, also acknowledges this shared legacy.

32. Yehuda Amichai, "Jerusalem, 1967," trans. Stephen Mitchell, in *The Poetry of Yehuda Amichai*, ed. Robert Alter (New York: Farrar, Straus and Giroux, 2015): 82.

33. The journal *Akhshav* was founded in 1957 and took its name from the title of Yehuda Amichai's first book of poems *Akhshav u-va-yamim ha-acherim* [*Now and in Other Days*], which was published in 1955. The journal brought together some of the major voices of the Statehood generation, notably Dahlia Ravikovitch. Poets affiliated with the journal included David Avidan, Yonah Wallach, Maya Bejerano, Roni Somek, Meir Wieseltier, and Aharon Shabtai.

34. Harold Schimmel, "Selected Poems," *Now*, ed. Maxim Ghilan (Jerusalem: Akhshav, 1964), 27–40.

35. In his introduction to the issue, Ghilan also asserts, somewhat optimistically, that "that an audience exists for these writers is attested by the fact that newspapers appear in some twenty languages here." Maxim Ghilan, "Editor's Note," *Now*, vol. 1 (1964): 5–6.

36. Harold Schimmel, *Ha-shirim* [*The Poems*] (Motsa: Get That, 1968). The National Library of Israel holds a very rare copy of this chapbook, a hand-stapled edition (now quite faded) printed on a Gestetner duplicator. Black and white reproductions of Jasper Johns's *In memory of my feelings I and II* (1968) feature, respectively, on both the front and back covers and the copyright page.

37. Chana Kronfeld, "Beyond Thematicism in the Historiography of Post-1948 Political Poetry," *Jewish Social Studies*, vol. 18, no. 3 (Spring/Summer 2012): 180–196.

38. Peter Cole, Email to author, December 2002 (original quote modified by Cole on July 24, 2017).

39. The Hebrew translations include "Construction: Without a Bikini" (trans. Aryeh Sachs and Yehuda Amichai), "Poetry Is Made Like This" (trans. Sachs) and "The Gentle Land of Siena" (trans. Sachs), which was first published in *Epoch*, in its Spring 1965 issue. Aryeh Sachs (1932–1992) was born in Mandatory Palestine and enjoyed a long literary career as a critic, theater director, poet, and translator. Sachs had studied English literature at Johns Hopkins and Fitzwilliam College, Cambridge, and was the author of the academic monograph *Passionate Intelligence: Imagination and Reason in the Work of Samuel Johnson* (Baltimore: Johns Hopkins Press, 1967). In addition to his own poetry,

he also published a Hebrew translation of John Berryman's *Dream Songs* (1978) and a collection of "imitations" of English Renaissance and Baroque poetry. Cf. Yuval Yavneh, "Me'ase ahava: 'al tirgumav shel Aryeh Zakhs le-'shirei chalom' shel Jon Beriman" ["A Labor of Love: On Aryeh Sachs's Translations of John Berryman's *Dream Songs*"], June 2006, *Makom le-shira* [*Poetry Place*], August 29, 2009, http://www.poetryplace.org/john-about.html.

40. See chapter 3, page 105.

41. Hanan Hever, "Shirei malon tsiyon le-Harold Shimel," 199.

42. Zukofsky, "Program," 268.

43. Helit Yeshurun, "Kol ha-be'erekh she-ata yode'a la'asot," 125. Schimmel was raised in a religiously observant household and initially studied Hebrew in this context.

44. William Carlos Williams stands out among the American modernists for his commitment to an idea of the American local and the American poetic idiom that rejected the (elective) exile and expatriate status of his contemporaries, notably T. S. Eliot. In a letter to the poet and translator Horace Gregory (dated May 5, 1944), Williams argued: "It is the poet who lives locally, and whose senses are applied no way else than locally to particulars, who is the agent and the maker of all culture. It is the poet's job and the poet lives on the job, on location." But Williams's local poetry was nonetheless invested in a reworking of the American past to include narratives that challenged English (and New England) hegemony. John Lowney's *The American Avant-Garde Tradition: William Carlos Williams, Postmodern Poetry, and the Politics of Cultural Memory* (Lewisburg, PA: Bucknell University Press, 1997) examines how Williams, the son of immigrants, was "especially sensitive to the widespread experience of dislocation" and resisted the canonization of American "national" poetry through heteroglossia and formal experimentation (16). In an unpublished dissertation, Keith Manecke characterizes the American modernist local as a "poetically generative site" that is transhistorical and transcultural and also invested in what is immediate and present. Schimmel's Hebrew poetry, particularly the early poems of *Shirei malon tsiyon* and *Ar'a*, advance a local poetry but bring to it a distinctly (American) modernist poetics of relation. Manecke, "On Location: The Poetics of Place in Modern American Poetry," diss. (The Ohio State University, 2003), ii. For the full text of Williams's letter to Gregory, see "145: To Horace Gregory," in *The Selected Letters of William Carlos Williams*, ed. John C. Thirwell (New York: New Directions, 1957), 225–226.

45. Daniel Weissbort, "Ted Hughes and the Translatable," *Comparative Critical Studies*, vol. 7, no. 1 (2010): 107.

46. Assia Wevill (née Gutmann), was born in Berlin in 1927 to a Jewish father and non-Jewish mother. Her family fled Berlin in 1933 and immigrated to Mandatory Palestine, where she lived until 1946, when she left for England. When she met Hughes, Wevill was working as a copywriter in the advertising industry, but was also drawn to poetry and translation. Though she remained technically married to the Canadian poet David Wevill, she elected to publish her translations under her maiden name Gutmann.

Following a six-year relationship with Hughes, Wevill committed suicide in 1969. Yehuda Amichai, *Poems*, trans. Assia Gutmann, introduction by Michael Hamburger (New York: Harper & Row, 1968). For a detailed account of Wevill's life and her correspondence with Amichai, see Yehuda Koren and Eilat Negev, *Lover of Unreason: Assia Wevill, Sylvia Plath's Rival and Ted Hughes's Doomed Love* (New York: Carroll & Graf, 2007).

47. Yehuda Amichai, *Selected Poems*, trans. Assia Gutmann and Harold Schimmel (with the collaboration of Ted Hughes) (Harmondsworth: Penguin, 1971), Modern European Poets Series. Amichai was born in Germany, so characterizing him as a "modern European poet" was not entirely off the mark.

48. See Yehuda Amichai, *Songs of Jerusalem and Myself*, trans. Harold Schimmel (New York: Harper & Row, 1973). Schimmel's translations have also been reprinted in expanded English editions of Amichai's poetry.

49. Frances McCullough, Letter to Yehuda Amichai, June 17, 1970. Yehuda Amichai Archive, Beinecke Rare Book and Manuscript Library at Yale University, Box 5, Folder 229. In the late 1960s and the 1970s, Harper & Row published several collections of Amichai's poetry in translation, including Schimmel's' translation of *Songs of Jerusalem and Myself* (New York: Harper & Row, 1973).

50. Amichai, "A Song of Praise to the Lovely Couple Varda and Schimmel," trans. Harold Schimmel, *The Early Books of Yehuda Amichai* (Riverdale, NY: Sheep Meadow, 1988), 68. Ted Hughes also translated "The Sweet Breakdown of Abigail," a poem dedicated to Schimmel's daughter (*TriQuarterly*, vol. 39 [1977]: 249).

51. Helit Yeshurun, "Kol ha-be'erekh she-ata yode'a la'asot: re'ayon 'im Harold Shimel" ["All the 'Sort Of' that You Know How to Make"], *Chadarim*, vol. 5 (Winter 1985/ 1986), 124.

52. After a long hiatus, Raab issued new collections of poetry and prose (*The Poems of Esther Raab* [1963], *Late Prayer* [1972] and *The Garden That Was Destroyed* [1983]). She remained, nevertheless, a marginal figure in Israeli letters, with most considerations of her oeuvre focusing on her first collection.

53. Schimmel, "Hedim (le-Ester Rab)" ["Echoes (for Esther Raab)"], *Shirei malon tsiyon*, 51–52.

54. Schimmel, "Introduction," in *Thistles: Selected Poems of Esther Raab* (Jerusalem: Ibis Editions, 2002), 20. In a short elegiac essay on Leah Goldberg (see "Afterword"), Schimmel also draws a comparison between Goldberg and Dickinson. Schimmel, "Leah Goldberg: ha-meshoreret" ("The Poet"), *Orot*, vol. 10 (1971): 20–27.

55. Helit Yeshurun, "Kol ha-be'erekh she-ata yode'a la'asot," 130.

56. Johannes Göransson, "Afterword," in Aase Berg, *Transfer Fat*, trans. Johannes Göransson (Brooklyn: Ugly Duckling Presse, 2012): 118.

57. Helit Yeshurun, "Kol ha-be'erekh she-ata yode'a la'asot," 126.

58. Schimmel, "His Commitment," *Epoch*, vol. 14, no. 1 (1964): 62.

59. The first mention of Jerusalem, in the spelling by which the city is known today, appears in Joshua 10:1. While the etymology of Jerusalem—in Hebrew, *Yerushalayim*—is unclear, the pseudo-double "ayim" is a late addition. An earlier version "yerushalem" is mostly like a compound of "yeru" (to lay the foundation) and "Shalem" (an Ugaritic deity). Following David's conquest of the city, the Israelites took over the name and transferred to it a Hebrew etymology (shalem, meaning "peace" and "whole").

60. According to the Talmud, Rabbi Akiva promised his wife a "Jerusalem of Gold" to compensate for her banishment from her wealthy father's home. Hayim Lapin, "Rabbis and Cities: Some Aspects of the Rabbinic Movement in Its Graeco-Roman Environment," in *The Talmud Yerushalmi and Graeco-Roman Culture*, vol. 2, ed. Peter Schäfer and Catherine Hezser, Texts and Studies in Ancient Judaism 79 (Tübingen: Mohr Siebeck, 2000): 47–48. Charles Reznikoff, "Jerusalem the Golden," *The Poems of Charles Reznikoff, 1918–1975*, ed. Seamus Cooney (Jaffrey, NH: Black Sparrow Books, 2005), 91–115. See also Robert Manaster, "Opening Up a Tradition, a Return from Exile: The Vision in Charles Reznikoff's Jerusalem the Golden," *Shofar: An Interdisciplinary Journal of Jewish Studies*, vol. 21, no. 1 (2002): 44–62; Ranen Omer-Sherman, "Revisiting Charles Reznikoff's Urban Poetics of Diaspora and Contingency," in *Radical Poetics and Secular Jewish Culture*, ed. Stephen Paul Miller and Daniel Morris (Tuscaloosa: University of Alabama Press, 2010), 103–126. Unrelated to Schimmel or Reznikoff, Naomi Shemer's 1967 song "Jerusalem the Golden" has achieved anthemic status in Israel.

61. Norman Finkelstein, "Tradition and Modernity, Judaism and Objectivism: The Poetry of Charles Reznikoff," in *The Objectivist Nexus: Essays in Cultural Poetics*, ed. Rachel Blau DuPlessis and Peter Quartermain (Tuscaloosa: University of Alabama Press, 1999): 202.

62. Schimmel, "His Commitment," in *Retrievements*, ed. Dennis Silk (Jerusalem: Keter Publishing House, 1977), 155.

63. In 1872, Conder led a Survey of Western Palestine for the British Society's Palestine Exploration Fund. The purpose of the survey was to provide detailed topographic and geographic descriptions and measurements of Ottoman Palestine, information that largely served military purposes. The drawing included in *Retrievements* is the cover illustration for Conder's *Tent Work in Palestine: A Record of Discovery and Adventure* (London: A. P. Watt & Son, Hastings House, 1895 [1878]).

64. The first scientifically accurate map of Jerusalem was made by Sir Charles W. Wilson of the British Royal Engineers, who conducted the Ordnance Survey in 1864–1865. See Dov Gavish, *A Survey of Palestine under the British Mandate, 1920–1948* (New York: Routledge, 2005).

65. Ibid., 101.

66. Cole, Email to author, December 2002.

67. Meron Benvenisti, *Sacred Landscape: The Buried History of the Holy Land Since 1948*, trans. Maxine Kaufman-Lacusta (Berkeley: University of California Press, 2000).

68. The discourse of Hebrew language "revival" took hold in the late nineteenth century but neglected the ways in which Hebrew had remained an active diasporic language for centuries. More recent studies that map this discourse and address how it continues to shape contemporary Israeli language politics include Ron Kuzar, *Hebrew and Zionism: A Discourse Analytic Cultural Study* (Berlin: Mouton de Gruyter, 2001), and Ghil'ad Zuckermann, *Language Contact and Lexical Enrichment in Israeli Hebrew* (London/New York: Palgrave-Macmillan, 2003). See also Saposnik, *Becoming Hebrew*.

69. Schimmel, "Translator's Foreword," xv.

70. Harold Schimmel, *Lo'el* [*Lowell*] (Tel Aviv: Chadarim, 1986), ii. See also, Yochai Oppenheimer, "Be-makom afus: 'al shirat Harold Shimel" ["In a Vacant Place: On Harold Schimmel's Poetry"], in *Chadarim*, vol. 7 (1988): 86–99.

71. This is not the case for the later books of *Ar'a*. *Lo'el*, for instance, is a collection of sonnets.

72. Gabriel Levin, "The Pleasures of an Earthly Vision: On Harold Schimmel's *Ar'a*, *Modern Hebrew Literature*, vol. 6, no. 1–2 (1980): 54.

73. Parts of the book of Ezra are also composed in Aramaic, as is the Zohar, a Jewish kabbalistic text. Its use as a vernacular has been attested as well by the Dead Sea Scrolls. "Aramaic Language Among the Jews," *Jewish Encyclopedia*, vol. 2 (London: Funk and Wagnalls, 1901–1906), 68–72.

74. Liora Halperin cites Yosef Y. Berlin's proposal that language study in the Hebrew gymnasium include Aramaic and Arabic as classical Semitic languages comparable to Greek and Latin in the European educational system. Halperin, *Babel in Zion*, 205–206.

75. Notably, the town of Jish in northern Israel received controversial funding from the Israeli government to support the study of the Aramaic language. Most of its residents are affiliated with the Maronite Church, where Aramaic is the primary liturgical language. Jonathan Lis, "Israel Recognizes Aramean Minority in Israel as Separate Nationality, *Haaretz* (September 17, 2014), http://www.haaretz.com/israel-news/1.616299. Discussing Amira Hess's poem "Kolot mesaprim" ("Voices Tell"), which is written predominantly in Aramaic, Lital Levy contends that Aramaic literary composition is "highly anomalous" and "virtually incomprehensible to the vast majority of the Israeli readership." Levy, *Poetic Trespass*, 247–253.

76. See the introduction for a discussion of Amichai's use of the Aramaic *turgeman*. Amichai, "Be-khol chumrat ha-rachamin" ("To the Full Severity of Compassion"), *Shirim: 1948–1962* (Tel Aviv: Schocken, 1977): 253.

77. H. W. F. Gesenius, *Hebrew and Chaldee Lexicon to the Old Testament* (Grand Rapids, MI: Baker Book House, 1979 [7th ed.]), 81, 598. Aramaic still preserves the three distinct phonemes associated with the letter *tsade*.

78. Daniel 5:1–31.

79. Gabriel Levin, "The Pleasures of an Earthly Vision," 231.

80. Harold Schimmel, *Ar'a* (Tel Aviv: Siman kri'a, 1979), 6.

81. I would like to thank C. D. Blanton for pointing out to me that these relations mark another moment of translation, of the classical elegy from Greek to Latin (mediated via Callimachus's influence). Callimachus (c. 305–240 BCE) was best known for the *Pinakes*, a catalog of all the works held in the Library of Alexandria. As a poet, he excelled at short poems and epigrams and rejected the Homeric epic. His influence on later Roman poetry was profound. The lines that Schimmel translates can be found among Callimachus's *epigrammatum fragmenta* (fragments of epigrams): "Momos himself used to write on the walls: 'Cronos is wise.' Look, even the crows on the roofs croak: 'what (different) things are joined together?' and 'how shall we be hereafter?'" Callimachus, Epigram #393, *Aetia, Iambi, Hecale and Other Fragments*, trans. C. A. Trypanis, T. Glezer, and Cedric H. Whitman, Loeb Classics Library (Cambridge: Harvard University Press, 1973), 246–247. In Greek mythology, Momos, a son of Nyx (Night), is a personification of reproach and mockery. Cronos was deposed by his son Zeus; therefore, Momos may be stirring up trouble with this declaration. But the name appears to refer to Diodorus Cronus, a third-century BCE Greek philosopher related to the Megarian school. For a detailed, historical reading of this fragment, see Vladimír Marko, "Callimachus' Puzzle about Diodorus," *Organon F*, vol. 4 (1995): 342–367.

82. Ezra Pound, "Homage to Sextus Propertius," *Poetry*, vol. 13, no. 6 (1919): 291–299. Scholars have pointed out Pound's (deliberate) misreading/mistranslation of Propertius's "Coi sacra Philetae" (*Elegies* III, I). Daniel M. Hooley, *The Classics in Paraphrase: Ezra Pound and Modern Translators of Latin Poetry* (London: Associate University Presses, 1988), 35–36.

83. Gabriel Levin, "What Different Things Link Up: Hellenism in Contemporary Hebrew Poetry," *Prooftexts*, vol. 5, no. 3 (1985): 234.

84. Walter Benjamin, "The Task of the Translator," trans. Harry Zohn, 262.

85. See Eisig Silberschlag, "Greek Motifs and Myths in Hebrew Literature," *Proceedings of the American Academy for Jewish Research*, vol. 44 (1977): 151–183.

86. Jacques Derrida, "Des Tours de Babel," 129.

87. Helit Yeshurun, "Kol ha-be'erekh she-ata yode'a la'asot," 119.

88. Gertrude Stein, *Paris France* (New York: Charles Scribner's Sons, 1940), 2.

89. Helit Yeshurun, "Kol ha-be'erekh she-ata yode'a la'asot," 130–131.

90. Schimmel, *Lo'el*, i.

91. Marjorie Perloff, "Realism and the Confessional Mode of Robert Lowell," *Contemporary Literature*, vol. 11, no. 4 (Autumn, 1970): 470–487.

92. Quoted in Perloff, "The Return of Robert Lowell," *Parnassus*, vol. 27, no. 1–2 (2004): 99.

93. Perloff, *The Poetic Art of Robert Lowell* (Ithaca, NY: Cornell University Press, 1973).

94. I discuss both sonnets later in this chapter. While the poems of *Lo'el* are untitled, for the sake of clarity, I will refer to them by their page number.

95. Hever, "Shirei malon tsiyon le-Harold Shimel," 199.

96. Schimmel, "#47: 'Kore Le-yad ha-okeyanus tari mi-nyu" [Reading Near the Ocean fresh from new], *Lo'el*, 47.

97. See chapter 3 for a discussion on Goldberg and the "blurred" line between translation and imitation.

98. Lowell, *Collected Poems*, 381.

99. The four poems, all from *History*, are "For Ann Adden I. 1958" (#15), "Coleridge" (#19), "Second Shelley" (#50), and "Lady Cynthia Asquith, 1916" (#93).

100. Shahar Bram, *'Al mabat ha-mufne le-achor: gilgulei ha-po'ema etsel Israel Pinkas, Harold Shimel, ve-Aharon Shabtai* [*A Backward Look: The Long Poem in the Writings of Israel Pincas, Harold Schimmel and Aharon Shabtai*] (Jerusalem: Magnes Press, 2005), 79.

101. Schimmel, "#21: 'Ha-magnoliya ha-yapanit shel Montale hishtanta" ["Montale's 'magnolia giapponese' became"], *Lo'el*, 21.

102. Eugenio Montale, *Poesie di Montale*, trans. Robert Lowell (Bologna: Edizioni della Lanterna, 1960).

103. Moriani, *Lost Puritan*, 214.

104. In 1933, Montale reportedly fell in love with Irma Brandeis, a Jewish American scholar, who became his muse. She appears in *Le Occasioni* as Clizia. Glauco Cambon, "Introduction," *Selected Poems*, by Eugenio Montale (New York: New Directions, 1965), ix–xxiv. For a fuller treatment of this relationship, see David Michael Hertz, Eugenio Montale, *The Fascist Storm and the Jewish Sunflower* (Toronto: University of Toronto Press, 2015).

105. Lowell, *Collected Poems*, 283–298.

106. Ibid., 283. Montale's lines read "La tua irrequietudine mi fa pensare/agli uccelli di passo che urtano ai fari/nelle sere tempestose," which David P. Young translates as "Your unrest reminds me of/of those great birds of passage/who brain themselves against beacons/during evening storms." Eugenio Montale, "Dora Markus," trans. David P. Young, *Selected Poems*, ed. Glauco Cambon (New York: New Directions, 1965), 46–47.

107. Robert Lowell, "1958" (in *Near the Ocean*), *Collected Poems*, 397; "For Ann Adden I. 1958" (in *History*), *Collected Poems*, 535. Another version titled "158" appears in *Notebook*, gathered with two other poems under the heading "Mania" (Notebook, 148).

108. Schimmel, "#15: 'At zokheret she-'amadet iti ba-choshekh'" ["Do you remember that you stood with me in the dark"], *Lo'el*, 15.

109. Schimmel, "#81: Ke-tsipor torefet metila et tsila" [Like a bird of prey casting its shadow], *Lo'el*, 81. The following biographies of Lowell offer accounts of this visit: Ian Hamilton, *Robert Lowell: A Biography* (New York: Random House, 1982), 389–390; Paul Moriani, *Lost Puritan: A Life of Robert Lowell* (New York: W. W. Norton, 1994), 370–371. Schimmel's own account of what sounds like a very disappointing encounter with his old mentor appears in his obituary for Lowell. Harold Schimmel, "R. L. z"l," *Haaretz* (October 21, 1977): 18.

110. Motti Regev and Edwin Seroussi, *Popular Music and National Culture in Israel* (Oakland: University of California Press, 2004), 16.

111. Helit Yeshurun, "Kol ha-be'erekh she-ata yode'a la'asot," 125.

112. Cole, "Translator's Note," 16.

113. Ibid., 15.

114. Lowell, *Collected Poems*, 421.

115. Frank Bidart, "Introduction: 'You Didn't Write, You Rewrote,'" *Collected Poems*, vii–xvi.

116. The translations are revealed only at the very end of the book.

117. See the introduction for a short discussion of the relation between translation and a poetics of cannibalism. Cf. Rachel Galvin, "Poetry Is Theft," *Comparative Literature Studies*, vol. 51, no. 1 (2014), 18–54.

118. Lowell's translation appeared in the collection *Poets on Street Corners: Portraits of Fifteen Russian Poets*, ed. Olga Carlisle (New York: Random House, 1968), 145. Vladimir Nabokov was very critical of Lowell's translations of Mandelstam in general, referring to one of them as "a farrago of error." Nadezhda Mandelstam, the poet's widow, came to Lowell's defense in a letter she exchanged with Robert Silvers, editor of *The New York Review of Books*. Nabokov, "On Adaptation," *New York Review of Books* (December 4, 1969), 50. Michael Wachtel and Craig Cravens, "Nadezhda Iakovlevna Mandel'shtam: Letters to and about Robert Lowell," *Russian Review*, vol. 61, no. 4 (October 2002): 529. For a fuller discussion of Lowell's translations of Russian poetry, particularly the work of Boris Pasternak, see Michael Wachtel, "Translation, Imitation, Adaptation, or Mutilation? Robert Lowell's Versions of Boris Pasternak's Poetry," in *Novoe o Pasternakakh:Materialy Pasternakovskoi konferentsii 2015 goda v Stenforde* [New Studies on Pasternak: Proceedings from the 2015 Pasternak Conference at Stanford], ed. Lazar Fleishman (Moscow: Azbukovnik, 2017), 592–655. Wachtel's chapter also includes facsimiles of Lowell's drafts, on yellow-lined paper.

119. Yehuda Amichai, "Chaval, hayinu amtsa'a tova," *Akhshav ba-ra'ash: 1963–1968* [*Now in the Storm*] (Tel Aviv: Schocken Books, 1968), 56.

120. Robert Lowell, "Preserve My Words Forever," *Collected Poems*, 909; Yehuda Amichai, "A Pity. We were a Good Invention," trans. Assia Gutmann, *Poems*, 11. The Mandelstam translation appears in the 1968 collection *Poets on Street Corners: Portraits of Fifteen Russian Poets*, edited by Olga Carlisle (New York: Random House, 1969).

121. In his introduction to *Imitations*, Lowell claims, "This book is partly self-sufficient and separate from its sources, and should be first read as a sequence, one voice running through many personalities, contrasts and repetitions." Lowell, *Collected Poems*, 196.

122. Harold Schimmel, "#60: Boston hi kula historiya ve-hizakhrut" ["Boston is entirely history and recollection"], *Lo'el*, 60. These lines appear in Schimmel's poem without any quotation marks but they adapt something that Lowell said in a 1964 interview with the poet Stanley Kunitz: "So much of the effort of the poem is to arrive at something essentially human, to find the right voice for what we have to say. In life we speak with many false voices; occasionally, if we are lucky, we find a true one in our poems. A poem needs to include a man's contradictions." Stanley Kunitz, "Talk with Robert Lowell," *Robert Lowell: Interviews and Memoirs*, ed. Jeffrey Meyers (Ann Arbor: University of Michigan Press, 1988), 85. Quoted in Bram, *'Al mabat ha-mufne le-achor*, 86.

Afterword

1. Israel literary journals have included translations for decades, so this statement does not disregard the ongoing presence of literary translation in the Hebrew literary field. But 2005 proved to be a pivotal year for Israeli literature, particularly in the field of poetry. The debut of a number of literary journals, notably *Ho!*, *Ma'ayan*, *Mita'am*, and *Urbania*, each one with its distinct aesthetic and political objectives, reenergized debates on the place and status of poetry in contemporary Israeli culture. The role of translation figured prominently in these discussions.

2. A look at the online catalogs for 'Am 'oved and Ha-kibbuts ha-me'uchad, two of the largest publishers in Israel, shows that poetry translations are published continuously but not prolifically. Most of these translations are of venerated poets like Rainer Maria Rilke, Sylvia Plath, and Czeslow Milosz, and very rarely fall under the category of contemporary poetry. In recent years, the publisher Ra'av has been promoting contemporary works in translation, and in 2016 published a collection of poems by the Nigerian American poet Chris Abani under the title *Shi 'ur ge'ografi* [*Geography Lesson*], a project in which multiple translators were involved.

3. One example is the second issue of *Ho!* (June 2005), which featured a section on seafaring literature and included both original Hebrew works and Hebrew translations. Adriana X. Jacobs, "*Ho!* and the Transnational Turn in Contemporary Israeli Poetry," *Prooftexts*, vol. 36, no. 1–2 (2017), 137–166.

4. Roni Hirsch, Eran Tzelgov, and Boaz Yaniv, "From the Editors," *Daka*, vol. 1 (Winter 2007): 5. *Daka's* regular contributors and editors began to organize in 2005 with a series of poetry readings in unconventional locales (e.g., kiosks).

5. The editors refused to name this person but described them as the editor of a literary journal. Eran Tzelgov, "Introduction to Octavio Paz's Essay," *Daka*, vol. 3 (Winter 2008): 33.

6. Ibid.

7. Anna Herman, *Chad Keren* (*Unicorn*) (Tel Aviv: Ha-kibbuts ha-me'uchad, 2002); *Sefer ha-refuot ha-peshutot* (*The Book of Simple Remedies*) (Tel Aviv: Ha-kibbuts ha-me'uchad, 2006); *Ha-yetuma ha-nireit* (*The Seen Twin*) (Tel Aviv: Ha-kibbuts ha-me'uchad, 2016); trans., *Ha-yomanim shel Sylvia Plath* (*Diaries*) (Tel Aviv: Yedi'ot achronot, 2002). My English translations of her poems have appeared in *Michigan Quarterly Review*, *Poetry International*, and more recently in *Ho!*

8. Herman's translation first appeared in *Haaretz* (February 25, 2003). Lord Alfred Tennyson, "Mariana," trans. Anna Herman, in Herman, *The Book of Simple Remedies*, 52–55.

9. E.g., "The Lady of Shalott" (1833) and "Oenone" (1829). "Mariana in the South" (1832) also revisits the figure of Mariana and offers a more conclusive ending. The full text of "Mariana" is available online on the *Poetry* magazine website: http://www.poetryfoundation.org/poems-and-poets/poems/detail/45365.

10. In Shakespeare's play, Mariana is reunited with her fiancé Angelo.

11. These words are spoken by Duke Vicentio in Act III, Scene I (l.265–266). William Shakespeare, "Measure for Measure," ed. N. W. Bawcutt (Oxford: Oxford University Press, 199), 163. Tennyson's epigraph "Mariana in the Moated Grange (Shakespeare, Measure for Measure)" is not an exact quotation. For a reading of this poem, the epigraph, and the relation between place and voice, see Matthew Rowlinson, "The Place of Voice," *Tennyson's Fixations: Psychoanalysis and the Topics of the Early Poetry* (Charlottesville: University of Virginia Press, 1994), 60–111.

12. Herman, *The Book of Simple Remedies*, 55.

13. Tennyson scholars have long argued that these, and other "rose" poems, were in part inspired by Tennyson's love for a woman named Rose Baring, with whom he was infatuated in his youth. See Ralph Wilson Rader, *Tennyson's* Maud: *The Biographical Genesis* (Berkeley: University of California Press, 1963).

14. For a discussion of these other "Marianas," see Matthew Reynolds, "Illustrations, Translations, and Interpretations," in *Likenesses: Translation, Illustration, Interpretation* (Oxford: Legenda, 2013): 3–9.

15. Harold Schimmel, *Lo'el*, 81. Harold Schimmel, "#81," in *From Island to Island*, trans. Peter Cole (Jerusalem: Ibis Editions, 1997), 84.

16. Harold Schimmel, "Lea Goldberg ha-meshoreret/Lea Goldberg, the Poet," *Orot*, vol. 10 (Jerusalem 1971): 21–27.

17. The poems draw from Goldberg's later collections and include "In the Jerusalem Hills" ["Be-harei yerushalayim"], "Last Words" ["Milim achronot"], "Don't Try to Move with the New Generation" ["Al tenase lalekhet 'im ha-dor"], "On Myself" ["'Al 'atsmi"], and "Mercy Doesn't Fall" ["Ha-rachamim einam chalim"]. Lea Goldberg, "Poems," trans. Harold Schimmel, *Orot*, vol. 10 (Jerusalem 1971): 3–19.

18. Dahlia Ravikovitch, "Bi-yerushalayim" (In Jerusalem), *Kol ha-shirim 'ad ko* (Tel Aviv: Ha-kibbuts ha-me'uchad, 1995): 185–186.

19. Schimmel, "Lea Goldberg," 21.

20. Ibid., 23.

21. Ibid., 25. Aleksandr Block's long poem "The Twelve" (Двенадцать) was composed soon after the October Revolution of 1917.

22. See chapter 3, page 130.

23. Translated by and quoted in Schimmel, "Lea Goldberg ha-meshoreret," 27. The stanza that Schimmel cites in his essay is from the second part of the poem "'Al 'atsmi" ("About Myself") from Goldberg's 1964 collection *'Im ha-layla ha-ze* (*With This Night*).

24. Leah Goldberg, *Shirim*, vol. 2, 232. In 1968, Avraham Shlonsky's collection *Mi-shirei ha-prozdor ha-arokh* (*Poems from the Long Corridor*) included a poem that reproduced almost verbatim these lines by Goldberg—replacing her "meshorer" (poet) with his "paytan" (liturgical poet). Giddon Ticotsky, "Ha-meshoreret she-lo ratsta lehizdaken" ("The Poet Who Did Not Want to Grow Old"), *Makor rishon*, vol. 718 (*Shabbat* supplement) (May 13, 2011), https://musaf-shabbat.com/2011/05/14/המשוררת-שלא-רצתה-להזדקן-גדעון-טיקוצקי/.

25. The poem appears in a group of poems titled *Milim achronot*, which were first published in Goldberg's 1959 compilation of selected poems, *Mukdam u-me'uchar*. Given that Goldberg lived until 1971 and continued writing until the end, the irony of this title must be noted.

26. Originally published in *Lustra* (1916). Ezra Pound, "Li Po," *Personae: The Shorter Poems*, ed. Lea Baechler and A. Walton (New York: New Direction Books, 1990), 122.

27. Li Bai, "Hard Road," trans. Geoffrey Waters, in *300 Tang Poems*, ed. Geoffrey Waters, Michael Farman, and David Lunde (Buffalo, NY: White Pine Press, 2011), 111. This is a translation, one of many that have appeared over the years, of an eighteenth-century compilation of Tang era poetry.

28. Wang Wei, "Crossing the Yellow River," in *Crossing the Yellow River: Three Hundred Poems from the Chinese*, trans. Sam Hamill (Rochester, NY: BOA Editions, 2000), 101.

29. Goldberg, "Al 'atsmi," *Shirim*, vol. 3, 86; Goldberg, "On Myself," *Orot*, vol. 10 (1971): 15.

30. Anne Carson, Conversation with Brighde Mullins, *Lannan Foundation Readings & Conversations Series* (March 21, 2001).

31. Benjamin, "The Task of the Translator," 16.

Bibliography

Abelard, Peter and Héloïse. *The Letters of Abelard and Héloïse*. Translated by Betty Radice. London: Penguin Classics, 2003.

Abu El-Haj, Nadia. *Facts on the Ground: Archeological Practice and Territorial Self-Fashioning in Israeli Society*. Chicago: University of Chicago Press, 2001.

Adorno, Theodor W. "On the Use of Foreign Words." In *Notes to Literature* [Noten zur Literatur], vol. 2, translated by Shierry Weber Nicholsen, edited by Rolf Tiedmann, 286–291. New York: Columbia University Press, 1992.

Agamben, Giorgio. *The End of the Poem: Studies in Poetics* [Categorie italiane: Studi di poetica]. Translated by Daniel Heller-Roazen. Stanford: Stanford University Press, 1999.

Agamben, Giorgio. *The Idea of Prose* [Idea della prosa]. Translated by Michael Sullivan and Sam Whitsitt. Albany: SUNY Press, 1995.

Albag, Ruhama. "'Od elef shanim omer shimekh" [To Say Your Name for Another Thousand Years]. *Haaretz*, September 27, 2009. Accessed December 30, 2017. http://www.haaretz.co.il/literature/1.1282492.

Alcalay, Ammiel. *After Jews and Arabs: Remaking Levantine Culture*. Minneapolis: University of Minnesota Press, 1993.

Alter, Robert. "Lea Goldberg: Poetry in Dark Times." *Defenses of the Imagination: Jewish Writers and Modern Historical Crisis*. Philadelphia: Jewish Publication Society of America, 1977.

Alter, Robert. *Hebrew and Modernity*. Bloomington: Indiana University Press, 1994.

Alter, Robert. *The Invention of Hebrew Prose: Modern Fiction and the Language of Realism*. Seattle: University of Washington Press, 1988.

Amichai, Yehuda. *Akhshav ba-ra'ash: 1963–68* [Now in the Storm]. Tel Aviv: Schocken Books, 1968.

Amichai, Yehuda. *The Early Books of Yehuda Amichai*. Translated by Harold Schimmel. Riverdale, NY: Sheep Meadow, 1988.

Amichai, Yehuda. *Patu'ach sagur patu'ach* [Open Closed Open]. Jerusalem: Schocken Books, 1998.

Amichai, Yehuda. *Poems*. Translated by Assia Gutmann. New York: Harper & Row, 1968.

Amichai, Yehuda. *The Poetry of Yehuda Amichai*. Edited by Robert Alter. New York: Farrar, Straus and Giroux, 2015.

Amichai, Yehuda. *Shirim 1948–1964* [Collected Poems]. Jerusalem: Schocken Books, 1962.

Amichay-Michlin, Dania. *Ahavat Aysh: Avraham Yosef Shtibel* [For the Love of A. Y. S.]. Jerusalem: Mossad Bialik, 2000.

Anderson, Benedict. *Imagined Communities: Reflections on the Origin and Spread of Nationalism*. 1983. London: Verso-New Left Books, 2003.

Andrade, Oswald de. "Manifesto antropófago" [Cannibal Manifesto], *Revista de antropofagia* 1, no. 1 (May 1928): 3, 7.

Appelfeld, Aharon. *The Story of a Life*. Translated by Jeffrey Green. New York: Schocken Books, 2004.

Apter, Emily. "Translation with No Original: Scandals of Textual Reproduction." *Nation, Language, and the Ethics of Translation*. Edited by Sandra Bermann and Michael Wood, 159–174. Princeton, NJ: Princeton University Press, 2005.

Aviv, Nurith. *From Language to Language*. Swan Productions, Paris, France, 2004.

Avneri, Shmuel. "Ha-neshika mi-ba'ad le-mitpachat: Bialik ke-metargem" [Kissing through a Veil: Bialik as Translator]. *NRG*, May 13, 2013. Accessed December 30, 2017. http://www.nrg.co.il/app/index.php?do=blog&encr_id=7b710fc4596b25648b444 72262adc013&id=4490.

"Avot Yeshurun, Berdichevsky 8." *Snunit*, January 26, 2010. Accessed December 30, 2017. http://www.snunit.k12.il/shireshet/tel_avot.htm.

"Avot Yeshurun, 88, Poet in Unusual Idiom." *New York Times*, February 24, 1992, B10.

Axelrod, Steven Gould. *Robert Lowell: Life and Art*. Princeton, NJ: Princeton University Press, 1978.

Back, Rachel Tzvia, trans., *Lea Goldberg: Selected Poetry and Drama*. London: Toby Press, 2005.

Baker, Deborah Lesko. "Volume Editor's Introduction." In *Complete Poetry and Prose: A Bilingual Edition*, by Louise Labé, edited by Deborah Lesko Baker, translated by Deborah Lesko Baker and Annie Finch, 1–12. Chicago, IL: University of Chicago Press, 2006.

Baker, Mona, ed., *Critical Readings in Translation Studies*. New York: Routledge, 2010.

Baker, Mona, ed., *Routledge Encyclopedia of Translation Studies*. London: Routledge, 1998.

Balbuena, Monique R. *Homeless Tongues: Poetry and Languages of the Sephardic Diaspora*. Stanford: Stanford University Press, 2016.

Bardenstein, Carol. "Threads of Memory in Discourses of Rootedness: Of Trees, Oranges and Prickly-Pear Cactus in Palestine/Israel." *Edebiyât: A Journal of Middle Eastern Literatures* 8 (1998): 1–36.

Bar-El, Yehudit. *Ha-poema ha-'ivrit: me-hithavuta ve-'ad reshit ha-me'a ha-'esrim* [The Hebrew Long Poem: From Its Emergence to the Beginning of the Twentieth Century]. Jerusalem: Mosad Bialik, 1995.

Bar-El, Yehudit. "The National Poet: The Emergence of a Concept in Hebrew Literary Criticism (1885–1905)." *Prooftexts* 6, no. 3 (September 1986): 205–220.

Barouch, Lina, and Galil Shahar. "Arie Ludwig Strauss: Between Hölderlin and Yehuda Halevi." *Naharaim* 8, no. 2 (2014): 246–252.

Bartov, Hanoch. "1878–1882, The Founding of Petach-Tikvah." *Ariel: A Quarterly Review of Arts and Letters in Israel* 48 (1979): 56–79.

Bar-Yosef, Hamutal. "Bialik and the Baudelairian Triangle: *Ennui*, Cats and Spider's Webs." *Jewish Studies Quarterly* 1 (1993/1994): 362–378.

Bar-Yosef, Hamutal. "De-Romanticized Zionism in Modern Hebrew Literature." *Modern Judaism* 16, no. 1 (1996): 67–79.

Bar-Yosef, Hamutal. "Ha-hitkablut shel Bodlir ba-sifrut ha-'ivrit: 'avar ve-hove." [The Reception of Baudelaire in Hebrew Literature: Past and Present]. *Dimui* 25 (Spring 2005): 43–49.

Bar-Yosef, Hamutal. "Ha-meshulash ha-bodleri: shimamon, chatul, kurei 'akavish" [The Baudelairean Triangle: Ennui, Cats and Spider's Webs]. In *Maga'im shel dekadens: Bialik, Berdichevsky, Brenner* [Decadent Trends in Hebrew Literature]. 86–105. Beer Sheva: Ben Gurion University, 1997.

Bar-Yosef, Hamutal. "Neo-Decadence in Israeli Poetry 1955–1965: The Case of Nathan Zach." *Prooftexts* 10 (1990): 109–128.

Bassnett, Susan. *Translation Studies*. Revised ed. London: Routledge, 1991.

Baudelaire, Charles. *Pirchei ha-ro'a: mivchar* [The Flowers of Evil: A Selection]. Translated by Dory Manor. Tel Aviv: Ha-kibbuts ha-me'uchad, 1997.

Baudelaire, Charles. *Pirchei ha-r'a: Mivchar shirim* [The Flowers of Evil: Selected Poems]. Translated by Eliahu Meitus. Tel Aviv: Yehusha Chachik, 1962.

Baudelaire, Charles. *Selected Poems*. Translated and edited by Joanna Richardson. London: Penguin Books, 1975.

Beaujour, Elizabeth Klosty. *Alien Tongues: Bilingual Russian Writers of the "First" Emigration*. Ithaca, NY: Cornell University Press, 1989.

Beaumont, Germaine. "De'avon" [Regret]. Translated by Esther Raab. *Moznayim* 28 (1969): n.p.

Behar, Almog. "'Al *Ha-kivun ve-Ho!*: Betokh ha-isre'eliyut u-michuts la" [On *Ha-kivun* and *Ho!*: Israeliness From Without and Within]. *Teoria u-vikoret* 35 (Fall 2009): 264–279.

Beinin, Joel. *The Dispersion of Egyptian Jewry: Culture, Politics, and the Formation of a Modern Diaspora*. Cairo: American University in Cairo Press, 1998.

Belitt, Ben. "*Imitations*: Translation as Personal Mode." In *Robert Lowell: A Portrait of the Artist in His Time*, edited by Michael London and Robert Boyers, 115–129. New York: David Lewis, 1970.

Bellow, Saul. *To Jerusalem and Back: A Personal Account*. New York: Viking Press, 1976.

Benbassa, Esther. *The Jews of France: A History from Antiquity to the Present* [Histoire des Juifs de France]. Translated by M. B. DeBevoise. 1997. Princeton, NJ: Princeton University Press, 1999.

Ben-Eliezer, M. "'Al ha-targumim" [On Translations]. In *Kneset*, edited by Ch. N. Bialik, n.p. Odessa: Moria, 1916.

Ben-Ezer, Ehud. *Yamim shel la'ana u-devash* [Days of Gall and Honey]. Tel Aviv: 'Am 'oved, 1998.

Benjamin, Walter. "Berlin Chronicle." Translated by Edmund Jephcott. In *Walter Benjamin: Selected Writings 1931–1934*, vol. 2, Pt. 2, edited by Michael W. Jennings, Howard Eiland, and Gary Smith, 594–637. Boston: Harvard University Press, 1999.

Benjamin, Walter. "On Language as Such and on the Language of Man" and "Paris, Capital of the Nineteenth Century." In *Reflections*, translated by Edmund Jephcott, 314–332, 146–162. New York: Schocken Books, 1978.

Benjamin, Walter. "The Task of the Translator." In *Walter Benjamin: Selected Writings, Vol. 1, 1913–1926*, translated by Harry Zohn, edited by Marcus Bullock and Michael W. Jennings, 253–263. Cambridge, MA: Belknap Press of Harvard University Press, 2004.

Ben-Porat, Ziva. *Ha-stav ba-shira ha-'ivrit* [Autumn in Hebrew Poetry]. Tel Aviv: Matkal/Ketsin rashi, 1991.

Benvenisti, Meron. *Sacred Landscapes: The Buried History of the Holy Land since 1948*. Translated by Maxine Kaufman-Lacusta. Berkeley: University of California Press, 2000.

Ben-Yehuda, Eliezer. *A Dream Come True*. Translated by T. Muroaka. Edited by George Mandel. Boulder: Westview Press, 1993.

Ben-Yehuda, Eliezer. *Ha-chalom ve-shivro: mivchar ketavim be-'inyenei lashon* [A Dream Fulfilled: Selection of Writings on Language Matters]. *Proyekt Ben Yehuda*. Accessed December 30, 2017. http://benyehuda.org/by/haidan_harishon.html.

Bergvall, Caroline. "Cat in the Throat." *Meddle English*, 156–158. Callicoon, NY: Nightboat Books, 2011.

Berlina, Alexandra. *Brodsky Translating Brodsky: Poetry in Self-Translation*. London/New York: Bloomsbury, 2014.

Berman, Antoine. *The Experience of the Foreign: Culture and Translation in Romantic Germany* [L'Épreuve de l'étranger]. Translated by S. Heyvaert. Albany: State University of New York, 1992.

Berman, Jessica. *Modernist Fiction, Cosmopolitanism, and the Politics of Community*. Cambridge: Cambridge University Press, 2001.

Bermann, Sandra L. *The Sonnet over Time: A Study in the Sonnets of Petrarch, Shakespeare, and Baudelaire*. Chapel Hill: University of North Carolina Press, 1988.

Bermann, Sandra and Michael Wood, eds, *Nation, Language, and the Ethics of Translation*. Princeton, NJ: Princeton University Press, 2005.

Berneker, Erich Karl, ed., *Russisches Lesebuch mit Glossar* [Readings in Russian with a Glossary]. Leipzig: Göschen, 1887.

Bernofsky, Susan. *Foreign Words: Translator-Authors in the Age of Goethe*. Detroit: Wayne State University Press, 2005.

Bernofsky, Susan. "Friedrich Schleiermacher." *Translationista*, February 4, 2011. Accessed July, 31, 2017. http://translationista.net/2011/02/friedrich-schleiermacher.html.

Bernstein, Charles. "Introduction to *Louis Zukofsky: Selected Poems*." *Jacket* 30 (July 2006). Accessed December 30, 2017. http://jacketmagazine.com/30/z-bernstein.html.

Bervin, Jen, and Marta Werner, eds, *The Gorgeous Nothings: Emily Dickinson's Envelope Poems*. New York: New Directions/Christine Burgin, 2013.

Bethea, David, and Clare Cavanagh. "Remembrance and Invention: Poetry and Memory in Modern Russia." *Russian Review* 53 (January 1994): 1–8.

Bhabha, Homi. *The Location of Culture*. New York: Routledge, 1994.

Bhabha, Homi, ed., *Nation and Narration*. London: Routledge-Taylor & Francis, 1990.

Bialik, Chaim Nachman. "Al Shalom Ash ve-Perets Hirshbein." *Proyekt Ben Yehuda*, Accessed December 30, 2017. http://benyehuda.org/bialik/dvarim_shebeal_peh83.html.

Bialik, Chaim Nachman. "Chevlei lashon" [Language Pangs]. *Kol kitvei Ch. N. Bialik*. Tel Aviv: Dvir, 1939.

Bialik, Chaim Nachman. *Devarim she-be-'al pe* [Lectures]. Tel Aviv: Dvir, 1935.

Bialik, Chaim Nachman. *Ketavim genuzim* [Unpublished Writings]. Tel Aviv: Beit Bialik and Dvir, 1970.

Bialik, Chaim Nachman. "Revealment and Concealment in Language" [Gilui ve-kisui ba-lashon]. In *Revealment and Concealment: Five Essays*, translated by Jacob Sloan, 11–26. Jerusalem: Ibis Editions, 2000.

Bidart, Frank. "Introduction: 'You Didn't Write, You Rewrote.'" In *Collected Poems*, edited by Frank Bidart and David Gewanter, vii–xvi. New York: Farrar, Straus and Giroux, 2003.

Biguenet, John, and Rainer Schulte, eds, *The Craft of Translation*. Chicago, IL: University of Chicago Press, 1989.

Biguenet, John, and Rainer Schulte, eds, *Theories of Translation: An Anthology of Essays from Dryden to Derrida*. Chicago, IL: University of Chicago Press, 1992.

Blanchot, Maurice. *The Space of Literature* [L'Espace littéraire]. Translated by Ann Smock. Lincoln: University of Nebraska Press, 1982.

Bloch, Chana. "The Politics of Translation: Amichai and Ravikovitch in English." *Tikkun* 4, no. 4 (1989): 70–76.

Bluwstein, Rachel. "'Al ot ha-zman" [On the Sign of the Times]. In *Rachel: Shirim, mikhtavim, reshimot, korot chayeyha* [Rachel: Collected Poems, Letters, Notes, Biography], edited by Uri Milstein, 325–326. Tel Aviv: Zmora, Bitan, 1985.

Bochbut, David (Neo). "Harold Shimel, meshorer shel meshorerim" [A Poet's Poet]. *Haaretz*, June 7, 2015. Accessed December 30, 2017. http://www.haaretz.co.il/literature/book-week/.premium-1.2648713.

Boele, Otto. "North and South." In *The North in Russian Romantic Literature*, 117–180. Amsterdam: Rodopi, 1996.

Booth, Allyson. *Postcards from the Trenches: Negotiating the Space between Modernism and the First World War*. Oxford: Oxford University Press, 1996.

Bougera, Mohamed Ridha. "La Permanence de la figure de la bohémien." In *La bohémienne: figure poétique de l'errance aux XVIIIe et XIXe siècles*, edited by Pascale Auraix-Jonchière and Gérard Loubinoux, 65–83. Clermont-Ferrand: Presses universitaires Blaise Pascal, 2005.

Boyarin, Jonathan. *Thinking in Jewish*. Chicago, IL: University of Chicago Press, 1996.

Braidotti, Rosi. *Nomadic Subjects: Embodiment and Sexual Difference in Contemporary Feminist Theory*. New York: Columbia University Press, 1994.

Bram, Shahar. "'Al Ar'a shel Harold Shimel" [Harold Schimmel's Ar'a]. In *Mechkrei yerushalayim be-sifrut 'ivrit* [Jerusalem Studies in Hebrew Literature], vol. 19, edited by Michal Arbel-Tor, Ariel Hirschfeld, and Yehoshua Levinson, 1–21. Jerusalem: Magnes Press, 2003.

Bram, Shahar. *'Al mabat ha-mufne le-achor: gilgulei ha-po'ema etsel Israel Pinkas, Harold Shimel, ve-Aharon Shabtai* [A Backward Look: The Long Poem in the Writings of Israel Pincas, Harold Schimmel and Aharon Shabtai]. Jerusalem: Magnes Press, 2005.

Brann, Ross. "The Arabized Jews." In *The Literature of Al-Andalus*, edited by Maria Rosa Menocal, Raymond P. Scheindlin, and Michael Sells, 435–454. Cambridge: Cambridge University Press, 2000.

Brann, Ross. *The Compunctious Poet: Cultural Ambiguity and Hebrew Poetry in Muslim Spain*. Baltimore, MD: Johns Hopkins University Press, 1991.

Brann, Ross. "'The Fire of Love Poetry Has Kissed Me, How Can I Resist?' The Hebrew Lyric in Perspective." In *Medieval Lyric: Genres in Historical Context*, edited by William D. Paden, 317–333. Chicago: University of Illinois Press, 2000.

Brenner, Naomi. *Lingering Bilingualism: Modern Hebrew and Yiddish Literatures in Contact*. Syracuse, NY: Syracuse University Press, 2015.

Brenner, Naomi. "A Multilingual Modernist: Avraham Shlonsky between Hebrew and Yiddish." *Comparative Literature* 61, no. 4 (2009): 367–387.

Brodsky, Joseph. "In a Room and a Half." In *Less Than One: Selected Essays*, 447–501. New York: Farrar, Straus and Giroux, 1986.

Brodsky, Patricia Pollock. *Russia in the Works of Rainer Maria Rilke*. Detroit: Wayne State University Press, 1984.

Brooks, Cleanth, and Robert Penn Warren, eds, *Conversations of the Craft of Poetry*. New York: Holt, Rinehart and Winston, 1961.

Burshtein, Dror. "Lilmod likhtov mi-chadash, be-khol shir: Shirato shel Harold Shimel" [To Learn to Write Anew—with Every Poem: The Poetry of Harold Schimmel]. *Haaretz*, May 30, 2007. Accessed December 30, 2017. http://www.haaretz.co.il/hasite/spages/864116.html.

Calder, Alex. "Notebook 1967–68: Writing the Process Poem." In *Robert Lowell: Essays on the Poetry*, edited by Steven Gould Axelrod and Helen Deese, 117–138. Cambridge: Cambridge University Press, 1986.

Calé, Walter. *Nachgelassene Schriften*. Edited by Arthur Brückmann. Berlin: S. Fischer, 1907.

Callimachus. *Aetia, Iambi, Hecale and Other Fragments*. Translated by C. A. Trypanis, T. Glezer, and Cedric H. Whitman. Cambridge: Harvard University Press, 1973.

Carlisle, Olga, ed., *Poets on Street Corners: Portraits of Fifteen Russian Poets*. New York: Random House, 1969.

Carne-Ross, Donald. "The Two Voices of Translation." In *Robert Lowell: A Collection of Critical Essays*, edited by Thomas Parkinson, 152–170. Englewood Cliffs, NJ: Prentice Hall, 1968.

Carson, Anne. "Conversation with Brighde Mullins." *Lannan Foundation Readings & Conversations Series*, Santa Fe, New Mexico, March 21, 2001.

Cavanagh, Clare. *Osip Mandelstam and the Modernist Creation of Tradition*. Princeton, NJ: Princeton University Press, 1995.

Caws, Mary Ann, and Hermine Riffaterre, eds, *The Prose Poem in France Theory and Practice*. New York: Columbia University Press, 1983.

Celan, Paul. *Collected Prose*. Translated by Rosemarie Waldrop. Manchester: Carcanet Press, 1986.

Cervantes, Miguel de. *Don Quijote de la Mancha*. Barcelona: Editorial Juventud, 1998 [1605].

Chaver, Yael. "Outcasts Within: Zionist Yiddish Literature in Pre-State Palestine." *Jewish Social Studies* 7, no. 2 (2001): 39–66.

Chaver, Yael. *What Must Be Forgotten: The Survival of Yiddish in Zionist Palestine*. Syracuse, NY: Syracuse University Press, 2004.

Chisholm, Hugh, ed., "Jean de Meun." *The Encyclopaedia Britannica: A Dictionary of Arts, Sciences, Literature and General Information*, vol. 15. Cambridge: University Press, 1911 (11th ed.).

Chow, Rey. "Reading Derrida on Being Monolingual." *New Literary History* 39 (2008): 217–231.

Chow, Rey. "Translator, Traitor; Translator, Mourner (or, Dreaming of Intercultural Equivalence)." *New Literary History* 37 (2007): 565–580.

Clanchy, M. T. "The Letters of Abelard and Heloise in Today's Scholarship." In *The Letters of Abelard and Heloise*, lvi–lxxxiv. London: Penguin Classics, 2003.

Clej, Alina. "The Debt of the Translator: An Essay on Translation and Modernism." *Symploke* 5, no. 1 (1997): 7–26.

Clifford, James. "Diasporas." *Cultural Anthropology* 9, no. 3 (1994): 302–338.

Cohen, Zafrira Lidovsky. *Loosen the Fetters of Thy Tongue, Woman: The Poetry and Poetics of Yona Wallach*. Cincinnati: Hebrew Union College Press, 2003.

Cole, Peter, ed., *Hebrew Writers on Writing*. San Antonio, TX: Trinity University Press, 2008.

Cole, Peter, ed., "Introduction." In *The Dream of the Poem: Hebrew Poetry from Muslim and Christian Spain 950–1492*, translated by Peter Cole, 1–20. Princeton, NJ: Princeton University Press, 2007.

Cole, Peter, ed., "Translator's Note." In *From Island to Island*, by Harold Schimmel, translated by Peter Cole, 13–17. Jerusalem: Ibis Editions, 1997.

Conder, Claude Reignier. *Tent Work in Palestine: A Record of Discovery and Adventure.* London: A. P. Watt & Son, Hastings House, 1895 [1878].

Cutter, William. "Ghostly Hebrew, Ghastly Speech: Scholem to Rosenzweig, 1926." *Prooftexts* 10 (1990): 413–433.

Darwish, Mahmoud. "A Letter from Exile." Translated by Ben Bennani. *Boundary 2* 8, no. 3 (Spring 1980): 203–206.

Dekel, Michal. *The Universal Jew: Masculinty, Modernity and the Zionist Moment.* Evanston, IL: Northwestern University Press, 2010.

Deleuze, Gilles, and Félix Guattari. *Kafka: Toward a Minor Literature.* Translated by Dana Polan. Minneapolis: University of Minnesota Press, 1986.

De Man, Paul. "Conclusions: Walter Benjamin's 'The Task of the Translator.'" In *The Resistance to Theory*, 73–105. Minneapolis: University of Minnesota Press, 1986.

Denham, Robert D. "An Interview by Morgan Lucas Schuldt." In *Charles Wright in Conversation: Interviews, 1979–2006*, 127–131. Jefferson, NC: McFarland, 2008.

Denham, Robert D. *The Early Poetry of Charles Wright: A Companion, 1960–1990.* Jefferson, NC: McFarland, 2009.

Derrida, Jacques. *Acts of Religion.* Edited by Gil Anidjar. New York: Routledge-Taylor & Francis, 2002.

Derrida, Jacques. *A Derrida Reader: Between the Blinds.* Edited by Peggy Kamuf. New York: Columbia University Press, 1991.

Derrida, Jacques. "Des Tours de Babel." Translated by Joseph F. Graham. In *Acts of Religion*, edited by Gil Anidjar, 104–134. New York: Routledge-Taylor & Francis, 2002.

Derrida, Jacques. "A Discussion with Jacques Derrida." *Theory & Event* 5, no. 1 (2001).

Derrida, Jacques. *Monolingualism of the other or the Prosthesis of Origin* [Le monolinguisme de l'autre, ou, La prothèse d'origine]. Translated by Patrick Mensah. Stanford: Stanford University Press, 1998.

Derrida, Jacques. *The Post Card: From Socrates to Freud and Beyond* [Carte postale]. Translated by Alan Bass. Chicago, IL: University of Chicago Press, 1987.

Dingwaney, Anuradha, and Carol Maier, eds, *Between Languages and Cultures: Translation and Cross Cultural Texts.* Pittsburgh: University of Pittsburgh Press, 1998.

DuPlessis, Rachel Blau, and Peter Quartermain, eds, *The Objectivist Nexus: Essays in Cultural Poetics.* Tuscaloosa: University of Alabama Press, 1999.

Dykman, Aminadav. "'Al Leah Goldberg ke-metargemet shira" [Leah Goldberg as a Translator]. In *Pegishot 'im meshoreret* [Encounters with a Poet], edited by Ruth Kartun-Blum and Anat Weisman, 218–248. Tel Aviv: Sifriyat po'alim, 2000.

Dykman, Aminadav, ed. and trans., *Dor sheli, chaya sheli: mi-shirat Rusiya be-me'a ha-'esrim* [My Generation, My Beast: Russian Poetry of the 20th Century]. Tel Aviv: Schocken, 2002.

"Editorial Comments." *Epoch* 15, no. 1 (1965): n.p.

Ehrenpreis, Irvin. "The Age of Lowell." In *Robert Lowell: A Portrait of the Artist in His Time*, edited by Michael London and Robert Boyers, 155–186. New York: David Lewis, 1970.

Epstein, Rabbi Isidore, ed., *Halakhah.com: The online Soncino Bablyonian Talmud*. London: Soncino Press, 1938–1961. Accessed December 30, 2017. http://www.halakhah.com.

Erdinast-Vulcan, Daphna. "Language, Identity, and Exile." *Policy Futures in Education* 8, no. 3/4 (June 2010): 251–257.

Eshel, Amir, and Na'ama Rokem. "Berlin and Jerusalem: Toward German-Hebrew Studies." In *The German-Jewish Experience Revisited*, edited by Steven E. Aschheim and Vivian Liska, 265–272. Berlin/Boston: Walter de Gruyter GmbH, 2015.

Even-Zohar, Itamar. Special Issue on Polysystem Studies. *Poetics Today* 11, no. 1 (1990).

Even-Zohar, Itamar. "Polysystem Theory." *Poetics Today* 1, no. 1–2 (1979): 287–310.

Even-Zohar, Itamar. "'Spleen' le-Bodlir ba-tirgum Leah Goldberg" [Baudelaire's "Spleen" in Leah Goldberg's Translation] *Ha-sifrut* 6, no. 21 (1975): 31–45.

Ezrahi, Sidra. *Booking Passage: Exile and Homecoming in the Modern Jewish Imagination*. Berkeley: University of California Press, 2000.

Fein, Richard J. "Family and History in Life Studies." *The New England Quarterly* 46, no. 2 (June 1973): 272–278.

Feldman, Sara. *Fine Lines: Hebrew and Yiddish Translations of Alexander Pushkin's Verse Novel Eugene Onegin, 1899–1937*. PhD diss., University of Michigan, 2014.

Feldman, Yael. *Modernism and Cultural Transfer: Gabriel Preil and the Tradition of Jewish Literary Bilingualism*. Cincinnati: Hebrew Union College Press, 1986.

Fernandes, Ana. "Les bohémiens de Baudelaire, une métamorphose possible" [Baudelaire's Gypsies, a Possible Transformation]. *Máthesis* 12 (2003): 233–243.

Fichman, Jacob. "Sharl Bodler" [Charles Baudelaire]. *Ha-tekufa*. Warsaw: Avraham Yosef Shteibel, 1924, 509–510.

Forster, Leonard. *The Poet's Tongue: Multilingualism in Literature*. London: Cambridge University Press, 1970.

Fraade, Steven D. "Language Mix and Multilingualism in Ancient Palestine: Literary and Inscriptional Evidence." *Jewish Studies* 48 (2012): 1–40.

François, Anne-Isabelle. "The Mother Tongue as Border." In *Minding Borders: Resilient Divisions in Literature, the Body and the Academy*, edited by Nicola Gardini, Adriana X. Jacobs, Ben Morgan, Mohamed-Salah Omri, and Matthew Reynolds, 115–134. Oxford: Legenda, 2017.

Fredman, Stephen. *A Menorah for Athena: Charles Reznikoff and the Jewish Dilemmas of Objectivist Poetry*. Chicago, IL: University of Chicago Press, 2001.

Freud, Sigmund. "The Uncanny" [Das Unheimliche]. *The Uncanny*. Translated by David McLintock, 121–162. London, Penguin Books, 2003.

Friedberg, Maurice. *Literary Translation in Russia: A Cultural History*. University Park: Pennsylvania State University Press, 1997.

Friedlander, Yehuda. "Letteris, Me'ir." *YIVO Encyclopedia of Jews in Eastern Europe*. Accessed December 30, 2017. http://www.yivoencyclopedia.org/article.aspx/Letteris_Meir.

Friedman, Rivka. "Anenet ha-tsemer ve-ha-ekaliptus ha-sav shela: 'iyun be-'nof'" shel Ester Raab" [A Wool Cloud and Her Aged Eucalyptus: A Study of Ester Raab's 'Landscape'] *Ha-do'ar* 28, no. 4 (1999): 18–19.

Frischmann, David (as Shaul Goldmann). "Sharl Bodlir (Part 1)" [Charles Baudelaire]. *Ha-dor* 32 (August 15, 1901: 6–8);

"Sharl Bodlir (Part 2)." *Ha-dor* 33 (August 22, 1901: 7–9); "Sharl Bodlir (Part 3)." *Ha-dor* 34 (August 29, 1901: 9–11).

Funk, Tiffany. "The Prosthetic Aesthetic: An Art of Anxious Extensions," Mid-America College Art Association Conference, Wayne State University, Detroit, MI, October 4, 2012. Accessed December 30, 2017. http://digitalcommons.wayne.edu/macaa2012scholarship/1.

Galvin, Rachel. "Poetry Is Theft." *Comparative Literature Studies* 51, no. 1 (2014): 18–54.

Gan, Shimon. "Leah Goldberg: Tirgum shira" [Poetry Translation]. *Moznayim* 7, no. 1 (June 1958): 41–43.

Garbarini, Alexandra. *Numbered Days: Diaries and the Holocaust.* New Haven: Yale, 2006.

Gautier, Théophile. "Charles Baudelaire." In *Les fleurs du mal*, by Charles Baudelaire, 17. Paris: Michel Lévy Frères, 1868.

Gavish, Dov. *A Survey of Palestine under the British Mandate, 1920–1948.* New York: Routledge, 2005.

Genette, Gérard. *Palimpsests: Literature in the Second Degree* [Palimpsestes]. Translated by Channa Newman and Claude Doubinsky. Lincoln: University of Nebraska Press, 1997.

Gentzler, Edwin. "The Poetics of Translation." In *Routledge Encyclopedia of Translation Studies*, edited by Mona Baker, 167–170. London: Routledge, 1998.

Gesenius, H. W. F. *Hebrew and Chaldee Lexicon to the Old Testament Scriptures.* Grand Rapids, MI: Baker Book House, 1979 (7th ed.).

Ghilan, Maxim. "Editor's Note." *Now* 1 (1964): 5–6.

Gilboa, Amir. *Shirim ba-boker, ba-boker* [Songs in the Early Morning]. Tel Aviv: Ha-kibbuts ha-me'uchad, 1953.

Gilman, Sander. "The Jewish Voice: Chicken Soup or the Penalties of Sounding Too Jewish." In *The Jew's Body*, 10–37. New York: Routledge-Routledge, Chapman & Hall, 1991.

Glissant, Édouard. *Poetics of Relation* [La poétique de la relation]. Translated by Betsy Wing. Ann Arbor: University of Michigan Press, 1997.

Gluzman, Michael. *Ha-guf ha-tsiyoni: le'umiyut, migdar u- miniyut ba-sifrut ha- yisra'elit ha-chadasha* [The Zionist Body: Nationalism, Gender and Sexuality in Modern Hebrew Literature]. Tel Aviv: Ha-kibbuts ha-me'uchad, 2007.

Gluzman, Michael. *The Politics of Canonicity: Lines of Resistance in Modernist Hebrew Poetry.* Stanford: Stanford University Press, 2003.

Gluzman, Michael. "Trauma ve-intertekstualiut be-shirat Avot Yeshurun: Kri'a be-'Balada shel Miryam ha-magdalit u-vena ha-lavan'" [Trauma and Intertextuality in the Poetry of Avot Yeshurun: A Reading of "'The Ballad of Mary Magdalene and Her White Son"]. Paper presented at the National Association of Professors of Hebrew Annual Conference, University College, London, July 7–9, 2009.

Gobles, Mark. *Beautiful Circuits: Modernism and the Mediated Life*. New York: Columbia University Press, 2010.

Gold, Nili Scharf. "And the Migration of My Parents Has Not Subsided in Me: Yehuda Amichai." *Middle Eastern Literatures* 8, no. 2 (2005): 171–185.

Gold, Nili Scharf. *Yehuda Amichai: The Making of Israel's National Poet*. Lebanon: University Press of New England, 2008.

Goldberg, Leah. "Ahavata shel Tereza di Mon" [The Love of Teresa de Meun]. *Molad* 9, no. 49 (1952): 33–35.

Goldberg, Leah. "'Al oto nose 'atsmo" [On the Very Same Subject]. *Ha-shomer ha-tsa'ir* (September 8, 1939): 9–10.

Goldberg, Leah. *Avedot* [Losses]. Edited by Giddon Ticotsky. Bnei Barak: Sifriyat po'alim, 2010.

Goldberg, Leah. "Avraham Shlonsky ke-metargem shira" [Avraham Shlonsky as a Translator of Poetry]. In *Yevul: Kovets le-divrei sifrut u-machshava 'im yovel Avraham Shlonsky* [Harvest: A Collection of Literature and Thought for Avraham Shlonsky's Jubilee], edited by Jacob Fichman, 31–37. Merchaviya: Sifriyat po'alim, 1950.

Goldberg, Leah. "Certain Aspects of Imitation and Translation in Poetry." In *Actes du IVe congrès de l'Association internationale de littérature comparée, Fribourg 1964* [Proceedings of the IVth Congress of the International Comparative Literature Association], edited by François Jost, 837–843. The Hague: Mouton, 1966.

Goldberg, Leah. "Eiropa shelakhem" [Your Europe]. *Mishmar* (April 30, 1945).

Goldberg, Leah. *Ha-omets le-chulin* [The Courage for the Ordinary]. Edited by A. B. Yoffe. Tel Aviv: Sifriyat po'alim, 1976.

Goldberg, Leah. *Kolot rechokim u-krovim* [Voices Far and Near]. Edited by Tuvia Ruebner. Tel Aviv: Sifriyat po'alim, 1975.

Goldberg, Leah., trans. and ed., *Lu'ach ha-ohavim: leket shirei ahava mi-shirat Yisrael ve-'amim le-12 chodshei ha-shana* [A Calendar of Lovers: An International Anthology of Love Poetry for the Twelve Months of the Year]. Tel Aviv: Amichai, 1966.

Goldberg, Leah. *Mi-dor u-me'ever: bechinot u-te'amim be-sifrut klalit* [Contemporary and Beyond: Perspectives and Trends in General Literature], edited by Orah Koris, 123–199. Tel Aviv: Sifriyat po'alim, 1977.

Goldberg, Leah. *Mikhtavim mi-nesi'a meduma* [Letters from an Imaginary Journey]. 1937. Bnei-Barak: Sifriyat po'alim-Ha-kibbuts ha-me'uchad, 2007.

Goldberg, Leah. *Ne'arot 'ivriyot: mikhtavei Leah Goldberg min ha-provintsiya 1923–1935* [Hebrew Youth: Leah Goldberg's Letters from the Province]. Edited by Yfaat Weiss and Giddon Ticotsky. Bnei-Brak: Sifriyat po'alim -Ha-kibbuts ha-me'uchad, 2009.

Goldberg, Leah. *Shirei ahava ve-zahav: Ha-sonetot shel Leah Goldberg* [Love and Gold Poems: The Sonnets of Leah Goldberg]. Edited by Ofra Yeglin. Bnei-Barak: Sifriyat po'alim and Ha-kibbuts ha-me'uchad, 2008.

Goldberg, Leah. *Shirim* [Poems]. Vols. 1–3. Edited by Tuvia Ruebner. Tel Aviv: Sifriyat po'alim, 1973.

Goldberg, Leah. *Yomanei Leah Goldberg* [Diaries]. Edited by Rachel and Arieh Aharoni. Bnei-Brak: Sifriyat po'alim -Ha-kibbuts ha-me'uchad, 2005.

Goldberg, Leah, and Avraham Shlonsky, eds, *Shirat Rusiya* [Russian Poetry]. 1942. Tel Aviv: Sifriyat po'alim, 1983.

Golomb, Jacob. *Nietzsche and Zion*. Ithaca: Cornell University Press, 2004.

Göransson, Johannes. "Afterword." In *Transfer Fat*, by Aase Berg, translated by Johannes Göransson, 15–18. Brooklyn: Ugly Duckling Presse, 2012.

Göransson, Johannes, and Joyelle McSweeney. "Manifesto of the Disabled Text." *Exoskeleton*, June 14, 2008. Accessed December 30, 2017. http://exoskeleton-johannes.blogspot.com/2008/06/manifesto-of-disabled-text.html.

Göransson, Johannes, and Joyelle McSweeney. *The Deformation Zone*. Brooklyn: Ugly Duckling Press, 2012.

Gordinsky, Natasha, and Joyelle McSweeney. "Homeland I Will Name the Language of Poetry in a Foreign Country—Modes of Challenging the Home/Exile Binary in Leah Goldberg's Poetry." In *Leipziger Beiträge zur jüdischen Geschichte und Kultur* [Leipzig Studies on Jewish History and Culture], vol. 3, edited by Markus Kirchhoff and Monika Heinker, 239–253. München: K. G. Saur Verlag, 2005.

Gordinsky, Natasha. *Bishelosha nofim: yetsirata ha-mukdemet shel Leah Goldberg* [In Three Landscapes: Leah Goldberg's Early Writings]. Jerusalem: Magnes Press, 2016.

Gouri, Haim. "Noshmim goral ve-adama" [Breathing Destiny and Earth]. *Haaretz Books* 528 (April 9, 2003): 12.

Graham, Joseph F., ed., *Difference in Translation*. Ithaca, NY: Cornell University Press, 1985.

Green, Jeffrey M. "Zionist Ideology and the Translation of Hebrew." *TTR: Traduction, Terminologie, Redaction* 13, no. 1 (2000): 81–93.

Greenwald, Roy. "Homophony in Multilingual Jewish Cultures," *Dibur* 1 (2015). Accessed December 30, 2017. http://arcade.stanford.edu/dibur/homophony-multilingual-jewish-cultures.

Grumberg, Karen. "Between the World and the Yishuv: The Translation of Knut Hamsun's Markens grøde as a Zionist Sacred Text." *Prooftexts* 36, no. 1–2 (2017): 111–136.

Grumberg, Karen. "Gothic Temporalities and Insecure Sanctuaries in Lea Goldberg's The Lady of the Castle and Edgar Allan Poe's 'Masque of the Red Death.'" *Comparative Literature* 68, no. 4 (2016): 408–426.

Guendler, Beatrice. "The Qasida." In *The Literature of Al-Andalus*, edited by Maria Rosa Menocal, Raymond P. Scheindlin, and Michael Sells, 211–231. Cambridge: Cambridge University Press, 2000.

Gurevitch, Zali, and Gideon Aran. "'Al ha-makom" [On the Place]. *Alpayim* 4 (1992): 9–44.

Gurevitch, Zali, and Gideon Aran. "The Double Site of Israel." In *Grasping Land: Space and Place in Contemporary Israeli Discourse and Experience*, edited by Eyal Ben-Ari and Yoram Bilu, 203–216. Albany: State University of New York, 1997.

Ha-am, Achad [Asher Ginzburg]. "Le-she'elat ha-lashon" [On the Question of Language]. In *Kol kitvei Achad Ha-am* [Complete Works], 93–103. Tel Aviv: Dvir, 1947.

Hallo, William W. *Origins: The Ancient Near Eastern Background of Some Modern Western Institutions*. New York: Brill Academic, 1996.

Halperin, Liora R. *Babel in Zion: Jews, Nationalism, and Language Diversity in Palestine, 1920–1948*. New Haven: Yale University Press, 2014.

Halsall, Peter, ed., *Medieval Sourcebook: Medieval Discussion of Heloise's Letters to Abelard*. Accessed December 30, 2017. http://sourcebooks.fordham.edu/source/heloisedisc1.asp.

Hamill, Sam, trans. *Crossing the Yellow River: Three Hundred Poems from the Chinese*. Rochester, NY: BOA Editions, 2000.

Hamilton, Ian. *Robert Lowell: A Biography*. New York: Random House, 1982.

Hang, Xing. *Encyclopedia of National Anthems*. Lanham, MD: Scarecrow Press, 2003. 645–647.

Hardie, Melissa Jane. "Late Modern Blog: Affect, Contagion and Flow from the Picture Postcard to the Blogosphere." *What Is the New Rhetoric?* Edited by Susan Thomas. Cambridge: Cambridge Scholars, 2007: 140–153.

Harel, Amir, dir. *Avot Yeshurun: A Documentary*. Tel Aviv: Eugene Wolf Productions, 1992.

Harshav, Benjamin. *Language in Time of Revolution*. Berkeley: University of California Press, 1993.

Harshav, Benjamin., ed., *Manifestim shel modernizm* [Modernist Manifestos]. Jerusalem: Karmel, 2001.

Harshav, Benjamin. *The Meaning of Yiddish*. Stanford: Stanford University Press, 1990.

Harshav, Benjamin. *The Polyphony of Jewish Culture*. Stanford: Stanford University Press, 2007.

Harshav, Benjamin. "Theses on the Historical Context of the Modern Jewish Revolution." *Jewish Studies Quarterly* 10 (2003): 300–319.

Hasan, Roy. "Medinat Ashkenaz." In *Ha-klavim she-navchu be-yalduteinu hayu chasumei pe* [The Dogs That Barked in Our Childhood Were Muzzled], 46–48. Tel Aviv: Tangier Press, 2014.

Hasan-Rokem, Galit. "Jews as Postcards, or Postcards as Jews: Mobility in a Modern Genre." *Jewish Quarterly Review* 99, no. 4 (Fall 2009): 505–546.

Ha-tsefira. "Natan Shapira eineno!" [Natan Shapira Is Gone]. *Ha-tsefira* (November 11, 1897): 2–3.

Heidegger, Martin. *On the Way to Language* [Unterwegs zur Sprache]. Translated by Peter D. Hertz. San Francisco: Harper, 1971.

Heller-Roazen, Daniel. "Des alterité de la langue: plurilinguismes poétiques au moyen age" [Of Otherness in Language: Poetic Plurilingualism in the Middle Ages]. *Littérature* 130 (2003): 75–95.

Heller-Roazen, Daniel. *Fortune's Faces: The Roman de la Rose and the Poetics of Contingency.* Baltimore, MD: Johns Hopkins University Press, 2003.

Herman, Anna. *Sefer ha-refu'ot ha-peshutot* [The Book of Simple Remedies]. Tel Aviv: Ha-kibbuts ha-me'uchad, 2006.

Hertz, David Michael. *Eugenio Montale: The Fascist Storm and the Jewish Sunflower.* Toronto: University of Toronto Press, 2015.

Hever, Hannan. "'Ha-zemer tam': Leah Goldberg kotevet shirei milchama." In *Pegishot 'im meshoreret* [Encounters with a Poet], edited by Ruth Kartun-Blum and Anat Weisman, 116–133. Tel Aviv: Sifriyat po'alim, 2000.

Hever, Hannan. *Nativism, Zionism and Beyond.* Syracuse, NY: Syracuse University Press, 2014.

Hever, Hannan. "Our Poetry Is Like an Orange Grove: Anthologies of Hebrew Poetry in Erets Israel." *Prooftexts* 17 (1997): 199–225.

Hever, Hannan. *Prichat ha-dumiya: Shirat Ben Yitzhak* [The Flowering of Silence: The Poetry of Ben Yitzhak]. Tel Aviv: Ha-kibbuts ha-me'uchad, 1993.

Hever, Hannan. *Producing the Modern Hebrew Canon: Nation Building and Minority Discourse.* New York: New York University Press, 2002.

Hever, Hannan. "Shirat ha-guf ha-le'umi: nashim meshorerot milchemet ha-shichror" [Poetry of the National Body: Women Poets and the War of Independence] *Teoria u-vikoret* 7 (Winter 1995): 99–123.

Hever, Hannan. "Shirei malon tsiyon le-Harold Shimel" [Harold Schimmel's Hotel Zion Poems]. *Akshav* 33–34 (1976): 196–202.

Hever, Hannan. *Suddenly, the Sight of War: Violence and Nationalism in Hebrew Poetry in the 1940s.* Stanford: Stanford University Press, 2016.

Hever, Hannan. "'The Two Gaze Directly into One Another's Face': Avot Yeshurun between the Nakba and the Shoah—An Israeli Perspective." *Jewish Social Studies* 18, no. 3 (Spring/Summer 2012): 153–163.

Hirschfeld, Ariel. "'Al mishmar ha-na'iviyut: 'Al tafkida ha-tarbuti shel shirat Leah Goldberg" [Guarding Naiveté: On the Cultural Role of Leah Goldberg's Poetry]. In *Pegishot 'im meshoreret* [Encounters with a Poet], edited by Ruth Kartun-Blum and Anat Weisman, 135–151. Tel Aviv: Sifriyat po'alim, 2000.

Hiu, Lydia, ed., *Tokens of Exchange: The Problem of Translation in Global Circulations.* Durham: Duke University Press, 1999.

Hochberg, Gil. "'Permanent Immigration'": Jacqueline Kahanoff, Ronit Matalon, and the Impetus of Levantinism." *Boundary 2* 31, no. 2 (Summer 2004): 219–243.

Holder, Alan. "The Flintlocks of the Fathers: Robert Lowell's Treatment of the American Past." *New England Quarterly* 44, no. 1 (1971): 40–65.

Holtzman, Avner. "Shapiro, Konstantin Abba." *YIVO Encyclopedia of Jews in Eastern Europe*, October 15, 2010. Accessed December 30, 2017. http://www.yivoencyclopedia.org/article.aspx/Shapiro_Konstantin_Abba.

Hooley, Daniel M. *The Classics in Paraphrase: Ezra Pound and Modern Translators of Latin Poetry*. London: Associate University Presses, 1988.

Houghton-Walker, Sarah. *Representations of the Gypsy in the Romantic Period*. Cambridge: Cambridge University Press, 2014.

Huntington, Ellsworth, and Sumner W. Cushing, eds, *Principles of Human Geography*. New York: John Wiley & Sons, 1922.

Jacobs, Adriana X. "The Go-Betweens: Leah Goldberg, Yehuda Amichai and the Figure of the Poet Translator." In *The Blackwell Companion to Translation Studies*, edited by Sandra Bermann and Catherine Porter, 479–491. Malden, MA: Blackwell.

Jacobs, Adriana X. "Hebrew Remembers Yiddish: The Poetry of Avot Yeshurun." In *Choosing Yiddish: Studies in Yiddish Literature, Culture and History*, edited by Lara Rabinovitch, Shiri Goren, and Hannah Pressman, 296–313. Detroit: Wayne State University Press, 2013.

Jacobs, Adriana X. "*Ho!* and the Transnational Turn in Contemporary Israeli Poetry." *Prooftexts* 36, 1–2 (2017): 137–166.

Jacobs, Adriana X. (Tatum). "Paris or Jerusalem? The Multilingualism of Esther Raab." *Prooftexts* 26 (2006): 6–28.

"Jacques Adout." *Bibliothèque nationale de France*. Accessed December 30, 2017. http://data.bnf.fr/12584887/jacques_adout.

Jain, Sarah S. "The Prosthetic Imagination: Enabling and Disabling the Prosthesis Trope." *Science, Technology, & Human Values* 24, no. 1 (Winter 1999): 31–54.

Jakobson, Roman. "On the Linguistic Aspects of Translation." 1959. In *The Translation Studies Reader*, edited by Lawrence Venuti, 113–118. London: Routledge-Taylor & Francis, 2000.

Jakobson, Roman. "What Is Poetry." In *Selected Writings: Poetry of Grammar and Grammar of Poetry*, vol. 3, translated by M. Heim, 740–750. The Hague: Mouton de Gruyter, 1981.

Jastrow, Marcus. *Dictionary of the Targumim, the Talmud Babli and Yerushalmi, and the Midrashic Literature*, vol. 2. New York: G. P. Putnam and Sons, 1903.

"Jean de Meun," In *The Encyclopaedia Britannica: A Dictionary of Arts, Sciences, Literature and General Information*, vol. 15, edited by Hugh Chisholm, 298. Cambridge: University Press, 1911 (11th ed.).

Johnson, Barbara. *Mother Tongues: Sexuality, Trials, Motherhood, Translation*. Cambridge: Harvard University Press, 2003.

Johnston, Allan. "Modes of Return: Memory and Remembering in the Poetry of Robert Lowell." *Twentieth Century Literature* 36, no. 1 (Spring 1990): 73–94.

Kafka, Franz. "Rede über die jiddische Sprache" [Speech on the Yiddish Language]. *Gesammelte Werke*. Edited by Max Brod. New York: Schocken, 1953: 421–426.

Kahn, Lily. *The First Hebrew Shakespeare Translations: A Bilingual Edition and Commentary*. London: University College London Press, 2017.

Kalston, David. "The Uses of History." *Robert Lowell*. New York: Chelsea House, 1987, 81–100.

Kartun-Blum, Ruth, and Anat Weisman, eds, *Pegishot 'im meshoreret* [Encounters with a Poet: Essays and Studies on the Work of Leah Goldberg]. Tel Aviv: Sifriyat po'alim, 2000.

Katz, David. *Words on FIRE: The Unfinished Story of Yiddish*. New York: Basic Books, 2004.

Katz, Shaul. "'Ha-telem ha-rishon: ideologiya, hityashvut, ve-chakla'ut be-Petach Tikva ba-'asor ha-shanim ha-rishon le-kiyuma" [The First Furrow: Ideology, Settlement and Agriculture in Petach Tikva in the First Decade of Its Founding]. *Cathedra* 23 (1982): 57–124.

Katznelson, Rachel. "Language Insomnia" [Nidudei lashon]. Translated by Barbara Harshav. In *Language in Time of Revolution*, by Benjamin Harshav, 183–194. Berkeley: University of California Press, 1993.

Katznelson, Rachel. "Nidudei lashon" [Language Wanderings]. In *'Al adamat ha-'ivrit* [On Hebrew Land], 231–241. Tel Aviv: 'Am 'oved, 1966.

Keane, Timothy. "No Real Assurances: Late Modernist Poetics and George Schneeman's Collaborations with the New York School Poets." In *Studies in Visual Arts and Communication: An International Journal* 1, no. 2 (2014). Accessed December 30, 2017. http://journalonarts.org/previous-issues/vol-1-2-dec2014/timothy-keane-abstract.

Keats, John. *Selected Poems*. Edited by John Barnard. London/NY: Penguin Books, 2007.

Kellman, Steven G., ed., *Switching Languages: Translingual Writers Reflect on Their Craft*. Lincoln: University of Nebraska Press, 2003.

Kellman, Steven G., ed., *The Translingual Imagination*. Lincoln: University of Nebraska Press, 2000.

Kenner, Hugh. *The Pound Era*. Berkeley: University of California Press, 1971.

Kessler, Sharon, trans., "Pine." By Lea Goldberg. *Fish Eye Press*. Accessed December 30, 2017. http://www.fisheyepress.com/Translations.html.

Koren, Yehuda, and Eilat Negev. *Lover of Unreason: Assia Wevill, Sylvia Plath's Rival and Ted Hughes' Doomed Love*. New York: Carroll & Graf, 2007.

Kramer, Shalom. "Eccentric Poetry." *Yedioth Achronot*, August 14, 1961.

Kronfeld, Chana. "Allusion: An Israeli Perspective." *Prooftexts* 5 (1985): 137–163.

Kronfeld, Chana. "Beyond Thematicism in the Historiography of Post-1948 Political Poetry." *Jewish Social Studies* 18, no. 3 (Spring/Summer 2012): 180–196.

Kronfeld, Chana. *The Full Severity of Compassion: The Poetry of Yehuda Amichai*. Stanford: Stanford University Press, 2016.

Kronfeld, Chana. "Making Honey from All the Buzz and Babble: Translation as Metaphor in the Poetry of Yehuda Amichai." Paper presented at conference Poetics and Politics in Yehuda Amichai's World, New Haven, Yale University.

Kronfeld, Chana. *On the Margins of Modernism: Decentering Literary Dynamics.* Berkeley: University of California Press, 1996.

Kronfeld, Chana. "Reading Amichai Reading." *Judaism* (1996): 311–323.

Kugel, James L. "Avot Yeshurun in English." *Prooftexts* 1, no. 3 (1981): 326–331.

Kunitz, Stanley. "Talk with Robert Lowell." In *Robert Lowell: Interviews and Memoirs.* Edited by Jeffrey Meyers, 84–90. Ann Arbor: University of Michigan, 1988.

Kuzar, Ron. *Hebrew and Zionism: A Discourse Analytic Cultural Study.* Berlin: Mouton de Gruyter, 2001.

Labé, Louise. *Complete Poetry and Prose: A Bilingual Edition.* Translated by Deborah Lesko Baker and Annie Finch. Edited by Deborah Lesko Baker. Chicago, IL: University of Chicago Press, 2006.

Lachman, Lilach. "'I Manured the Land with My Mother's Letters': Avot Yeshurun and the Question of the Avant-Garde." *Poetics Today* 21, no. 1 (2000): 61–93.

Lamm, Maurice. *Consolation: The Spiritual Journey beyond Grief.* Philadelphia: Jewish Publication Society, 2004.

Laor, Dan. "Prodigal Sons: Desertion and Reconciliation in Contemporary Israeli Writing." *Midstream* 50, no. 4 (May 1, 2004): 33–38.

Lavrenova, Olga. "Nature and Environment in Russian Poetry." In *Literature of Nature: An International Sourcebook,* edited by Patrick D. Murphy, 229–235. Chicago, IL: Fitzroy Dearborn, 1998.

Layton, Susan. *Russian Literature and Empire: Conquest of the Caucasus from Pushkin to Tolstoy.* Cambridge: Cambridge University Press, 1995.

Lefevere, André. *Translating Literature: The German Tradition from Luther to Rosenzweig.* Assen/Amsterdam: Van Gorcum, 1977.

Lefevere, André. *Translation, Rewriting and the Manipulation of Literary Fame.* London: Routledge, 1992.

Lehmann, Sophia. "In Search of a Mother Tongue: Locating Home in Diaspora." *MELUS: Multi-Ethnic Literature of the United States* 23, no. 4 (1998): 101–118.

Lerner, Anne Lapidus. "The Naked Land: Nature in the Poetry of Esther Raab." In *Women of the Word, Jewish Women and Jewish Writing,* edited by Judith R. Baskin, 236–257. Detroit: Wayne State University Press, 1994.

Lerner, Anne Lapidus. "'A Woman's Song': The Poetry of Esther Raab." In *Gender and Text in Modern Hebrew and Yiddish Literature,* edited by Naomi B. Sokoloff, Anne Lapidus Lerner, and Anita Norich, 27–37. New York: Jewish Theological Seminary of America, 1992.

Letteris, Meir. *Ayelet ha-shachar* [Morning Star]. Zolkiev: G. Letteris, 1824.

Letteris, Meir. *Divrei shir* [Lyrics]. Zolkiev: G. Letteris, 1822.

Letteris, Meir. *Tofes kinor ve-ugav* [The Harp and Organ Player]. Vienna: Druck und Typografisch-literarisch-artistisch Anstalt, L. C. Zamarski & C. Dittmarsch, 1860.

Levin, Gabriel. "Essential Vertigo." *PN Review* 127 (2000): 42–46.

Levin, Gabriel. "The Pleasures of an Earthly Vision: on Harold Schimmel's *Ar'a*." *Modern Hebrew Literature* 6, no. 1–2 (1980): 54–57.

Levin, Gabriel. "What Different Things Link Up: Hellenism in Contemporary Hebrew Poetry." *Prooftexts* 5, no. 3 (1985): 221–243.

Levinson, Avraham, trans., *Yevgeni Onyegin: roman be-charuzim* [Eugene Onegin: Novel in Rhyme]. Jerusalem: Vays, 1937.

Levy, Lital. "Exchanging Words: Thematizations of Translation in Arabic Writing from Israel." *Comparative Studies of South Africa, Asia, and the Middle East* 23, no. 1–2 (2003): 106–127.

Levy, Lital. *Poetic Trespass: Writing between Hebrew and Arabic in Israel and Palestine.* Princeton, NJ: Princeton University Press, 2014.

Levy, Lital. "Self-Portraits of the Other: Toward a Palestinian Poetics of Hebrew Verse." In *Transforming Loss into Beauty: Essays in Honor of Magda al-Nowaihi*, edited by. Marlé Hammond and Dana Sajdi. Cairo: American University in Cairo Press, 2008, 343–402.

Lieblich, Amia. *El Leah* [Toward Leah]. Tel Aviv: Ha-kibbuts ha-me'uchad, 1995.

Lindsay, Geoffrey. "Drama and Dramatic Strategies in Robert Lowell's Notebook 1967–68." *Twentieth Century Literature* 44, no. 1 (1998): 53–81.

Litvin, Rina. "Shtei shemi'ot: 'al omanuto shel metargem ha-shir" [Double Hearing: On the Art of the Poetry Translator]. *Haaretz*, September 18, 2009. Accessed December 30, 2017. http://www.haaretz.co.il/literature/1.1281373.

López-Morillas, Consuelo. "Language." In *The Literature of Al-Andalus*, edited by Maria Rosa Menocal, Raymond P. Scheindlin, and Michael Sells, 33–57. Cambridge: Cambridge University Press, 2000.

Lowell, Robert. *Collected Poems.* Edited by Frank Bidart and David Gewanter. New York: Farrar, Straus and Giroux, 2003.

Lowell, Robert. *Near the Ocean.* New York: Farrar, Strauss and Giroux, 1967.

Lowell, Robert. *Notebook.* London: Faber & Faber, 1970.

Lowney, John. *The American Avant-Garde Tradition: William Carlos Williams, Postmodern Poetry, and the Politics of Cultural Memory.* Lewisburg, PA: Bucknell University Press, 1997.

Luz, Zvi. *Shirat Ester Rab: monografiya* [The Poetry of Esther Raab: A Monograph]. Tel Aviv: Ha-kibbuts ha-me'uchad, 1997.

Lytton, Edward Bulwer, trans., *The Poems and Ballads of Schiller.* Leipzig: Bernhard Tauchnitz, 1844.

Macrakis, Kristie. *Prisoners, Lovers and Spies: The Story of Invisible Ink from Herodotus to al-Qaeda.* New Haven: Yale University Press, 2014.

Manaster, Robert. "Opening up a Tradition, a Return from Exile: The Vision in Charles Reznikoff's Jerusalem the Golden." *Shofar: An Interdisciplinary Journal of Jewish Studies* 21, no. 1 (2002): 44–62.

Mandelshtam, Nadezhda. *Hope against Hope: A Memoir.* Translated by Max Hayward. New York: Modern Library, 1999.

Mandelstam, Osip. *The Complete Critical Prose and Letters.* Translated by Jane Gary Harris and Constance Link. Edited by Jane Gary Harris. Ann Arbor: Ardis, 1979.

Mandelstam, Osip. *Complete Poetry of Osip Emilevich Mandelstam.* Translated by Burton Raffel. New York: State University of New York Press, 1973.

Mandelstam, Osip. "The Horseshoe Finder: A Pindaric Fragment." Translated by Steven J. Willett. *Arion* 9, no. 2 (Fall 2001): 90–93.

Manecke, Keith. *On Location: The Poetics of Place in Modern American Poetry.* PhD. diss., Ohio State University, 2003.

Itzik Manger. "Destiny of a Poem," trans. Murray Citron. *Pakn-Treger: Magazine of the Yiddish Book Center* (Summer 2016). Accessed December 30, 2017. http://www.yiddishbookcenter.org/destiny-poem.

Mann, Barbara. "Framing the Native: Esther Raab's Visual Poetics." *Israel Studies* 4, no. 1 (1999): 234–257.

Mann, Barbara. *A Place in History: Modernism, Tel Aviv, and the Creation of Jewish Urban Space.* Stanford: Stanford University Press, 2006.

Mann, Barbara. "The Vicarious Landscape of Memory in Tel Aviv Poetry." *Prooftexts* 21, no. 3 (2001): 350–378.

Manor, Dory. "'Im targum 'hitkansut' o: ha-neshika mi-ba'ad le-takhrikh" [With Translation, a "Gathering" or a Kiss through a Veil]. *Ev* 2 (1994): 43–44.

Marko, Vladimír. "Callimachus' Puzzle about Diodorus." *Organon F* 4 (1995): 342–367.

Masalha, Salman. *Echad mi-kan* [In Place]. Tel Aviv: 'Am 'oved, 2004.

Matan, Nimrod. *'Al pi* [As Per]. Jerusalem: Mossad Bialik, 2013.

McHale, Brian. "Poetry as Prosthesis." *Poetics Today* 21, no. 1 (2000): 1–32.

McHugh, Heather. "A Stranger's Way of Looking." *Broken English: Poetry and Partiality.* Middletown, CT: Wesleyan University Press, 1993, 41–67.

"Meïr Halevi (Max) Letteris." *Jewish Encyclopedia.* Accessed December 30, 2017. http://www.jewishencyclopedia.com/articles/9791-letteris-meir-halevi-max.

Menocal, Maria Rosa, Raymond P. Scheindlin, and Michael Sells, eds, *The Literature of Al-Andalus.* Cambridge: Cambridge University Press, 2000.

Meravi, S. T. "Small but Memorable." *Jerusalem Post,* July 31, 1998, 5.

Mermin, Dorothy. *Elizabeth Barrett Browning: The Origins of a New Poetry.* Chicago, IL: University of Chicago Press, 1989.

Mermin, Dorothy. "The Female Poet and the Embarrassed Reader: Elizabeth Barrett Browning's Sonnets from the Portuguese." *English Literary History* 48, no. 2 (Summer 1981): 351–367.

Miller, Elaine R. *Jewish Multiglossia: Hebrew, Arabic, and Castilian in Medieval Spain*. Newark, Delaware: Juan de la Cuesta, 2000.

Milne, Esther. *Letters, Postcards, Email: Technologies of Presence* . London: Routledge, 2013.

Milne, Esther. "Postcards." In *The Routledge Handbook of Mobilities*, edited by Peter Adey, et al., 306–315. New York: Routledge, 2014.

Mintz, Alan. *Sanctuary in the Wilderness: A Critical Introduction to American Hebrew Poetry* (Stanford: Stanford University Press, 2012).

Mintz, Alan. *Translating Israel: Contemporary Hebrew Literature and Its Reception in America*. Syracuse, NY: Syracuse University Press, 2001.

Miron, Dan. *Bodedim be-mo'adam: li-deyokana shel ha-republika ha-sifrutit ha-'ivrit bi-techilat ha-me'a ha-'esrim* [When Loners Come Together: Toward a Portrait of the Republic of Hebrew Letters at the Bginning of the Twentieth Century]. Tel Aviv: 'Am 'oved, 1987.

Miron, Dan. "Ha-omets le-chulin u-kerisato: 'Al Taba'ot 'ashan me'et Leah Goldberg ke-tachanat tsomet be-hitpatchut ha-shira ha-'ivrit ha-modernit" [The Courage for the Ordinary and Its Collapse: On Leah Goldberg's *Smoke Rings* as a Major Junction in the Development of Modern Hebrew Poetry]. In *Ha-adam eyno ela ... chulshat-ha-ko'ach, 'otsmat-ha-chulsha: 'iyunim be-shira* [Man Is Nothing but ... the Weakness of Being Strong, the Strength in Weakness: Studies in Modern Hebrew Poetry], 309–388. Tel Aviv: Zmora, Bitan, 1999.

Miron, Dan. *Harpaya le-tsorekh negi'a: likrat chashiva chadasha 'al sifruyot ha- yehudim* [From Continuity to Contiguity: Towards a New Theorizing of Jewish Literatures]. Tel Aviv: 'Am 'oved, 2005.

Miron, Dan. *Imahot meyesadot, achayot chorgot* [Founding Mothers, Step-Sisters]. Tel Aviv: Ha-kibbuts ha-me'uchad, 1991.

Miron, Dan. "La poésie hébraïque de Bialik à nos jours" [Hebrew Poetry from Bialik to the Present Day]. In *Anthologie de la poésie en hébreu modern*, translated by Laurence Sendrowicz, edited by Emmanuel Moses, 9–89. Paris: Gallimard, 2001.

Miron, Dan. "Neharot me'avshim: Ester Rab ve-shirata" [Rustling Rivers: Esther Raab and Her Poetry]. In *Ha-adam eyno ela ... chulshat-ha-ko'ach, 'otsmat-ha-chulsha: 'iyunim be-shira* [Man Is Nothing but ... the Weakness of Being Strong, the Strength in Weakness: Studies in Modern Hebrew Poetry], 259–307. Tel Aviv: Zmora, Bitan, 1999.

Mishol, Agi. "Galop." In *Mivchar ve-chadashim* [New and Selected Poems], 24–31. Jerusalem: Mosad Bialik and Ha-kibbuts ha-me'uchad, 2003.

Monroe, Harriet. "Editorial Comment: The Question of Prizes." In *Poetry: A Magazine of Verse* 7 (October–March 1915–1916): 249.

Montale, Eugenio. *Poesie de Montale* [Montale's Poetry]. Translated by Robert Lowell. Bologna: Edizioni della Lanterna, 1960.

Montale, Eugenio. *Selected Poems*. Edited by Glauco Cambon. New York: New Directions, 1965.

Moreh, Shmuel. *Modern Arabic Poetry, 1800–1970*. Leiden: E. J. Brill, 1976.

Moriani, Paul. *Lost Puritan: A Life of Robert Lowell.* New York: W. W. Norton, 1994.

Moss, Kenneth B. "Not the Dybbuk but Don Quixote: Translation, Deparochialization, and Nationalism in Jewish Culture, 1917–1919." In *Culture Front: Representing Jews in Eastern Europe,* edited by Benjamin Nathans and Gabriella Safran, 196–240. Philadelphia: University of Pennsylvania Press, 2008.

Moss, Kenneth B. "Stybel." *YIVO Encyclopedia of Jews in Eastern Europe,* October 21, 2010. Accessed December 30, 2017. http://www.yivoencyclopedia.org/article.aspx/Stybel.

Myers, Diana. "The Hum of Metaphor and the Cast of Voice. Observations on Mandel'shtam's 'The Horseshoe Finder.'" *Slavonic and East European Review* 69, no. 1 (1991): 1–39.

Nabokov, Vladimir. "The Art of Translation." *New Republic* (August 8, 1941): 160–162.

Nabokov, Vladimir. "On Adaptation." *New York Review of Books* 13, no. 10 (December 4, 1969): 50–51.

Neri, Barbara. "*Cobridme de flores*: (Un)Covering Flowers of Portuguese and Spanish Poets in Sonnets from the Portuguese." *Victorian Poetry* 44, no. 4 (2006): 571–583.

Niger, Shmuel. *Bilingualism in the History of Jewish Literature* [Tsveyshprakhikeyt fun undzer literatur]. Translated by Joshua A. Fogel. Lanham, MD: University Press of America, 1990 [1941].

Niranjana, Tejaswini. *Siting Translation: History, Post-Structuralism, and the Colonial Context.* Berkeley: University of California Press, 1992.

Nissenbaum, Dion. *A Street Divided: Stories from Jerusalem's Alley of God.* New York: St. Martin's Press, 2015.

Noland, Carrie. "Digital Gestures." In *New Media Poetics: Contexts, Technotexts and Theories,* edited by Adelaide Morris and Thomas Swiss, 217–243. Cambridge: MIT Press, 2005.

Noy, Amos. "'Al ha-poschim: 'Yahndes lo-lishko'ach'? 'Iyun be-mila achat shel Avot Yeshurun" [On Those Who Pass Over: Don't Forget Yahndes? A Close Reading of Single Word in Avot Yeshurun's Poetry]. *Teoria u-vikoret* 41 (Summer 2013): 199–221.

Olmert, Dana. *Bitenu'at safa 'ikeshet: ketiva ve-ahava be-shirat ha-meshorerot ha-'ivryot ha-rishonot* [Predicaments of Writing and Loving: The First Hebrew Women Poets]. Tel Aviv: University of Haifa University Press, 2012.

Omer-Sherman, Ranen. "Revisiting Charles Reznikoff's Urban Poetics of Diaspora and Contingency." In *Radical Poetics and Secular Jewish Culture,* edited by Stephen Paul Miller and Daniel Morris, 103–126. Tuscaloosa: University of Alabama Press, 2010.

Oppenheimer, Yochai. "Be-makom afus: 'al shirat Harold Shimel" [In a Vacant Place: On Harold Schimmel's Poetry]. *Chadarim* 7 (1988): 86–99.

Oppenheimer, Yochai. "Mukhrachim hayinu lisno gam et asher ahavnu"? Galutiyot ve-evel ba-shirat ha-'aliya ha-shlishit" [Did We Also Have to Hate What We Loved?

Exile and Mourning in the Poetry of the Third Aliya]. *Teoria u-vikoret* 42 (Spring 2014): 175–206.

Oppenheimer, Yochai. *Tenu li ledaber kmo she-ani: shirat Avot Yeshurun* [Let Me Speak As I Am: The Poetry of Avot Yeshurun]. Tel Aviv: Ha-kibbuts ha-me'uchad, 1997.

Ozick, Cynthia. "Toward a New Yiddish." In *Art and Ardor: Essays*, 154–177. New York: Alfred A. Knopf, 1983.

Pagis, Dan. *Chidush ve-masoret be-shirat-ha-chol: Sefarad ve-Italiya* [Change and Tradition in the Secular Poetry of Spain and Italy]. Jerusalem: Keter, 1976.

Pagis, Dan. *Gilgul*. Ramat Gan: Masada, 1970.

Pagis, Dan. *Mi-chuts la-shura: masot u-reshimot 'al ha-shira ha-'ivrit ha-modernit* [Outside the Line: Essays on Modern Hebrew Poetry]. Jerusalem: Keshev, 2003.

Pappas, Sara. "Managing Imitation: Translation and Baudelaire's Art Criticism." *Nineteenth-Century French Studies* 33, no. 3–4 (Spring–Summer 2005): 320–341.

Pasternak, Yevgeny et al., eds, *Letters: Summer 1926, Boris Pasternak, Marina Tsvetayeva, Rainer Maria Rilke*. New York: New York Review of Books, 2001.

Patterson, David. "Moving Centers in Modern Hebrew Literature." In *The Great Transition: The Recovery of the Lost Centers of Modern Hebrew Literature*, edited by Glenda Abramson and Tudor Parfitt, 1–10. Totowa, NJ: Rowman & Allanheld, 1985.

Paz, Octavio. *Traducción: literatura y literalidad* [Translation: Literary and Literality]. Barcelona: Tusquets Editores, 1980.

Paz, Octavio. "Translation: Literature and Letters." Translated by Irene de Corral. In *Theories of Translation: An Anthology of Essays from Dryden to Derrida*, edited by John Biguenet and Rainer Schulte, 152–162. Chicago, IL: University of Chicago Press, 1992.

Pelli, Moshe. *The Age of Haskalah: Studies in Hebrew Literature of the Enlightenment in Germany*. Leiden: Brill, 1979.

Pelli, Moshe. *Haskalah and Beyond: The Reception of the Hebrew Enlightenment and the Emergence of Haskalah Judaism*. Lanham, MD: Rowman & Littlefield, 2010.

Penslar, Derek. "Hashpa'ot tzorfatiyot 'al ha-hityashvut ha-hakla'it ha-yehudit be-erets yisra'el (1870–1914)" [French Influences on Jewish Agricultural Settlement in Eretz Israel]. *Cathedra* 62 (1992): 54–66.

Penslar, Derek. *Zionism and Technocracy: The Engineering of Jewish Settlement in Palestine (1870–1918)*. Bloomington: Indiana University Press, 1991.

Perloff, Marjorie G. *The Poetic Art of Robert Lowell*. Ithaca, NY: Cornell University Press, 1973.

Perloff, Marjorie G. "Realism and the Confessional Mode of Robert Lowell." *Contemporary Literature* 11, no. 4 (Autumn 1970): 470–487.

Perloff, Marjorie G. "The Return of Robert Lowell." *Parnassus* 27, no. 1–2 (2004): 76–102.

Petrarca, Franceso. *Petrarch's Lyric Poems: The Rime Sparse and Other Lyrics*, translated and edited by Robert M. Durling. Cambridge: Harvard University Press, 1976.

Pinsker, Shachar. "Deciphering the Hieroglyphics of the Metropolis: Literary Topographies of Berlin in Hebrew and Yiddish Modernism." In *Yiddish in Weimar Berlin*, edited by Gennady Estraikh and Mikhail Krutikov, 28–53. Oxford: Legenda, 2010.

Pinsker, Shachar. *Literary Passports: The Making of Modernist Hebrew Fiction in Europe.* Palo Alto: Stanford University Press, 2010.

Pound, Ezra. "Homage to Sextus Propertius." *Poetry* 13, no. 6 (1919): 291–299.

Pound, Ezra. *Personae: The Shorter Poems.* Edited by Lea Baechler and A. Walton. New York: New Direction Books, 1990.

Powelstock, David. "'Fierce Integrity': Inner Freedom and Poetic Potentials." In *Becoming Mikhail Lermontov: The Ironies of Romantic Individualism in Nicholas I's Russia*, 398–459. Evanston: Northwestern University Press, 2005.

Presner, Todd S. *Mobile Modernity: Germans, Jews, Trains.* New York: Columbia University Press, 2007.

Presto, Jenifer. "Reproductive Fantasies: Blok and the Creation of the *Italian Verses*." In *Beyond the Flesh: Alexander Blok, Zinaida Gippius and the Symbolist Sublimation of Sex*, 70–105. Madison: University of Wisconsin Press, 2008.

Prince, Gerald. "Foreword." In *Palimpsests: Literature in the Second Degree* [Palimpsestes], by Gérard Genette, translated by Channa Newman and Claude Doubinsky, ix–xi. Lincoln: University of Nebraska Press, 1997.

Prigozhina, Mariana. "Bialik's Translation of *Don Quixote* (1912/23)." In *The Russian Jewish Diaspora and European Culture, 1917–1937*, edited by Jörg Schulte, Olga Tabachnikova, and Peter Wagstaff, 25–36. Leiden/Boston: Brill, 2012.

Procopiow, Norma. "The Poetics of Imitation." In *Robert Lowell: The Poet and His Critics*, 42–108. Chicago, IL: American Library Association, 1984.

Raab, Esther. *Kol ha-proza* [Collected Prose]. Edited by Ehud Ben-Ezer. Hod Ha-Sharon, Israel: Astrolog, 2001.

Raab, Esther. *Kol ha-shirim* [Collected Poems]. Edited by Ehud Ben-Ezer. Tel Aviv, Israel: Zmora, Bitan, 1988.

Raab, Esther. *Machberot Kimshonim* [The *Kimshonim* Notebooks]. Collection of Ehud Ben Ezer, Tel Aviv.

Raab, Esther. "Sicha be-Tiv'on (December 12, 1980)" [A Conversation in Tivon]. *Chadarim* 1 (1981): 117–118.

Raab, Esther. *Thistles: Selected Poems of Esther Raab.* Translated by Harold Schimmel. Jerusalem: Ibis Editions, 2002.

Raab, Yehuda. *Ha-telem ha-rishon: zikhronot 1862–1930* [The First Furrow: Recollections]. Jerusalem: Ha-sifriya ha-tsiyonit, 1956.

Rabinovitch, Lara, Shiri Goren, and Hannah S. Pressman, eds, *Choosing Yiddish: New Frontiers of Language and Culture.* Detroit: Wayne State University Press, 2013.

Rader, Ralph Wilson. *Tennyson's Maud: The Biographical Genesis.* Berkeley: University of California Press, 1963.

Ramazani, Jahan. "Modernist Bricolage, Postcolonial Hybridity. *Modernism/Modernity* 13, no. 3 (2006): 445–463.

Ramazani, Jahan. "A Transnational Poetics." *American Literary History* (2006): 332–359.

Ramazani, Jahan. *A Transnational Poetics*. Chicago, IL: University of Chicago Press, 2009.

Ramon, Einat. *Chayim chadashim: dat, imahut, ve-ahava eliyona be-haguto shel Aharon David Gordon* [New Life: Religion, Motherhood and Supreme Love in the Thought of A. D. Gordon]. Jerusalem: Karmel Books, 2007.

Ramras-Rauch, Gila. "Review of Harold Schimmel's *Shirei Malon Tsiyon*." *Books Abroad* 50, no. 1 (1976): 233–234.

Regev, Motti, and Edwin Seroussi, *Popular Music and National Culture in Israel*. Oakland: University of California Press, 2004.

Reich, Asher, ed., *Neshika mi-ba'ad la-mitpachat: mivchar hashva'ot targumei shira* [A Kiss through the Veil: A Selection of Comparative Studies on the Translation of Poetry]. Tel Aviv: Am 'oved, 2001.

Ruebner, Tuvia, ed., In *Kolot rechokim u-krovim* [Voices Far and Near]. Tel Aviv: Sifriyat po'alim, 1975.

Ruebner, Tuvia. *Leah Goldberg: Monografiya* [Monograph]. Tel Aviv: Sifriyat po'alim, 1980.

Reynolds, Matthew. *Likenesses: Translation, Illustration, Interpretation*. Oxford: Legenda, 2013.

Reynolds, Matthew. *The Poetry of Translation*. Oxford: Oxford University Press, 2011.

Reznikoff, Charles. "Jerusalem the Golden." In *The Poems of Charles Reznikoff, 1918–1975*, edited by Seamus Cooney, 91–115. Jaffrey, NH: Black Sparrow Books, 2005.

Rich, Adrienne. *Poetry and Commitment*. New York: W. W. Norton, 2007.

Richardson, Joanna. "Introduction." In *Selected Poems*, by Charles Baudelaire, translated and edited by Joanna Richardson, 9–21. London: Penguin Books, 1975.

Rilke, Rainer Maria. *The Book of Hours: Prayers to a Lowly God*. Translated by Annemarie S. Kidder. Evanston: Northwestern University Press, 2001.

Rilke, Rainer Maria. *Diaries of a Young Poet*. Translated by Edward Snow and Michael Winkler. New York: W. W. Norton, 1997.

Rilke, Rainer Maria. *Sämtliche Werke*. Edited by Ruth Rilke Sieber. Frankfurt: Insel Verlag, 1955–1997.

Rilke, Rainer Maria. *The Selected Poetry of Rainer Maria Rilke*. Translated by Stephen Mitchell. New York: Vintage International-Random House, 1989.

Robinson, Douglas. "Proprioception of the Body Politic: 'Translation as Phantom Limb' Revisited." *Translation and Interpreting Studies* 1, no. 2 (2006): 43–71.

Rokem, Na'ama. *Prosaic Conditions: Heinrich Heine and the Spaces of Zionist Literature*. Evanston, IL: Northwestern University Press, 2013.

Ronsard, Pierre de. *Les Amours de P. de Ronsard nouvellement augmentées par lui et commentées par Marc-Antoine de Muret* [The Loves of P. de Ronsard in an Expanded Edition by the Author and Commentary by Marc-Antoine de Muret]. Paris: Veuve

Maurice de La Porte, 1553. In *Gordon Collection*, University of Virginia. Accessed December 30, 2017. http://search.lib.virginia.edu/catalog/u2360414.

Rowlinson, Matthew. *Tennyson's Fixations: Psychoanalysis and the Topics of the Early Poetry*. Charlottesville: University of Virginia Press, 1994.

Rubin, Adam. "'Like A Necklace of Black Pearls Whose String Has Snapped': Bialik's 'Aron ha-sefarim' and the Sacralization of Zionism." *Prooftexts* 28, no. 2 (Spring 2008): 157–196.

Sachs, Arieh. "Meshorerei ha-anti-metafora: Aharon Shabtai ve-Harold Shimel" [The Poets of the Anti-Metaphor]. *Divrei ha-kongres ha-'olami ha-shlishi le-m'adei ha-yahdut* [Proceedings of the Third World Congress of Jewish Studies], vol. 3, 171–177. Jerusalem: Ha-igud ha-'olami le-m'adei ha-yahdut, 1973.

Said, Edward. *Orientalism*. New York: Vintage Books, 1978.

Salines, Emily. *Alchemy and Amalgam: Translation in the Works of Charles Baudelaire*. Amsterdam and New York: Rodopi, 2004.

Sallis, John. *On Translation*. Bloomington: Indiana University Press, 2002.

Sammons, Jeffrey L. *Heinrich Heine: Alternative Perspectives 1985–2005*. Würzburg: Verlag Königshausen & Neumann, 2006.

Sand, Shlomo. *The Invention of the Land of Israel*. Translated by Geremy Forman. London: Verso, 2012.

Sandbank, Shimon. *Ha-kol hu ha-acher: 'Od masot 'al kesherim u-makbilot bein ha-shira ha-'ivrit ve-ha-eiropit* [The Voice Is the Other: Hebrew Poetry and the European Tradition]. Jerusalem: Karmel, 2001.

Sandbank, Shimon. "Ha-ta'arikh, Celan, Derrida, Yeshurun" [The Date]. In *Eikh nikra Avot Yeshurun* [How Does It Read], edited by Lilach Lachman, 97–106. Tel Aviv: Ha-kibbuts ha-me'uchad, 2011.

Sandbank, Shimon. "Leah Goldberg ve-ha-sonet ha-petrarki" [Leah Goldberg and the Petrarchan Sonnet]. *Ha-sifrut* 6, no. 1 (1975): 19–31.

Sandbank, Shimon. "Paul Celan kotev le-imo ha-meta" [Paul Celan Writes to His Dead Mother]. *Mita'am* 5 (2006): 85–94.

Sandbank, Shimon. *Shtei brekhot ba-ya'ar: kesharim u-magbilot bein ha-shira ha-'ivrit ve-ha-shira ha-eiropit* [Two Pools in the Woods: Connections and Parallels between Hebrew and European Poetry]. Tel Aviv: Ha-kibbuts ha-me'uchad, 1976.

Sanders, Janet. "Divine Words, Cramped Actions: Walter Benjamin—An Unlikely Icon in Translation Studies." *TTR: Traduction, Terminologie, Rédaction* 16, no. 1 (2003): 161–183.

Saposnik, Arieh B. *Becoming Hebrew: The Creation of a Jewish National Culture in Ottoman Palestine*. Oxford: Oxford University Press, 2008.

Schachter, Allison. *Diasporic Modernisms: Hebrew and Yiddish Literature in the Twentieth Century*. Oxford: Oxford University Press, 2011.

Schachter, Allison. "Orientalism, Secularism, and the Crisis of Hebrew Modernism: Reading Leah Goldberg's Avedot." *Comparative Literature* 65, no. 33 (2013): 345–362.

Schafer, Elizabeth O. "Red Cross." In *World War II in Europe: An Encyclopedia*, edited by David T. Zabecki, 753–775. New York: Routledge, 1999.

Schatz, Zvi. *'Al gevul ha-demama: ketavim* [On the Edge of Silence: Collected Writings]. Tel Aviv: Tarbut ve-chinukh, 1967.

Schimmel, Harold. "His Commitment." *Epoch* 14, no. 1 (Fall 1964): 62.

Schimmel, Harold. *Ar'a*. Tel Aviv: Siman Kri'a, 1979.

Schimmel, Harold. "Esther Raab: The First Native-Born Hebrew Woman-Poet." *Jerusalem Post Magazine*, August 22, 1986, 11–12.

Schimmel, Harold. *First Poems*. Milan: Edizioni Milella, 1962.

Schimmel, Harold. *From Island to Island*. Translated by Peter Cole. Jerusalem: Ibis Editions, 1997.

Schimmel, Harold. *Ha-sifriya* [The Library]. Ra'anana: Even Choshen, 1999.

Schimmel, Harold. "Katsida" [Qasida]. *Chadarim* 10 (1993): 65–80.

Schimmel, Harold. "Leah Goldberg: ha-meshoreret" [The Poet]. *Orot* 10 (1971): 20–27.

Schimmel, Harold. *Lo'el* [Lowell]. Tel Aviv: Chadarim ve-Galeriya Gordon, 1986.

Schimmel, Harold. "Mishpacha" [Family]. *Nekudatayim*, January 27, 2013. Accessed December 30, 2017. https://nekudataim.wordpress.com/2013/01/27/schimmel.

Schimmel, Harold. "Note to Fathers and Teachers." *Judaism* 14, no. 4 (Fall 1965): 498–500.

Schimmel, Harold. *Now*. Edited by Maxim Ghilan, 27–40. Jerusalem: Akhshav, 1964.

Schimmel, Harold. *Qasida*. Translated by Peter Cole. Jerusalem: Ibis Editions, 1997.

Schimmel, Harold. "R. L. z"l." *Haaretz* (October 21, 1977): 18.

Schimmel, Harold. *Shirei malon tsiyon* [The Hotel Zion Poems]. Tel Aviv: Ha-kibbuts ha-me'uchad, 1974.

Schimmel, Harold. "Translator's Foreword." In *The Syrian-African Rift and Other Poems*, by Avot Yeshurun, translated by Harold Schimmel, xi–xxi. Philadelphia: Jewish Publication Society of America, 1980.

Schimmel, Harold. "Two Views of Jerusalem." *Epoch* 13, no. 1 (Fall 1963): 45–46.

Schimmel, Harold. "Zuk. Yehoash David Rex." *Paideuma* 7, no. 3 (Winter 1978): 559–569.

Schleiermacher, Friedrich. "On the Different Methods of Translating." Translated by Susan Bernofsky. In *The Translation Studies Reader*, edited by Lawrence Venuti, 43–63. New York: Routledge, 2012 (3rd ed.).

Schweid, Eli. "El ha-shir u-mimenu ve-hala: Ahavata shel Tereza di Mon me'et Leah Goldberg [Toward the Poem and Onwards: Leah Goldberg's "The Love of Teresa de Meun"]. In *Leah Goldberg: mivchar ma'amarim 'al yetsirata* [A Selection of Critical Essays on Her Writings], edited by A. B. Yoffe, 110–118. Tel Aviv: 'Am 'oved, 1980.

Scott, Clive. "Engendering the Sonnet, Loving to Write/Writing to Love: Louise Labé's 'Tout aussi tot que je commence a prendre.'" *Modern Language Review* 92, no. 4 (October 1997): 842–850.

Seelig, Rachel. "The Middleman: Ludwig Strauss's German-Hebrew Bilingualism," *Prooftexts* 33, no. 1 (Winter 2013): 76–104.

Segal, Miryam. *A New Sound in Hebrew Poetry: Poetics, Politics, Accent.* Bloomington: Indiana University Press, 2010.

Segal, Nina. "Velimir Khlebnikov in Hebrew." *Partial Answers: Journal of Literature and the History of Ideas* 6, no. 1 (2008): 81–109.

Sela, Maya. "Who Touches This Touches a Man." *Haaretz,* September 27, 2009. Accessed December 30, 2017. http://www.haaretz.com/who-touches-this-touches-a-man-1.7101.

Seidman, Naomi. *Faithful Rendering: Jewish–Christian Difference and the Politics of Translation.* Chicago, IL: University of Chicago Press, 2007.

Seidman, Naomi. "Lawless Attachments, One-Night Stands: The Sexual Politics of the Hebrew–Yiddish Language War." In *Jews and Other Differences: The New Jewish Cultural Studies,* edited by Jonathan Boyarin and Daniel Boyarin, 279–305. Minneapolis: University of Minnesota Press, 1997.

Seidman, Naomi. *A Marriage Made in Heaven: The Sexual Politics of Hebrew and Yiddish.* Berkeley: University of California Press, 1997.

Sells, Michael, Translated by *Desert Tracings: Six Classic Arabian Odes.* Middletown, CT: Wesleyan University Press, 1989.

Sells, Michael. "The Qasida and the West: Self Reflective Stereotype and Critical Encounter." *Al'-Arabiyya* 20 (1987): 307–357.

Seyhan, Azade. *Writing Outside the Nation.* Princeton, NJ: Princeton University Press, 2000.

Shacham, Chaya. "Be-tsomet meshulash—ha-viku'ach sviv 'Pesach 'al kukhim' le-Avot Yeshurun" [At a Triple Crossroads: The Polemic on Avot Yeshurun's "Passover on Caves"]. *Dapim le-mechkar be-sifrut* 10 (1995–1996): 47–65.

Shamir, Ziva. "Baudelaire's Translations into Hebrew and Modern Hebrew Poetry. *TRANS: Internet-Zeitschrift für Kulturwissenschaften* 16 (2006). Accessed December 30, 2017. http://www.inst.at/trans/16Nr/09_4/shamir16.htm.

Shamir, Ziva. "Ne'urei ha-shira be-arets lo zeru'a" [The Youth of Poetry in an Unsowed Land: An Interview with Esther Raab], *Chadarim* 1 (1981): 101–118.

Shandler, Jeffrey. *Adventures in Yiddishland: Postvernacular Language and Culture.* Berkeley: University of California Press, 2006.

Shapira, Anita. *Land and Power: The Zionist Resort to Force, 1881–1948.* Palo Alto: Stanford University Press, 1992.

Shapira, Avner. "Be-Germaniya lifnei ha-milchama: ha-roman ha-ganuz shel Goldberg" [Germany before the War: Leah Goldberg's Unpublished Novel]." *Akhbar ha-'ir,* January 15, 2010. Accessed December 30, 2017. http://www.mouse.co.il/gallery/1.3322813.

Shapira, K. A. "Amarti yesh-li tikva" [I Said, I Have Hope]. *Ha-asif* 3 (1887): 706–713.

Shapira, Natan. "Tochelet nikhzava" [Hope Deceived]. *Ha-asif* 2 (1885): 565–568.

Shavit, Zohar. *Ha-chayim ha-sifrutiyim be-erets yisra'el, 1910–1933* [Literary Life in Palestine]. Tel Aviv: Porter Institute for Poetics and Semiotics, 1982.

Shavit, Zohar. "The Status of Translated Literature in the Creation of Hebrew Literature in Pre-State Israel." *Meta* 43, no. 1 (1998): 46–53.

Shavit, Zohar, and Yaakov Shavit. "Lemale et ha-arets sefarim" [To Fill the Country with Books: Translated vs. Original Literature in the Creation of the Literary Center in Erets Israel]. *Ha-sifrut* 25 (1977): 45–68.

Shemtov, Vered Karti. "Dwelling in the Stanzas of the Text: The Concept of 'Bayit' in Hebrew Poetry." *Shm'a: A Journal of Jewish Responsibility* (June 2012): 4–5.

Shlonsky, Avraham. "'Al 'shalom'" [On "Peace"]. *Ketuvim* 34–35 (May 18, 1927): 1.

Shlonsky, Avraham., trans. *Yevgeny Onigin (roman be-charuzim)* [Eugene Onegin: A Novel in Verse]. Tel Aviv: Va'ad Ha-yovel, 1937.

Shoham, Chaim. "Oren ve-nof: Model romanti u-model tsiyoni" [Pine and Landscape: A Romantic Model and a Zionist Model]. *Alei si'ach* 15–16 (1982): 22–38.

Shoham, Reuven. "Ha-ritmos ha-chofshi be-shirat Ester Rab" [Free Rhythm in the Poetry of Esther Raab]. *Ha-sifrut* 24 (1977): 84–91.

Shteinberg, Yaakov. "Hirhurai ('al ha-tirgumim)" [Reflections: On Translation]. *Ha-arets ve-ha-'avoda* 5 (January/February, 1919): 41–45.

Siegert, Bernhard. *Relays: Literature as an Epoch of the Postal System*. Translated by Kevin Repp. Stanford: Stanford University Press, 1997.

Silberschlag, Eisig. "Greek Motifs and Myths in Hebrew Literature." *Proceedings of the American Academy for Jewish Research* 44 (1977): 151–183.

Silk, Dennis, ed., *Retrievements: A Jerusalem Anthology*. Jerusalem: Keter Publishing House Jerusalem, 1977.

Simon, Sherry, and Paul St-Pierre. *Changing the Terms: Translating in the Postcolonial Era*. Ottowa: University of Ottowa Press, 2000.

Sin, Y. [Yosef Saaroni]. "Be-kele ha-intimiyut: *Taba'ot 'ashan* me'et Leah Goldberg" [In the Prison of Intimacy: Leah Goldberg's *Smoke Rings*]. *Ha-boker*, October 25, 1935, 3.

Singerman, Robert, ed., *Jewish Translation: A Bibliography of Bibliographies and Studies*. Amsterdam/Philadelphia: John Benjamins, 2002.

Sobchack, Vivian. *Carnal Thoughts: Embodiment and Moving Image Culture*. Berkeley: University of California Press, 2004.

Sokolow, Nachum. "He'arat ha-mul" [Editorial Comment]. *Ha-asif* 3 (1887): 707.

Sommer, Doris, ed., *Bilingual Games: Some Library Investigations*. New York: Palgrave Macmillan, 2003.

Sonis, Ronen "*Make it New*: Magamot chadashot be-tirgumei hashira ha-'ivri'im me-anglit u-me-rusit bishnot ha-shivi'im ve-ha-shmonim [New Trends in Poetic Translation from English and Russian into Hebrew in the 1970s and 1980s]. PhD diss., Hebrew University of Jerusalem, 2013.

Spector, Scott. *Prague Territories: National Conflict and Cultural Innovation in Franz Kafka's Fin de Siècle*. Berkeley: University of California Press, 2000.

Spivak, Gayatri Chakravorty. "The Politics of Translation." In *Outside the Teaching Machine*, 179–200. New York: Routledge, 1993.

Staff, Frank. *The Picture Postcard and its Origins*. London: Lutterworth Press, 1966.

Starr, Deborah A. and Sasson Somekh, eds, *Mongrels or Marvels: The Levantine Writings of Jacqueline Shohet Kahanoff*. Stanford: Stanford University Press, 2011.

Stein, Gertrude. "An American and France (1936)." In *What Are Masterpieces*, 59–70. New York: Pitman, 1970.

Stein, Gertrude. *Paris France*. New York: Liveright, 1970 [1940].

Steiner, George. *After Babel: Aspects of Language and Translation*. Oxford: Oxford University Press, 1998 (3rd ed.).

Steiner, George. *Extraterritorial: Papers on Literature and the Language Revolution*. New York: Atheneum, 1971.

Steiner, George. "Our Homeland, the Text." *Salmagundi* 66 (1985): 4–25.

Stevens, Wallace. "A Postcard from the Volcano." In *The Collected Poems of Wallace Stevens*, 158–159. New York: Alfred A. Knopf, 1971.

Stewart, Susan. *On Longing: Narratives of the Miniature, the Gigantic, the Souvenir, the Collection*. Durham: Duke University Press, 1993 [1984].

Stewart, Susan. *Poetry and the Fate of the Senses*. Chicago, IL: University of Chicago Press, 2002.

Still, Judith, and Michael Worton, eds, *Intertextuality: Theories and Practices*. New York and Manchester: Manchester University Press, 1990.

Stundzhiene, Brone. "The Depiction of Trees in Lithuanian Folk Songs." *Journal of the Baltic Institute of Folklore*, 1 (1997). In *Baltic Institute of Folklore*. Accessed December 30, 2017. http://www.folklore.ee/rl/pubte/ee/bif/bif1/stund.html.

Sturm-Maddox, Sara. *Ronsard, Petrarch, and the 'Amours.'* Gainesville: University Press of Florida, 1999.

Sturrock, John. "Writing between the Lines: The Language of Translation." *New Literary History* 21, no. 4 (1990): 993–1013.

Sullivan, Edward J. "Jacques Callot's Les Bohémiens." *Art Bulletin* 59, no. 2 (June 1977): 217–221.

Szondi, Peter. *Celan Studies*. Translated by Susan Bernofsky and Harvey Mendelsohn. Stanford: Stanford University Press, 2003.

Tamari, Salim. "Ishaq al-Shami and the Predicament of the Arab Jew in Palestine." *Jerusalem Quarterly File* 21 (August 2004): 10–26.

Ticotsky, Giddon. "Boker afel ba-bira: acharit devar" [Gray Morning in the Capital: Afterword]. In *Avedot*, edited by Leah Goldberg, 317–353. Tel Aviv: Sifriyat po'alim, 2010.

Ticotsky, Giddon. "Ha-meshoreret she-lo ratsta lehizdaken" [The Poet Who Did Not Want to Grow Old]. *Makor rishon* 718 (May 13, 2011). Accessed December 30, 2017. https://musaf-shabbat.com/2011/05/14/המשוררת-שלא-רצתה-להזדקן-גדעון-טיקוצקי/

Ticotsky, Giddon. "Ha-nishkachot--she-i-efshar lishko'ach" [The Forgotten Things that One Can't Forget]. *Mikhtavim mi-nesiy'a meduma* [Letters from an Imaginary

Journey], by Leah Goldberg, 133–170. Bnei-Barak: Sifriyat poʻalim-Ha-kibbuts ha-meʻuchad, 2007 [1937].

Ticotsky, Giddon. "Mi-chaloni ve-gam mi-chalonkha: hitkatvut dialektit ʻim muskamot sifrutiyot be-shir shel Leah Goldberg" [From my Window and Also from Yours: A Dialectical Correspondence with Literary Conventions in a Poem by Leah Goldberg]. *Alei siʻach* 53 (2005): 69–83.

Toury, Gideon. "Translation and Reflection on Translation: A Skeletal History for the Uninitiated." In *Jewish Translation: A Bibliography of Bibliographies and Studies*, edited by Robert Singerman, ix–xxxi. Amsterdam/Philadelphia: John Benjamins, 2002.

Tsamir, Hamutal. "Ahavat moledet ve-siʻach chershim: shir echad shel Ester Rab ve-hitkabluto ha-gavrit" [Love of Homeland and a Deaf Conversation: A Poem by Esther Raab and Its Masculine Reception]. *Teoria u-vikoret* 7 (1995): 125–145.

Tsamir, Hamutal. *Be-shem ha-nof: leʻumiut, migdar u-sovyektibiyut ba-shira ha-isrealit bishenot ha-chamishim ve-ha-shishim* [In the Name of the Land: Nationalism, Subjectivity and Gender in the Israeli Poetry of the Statehood Generation]. Jerusalem and Beer Sheva: Keter Books/Heksherim, 2006.

Tsur, Reuven. "ʻOd ʻal tirgumei Leah Goldberg ve-shirata ha-mekorit" [More on Leah Goldberg's Translations and Original Poetry]. *Ha-sifrut* 24 (1977): 117–133.

Tsvetaeva, Marina. *Earthly Signs: Moscow Diaries, 1917–1922*. Translated and edited by Jamey Gambrell. New Haven: Yale University Press, 2002.

Tymoczko, Maria. "Ideology and the Position of the Translator: In What Sense Is a Translator ʻIn Between.'" In *Critical Readings in Translation Studies*, edited by Mona Baker, 213–228. New York: Routledge, 2010.

Tzelgov, Eran. "Introduction to Octavio Paz's Essay." *Daka* 3 (Winter 2008): 32–34.

Ungar, Steven. "Writing in Tongues: Thoughts on the Work of Translation." In *Comparative Literature in an Age of Globalization*, edited by Haun Saussy, 127–138. Baltimore, MD: Johns Hopkins University Press, 2006.

Vaitsman, Eldeʻah, ed., *Mavo le-torat ha-tirgum: mikraʻa la-shiʻurim shel Prof. Hayim Rabin ve-Dr. Shoshana Blum* [An Introduction to Translation Studies: Course Readings]. Jerusalem: Hebrew University of Jerusalem, 1975.

Varela, María Encarnación. "Hypotexts of Lea Goldberg's Sonnets *Ahabatah shel Tereza di Mon*." In *Jewish Studies at the Turn of the 20th Century. Vol. II: Judaism from the Renaissance to Modern Times*, edited by Judit Targarona Borrás and Ángel Sáenz-Badillos, 236–243. Leiden: Brill, 1999.

Varon, Miri. "Esther Rab—shira, pirkeiyoman ve-proza ba-ʻarov ha-yom" [Poetry, Journal Writings, and Prose When the Sun Goes Down]. In *Ba-ʻarov ha-yom: ʻiyun be-yetsirot meʻucharot* [When the Sun Goes Down: Studies in Late Writing], 39–74. Beer Sheva: Ben Gurion University, 2001.

Venuti, Lawrence. *Rethinking Translation: Discourse, Subjectivity, Ideology*. New York: Routledge-Taylor & Francis, 1998.

Venuti, Lawrence. "Strategies of Translation," In *Routledge Encyclopedia of Translation Studies*, edited by Mona Baker, 240–244. London: Routledge, 1998.

Venuti, Lawrence., ed., *The Translation Studies Reader*. London: Routledge-Taylor & Francis, 2000.

Venuti, Lawrence. *The Translator's Invisibility: A History of Translation*. New York: Routledge, 1995.

Vogel, Lucy E. *Aleksandr Blok: The Journey to Italy*. Ithaca, NY: Cornell University Press, 1973.

Wachtel, Michael, and Craig Cravens. "Nadezhda Iakovlevna Mandel'shtam: Letters to and about Robert Lowell." *Russian Review* 61, no. 4 (2002): 517–530.

Wachtel, Michael, and Craig Cravens. "Translation, Imitation, Adaptation, or Mutilation? Robert Lowell's Versions of Boris Pasternak's Poetry." In *Novoe o Pasternakakh: Materialy Pasternakovskoi konferentsii 2015 goda v Stenforde* [New Studies on Pasternak: Proceedings from the 2015 Pasternak Conference at Stanford], edited by Lazar Fleishman, 592–655. Moscow: Azbukovnik, 2017.

Wallach, Yona. *Tat hakara niftachat kemo menifa: mivchar shirim 1963–1985* [Subconscious Opens Like a Fan: Selection of Poems]. Tel Aviv: Ha-kibbuts ha-me'uchad, 1992.

Wanner, Adrian. *Baudelaire in Russia*. Gainesville: University Press of Florida, 1996.

Warnke, Frank J. "Aphrodite's Priestess, Love's Martyr." In *Women Writers of the Renaissance and Reformation*, edited by Katharina M. Wilson, 3–21. Athens: University of Georgia Press, 1987.

Waters, Geoffrey, Michael Farman, and David Lunde, eds, *300 Tang Poems*. Buffalo, NY: White Pine Press, 2011.

Weinfeld, David. "Shirei Harold Shimel" [Poems by Harold Schimmel]. *Siman kri'a* 5 (February 1976): 456–459.

Weingrad, Michael, ed. and trans., *Letters to America: Selected Poems of Reuven Ben-Yosef*. Syracuse, NY: Syracuse University Press, 2015.

Weinreich, Max. "Der Yivo un ki problemen fun undzer tsayt" [YIVO and the Problems of Our Time]. *YIVO-Bleter* 25, no. 1 (1945): 3–18.

Weinreich, Max. *History of the Yiddish Language* [Geshikhte fun der yidisher shprakh]. Translated by Shlomo Noble and Joshua A. Fishman. Chicago, IL: University of Chicago Press, 1980.

Weiss, Haim. "Le-fet'a hukam gesher el me'ever le-alpayim shana: mi-arkhi'ologiya mechulenet le-arkhi'ologiya datit: ha-mikre shel Bar-Kosiba, Yigal Yadin u-Shlomo Goren" [From Secular to Religious Archeology: The Case of Bar-Kosiba, Yigal Yadin and Shlomo Goren], *Teoria u-vikoret* 46 (2016): 143–167.

Weiss, Yfaat. "'Nothing in my life has been lost.' Lea Goldberg Revisits her German Experience." *Leo Baeck Institute Year Book* 54 (2009): 357–377.

Weiss, Yfaat. "A Small Town in Germany: Leah Goldberg and German Orientalism in 1932." *Jewish Quarterly Review* 99, no. 2 (2009): 200–229.

Weissbort, Daniel. "Ted Hughes and the Translatable." *Comparative Critical Studies* 7, no. 1 (2010): 107–119.

Weissbort Daniel, and Astradur Eysteinsson, eds, *Translation—Theory and Practice: A Historical Reader*. Oxford: Oxford University Press, 2006.

Wettstein, Howard. *Diasporas and Exiles: Varieties of Jewish Identity*. Berkeley: University of California Press, 2002.

Whitman, Ruth. "Motor Car, Bomb, God: Israeli Poetry in Translation." *Massachusetts Review* 23, no. 2 (1982): 309–328.

Willett, Steven J. "Wrong Meaning, Right Feeling: Ezra Pound as Translator." *Arion* 12, no. 3 (2005): 149–189.

Williams, William Carlos. *The Selected Letters of William Carlos Williams*. Edited by John C. Thirwell. New York: New Directions, 1957.

Wills, David. "Post/Card/Match/Book/'Envois'/Derrida." *SubStance* 43 (1984): 19–38.

Wills, David. *Prosthesis*. Stanford: Stanford University Press, 1995.

Wills, David. "Two Words Pro-Derrida," *Tympanum* 4 (2000).

Winchester, Atira. "Abu Tor: Creativity on the Cusp." *Jerusalem Post*, March 27, 2005, 12+.

Wirth-Nesher, Hana. "Between Mother Tongue and Native Language: Multilingualism in Henry Roth's Call It Sleep." *Prooftexts* 10 (1990): 297–312.

Wirth-Nesher, Hana., ed., *What Is Jewish Literature?* Philadelphia: Jewish Publication Society, 1994.

Wise, Michael Owen. *Language and Literacy in Roman Judaea: A Study of the Bar Kokhba Documents*. New Haven: Yale University Press, 2015.

Wright, Charles. *Country Music: Selected Early Poems*. Middletown, CT: Wesleyan University Press, 1991 (2nd ed.).

Wright, Charles. "The Poem as Journey." *Southern Review* 29, no. 22 (1993): 259–273.

Yadin, Yigael. *Bar-Kokhba: The Rediscovery of the Legendary Hero of the Last Jewish Revolt against Imperial Rome*. New York: Random House, 1971.

Yavneh, Yuval. "Me'ase ahava: 'al tergumav shel Aryeh Zakhs le-'shirei chalom' shel Jon Beriman" [An Act of Love: On Aryeh Sachs Translations of John Berryman's *Dream Songs*]. *Makom le-shira*. Accessed December 30, 2017. http://www.poetryplace.org/article/מעשה-אהבה

Yeglin, Ofra. "The Sonnets of Lea Goldberg." *Hebrew Studies* 50 (2009): 265–276.

Yeglin, Ofra. *Ulai mabat acher: klasiyut modernit ve-modernizm klasi be-shirat Leah Goldberg* [Modern Classicism and Classical Modernism in Lea Goldberg's Poetry]. Tel Aviv: Ha-kibbuts ha-me'uchad, 2002.

Yenser, Stephen. "Imitations." *Robert Lowell*. New York: Chelsea House, 1987, 73–80.

Yeshurun, Avot. "Hebrew Literature Will Set the Prayer." Translated by Lilach Lachman and Gabriel Levin. *PN Review* 33, no. 4 (March–April 2007): 28.

Yeshurun, Avot. *Kol shirav, vol. 1* [Collected Poems]. Tel Aviv: Ha-kibbuts ha-me'uchad, 1995.

Yeshurun, Avot. *Kol shirav, vol. 2*. Tel Aviv: Ha-kibbuts ha-me'uchad, 1997.

Yeshurun, Avot. *Kol shirav*, vol. 3. Tel Aviv: Ha-kibbuts ha-me'uchad, 2001.

Yeshurun, Avot. *Kol Shirav*, vol. 4. Tel Aviv: Ha-kibbuts ha-me'uchad, 2001.

Yeshurun, Avot. "Memories are a House." Translated by Leon Wieseltier. *Poetry* 192, no. 1 (2008): 109.

Yeshurun, Avot. *Milvadata* [Selected Poems]. Edited by Helit Yeshurun and Lilach Lachman. Ha-kibbuts ha-me'uchad, 2009.

Yeshurun, Avot. *The Syrian-African Rift and Other Poems*. Translated by Harold Schimmel. Philadelphia: Jewish Publication Society of America, 1980.

Yeshurun, Helit. "Ani holekh el ha-kol: re'ayon 'im Avot Yeshurun" [I Walk toward Everything: Interview with Avot Yeshurun]. *Chadarim* 3 (1982): 92–109.

Yeshurun, Helit. "Kol ha-be'erekh she-ata yode'a la'asot: re'ayon 'im Harold Shimel" [All the Approximately You Know How to Do: An Interview with Harold Schimmel] *Chadarim* 5 (1985/1986): 118–131.

Yoffe, A. B. *Pegishot 'im Leah Goldberg* [Encounters with Leah Goldberg]. Tel Aviv: Cherikover, 1984.

Yudkoff, Sunny. *Let it Be Consumption! Modern Jewish Writing and the Literary Capital of Tuberculosis*. PhD diss., Harvard University, 2015.

Zach, Nathan. "Nofa shel meshoreret nof" [The Landscape of a Landscape Poet]. *Amot* 2, no. 4 (1964): 86–91.

Zerubavel, Yael. "Desert and Settlement: Space Metaphors and Symbolic Landscapes in the Yishuv and Early Israeli Culture." In *Jewish Topographies: Visions of Space, Traditions of Place*, 201–222. Burlington and Hampshire: Ashgate, 2008.

Zerubavel, Yael. *Recovered Roots: Collective Memory and the Making of Israeli National Tradition*. Chicago, IL: University of Chicago Press, 1995.

Ziegler, Heide, ed., *The Translatability of Cultures*. Stuttgart: J. B. Metzler, 1999.

Zierler, Wendy I. *And Rachel Stole the Idols: The Emergence of Modern Hebrew Women's Writing*. Detroit: Wayne State University Press, 2004.

Zoritte, Eda. *Shirat ha-pere he-atsil: biografiya shel ha-meshorer Avot Yeshurun* [The Song of the Noble Savage: A Biography of the Poet Avot Yeshurun]. Tel Aviv: Ha-kibbuts ha-me'uchad, 1996.

Zuckermann, Ghil'ad. *Language Contact and Lexical Enrichment in Israeli Hebrew*. London/New York: Palgrave Macmillan, 2003.

Zukofsky Louis. *"A."* New York: New Directions Books, 2011.

Zukofsky Louis. "Program: 'Objectivists' 1931." *Poetry* (February 1931): 268–272.

Index